# Chernyshevskii

*The Man and the Journalist*

Russian Research Center Studies 67

# Chernyshevskii

## The Man and the Journalist

## William F. Woehrlin

Harvard University Press
Cambridge, Massachusetts
1971

*The Russian Research Center of Harvard University is supported by a grant from the Ford Foundation. The center carries out inter-disciplinary study of Russian institutions and behavior and related subjects.*

Library of Congress Catalog Card Number 73–156137

SBN 674–11385–3

*To Frederick and Augusta*

# *Acknowledgments*

I owe a special debt of gratitude to the late Laurence B. Packard of Amherst College, whose intellectual integrity and intense concern with the past first engaged my interest in history, and to the late Michael Karpovich of Harvard University, whose rare combination of knowledge and wisdom represented the best of American graduate education.

In preparing this book, I was greatly aided by the criticisms of Richard Pipes and Robert L. Wolff made on an earlier version submitted as a doctoral dissertation.

In 1966–1967 I was privileged to use the facilities of Harvard's Russian Research Center and, as a research associate, to have access to the rich resources of Widener Library.

# Contents

# Illustrations

*Chernyshevskii*

*The Man and the Journalist*

# Introduction

In several significant ways, there is an affinity between mid-nineteenth century Russia and our own day. Then, too, the atmosphere was one of social unrest fostered by technological and economic change, of challenge to long-established political arrangements and traditions, and of strenuous and bitter ideological debate. Men of that time, often with considerable passion and anger, found themselves divided over issues that ranged from attempts to introduce new elements of justice and human dignity into society to renewed efforts at maintaining Russia's great-power status, especially after that status had been threatened by her humiliating defeat in the Crimean War. All who were alert to conditions around them realized that it was a time of change. Though they responded to the situation with either hope or fear, anticipation or foreboding, they generally shared an appropriate sense of the importance of current issues. They therefore engaged each other with an intensity of conviction, and for some a commitment to action, that gave excitement to the period and established its importance in Russian history.

The career and writings of N. G. Chernyshevskii represented a relatively small part of this period. Yet shortly after his arrest in 1862, which brought to a sudden halt the most active and productive period of his public career, he flung out a challenge about his historical importance. Writing to bolster the flagging spirits of his wife, he claimed that in a hundred years their names would be remembered with thanks by people who had forgotten nearly all of their contemporaries (XIV, 455–456).* On the face of it, Chernyshevskii's claim would seem to be denied by the facts of his life: an obscure background, a period of hard-won success in Russian journalism that was cut off just as his influence began to be felt, some attempts at direct action that bordered on disaster and farce, and finally almost half a lifetime spent in prison or exile, in a bitter tragedy of unfulfilled dreams and personal hardship. Still, to a considerable extent Chernyshevskii was right in his claim, as this study will show, for his career was of major significance to developments in nineteenth century Russia.

There can be little question about which aspect of Chernyshevskii's life requires greatest attention. His personal influence on all but a few men in society was inconsequential, and his role as a participant in any important sequence of events is barely worthy of mention. But in his chosen role as a publicist, he made a considerable mark. As a member of an intellectual elite, he fully acknowledged the importance of ideas in history and therefore tried to influence the thoughts of other men in the widest possible sphere. Choosing the role of publicist rather than of specialized scholar, he wrote extensively on a broad variety of subjects. These were not all-inclusive, as Chernyshevskii paid no serious attention to the natural sciences, but he did touch on vital problems facing man and society. He attacked the most important questions that men must answer in their personal and social lives, whether by conscious choice or by the thoughtless, uncritical exercise of tradition: How are power and authority in society to be organized? With what rights, privileges, and obligations should men relate to each other in their social and economic roles? How ought men to determine the meaning of their lives in relation to God or nature and then derive from that decision a morality or basis for judging human actions? And finally,

---

* This form will be used throughout for references to N. G. Chernyshevskii, *Polnoe sobranie sochinenii*, ed. V. Ia. Kirpotin et al. (16 vols.; Moscow, 1939–1953). The translations are mine.

by what standards should men evaluate the merits of their creativity? Chernyshevskii approached these questions not only with a passion appropriate to the times, but also with a sense that the answers must be part of a coherent, logically consistent world view. He sought an ideology wherein the parts would have relation to each other and to the whole.

Although Chernyshevskii could lay claim to original thinking in some areas, his more important function was to popularize ideas of others that he believed deserved a wider audience. He made no apology for this role; its importance to him was self-evident. If ideas were to be operative in society, they had to be shared by greater numbers of men. Furthermore, he believed that in some areas of human thought major break-throughs had occurred, which had important implications elsewhere. He sought to work through these implications and make them known. Thus, in the greater part of his activity, Chernyshevskii chose the role of intermediary between the philosophers and theorists, who were intellectual innovators, and the larger audience of men whose way of thought would have to change if new ideas were to have effect on human affairs. He made this choice in a society whose woefully inadequate eduational system placed an automatic restriction on the literate audience he might reach. Naturally, this role affected the character and quality of what he wrote, and it suggests criteria by which the significance of his career ought in fairness to be judged. Viewed within the general context of intellectual history, Chernyshevskii's career must be examined for the particular ideas he favored, their relative emphasis, and his attempts to establish a relationship between them. But one must also be concerned with the effectiveness of his effort to give those ideas greater popularity.

Another context within which to evaluate Chernyshevskii's career is the particular area of public debate in which he engaged. The years of Chernyshevskii's active career, covering the decade from the closing years of the reign of Nicholas I and the Crimean War through the liberation of the serfs under Alexander II, constitute an intelligible and coherent unit. It began in the shock of military defeat, with severe limitations in effect on public expression. During the subsequent preparations for reform amid a relaxed censorship, there took place the most active and exciting public debate of current issues that Russia had ever experienced. After a brief flowering, the period ended with renewed restrictions, which appeared to many as an attempt to set back the clock.

The debate was especially lively because of the wide disparity between sides and because of the high stakes. Defeat in war had precipitated a serious crisis of confidence in long-established institutions and relationships in both society and politics. If the autocracy was prepared to lead in reforming the institution of serfdom that stood at the core of Russian society, others were willing to go beyond that leadership to more profound criticism of different aspects of Russian life. Nor was military defeat and concern for Russia's national strength the only impetus to change. Some participants in the debate would have written and acted in defiance of tradition regardless of the outcome of the Crimean War. These men had already developed new sensitivities and understandings that perceived Russia's social and political structure as largely inappropriate to their time. The sources of dissatisfaction were many, including both moral outrage and hard-headed, amoral calculation of the degree to which the system worked to their personal benefit. Among the opponents of serfdom, for example, were representatives of both these types.

Because of the real possibility of change, the period was not easily satisfied with contemplation or with the delights of philosophy for its own sake. In the enthusiasm that accompanied new opportunities to speak out, many intellectuals overestimated the power of words to influence government policy and the course of events. But because they valued their ideas as a directing force for change, and because so much appeared to depend on the outcome, they argued with passion and intensity, and often with intolerance. This mood had implications for the choice of ideas discussed, their method of presentation, and their evaluation. The close relationship of ideas to an expectancy of change may also explain the intrusion of pragmatic calculations into an age that otherwise found fascination in systems of thought and ideologies. What mattered was the ability of ideas to work toward a chosen end. To be inconsistent was less of a sin than to be ineffective.

Much of the significance of Chernyshevskii's career and writings is found in this area of public debate. He was one of the leading representatives of the left wing or radical point of view. Not all radicals were alike, since this period predated the establishment of strictly defined party lines. Yet they held enough views in common so that a detailed study of one representative illuminates the whole movement. Moreover, Chernyshevskii did not merely reflect the movement; he made an important contribution to its formation. There was every likelihood, because of current conditions and the availability of models from Western Europe, that extreme solutions would be proposed. But variation was still possible in combining attitudes and prescriptions so as to catch the imagination of a sizable group of supporters. In this regard, the access that Chernyshevskii managed to gain to a reading public for himself and for those who thought like him had considerable influence.

At another level, the scope of polemics in which Chernyshevskii engaged was so broad that his writings illuminate the entire period, reflecting significant issues whose discussion enlivened the times. On this level it is also possible to speak of his influence beyond the circle of those who agreed with him. He wrote, after all, in a situation of argument and debate, where participants interacted with each other. Once he had gained a measure of influence, the statements of his own position necessarily affected the thought of his opponents and how it was expressed.

Still another context in which to weigh the significance of Chernyshevskii's career and writings is the attempt of succeeding generations of alienated intellectuals throughout the eighteenth and nineteenth centuries to find a basis for protest against the established ideology supporting Russia's social and political institutions. This movement provided a measure of continuity to an important segment of Russia's intellectual life. Often united by no more than a common enemy, uniformly unfavorable conditions, and despair, these men tried in many different ways to fashion a counter-ideology, and a small number went on to seek a rationale for revolutionary action. In retrospect, the temptation is great to read more coherence into this movement than perhaps existed, but within the lines of continuity that can be established, Chernyshevskii's career is notable. He was both a reflection of one stage in the movement and a factor of change in his own right, having an influence on those who followed him.

The most fundamental institutions of Russian life in the eighteenth century and well into the nineteenth—comprising the autocracy, the caste organization of society with a strict assignment of privileges and responsibilities, and serfdom—were inherited from an earlier Muscovite period. Within the earlier context these institutions had proven functional and they found legitimacy in a system of thought dominated by the authority of a revealed religion. In the course of time, however, especially with westernization and the development of a secular, rational culture encouraged by Peter the Great, the functional utility of these institutions became less apparent, and the beliefs that justified them less easy to accept.

The rich and complex movement toward alternative institutions and new legitimizing beliefs is easily distorted if given too precise or narrow a definition. But there were several aspects of the general undertaking that gave it a particular character. First among these was the understandably ambivalent attitude of the Russian autocracy toward innovation. From the time of Peter's selective westernization, Russian rulers were often the leading factors of change. Insofar as the traditional Russian culture contained few of the bases for national power or technological and economic advance that were needed to compete in the eighteenth and nineteenth centuries, the autocracy had to be innovative. Yet Peter and his successors faced a dilemma, because most of the changes they considered useful were the products of a secular and rational culture in Western Europe that came increasingly to condemn divine right monarchy as a hopeless anachronism. So long as the Russian rulers clung to this justification for power—as they did, in effect, to the very end—they were forced into a vacillating policy of encouragement and repression, a bewildering alternation of enlightened policy with official obscurantism. The result, in time, was to alienate many of the best Russian thinkers and literally force them into a position of opposition.

An equally prominent characteristic of the movement was the input of Western ideas into the development of Russia's secular thought. The contact with the West established by Peter had made isolated development impossible, so that Russians necessarily thought through secular alternatives to their traditional culture under an influence from abroad. The nature of that influence was complex, because the West did not speak with a single voice, and because transplanted ideas did not necessarily take root in like form in Russian soil. Nor was the influence present with constant intensity. Restrictions placed on foreign contact were erratically applied, and generations differed in the seriousness of their interest and ability to comprehend.

On the whole, however, this foreign influence served to stimulate lively currents of thought in Russia. It is no doubt true that for some time the weakness of Russia's philosophical tradition allowed imported ideas to be approached uncritically. But with each new generation, the specifically Russian tradition of secular thought grew. Certainly the process of selection had a creative aspect, if it occasionally distorted new ideas as well. Men tended to emphasize what seemed relevant to their own situation, and the cumulative effect was to give Russian intellectual life a distinctive flavor.

In any society, those who seek consciously to break from tradition are few in number, and their position is often one of isolation. In Russia, this isolation was compounded by the Western influence, which widened the expected separation between the literate and illiterate segments of society, and between those who could think abstractly and those who could not. Possessors of a cosmopolitan education were suspect, considered to be representatives of another culture and hence foreigners in their own country. Especially in the nineteenth century, men who tried to turn dissenting thought into effective action faced this serious handicap. They met an obscurantism from below to match the official obscurantism from above.

The Russian social and class structure also affected the character of oppositional thought. Russia's general pattern of economic development differed significantly from the West's in that it did not have a dynamic and powerful middle class whose interests were served by challenging tradition. Until the middle decades of the nineteenth century, the main burden of intellectual dissent was carried by representatives of the privileged order of society, who had easiest access to adequate education. The absence of support from a dynamic, self-seeking social group added a note of futility to the movement, though it added an attractive, ingenuous quality as well. An unfortunate counterpart to ingenuousness was often impracticality.

By the time of Chernyshevskii's involvement, the movement for reform had acquired additional characteristics. Chief among them was the change in mood of the system's opponents brought on by the impact of the reign of Nicholas I. Under the label "official nationality," government-inspired proponents of autocratic rule had made exalted claims for the tsar's God-given authority and Russia's mission. Religious orthodoxy and the autocrat's wise, benign intentions were placed above question. With absurd pretension in terms of other nineteenth century views, this official ideology was offered as a comprehensive answer to Russia's needs. But however exalted or total in aim, the doctrine of "official nationality" could not justify the reality of Russian life, which offered no more than a shabby caricature of the ideal. For men who were sensitive to the manifold inadequacies of Russian society, the doctrine served merely as a challenge to form their own counterstatements. Perhaps, in a situation of interaction, such qualities as intolerance, comprehensiveness, and exalted pretense are infectious. In any event, the angry, alienated writers sometimes displayed the same qualities, as if in inverted imitation of the system they opposed.

During the reign of Nicholas I, the tendency toward total solutions was reinforced by the prevailing wave of Western thought. The idealistic systems of Schelling and Hegel, which found enthusiastic audience in Russia, suited the mood and circumstances of intellectuals in the period of reaction and repression following the failure of the quixotic Decembrist revolt in 1825. Grand speculation about how to interpret the world provided a fitting pastime for men who saw no opportunity to change it. An element of escapism was apparent in the way such intellectuals passionately sought communion with the Absolute, pursued higher intuitive truths in the realm of art, and somewhat later tried to rationalize the sad conditions of Russia by reference to Hegelian determinism. To a later generation, this activity seemed like self-indulgent play, amusing rather than useful, but that judgment was shallow. Though Russia's political and social system could certainly not be overthrown by conversation, the discussion circles of Nicholas' time, stimulated by German idealism, helped to develop an intensity of concern and involvement that scorned apathy and earnestly sought truth without embarrassment or cynicism. The involvement with German idealism also introduced issues and questions into Russian intellectual life that later generations felt obliged to answer. One result was a general growth in philosophical sophistication; another was the strong imperative to determine the relatedness of things and to seek explanations in terms of total systems.

By the 1850's the influence of idealistic philosophy had waned significantly. Many in the next generation followed new gods. This shift reflected the larger change of emphasis in European thought that had taken place on the eve of 1848. In Germany, the criticism of left-wing Hegelians had undercut the idealistic framework of their master's teachings, and overall there was a new concern for social problems, which found expression in literature and in an outpouring of social and economic theory. Moreover, there were growing signs of a new reverence for science as the ultimate intellectual authority. Scientific method and its assumptions about the nature of reality seemed to promise answers, where divine revelation and the idealistic speculation of the past had failed. Chernyshevskii took part in Russian intellectual life as the representative and manipulator of many of these new ideas. Through them he contributed to the movement of secular thought toward alternative social and political systems. In this context, he fought not only against established tradition but also against the alternatives suggested by his immediate forebears.

A final area in which to assess Chernyshevskii is his contribution as a revolutionary. Among the alienated intellectuals there was a small number who engaged directly in the formation of revolutionary strategy, and who tried themselves to translate word into deed. The appreciation of Chernyshevskii in the Soviet Union today is based largely on the fact that he is rightfully considered a member of his country's revolutionary tradition.

Prior to the nineteenth century, with the sole exception of the short-lived constitutional crisis of 1730, there had been only two kinds of challenge to the royal power of the Romanovs. Neither of these proved ultimately effective, perhaps because neither seriously challenged the ideological basis of autocracy. The first was the palace coup d'état, which in the eighteenth century resulted in periodic disorder at the core of the system. Yet in the coups that spanned the period from Peter's immediate successors to the murder of Paul I, the key issue was not principles but persons. All parties agreed essentially on the fundamental character of royal power; the issue was simply who would wield that power. Temporary chaos at the center rarely touched more than the small groups directly involved and therefore left the system itself blemished but intact.

More threatening were the periodic outbursts of peasant unrest which, as in the case of the Pugachev rebellion, could be widespread and directly affect many hundreds of thousands. But here, too, serious threat was tempered by the absence of a progressive, alternative ideology. There is no question as to the social and economic exploitation that caused the unrest, but the ideals and specific programs of the rebels more often looked backward than forward. The protest itself frequently lacked coherence, or it was based on traditional concepts and beliefs that actually reinforced the system.

An overview of the revolutionary tradition during most of the nineteenth century indicates a serious and recurring problem. How could a progressive ideology be combined with a major source of unrest and active discontent? Until the economic development near the end of the century had widened the possible base of revolutionary unrest, the source of discontent must necessarily be the peasantry, whether serf-bound or ambiguously and inadequately freed. This problem was slow to be realized and came sharply into focus only after the Crimean War, during the period of preparation for the serf reform and of Chernyshevskii's active career. Prior to that time, although blind outbursts of peasant anger had continued and even become more numerous, leadership and progressive ideologies had remained fully divorced from the potentially explosive locus of mass discontent. The Decembrist fiasco was ample evidence of this; despite all its other weaknesses of disunity, romantic naiveté, and failure of nerve, its greatest failing was the lack of any workable tie between those who wanted to lead and a mass force capable of challenging the established power.

The central problem of the revolutionary movement was thus the need to join leaders and followers across two cultures that barely communicated with each other. One group could not realize its schemes except in a mass movement, where it often had the least chance of being understood. The other group could not utilize its potential force without organizational and ideological guidance, yet it suspected all schemes that were beyond its immediate ken. The peasants had tragically little ability to distinguish between friends and enemies, when both came from an outside, unknown world. This problem, and other problems of revolutionary strategy and tactics, were first confronted with any degree of seriousness by the radical generation in which Chernyshevskii played a leading role.

Chernyshevskii's life itself reflected several of the most interesting and exciting aspects of his nation's past: the process of working out long-overdue reforms, with the accompanying public debate; the development of a native intellectual tradition under the selective influence of foreign ideas; the generational struggle between exponents of different phases of that tradition; the problems of alienated intellectuals in a largely illiterate society; and finally, the search for an ideological basis for political protest and a strategy for revolution. Furthermore, his career had varying consequences in defining the character and determining the outcome of these issues. There was a considerable degree of probability in the main outlines of nineteenth century Russian history. The imperatives to modernization in economic terms were everywhere apparent in Europe, and in its traditional form the tsarist autocracy was a hopeless anachronism. In this setting it was more than likely that a radical prescription for Russia's ills would develop, and it was also likely that the radical view would include socialism, a philosophy of materialism, and a demand for immediate action. But within that probability, there was also an area of possible variation, and it was here that Chernyshevskii figured. By his choices and emphases, by the varied pattern of his successes and failures, he became an independent factor for change.

I have placed my investigation of Chernyshevskii's writings in the setting of a relatively detailed account of his life. The study makes no claim to be either a sociological analysis or a psychological portrait. Yet along with the external facts of his life that parallel the trend of his thought, I have tried to give as coherent a picture as possible of the view Chernyshevskii held of himself and of how he rationalized his actions. Rounding out the portrait are personal impressions he left on his contemporaries and certain patterns of behavior that are discernible in him from a modern perspective.

# I. Boyhood in Saratov
## (1828–1846)

As far as Nikolai Chernyshevskii knew of both branches of his family, his direct forebears were minor provincial clergy in the area of the middle Volga. Although sources are scanty, enough is known to describe the immediate background of his family in Saratov.[1] Nikolai's father, Gavriil Ivanovich, the son of a village deacon, was born in 1793 in Chernyshev, in the province of Penza (I, 566–567). Left destitute by the early death of her husband, Gavriil's mother secured her son's admittance to the ecclesiastical school in Tambov, where Gavriil apparently assumed the name Chernyshevskii, after his native village. Proving to be a promising student, he went on to the seminary at Penza, where he achieved an excellent record. He probably expected to continue in a scholarly or teaching career, because at the conclusion of the seminary course he taught Greek language and literature and for a short time was employed as seminary librarian. Then in 1818 an unusual circumstance brought about a sudden change in his career.[2]

In that year Egor Ivanovich Golubev, the priest of the Sergievskaia Church in Saratov, died, leaving an opening in one of the oldest and best situated churches in the city as well as an unmarried fifteen-year-old daughter. The governor of Saratov intervened personally to find a replacement, appealing to the bishop of Penza to send his best recent graduate from the seminary. The bishop responded with the appointment of Gavriil Ivanovich Chernyshevskii, who received the position on condition that he marry the young Evgeniia Egorovna Golubeva. Gavriil thus received a dramatic boost in a career that had seen rather humble beginnings and in addition came into possession of a comfortable family home.

During the following decades, Gavriil Ivanovich made a secure and honored place for himself in Saratov society and the church organization. One of only three parish priests in the city to have completed seminary, he displayed an administrative ability and tact that brought him increasing responsibilities. He taught at a boarding school for noble girls as well as at the local ecclesiastical school, which he also helped to administer. In 1825 he achieved the rank of archpriest, and in 1828 he was named to the local consistory. A. N. Pypin, Gavriil's nephew by marriage who later became a literary historian, noted in his memoirs the reputation his uncle had enjoyed in Saratov and the important work he had done as ecclesiastical superintendent, acting as mediator between the other clergy and the office of the bishop.[3] The year 1828 also saw the birth of his only child to survive infancy, Nikolai, whose first inheritance was thus membership in a family with a respected, though modest, position in the Saratov community.[4]

It was in the more intimate setting and values of his family life, however, that young Nikolai was most favored. The Chernyshevskii family lived in the former Golubev home as part of a larger household.[5] In addition to Nikolai's grandmother, who lived on until 1847, they shared the home with the family of his aunt, who by her second marriage was the wife of a petty nobleman, N. D. Pypin. The Pypin fortunes were such as to require service in the provincial bureaucracy and thus demanded residence in town. Together, the heads of these two families represented the best type of service that could be found in provincial church and government administration. Despite the well-deserved criticism of petty officialdom in the Russia of that time, Nikolai grew up with knowledge of two avenues of service which, as performed by his father and uncle, possessed integrity and dedication.[6]

Life in the joint household, though far from luxurious, knew none of the serious want Gavriil had experienced in his own youth. According to one of Nikolai's estimates, his father had an income amounting to some fifteen hundred paper rubles a year, on which they lived without need. In fact, they lived in a class above Nilolai's schoolmates when he was attending the seminary (X, 17). In another description that Nikolai gave of his family life, however, he spoke of it as a "moneyless" household. They valued a ten-kopek piece more than a St. Petersburg pauper. To provide a life of simple comforts, his mother and aunt had to work regularly beside the house serfs supplied by the Pypins (XV, 152–153).

The attitudes and relationships within this tightly knit family offered a healthy and stable setting for Nikolai's childhood and youth. According to his memories of his earliest years, the children of the two families were often left to themselves and allowed to fashion their own lives after the models of sound industry set forth by their elders. With the fathers at work all day on official business, and the mothers and servants busy with concerns of household, the children received attention only in moments of relaxation or when they had a pressing need (XV, 152–153).

The recollections of Nikolai and his cousin A. N. Pypin agree that their families lived by a strict moral code and according to high standards of personal conduct. Nikolai once referred to this "modest and strictly moral manner of life" as the reason that all his life he had found coarse pleasures, like heavy drinking, repulsive (XV, 372–373). Gavriil held the position of prime importance in the joint household, and some contemporaries claimed his word was law, even for the Pypins. But if so, this did not mean that limited clerical values dominated the home. Indeed, the Pypins introduced to it a considerable element of secular concern and contact that the household might otherwise have lacked. Moreover, the Chernyshevskii family itself, while sincere in church service, was not narrow in outlook. Gavriil's intellectual interests extended beyond his religious concerns, and the family appears to have regarded his role in the church as a living or career as much as a calling. They did not scruple for long when it seemed possible that their only son would seek a more illustrious career outside the church.

As head of the household, and as a person of consequence in the church affairs of Saratov, Gavriil had an enviable reputation. The testimony of contemporaries who knew him in various capacities provides a remarkably uniform impression.[7] They recognized and respected his intelligence and education, which stood out noticeably in the surrounding context.[8] He was described as honorable, kind, and generally beloved, a fact further evidenced by his apparent success in missionary work for the church. Yet he was modest in displaying his talents. Some who knew him did not even suspect that he commanded a thorough knowledge of classical languages, and as a result they did not think he could possibly prepare his son at home for entrance into the seminary. This same modesty enabled Gavriil to be a wisely permissive guide for his son's self-education. In 1848, Nikolai recorded in his diary an evaluation of his father, in which he expressed an ever-growing appreciation of his father's good qualities: Christian kindness and humanity, absence of malice, and a firm nobility of character. "More and more," Nikolai wrote, "I recognize a similarity between him and me in the best moments of my life, or, in any case, between him and what I consider to be the best in man" (I, 64). In the same passage he spoke of his mother with only slightly less generous praise, recognizing her love of his father and complete devotion to her son.

Much less is known of Evgeniia Egorovna than of Gavriil. She appears in the memoir literature of the time as a good but limited woman who, as Iu. M. Steklov noted, could exert little intellectual influence on her son. Anxious and nervous, she suffered from chronic poor health and gave herself over completely to household affairs. She lavished a loving and doubtless overprotective care on her son, which probably helped to cultivate a reticence and dependence in his character that lasted into young manhood. Nikolai once wrote that "it lies in Mother's character to interfere in everything," but his own willingness to indulge her excessive worry and concern also became family legend.[9]

On the whole, the immediate family surroundings of Nikolai's childhood gave him a secure and privileged start in life. From his family he knew modest comfort and love, and he saw before him examples of conduct which, within the terms of that society, were worthy of emulation. In later life, even complete estrangement from the religious and intellectual beliefs of his parents never threatened these bonds of affection or clouded his memory of early family happiness.

Another aspect of Nikolai's early background is more difficult to evaluate: the effect of an unjust and obviously oppressive social environment on his youthful development. The Saratov of his childhood was a relatively large provincial city of about fifty thousand, which served as a trade and administrative center for a large border region between European and Asiatic Russia. There is no question that young Nikolai was exposed there to many of the darker aspects of Russian life that he later opposed. In the thirties and forties Saratov was not far removed in time or distance from scenes of violent peasant disorder. Life in the town gave frequent examples of the arbitrary use of authority, of class injustice, unbridled privilege, and the terrible cruelties of recruitment for twenty-five years of degrading military service. Nikolai could observe a lower-class town population which was brutal in habit yet intimidated by the merest show of police power. Finally, he could witness the widespread poverty and despair that for many made survival itself a demanding task. In later writings Chernyshevskii referred to all these aspects of Russian life as recollections of his childhood and thereby led at least one biographer to ask whether such a youth could be called idyllic and happy. Was it not rather a time he remembered with sadness? [10]

This question is important because it suggests an interpretation of Chernyshevskii's life that could place his disaffection from Russian society at a considerably earlier date than seems reasonable. His comments on the unpleasant realities of Saratov life are taken from semiautobiographical literary works or from incomplete sketches for an autobiography written in prison or exile at the end of his active career, when his mature ideas were fully formed. [11] The autobiographical fragments in particular show a mature man, already in possession of a world view for which he had sacrificed comfort and freedom, reaching back into the impressions of childhood to find recollections in support of that world view. Thus, among other things, he wrote of being close to the life of the people and offered as supporting evidence examples of social injustice and the poverty of life in Saratov (I, 614). These recollections reveal that he was not blind to life outside of the comfort and security of his own home, but they do not tell much about his reactions to what he saw at the time. To read back into the young Nikolai an angry sense of social protest seems unjustified and would make unintelligible his painful search for identity and an independent scale of values during his years at the university.

Perhaps it is best to conclude that in childhood he, like all children, possessed a marvelous facility in recording the most diverse impressions at the same time as he experienced only what was compatible with his current needs and values. The other impressions, if not of immediate relevance, later became part of his mature view of life within a different framework of values and ideas. Probably Chernyshevskii himself meant something like this when, in these same autobiographical fragments, he wrote of the "chaos" of impressions and convictions a child could gain from an experience like his own in Saratov. The kaleidoscopic impressions, he claimed, were nonetheless useful for achieving an "understanding" later on (I, 671–672).

The earliest years of Nikolai's education consisted of study at home under the guidance of his father. Although in September 1836 he was enrolled officially at the local ecclesiastical school, he never in fact attended but merely appeared there from time to time to take examinations. From what is known of the school, Gavriil's decision to keep his son at home is understandable. None of the teachers would have measured up to the father's own ability and level of education, and conditions at the school were shabby and uncomfortable. Old-fashioned methods of rote learning and the use of physical punishment may also have influenced the decision.

Unlike the prevailing techniques of strictly enforced study, Gavriil's methods of teaching emphasized encouragement and example. He gave Nikolai a firm grounding in classical languages, beginning Latin at age seven and Greek at eight, and he required copybook exercises right up to the time Nikolai entered the seminary.[12] But in large part his guidance was permissive, allowing Nikolai enough time to follow his own interests and to develop a self-generating intellectual curiosity. There is evidence that this apparently excessive freedom troubled his mother, who was ambitious for her son and feared that he was not making adequate progress.[13] But her fears proved groundless. A. N. Pypin described his cousin as possessing a strong and many-sided curiosity, quick to grasp what he studied and, with the help of an extraordinary memory, able to retain it. In fact, young Nikolai showed an easy ability to learn languages and a desire to read whatever he could get his hands on.[14]

If, as Chernyshevskii later claimed, most of his education derived from his own independent reading, he was favored by the respect for books felt in his home (XV, 21). Gavriil's library has been the subject of considerable comment, even attracting the attention of the historian N. I. Kostomarov when he was in exile in Saratov. It contained secular and religious books in numbers one would not expect to find in the home of a provincial clergyman. A. N. Pypin recalled some of its contents, which ranged from older religious books and church and secular histories to the recent works of Pushkin, Zhukovskii, and Gogol. In addition to Gavriil's theological journals, other periodical literature came into the house. Nikolai is said to have read the *Moscow Gazette* avidly from age ten, and family members read *Notes of the Fatherland,* which in the early forties contained articles by Herzen and Belinskii.[15] In later years, a mature Chernyshevskii would write with obvious amusement about the haphazard choice of his childhood reading.[16] By the time he entered the seminary in 1842, however, the sheer bulk of his reading had overcome the shortcomings of disorder. Nikolai not only met the school's requirements easily but, largely through his own efforts, was educated well beyond his fourteen years.

Nikolai completed only four of the six years of course work

offered at the seminary in Saratov. It is difficult to evaluate the impact of that experience on him at the time, as he left no diary comparable to the one describing his later university years, and he had few occasions to write letters describing his schoolwork. His evaluations of the seminary made in later life were naturally colored by the fact that he had since come to reject all that the seminary stood for.

The recently established seminary at Saratov nevertheless did have some teachers of scholarly ability and renown. Thus, Nikolai was able to study the Tartar language from the orientalist G. S. Sablukov, who may have been the first to arouse his interest in scholarship and a teaching career. Twenty years later, Chernyshevskii called Sablukov one of the most conscientious scholars and purest persons he had ever known (I, 702).[17] But generally the seminary course left much to be desired from his point of view. When after only two years he wrote to a relative in St. Petersburg for information about admittance to the university in the field of Eastern languages, Nikolai complained about the students and told of backbiting among the teachers and administration (XIV, 5–7). Probably most serious was the limited scope of intellectual concern found at the seminary in a time when his own horizons had been widened by extensive reading. In the memory of one contemporary, the word politics was never heard at the seminary, and scarcely one in a hundred students saw in print the fables of Krylov or the poetry of Pushkin or Zhukovskii, whose works were not available in the seminary library.[18] The low quality of seminary education, along with Nikolai's preference for a scholarly career, may have influenced his desire to transfer to a university, but at the time he gave no further evidence of alienation from the values and the hierarchy of authority represented by the seminary.[19]

Indeed, throughout his stay at the seminary, Nikolai proved to be a model student. Unlike the families of other students, his parents showed concern for his success and conduct in school, and he in no way disappointed them. His name frequently appeared on lists of honor students, and he usually received the highest grades. Memoirs of those who knew him at the seminary describe their amazement at the answers he gave in class and their wonder at the information at his command. If young Nikolai in any way went against the grain of the system, it was probably in writing themes that were too long and in being overly zealous in speaking in class.[20]

Further insight into the character of Nikolai's work at the seminary may be gained from his theme notebooks, which are especially interesting to compare with his adult views.[21] In one of them, for example, he wrote in favor of private rather than public schooling because the former seemed best able to foster individual development. Another exercise, which included his own Russian version of one of the Psalms of David, evoked the teacher's comment that he had written in true meter but not poetically. Other themes ranged from biblical history to religious affirmations, and in one essay he dealt with the philosophical problem of the validity of sense perception. He argued that human perception must be valid because God, the author of this gift, would not betray man. Not only did this draw his teacher's favorable comment, but it showed more generally that his views at the time, so far as they can be known, remained well within the accepted bounds for one preparing to undertake a career in the church.

The reports on Nikolai's standing among his peers are contradictory. A. F. Raev, a second cousin who was also raised in Saratov and claimed to have been close to the Chernyshevskii family in the early 1840's, spoke of young Nikolai as not at all like the other boys his age. Rarely did he engage in games and sports with other children. Other accounts, however, read quite differently. V. D. Chesnokov, for example, described with evident fondness his own experience with Nikolai in a group of active young boys vigorously involved in outdoor play. In this group Nikolai showed his liveliness and kindness by wanting to include the servants' children and by making room for the younger ones who might otherwise have been left out.[22]

Nikolai's relation to other children probably changed with growth. As reading became more of a passion for him—and he was rarely found without a book in hand—he developed a seriousness and level of knowledge that set him apart from others his age.[23] Furthermore, as he grew older, he became increasingly sensitive about the extreme nearsightedness that all his life affected his self-confidence in strange situations and among new people. He once noted how difficult it was for him to keep up in some games because of the handicap of his sight.[24]

By the time he reached the seminary, Nikolai stood out among his contemporaries in several ways. From memoir accounts a portrait emerges showing personality features that remained with him throughout his career—features that seem, by their mildness, utterly different from the severity of much of his later writing. One seminary friend, A. I. Rozanov, described him as follows: "At that time he was a little more than average height with an unusually delicate feminine face; his hair light blond, but wavy, soft and beautiful; his voice was quiet, his speech pleasant. In general this was a youth resembling the most modest, sympathetic girl who unwillingly attracts approval. Unfortunately for him he was extremely nearsighted; he always held a book or notebook right up to his eyes and always wrote bent right down to the table."[25] Other reports stressed his retiring, modest character, describing him as extremely timid, bashful, gentle, and mild. He was said to blush easily and not to venture readily into open conversation. Indeed, one account revealed that the other students reacted to his "maidenlike modesty, pure heart, and gentle timidity" by referring to him among themselves as the "pretty maid" (krasnaia devitsa).[26]

These retiring ways, along with his obvious intellectual superiority, probably stood in the way of close friendship with the seminarists; and there were other obstacles as well. As the son of an archpriest, who was respected by the school administration and even the bishop, Nikolai seemed to many to be of a higher social class. He wore better clothes than the others, and it was said that he often indulged in the "aristocratic" practice of riding to school on horseback, for which he was sometimes called the "young nobleman."[27] Years later, Chernyshevskii claimed he had been friends with all of his school comrades, and intimate with about ten of them. He felt he had been treated equally by the other boys at school, yet admitted that his family situation made the poorer students feel ill at ease, so that only two or three ventured to visit him in his home. Nor were they his closest friends, but rather those who were not ashamed of their clothing (X, 17).

Nikolai's shyness and his intellectual and social differences did not necessarily alienate him from his fellows, for the same contemporary reports indicate his readiness to assist less able classmates having difficulties with translations and problem assignments, and their willingness to turn to him for help.[28] Furthermore, there was the possibility of relationships outside the seminary. A. N. Pypin remained in close contact with his cousin and in his memoirs indicated that Nikolai also knew and had long conversations with young people from a circle of noblemen known to Gavriil. Pypin suggested that these contacts might have provided the seminarist with his first exposure to "idealistic" and "social" topics.[29]

The one known seminary friendship was with M. D. Levitskii, a bright, rebellious priest's son, who attended the school on public assistance and seems to have made his mark by chafing at the narrow confines of official interpretations.[30] Once contact was broken, this school relationship left few traces. Yet during his bitter years of prison and exile, when Chernyshevskii wrote the novel *Prologue,* he gave the name Levitskii to the character modeled on his life's only intimate friend, N. A. Dobroliubov.[31]

If one can speak of significant turning points in a career, the decision to send Nikolai to a secular university for his higher education was surely one. The natural course for a very able student who had completed the seminary would have been to go on to a theological academy, such as that in Kazan, to prepare for a scholarly career within the church. Instead, Nikolai was withdrawn from the seminary before completing the course and was exposed to four years of secular learning and life in St. Petersburg. From this experience he emerged transformed in a way that no one who had known him earlier would have anticipated.

The decision to break the tradition of church service dating back on both sides of his family could not have been taken lightly, but in one regard at least, an early recognition of Niko-lai's abilities helped to pave the way. Before there was any thought of removing him from the church's educational system, his parents doubtless realized that his rightful calling was in scholarship rather than in parish service and administration in the manner of Gavriil himself. Thus, ambition for his career overcame any sentimental or practical desire they might have had to see their son inherit the family church, and the problem became one of finding the best education to suit Nikolai's talents and inclinations. When, under the guidance of G. S. Sablukov, the boy showed ability in Eastern languages, his parents de-termined to find the best way for him to continue those studies.

Chernyshevskii's later writings say surprisingly little on this question, except that the decision for him to attend a uni-versity was made a full year before his departure (I, 627). This would have been the spring of 1845, and in fact, the memoirs of the Chernyshevskiis' relative in St. Petersburg, A. F. Raev, quote a letter he received from Gavriil in April of that year, noting his intention to send Nikolai to the university a year hence, "if God favors and blesses his purpose." [32]

It would appear that another factor in the decision was diffi-culties encountered by Gavriil with local church authorities at the end of 1843 and in early 1844, at just the time when the issue first came under serious discussion. Because of an error he had made in keeping the baptismal records, Gavriil suffered the loss of his position on the Saratov consistory. There is no question that he felt this blow keenly and believed he had been unjustly treated. Although there is no evidence that Gavriil retained a lasting antagonism toward the church, the episode may have made the break in family tradition easier for him. This was surely true of Nikolai's mother who, being less aware of the educational issues involved, had at first offered greater resistance to the shift. But the blow to her husband, which she felt had caused him to "turn grey," affected her view of her son's career. Early in 1844 she wrote, "My wish was, and is, for him to remain in the clerical calling, but I am offended; the present unpleasantness shakes my determination. All poor clergymen work, toil, endure poverty and this is the reward to the very best of them. May God forgive them such injustice." These feelings lasted throughout the period of decision, and when she later confronted the seminary inspector, who asked why they wanted to withdraw Nikolai, she answered that the clerical career was too "humble." [33]

Once the decision for a secular education had been made, the family still had to choose a university. Each of the obvious alternatives—St. Petersburg, Moscow, and Kazan—must have seemed worlds away from Saratov, but the university in St. Petersburg, although the most distant, offered some clear advantages. Its reputation had grown during the 1840's, so that it probably surpassed Moscow as a center of learning. The university's location in the capital city equipped it best as a stepping-stone to state service, a consideration of which Gavriil was aware. But the overriding concern seems to have been finding someone to look after Nikolai in a far-off city, and in this regard the presence of the Chernyshevskiis' distant relative, A. F. Raev, in the capital proved decisive. Raev, five years Nikolai's senior, had left the seminary in Saratov in 1842 to study at the university in St. Petersburg. He informed the Chernyshevskii family of the steps that had to be taken for Nikolai's enrollment, and when the choice of St. Petersburg had been made, Gavriil took comfort in appealing to Raev to watch over his son.[34]

Nikolai encountered no difficulties with his request for release from the seminary. He submitted his appeal late in December 1845; a month and a half later he received permission to withdraw. Admittance to the university in the fall of 1846 depended upon qualifying examinations given to new students during the summer. To allow time to prepare for these examinations, and to rest after the long and arduous journey to St. Petersburg, the family decided that Nikolai, accompanied by his mother, would set out for the capital in the middle of May.

Without question, Nikolai was overjoyed with the change of schools. His anticipation of an exciting new intellectual experience was combined with an exalted sense of mission, as shown by his reactions to remarks of well-wishers at the time of his journey to the capital. He wrote that his soul had been touched by the hope expressed by one Saratov priest that he would return from St. Petersburg a "professor" and a "great man." During the journey, Nikolai also thrilled to the wish of a village priest that someday he might prove useful to the cause of enlightenment in Russia. Both these men, Nikolai felt, understood what is meant by striving for the glory and well-being of all mankind. They helped him to understand that one must serve not only one's family but also one's native land (I, 562).

These high-flown sentiments remained with Chernyshevskii throughout his life, though at the beginning of his university career he saw the advancement of learning in Russia as the first order of the day and aspired to a scholarly career that would contribute to this advancement. He expressed his ambition for Russia, and thereby indirectly for himself, best in a letter to his cousin A. N. Pypin in August 1846. After a damning contrast of Russia's minimal contribution to learning with its strong military power, he wrote: "Is this our destiny? To be all powerful in political and military relations and inconsequential in other higher elements of national life? In that case, it would be better not to be born than to be born a Russian, just as it would be better not to be born than to be born a Hun, an Attila, a Genghis Khan, a Tamerlane, or one of their warriors or subjects." Noting how Russia had delivered the world from the yoke of both the Mongols and the French under Napoleon, he continued:

We will firmly resolve, with all the strength of our soul to work together with others in order to end this period in which learning has been foreign to our spiritual life, that it may cease to be a strange coat, a sorrowful, impersonal aping for us. Let Russia also contribute what it should to the spiritual life of the world, as it has contributed and contributes to political life; to enter powerfully, in its own way, a saving way for humanity, in another great arena of life—learning, as it has already done in the arena of state and political life. Yes, and may this great event be achieved through us, even if only in part. Then we will not have lived in vain; we may then view this life of ours on earth with tranquillity and, with tranquillity, move on to life beyond the grave. To work together with others for glory, which does not pass, but is eternal for one's native land and the good of mankind, what can be higher and more desirable than that?

We pray to God He will grant this as our destiny. Will it be? Yes, say it will! (XIV, 48).

More than any other passage of Chernyshevskii's writings, these lines show his values and ambitions at the time he began his study at the university. He was then eighteen years old, a shy and retiring personality, precocious well beyond his years. His childhood in Saratov had given him an excellent start toward a scholarly career. Despite family precedent and a heavy dose of clerical education, he clearly preferred secular studies, although there is no contemporary evidence that he felt alienated in any other way from religion or the church. From a secure and happy family situation, he had been able to observe many darker aspects of Russian provincial life. But he was still a long way from the mood of an angry social reformer or revolutionary, and in 1846, he saw his own career, indeed his mission, as contributing to the important and formidable task of Russian enlightenment.[35]

# II. University Years: The Making of a Radical (1846–1851)

In 1846, the trip from Saratov to St. Petersburg was expensive and exhausting. Unable to afford the more rapid but costly post coach, Chernyshevskii and his mother traveled in a small hired buggy as far as Moscow, where difficulty with the driver and extreme discomfort caused them to transfer to a larger public stagecoach. In all, the trip lasted thirty-two days and, according to Chernyshevskii's estimate, cost five hundred paper rubles, fully a third of his father's annual income (XIV, 17).

For mother and son this journey was their first excursion into the wider world. In letters home they reported on the sights and gave their impressions of city life. Evgeniia Egorovna appeared uncomfortable in the strange context and characteristically felt that large cities would be no place to keep house. Her letters to Gavriil lamented the difficulties of the journey and the unpleasant weather; in St. Petersburg, she complained, everyone seemed to hustle about with fixed stares. This sense of despondency even characterized her evaluation of young Chernyshevskii's mood in St. Petersburg, which, she said, was sad, as it had been on the journey before they reached Moscow.[1]

If, in fact, her son felt remorse at making the break with his family, his letters certainly did not show it. He wrote to his relatives with a keen sense of their individual interests. To his father, he dutifully described the churches and holy places they visited, and to his young cousin, A. N. Pypin, he marveled at the wonders of the city. As a wide-eyed provincial, he found the people of Moscow bigger, healthier, better educated, and morally superior to those of Saratov. He described goods in expensive shops that were unobtainable in Saratov. To another young cousin he boasted that someday, not far off, he would be earning a fifty-thousand-ruble income (XIV, 14–33).

Once he was established, excitement over his immediate prospects took precedence over fanciful dreams of future success. He wrote with delight of touring the bookstores, which seemed to be everywhere, and the lending and public libraries. However great the shock of leaving the confines of family life in the provinces, Chernyshevskii expressed nothing but gratitude for the opportunity to attend the university. Soon after his arrival in St. Petersburg, he wrote to his father, "To live here and especially to study is excellent, although one must be a little cautious. I am pleased as I can be, and I do not know how to tell you dear Papa how thankful I am to you that I am here" (XIV, 19).

With over a month to prepare for the university's qualifying examinations, scheduled for early August, Chernyshevskii felt confident of success, more so than his fretful mother, who feared lest they had taken the trip in vain. At this time, Evgeniia Egorovna was especially concerned about her son's career. On arrival in St. Petersburg, she had apparently tried to speak on her husband's behalf before the Synodal authorities. Feeling rebuffed, she had written home that their son's career was now their only consolation. So eager was she to see young Nikolai established in the new situation to which God had called him that were it possible, she wrote, despite her obvious dislike of the capital, she would stay with him all four years.[2] This protective attitude soon led to an incident that caused Chernyshevskii no little embarrassment. Near the end of July, Evgeniia Egorovna, feeling that a kindly disposition of the professors toward her son would help insure his success, visited alone with a professor of theology, A. I. Raikovskii, in an attempt to secure special consideration for Nikolai. Her son's report of the incident to his father showed carefully controlled indignation. Without criticizing his mother openly, he argued that such solicitude was out of place and, in any case, unnecessary. He had no desire to be labeled the fool from afar who needed generous treatment (XIV, 31–32).

The examinations showed that Chernyshevskii could easily stand on his own feet. For entry into the history and philology section of the philosophical faculty, he was tested in physics, mathematics, literature, Latin, German, French, logic, geography, theology, and universal and Russian history. He scored forty-nine out of a possible fifty-five points, well above the qualifying score of thirty-three (XIV, 42). With this impressive beginning, his student uniform was ordered. A few days before the beginning of classes in late August, Evgeniia Egorovna left for Saratov. Her departure, as Chernyshevskii described it, was quieter than expected, for they "almost" avoided tears (XIV, 41).

The next four years witnessed a dramatic transformation in the life of this timid, naive provincial. At first, Chernyshevskii appeared the model of his home training, but by degrees he found a new identity, working out a world view in total opposition to that of his parents. By graduation, he had not yet settled on his ultimate career, and he still showed signs of indecision. But intellectually he had become a man, reaching an ideological position that he would amplify and develop with surprisingly little change throughout the rest of his life. As a phase in Chernyshevskii's career, therefore, these university years were of prime importance. Yet growing up did not come easily for him. It proved difficult to break the pattern of overprotection and dependence that had characterized his childhood, and perhaps a radical break with the values of his home environment was necessary for the break to occur at all.

During these years, however, Chernyshevskii showed few outward signs of rebelliousness. He continued his course of studies and shared his new-found world of radical ideas with a limited circle of acquaintances. A full consistency of ideas and action came only later. This fact makes it possible to treat separately his life as a student, preparing for an academic career, and the intellectual transformation that eventually alienated him from official Russia to the point of wishing to destroy it.

When Chernyshevskii arrived in St. Petersburg, the university he entered with an almost religious sense of awe and respect was only a few decades old. The "official nationality" of Nicholas I and his Minister of Public Education, S. S. Uvarov, set clearcut limits to freedom of inquiry in educational institutions. Science and learning were expected to advance within a framework of known truths and of social and political relationships that could not seriously be questioned. Moreover, after the European upheavals of 1848, when Chernyshevskii was still a student, the government took further steps in the direction of obscurantist regulation of university life, so that Uvarov himself was dropped for inadequate zeal.

Within these limitations, however, serious work went on at the university. A. N. Pypin, who enrolled in the historical-philological faculty just as Chernyshevskii was finishing there, and who later became one of Russia's most able scholars, wrote of the school with qualified respect. Pypin knew essentially the same faculty that had taught his cousin and felt that, although their scholarly level was not especially high, they performed the useful function of widening the horizon of knowledge and urging Russians to undertake scholarly work.[3]

Although Chernyshevskii later rejected much of the formal education offered him at the university, there were men on the faculty from whom he did learn. Two months after beginning school, for example, he wrote to his seminary teacher, G. S. Sablukov, in praise of the professor M. S. Kutorga, whose approach, he claimed, played down straight political history in favor of the history of literature and learning and relating these matters to general history and to the spirit of the times (XIV, 71–72). All these considerations reappear in Chernyshevskii's later writings. In the study of literature he received sympathetic attention, though rarely inspiration, from A. V. Nikitenko who, unlike most of his colleagues, allowed his students to develop their own points of view and gave Chernyshevskii in particular an opportunity to pursue his interest in the relationship between literature and society.[4] But the most serious and lasting scholarly influence came from I. I. Sreznevskii, the Slavic philologist, for whom Chernyshevskii did more work than for any other teacher. Under Sreznevskii's direction he spent many dreary hours in the unimaginative job of compiling word lists for old Russian chronicles. This work led in 1853 to publication by the Imperial Academy of Science of his lexicon for the Ipat'evskaia chronicle. Up to the early 1850's Chernyshevskii could still on occasion call himself a devoted student of Sreznevskii and freely express his appreciation for the many kindnesses shown him by his teacher (I, 365; XIV, 221).

In spite of this evidence that some of the formal course work influenced his development, the general story of his university years was one of disillusionment. From his early mood of hope in the power of education, he changed to a rather perfunctory attitude toward the university, preferring to find excitement and intellectual fulfillment in his own reading and discussions apart from class work. His disillusionment was not simply a reflection of the radicalization of his thought, which would naturally turn him against an official institution of the establishment. Though in time, ideological alienation played a part, the initial impetus to dissatisfaction did not originate there, because before Chernyshevskii reevaluated his own thought, he had already found much to criticize in the university. Not long after arriving in St. Petersburg, he expressed misgivings about the quality of education offered and the relevance of the required courses.

Chernyshevskii criticized the university in several areas and with varying degrees of fairness. One of his earliest complaints was the poverty of the library holdings, which lacked even a complete edition of Hegel. Three years later he reversed this severe judgment upon discovering that earlier he had been looking at an outdated catalogue, but by then he had more serious objections (XIV, 56, 156).

One of these was the failure of some teachers to keep abreast of their fields. After no more than a few weeks of classes he lamented that A. I. Raikovskii, the professor of theology, wasted his time on trifles and outworn phrases, defending the faith against outmoded challenges. How was it possible, Chernyshevskii asked, for an intelligent man, who realized the present state of Christianity and Orthodoxy, to dwell on ancient paganism or popery and not face up to the present-day threats of deism, Hegelianism, and neologism? He saw no other outcome for this sad state of affairs than that hundreds of young men, not hearing effective words in defense of religion, would all their lives retain no more than a formal faith masking inner disbelief or skepticism (XIV, 51–52).

His most persistent complaint, however, seems to have been the large number of lectures, which he soon decided were not worth the time they took from reading. After one week he became convinced that the Greek and Latin lectures had little value, though he hastened to assure his father that he would not cut classes—a resolve not easily kept once his initial zeal had weakened (XIV, 46, 128). Having experienced so much self-education in Saratov, he found it difficult to reconcile the sacrifices his parents made to send him to school with the little he got out of classes. After noting that only five of his twenty-one weekly class lectures were worthy of attention, he lamented the cost of attending the university. "My God, how expensive! If I had known, I would not have come here. Any why all this great expense? For nonsense! With a hundred silver rubles spent on books in Saratov, more would have been learned" (XIV, 63).

Furthermore, the lecture system offered little opportunity for the professors to have contact with their students. Chernyshevskii noted with regret that a number of his teachers would enter the class, go to the lectern, read their lectures, and then leave without speaking further to anyone. Thus, four months after entering school, he concluded that the main form of university instruction had value only for those students who were unwilling or unable to read for themselves. How much better was the English system, where professors published books and helped students mainly with bibliography (XIV, 86, 91).

Over the next few years, especially as his independent reading involved him with contemporary problems and new ideas, he questioned more severely the relevance of what he heard in class. Lectures at the university seemed "abominable," and his

Greek and Latin professors "childish" (I, 105). With his mind turned to events of 1848 in France, he felt impatience even with the lectures of Sreznevskii, his most respected teacher (I, 143). The school administration also drew comment in his letters home and in his diary. He found occasion both to praise the university rector, P. A. Pletnev, and to rage against the school warden and petty inspectors who kept official watch over classroom teaching and student conduct (XIV, 163; I, 141, 159, 363).

But even when feeling most critical, Chernyshevskii generally avoided an outward show of rebellion and prudently kept his resentment to himself. He complied with the system to the extent of devoting routine effort to course work, while giving major attention to his own reading. Thus, at the end of his university career he could readily apply for, and receive, official guidance and recommendations in connection with securing a teaching position (XIV, 166; I, 370).

Chernyshevskii's performance as a student nevertheless reflected his decision to find intellectual fulfillment outside the formal structure of the university. Because of his superior abilities and wide reading, he was able to achieve an adequate academic record, but he would not make the commitment of time necessary to achieve schoolwork of highest distinction. He did not, for example, enter the annual gold medal competitions for essays of the most able students, since work on an essay in 1848 would have taken him away from his close following of the revolutionary events of western Europe. When the results were announced in February 1849, his diary entry showed that he regretted losing out on the acclaim enjoyed by his winning classmate, who would now be considered the best student in the philological faculty (I, 237–238). He found temporary solace by wondering if it might be possible to write two essays the following year and win two medals, but nothing came of this. Such competition required time that Chernyshevskii was simply not willing to give up; if his self-esteem suffered, he knowingly paid the price to develop independence.

A similar impression of perfunctory attention to schoolwork is gained from viewing the closing months of his university career when he was writing his bachelor's thesis, a study of

D. I. Fonvizin, and preparing for final examinations. Neither of these undertakings ranked uppermost in his mind at the time. Although he placed close to top of the class in his final examinations, he had lost the hopeful enthusiasm with which he entered the university four years earlier (XIV, 202).

Outwardly, much of Chernyshevskii's life as a university student was drab and, apart from his intellectual enthusiasms, uneventful. In his first year he shared quarters with A. F. Raev, who was then finishing his course work in the juridical faculty and about to enter a bureaucratic career. For some time during Chernyshevskii's second year he lived alone, and then, in his last two years, he lived with his cousin Liubov Nikolaevna (Kotliarevskaia), whose husband, I. G. Tersinskii, had recently moved to the capital to enter government service.[5]

Financing his son's studies proved no easy task for Gavriil, but he managed to send enough money to support a decent, if modest, standard of living. Furthermore, from late 1847 to the end of his university course, Nilolai earned additional income by tutoring K. S. Voronin, the son of a St. Petersburg official (XIV, 141, 785). Although his letters home and his diary are filled with minute calculations of expenditures and frequent complaints about high living costs, Chernyshevskii would have had enough for a reasonably comfortable existence if, during his last two years, he had not helped to support an impoverished acquaintance, V. P. Lobodovskii, at considerable sacrifice to himself. With this added burden, he often found it difficult to make ends meet (I, 791).

Except for a few acquaintances whose contact with Chernyshevskii definitely influenced his intellectual development, he did not enjoy a wide circle of school friends. Generally, ideas rather than personal affinity provided the essential link in his personal relationships, and compatibility of views was the main consideration in all his friendships. Perhaps the fact that he was ill at ease and not outgoing in human relations caused him to define them in intellectual terms.[6] In his eyes, a person was the sum of the beliefs that he held, so that, acceptance or rejection, indeed like or dislike, was an intellectual calculation. On these grounds, he could feel confident and secure.

During and after 1848, as Chernyshevskii's ideas were acquiring definition, he found himself becoming alienated from most of those with whom circumstances threw him in greatest contact. In a revealing diary entry for December 1848, he noted that there was only one friend, V. P. Lobodovskii, with whom he could speak with pleasure. For the rest, they bored him with their banality. In discussion, he found his own enthusiasm for a subject being destroyed by the views of the person with whom he spoke. The best he could say for his two closest school acquaintances, N. P. Korelkin and I. S. Slavinskii, was that they were less unpleasant than Tersinskii and Raef, the older countrymen from Saratov with whom he lived at different times (I, 201). A year and a half later, at the time of his graduation, he wrote to his parents that among his schoolmates he might keep up an acquaintance with Korelkin and Slavinskii. For the others, he apparently had no concern (XIV, 189).

It is difficult to illuminate other aspects of Chernyshevskii's social life during his university years—his entertainments or relations with women—because his diary and letters give such matters scant attention. Apparently he adhered closely to the demands of schoolwork and of his insatiable passion for reading and discussion. Early in his academic career, he wrote a revealing self-characterization in letters to his overanxious parents, who were apparently finding it difficult to have confidence in their young son's ability to make decisions. He chided them for their worry and insisted that he had not the temperament to expose himself to the dangers faced by young people in St. Petersburg (XIV, 82, 123).

Chernyshevskii's demand for trust was more than justified by the tight control he exercised over his own conduct. For example, many years later, in 1877, he wrote to one of his sons that as a young man he had been attracted to the theater, but for most of his student years he refrained from attending, for fear that he would go too often and take too much time away from his work. He relented only in his senior year, and then regretted that time and money should be spent for entertainment. "What an eccentric (chudak) I was in those days," he concluded (XV, 48).

Something similar might be said of his awakening interest in women, which offered him little diversion, perhaps because of self-restraint, but also because of social ineptitude. During his student years, he had very little to report about social affairs. Apparently he did his best to avoid such gatherings. One party, however, which took place in December 1848 at the lodgings of I. V. Pisarev, an acquaintance from Saratov, made a disturbing impression on Chernyshevskii. At the beginning of a long diary account, he claimed that he would never have attended had he known that young ladies would be present and dancing. Yet his subsequent, meticulous description of his every move over several hours showed that he was both fascinated by the event and troubled by the fact that he did not know how to conduct himself. That evening he had been "a post—nothing more," hardly a satisfactory role. He realized that he must learn to dance, so that he might more often enter into the company of young women, and to play some instrument, draw, and converse in French and German. All this was necessary, he wrote, because he felt that he had begun a new period in his life, a period in which the physical and spiritual needs of love would grow stronger (I, 208–213).

As far as can be gathered from Chernyshevskii's diary for his remaining student years, practically nothing came of this surge of interest in women. Continuing a detailed, day-by-day description of this activities, he left no mention of a more active social life or of any serious attempts to develop social graces. Two months after this party, he found all kinds of excuses to turn down an invitation to be introduced to a family with an attractive eighteen-year-old daughter (I, 249–250). It was as if Chernyshevskii had briefly revealed to himself a little-known side of his personality and then, because he felt awkward and insecure, and because there were other things to think about, he again became the no-nonsense seeker of truth, more concerned with the question of woman's place in society than with social life itself. Except for an occasional diary reference to a girl who caught his eye, he maintained this stance until after graduation (I, 290–291, 301).

Despite Chernyshevskii's apparently dull, sullen conformity to school regulations and his withdrawn social existence during these years, he was experiencing a dramatic intellectual transformation of great significance to his later career, and thus to the course of Russian history. After a painful process of re-evaluation, he reached a position profoundly critical of the society to which he outwardly conformed. Given the conditions of the time and the particular cast of his own personality and early education, Chernyshevskii's intellectual transformation was perforce a lonely, individual experience. For the young man who arrived at the university in 1846, firm in the traditional view that the tsar sat rightfully on the throne and that God reigned on high, there was available no fully developed alternative that might be comfortably adopted. Although critical ideas existed, based on a native rejection of different aspects of Russia's traditional system or on diverse waves of thought from western Europe, they had yet to be sifted and integrated into a prescription for the ills of Russian society. This, indeed, was to be Chernyshevskii's achievement, which a decade or so later would provide young people with a system of thought that could be used as a basis of action. In his own student career, under a flood of divergent influences, Chernyshevskii had to define for himself the inadequacies of his earlier thought and to choose and integrate new values and ideas. Although he worked most often with borrowed ideas, he made a contribution through his unique formulation of these ideas into a world view.

Chernyshevskii's wide reading proved to be his major source of inspiration, but a few personal relationships also had significant impact. Unlike his classmates, teachers, and older family relations, who served as little more than foils for the development of his daring opinions, four of his friends played important roles in assisting his intellectual growth: M. I. Mikhailov, V. P. Lobodovskii, A. V. Khanykov, and I. I. Vvedenskii. The first of these influences, that of M. I. Mikhailov, the future poet and revolutionary, is the most difficult to document specifically from Chernyshevskii's writings of the time, although he did identify Mikhailov as his closest friend during his first year and a half at school (XIV, 189). In addition, one contemporary referred to Chernyshevskii's frequent claim that Mikhailov had given him his "first push on the path to development."[7]

Mikhailov came from the family of an Orenburg official who, in one generation as the reward for state service, had risen from the status of freed serf to a title of nobility. At home he received an excellent education and commanded several foreign languages. He began at the university at the same time as Chernyshevskii but, because of low scores on his entrance examinations, attended only as an auditor. According to N. V. Shelgunov, who later knew both men well, the two met on their first day of classes.[8] From all reports the young students were quite different in personality and behavior, as Mikhailov was more open and outwardly emotional. Yet in February 1847, Chernyshevskii wrote to his parents that he saw Mikhailov often and felt less restrained with him than with any of the other students. Even if he did not approve of everything about this young man with "such a kind heart," Chernyshevskii clearly valued his friendship (XIV, 110).

A. N. Pypin, who met Mikhailov a few years later through Chernyshevskii, felt that their main tie was a common interest in literature, noting that Mikhailov had a knowledge of foreign literature shared by few in his generation.[9] This would have been a great attraction for Chernyshevskii, who also spent much time reading both Russian and Western writers. Nor should an interest in literature be considered a detraction from Chernyshevskii's growing social and political concerns, for the works of Eugene Sue, George Sand, and Dickens served both ends.

Beyond this, although it is difficult to establish definitely, Mikhailov may have served to encourage a more secular turn of mind in the former seminary student. On at least one occasion they read together from the current periodicals *The Contemporary* and *Notes of the Fatherland,* and probably Mikhailov was able to help his friend see reality through more critical and worldly eyes (XIV, 99). Early in 1848, some months after Mikhailov had left the university for lack of money, Chernyshevskii recalled with apparent acceptance Mikhailov's frequent reproach of him for being insufficiently perceptive and taking a year to recognize things other men recognized at once (I, 145). Clearly Chernyshevskii found in the future poet a friend who matched his own ability to read widely and who offered him an opportunity to share ideas and impressions, at the very time that university work first fell short of his expectations. How much this must have meant to Chernyshevskii can be seen in the warmth and concern displayed in a series of letters he wrote to Mikhailov in the early 1850's, after hearing that his friend might return to St. Petersburg. After a lapse of time, during which his own views had changed greatly, Chernyshevskii still wrote with openness and surprising frankness about newly formed convictions that in the Russia of Nicholas I one could share only with intimate and trusted friends (XIV, 198–199, 204–219).

If frequency of contact, in a relationship that bordered on infatuation, can be taken as an indication of influence, then Chernyshevskii's acquaintance with V. P. Lobodovskii must be considered one of the most important of his later student years. He met Lobodovskii in the spring of 1848 and, in the course of two years, filled his diary with so much praise of his new friend's intellectual and moral superiority that one can scarcely consider it a friendship of equals. The relationship rather showed a young provincial awestruck at contact with a personality more worldly than himself and, initially at least, more daring in his views. Only gradually did Chernyshevskii come to see his idol in a truer, less flattering light. Although Lobodovskii cannot be credited with instilling in his young ad-mirer his own set of convictions, there were several aspects of Chernyshevskii's development that clearly showed Lobodov-skii's influence.[10]

Chernyshevskii began to show a cooling of affection by 1850, but there is no doubt about the strength of his earlier attach-ment. He told his parents that when he was living close to Lo-bodovskii, he visited him as often as four times a week and con-sidered him to be the brightest of all the young people he had met and the one with the best character. He made the same statement in a letter to Mikhailov and even called Lobodovskii the only person for whom he had respect (XIV, 189, 210). In his diary, he described his willingness to sacrifice himself to help his friend out of pressing financial difficulties, calling himself a useless person, whereas Lobodovskii was a person of significance (I, 194–195).

It is difficult to share the author's evaluation of the relationship. While the young student spared no effort to take on the financial burdens of the older man, self-centered Lobodovskii appeared unwilling to do much to help himself and thus took unfair advantage of a friend (I, 320–321). In unintended and unexpected ways, however, Lobodovskii probably repaid his benefactor. His own life experience, including dismissal from a seminary, petty government service, tramps about Russia, experience with women, and finally marriage, opened a new world of considerations for the more sheltered Chernyshevskii. When, for example, Lobodovskii admitted that he was becoming bored with the banality of family life, the wide-eyed diarist noted that he was hearing such words for the first time. Similarly, he devoted many pages to recording the story of Lobodovskii's past, which obviously impressed him (I, 260–264).

Most important for Chernyshevskii's development was the fact that Lobodovskii was an interesting and critical person with whom to discuss literature and the current issues of philosophy and politics claiming his attention. Unfortunately, these conversations were mentioned in Chernyshevskii's diary with only a brief indication of Lobodovskii's views. Yet it seems reasonable to assume that his remarks made a considerable impression on the young admirer, if only to reinforce an opinion Chernyshevskii was working toward himself. Thus, they are known to have shared a high opinion of Gogol and, along with many of their generation, preferred Lermontov to Pushkin (I, 50, 54, 67). Similarly, in the spring of 1849, just as Chernyshevskii was beginning to read Ludwig Feuerbach, he heard Lobodovskii speak of Feuerbach in words of praise (I, 251, 253). By the following year, when he had started to reconsider his earlier uncritical acceptance of Lobodovskii, he could still write, "As before, I consider him, if not brighter than myself, then in any case more penetrating and much more mature of mind in many respects. I cannot defend myself against his influence when he gives his judgment on some work, especially if it is literary" (I, 358–359).

One further consideration is often mentioned by Soviet writers who see Lobodovskii as having helped direct Chernyshevskii's attention to the prospect of revolution in Russia, later only to turn away himself and become a government official.[11] There are several diary references to discussions between the two men on the possibility of revolution in Russia. The first of these, dated August 1848, is the earliest reference to the subject in all of Chernyshevskii's writing. For some time the impressionable student even thought that Lobodovskii might play a role as a revolutionary leader, only slowly coming to realize that his improvident friend scarcely possessed the stuff of which revolutionaries are made (I, 67, 237, 253).

Unlike his acquaintance with Mikhailov and Lobodovskii, which showed some personal concern, Chernyshevskii's relationship with A. V. Khanykov remained on a purely intellectual level. Their paths crossed for a brief five months, from late November 1848 to the following April, yet the importance of this contact can hardly be overemphasized.

Khanykov, an ardent supporter of Fourierism, had been dismissed as a student in the university the previous year for bad conduct. He remained at the university as an auditor and took active part in the weekly discussion meetings of the Petrashevskii circle, where radical ideas were openly considered. Apparently intent on making converts, after one of the university lectures he took the initiative in introducing himself to Chernyshevskii and identifying the socialist cause he represented. At first Chernyshevskii was put off by this show of zeal, but he appreciated the honesty of Khanykov's convictions and agreed to visit him and borrow some of the writings of Fourier and his disciples. Within a week of this meeting, he was describing Khanykov as an intelligent man of convictions, with whom he felt like a student before a teacher. He valued the commitment and ardor of this "propagandist," whose new ideas were not limited to Fourierism. Soon he noted that books borrowed from Khanykov had become the major part of his reading (I, 178, 182–183, 200).

For several months before his arrest, therefore, Khanykov helped to influence Chernyshevskii's reading at a critical time in his development. Although Chernyshevskii may already have known about Fourier, with Khanykov he first was obliged to make a judgment on the writings.[12] Fourierism thus became the source for one major component of his socialist position and the inspiration for some of his later writings. The influence of Khanykov proved equally decisive in the fields of philosophy and religion. In January 1849, Khanykov asked Chernyshevskii to make a translation from Hegel's *Rechtsphilosophie,* and this experience led Chernyshevskii to reject the smattering of Hegel he had gathered from secondary sources (I, 229–230). Khanykov subsequently urged Chernyshevskii to read a book more to his own liking, Ludwig Feuerbach's *Das Wesen des Christentums.* Feuerbach in turn became Chernyshevskii's most consistent guide throughout his life (I, 248).

In urging Chernyshevskii to read Fourier and Feuerbach, Khanykov's influence was probably decisive. In one other important area he merely reinforced a point of view that his young friend had heard elsewhere, regarding the possibility of revolution in Russia. Earlier, Chernyshevskii in almost an offhand fashion had recorded remarks by Lobodovskii to the effect that Russia might experience revolution. In December 1848, however, Khanykov made a far stronger impression when he listed the elements of unrest in Russia: the schismatics, the communal organization of the appanage peasants, the dissatisfaction of large parts of the service class, and so on. He argued that these conditions made revolution not only possible but perhaps imminent. Chernyshevskii's response was one of admiration for Khanykov's ability to see things he had not seen, or had not wanted to see, himself. The new insights troubled him, making it seem that the ground beneath his feet, which had always appeared so firm, was turning to water (I, 196). Some weeks later, describing another conversation about revolution and the feebleness of the government, Chernyshevskii identified Khanykov as the one who had planted these ideas in his mind (I, 235).

Through Khanykov, Chernyshevskii met I. M. Debu, a member of the Petrashevskii circle; he then discovered that another student acquaintance, P. N. Filippov, was also a member. Despite these contacts, and the fact that his own thought was tending in the same direction, he did not himself attend their gatherings. When news came of the group's arrest, in April 1849, Chernyshevskii thanked his good fortune, realizing that he had only been spared by the chance timing of the police attack. "In time," he wrote, "I would naturally have been involved." For those government officials responsible for the suppression, his judgment was unequivocal: the beasts should have been hanged (I, 274).

These months of contact with Khanykov thus brought Chernyshevskii to the threshold of involvement with a group considered by the government to be dangerous and subversive. By the spring of 1849, however, he still had not been subject to the challenge and stimulation of a larger, cosmopolitan society of intellectuals. This experience he received in the so-called Vvedenskii circle. I. I. Vvedenskii, also a native of Saratov, was fifteen years Chernyshevskii's senior.[13] After completing the local seminary in 1832, he attended the theological academy in Moscow, although he showed little desire to follow a clerical calling. Before finishing the course, he decided to pursue a secular education in St. Petersburg. In the capital, after his graduation in 1842, Vvedenskii taught Russian language and literature at two military academies, and in time he became known for his translations of Dickens and Thackeray. Beginning in 1847, he opened his home to weekly discussions that attracted other teachers, writers, students, and interested young intellectuals. The conversations usually turned on matters of literature, but frequently, in the critical atmosphere of the late forties, other social and political themes were heard. No single philosophy or political tendency dominated the group, but a generally critical attitude toward existing authority in Russia allowed discussion of even the most radical ideas and programs, apparently without restraint.

There is some question as to when Chernyshevskii began to attend these discussions.[14] Although he had made the acquaintance of Vvedenskii at least a year and a half earlier, it was only in December 1849 that he began to attend some of the Wednesday evening gatherings (I, 49, 271, 340–343). From this time until Chernyshevskii left St. Petersburg to teach in Saratov in April 1851, frequent references to discussions of the circle appear in his diary, although he did not attend every week. At the same time, he enjoyed a growing friendship with Vvedenskii himself.[15]

To judge from several memoir accounts, Chernyshevskii stood out in the Vvedenskii group because of the extreme views he expressed. One member, A. P. Miliukov, later noted a contradiction in young Chernyshevskii, between the mildness of his manner and the harshness of his views.[16] An anonymous account later described him as the "red-headed youth who, with a petulant and shrill voice, defended the fantasies of the communists and socialists." Vvedenskii, this writer continued, in no way shared his opinions.[17] A third report claimed that for some time Chernyshevskii bore the name "St. Just," because of his reaction to a tearful show of sympathy for the family of Louis XVI during a group reading at Vvedenskii's. "You women are strange," he is reported to have said, "yesterday you cried about the lambs who were eaten by the wolf, and today about the wolf who ate the lambs." [18]

Vvedenskii's opinion of his young visitor is revealed in a secondhand account written in 1890. According to this report, Vvedenskii found the young Chernyshevskii somewhat puzzling but also sympathetic, hard-working, and gifted. He predicted, in 1851, that someday Chernyshevskii would play a prominent role in Russian literature, perhaps even surpassing Belinskii.[19] The fact that Vvedenskii held his younger friend in high regard is shown by his efforts to help him find his first job. Chernyshevskii responded by helping Vvedenskii prepare for his master's degree examinations (I, 378, 390, 399).

Chernyshevskii clearly gained as much from the group discussions as he contributed to them. Primarily, they gave him stimulating contact with a wider circle of intellectuals, who discussed questions that had troubled him for some time. Apart from literature, he noted the group's concern with revolution and the socialist theory of Western Europe, different interpretations of religion, the fate of the Petrashevskii circle, criticism of the tsarist government, and even regicide (I, 346, 362, 373, 395, 401). He had the opportunity not only to test his ideas, but also to make himself heard and respected in a larger gathering. Initially, he seemed insecure and even intimidated by the situation: the first evening he did not enter the conversation at all. But by degrees, he came to feel more at home, and by mid-March 1850, he stated with some pride that he was becoming a stronger voice in the group (I, 343, 365). Outside of the classroom, where many of his most cherished thoughts could not be mentioned, no other situation offered him this needed opportunity to build his confidence and test his ideas.

The diversity of opinion among those who visited Vvedenskii makes it difficult to determine their exact effect on Chernyshevskii's thinking. Only once did he identify a general tendency, when in May 1850 he wrote that the group spoke against religion, which forced him also to speak against it, although clearly he had not yet made up his own mind (I, 373). He described his compliance as evidence of "weakness of character," but since he reached a similar view himself not long afterward, these discussions probably had some influence.

The Vvedenskii circle may also have affected Chernyshevskii's appreciation of Belinskii and Herzen, whose influence on his early thought is often exaggerated.[20] While still in Saratov, Chernyshevskii had admittedly read *Notes of the Fatherland,* which in the early and mid-forties, under A. A. Kraevskii's direction, carried articles by Belinskii and Herzen. Later in life he once mentioned Belinskii among the hodgepodge of writers he had read while still a seminary student, and another time he wrote of having familiarity with the Russian expositions of left-wing Hegelianism while still in Saratov (I, 597; II, 121). Yet neither of these references is sufficient grounds to claim that Belinskii and Herzen were important to him during most of his university career, prior to the time of his involvement with the Vvedenskii circle in late 1849.

In the case of Belinskii, the young Chernyshevskii even recorded some strongly negative comments in response to Belinskii's bitter attacks on Gogol's *Selected Passages from Correspondence with Friends.* Chernyshevskii could scarcely appreciate the views expressed in *Selected Passages,* but neither could he abide so rapid and total an attack on one of his favorite writers (XIV, 105–106). Perhaps because of this resentment, Chernyshevskii did not react to the news of Belinskii's tragic early death in May 1848, which came as such a blow to those who knew him or valued his work. Indeed, six months later, the young student could still refer to parts of his future idol's final articles as "hackneyed" (I, 161).

Within a year after he first attended the discussions at Vvedenskii's, however, Chernyshevskii's views on Belinskii had come full circle to an appreciation that resembled discipleship. At the end of 1850 he wrote to Mikhailov that the works of Belinskii were the only things worth reading in preparation for a qualifying examination as a teacher of literature. Other works were "nonsense" (XIV, 211). It is not possible from Chernyshevskii's writing to identify the source of his newly found appreciation of Belinskii, but A. P. Medvedev's study of the circumstantial evidence points convincingly to some members of the Vvedenskii group. Medvedev identifies A. P. Miliukov, A. A. Chumikov, M. B. Chistiakov, and Vvedenskii himself as those who encouraged Chernyshevskii to study Belinskii further, and who may first have acquainted him with the famous denunciatory "letter to Gogol." [21]

With regard to Chernyshevskii's acquaintance with the works of Herzen, it is significant that he made so little mention of Herzen prior to his contact with the Vvedenskii circle. In January 1847, he had apparently read the first part of *Who Is To Blame?* in a supplement to *The Contemporary,* but he made no further reference to the work at that time (XIV, 99, 781). During 1848 and 1849, although he filled his diary with references to the Russian and European writers he was reading, he made no mention of Herzen. In November 1849, on the eve of his active participation in the Vvedenskii group, he did make an off-hand comment on *Who Is To Blame?* and Goncharov's *A Common Story* suggesting that these two works were standards of quality in recent literature (I, 336). But nothing in these brief references prepares one for the warm statements of appreciation Chernyshevskii made during and after his attendance at

Vvedenskii's, where Herzen was often read aloud and had strong support (I, 395; XIV, 215). Six months after he had joined the circle, Chernyshevskii, perhaps carried away by what he liked to call his "usual enthusiasm," remarked that he valued Herzen above all other Russians and that there was nothing he would not do for him (I, 381). The group's discussions had thus stimulated his interest in a second leading critic of Russian society whose ideas and attitudes were to influence his own.

Any discussion of the intellectual transformation of Chernyshevskii during his final years at the university necessarily rests on the evidence of his student diary, recorded originally in his own cipher, and a few of his letters.[22] For providing insight into his ideas and his view of himself, the diary is invaluable, especially when he occasionally tried to sum up his progress, as if to find his bearings in a sea of confusion and doubt. However, the diary also has serious limitations, most noticeably the fact that it deals only with his last two years at school. Admittedly this was the time of greatest change, but the diary's limited scope means that little is known of what led up to the changes that began in 1848. A further problem is that he tended to make off-hand statements of partisanship rather than arguing a particular point of view, so that one is frequently unsure of his understanding of the men or schools of thought treated. Finally, he often buried his opinions in a mass of trivia.

But there can be no doubt of the major lines of Chernyshevskii's development. By 1850, philosophical materialism had replaced his earlier religious beliefs; he considered himself a socialist, and he was unalterably opposed to Russia's traditional structure of political power. Unlike Belinskii, whose intellectual life was troubled by recurring doubt and a restless search for truth, Chernyshevskii found his truth earlier in his career and spent the rest of his life defending and elaborating his basic views, or working out their implications in other areas of concern.

Of all the changes he experienced, the collapse of his faith in Orthodoxy proved the most difficult, and yet, because Orthodoxy included a total view of man and nature, this change was logically necessary for many of the others. Attempts have been made to find traces of materialism in his early seminary writings, but they remain unconvincing.[23] It is likely that his early religious training consisted in large part of uninspired, routine arguments, so that his religious beliefs may never have been very profound, nor personally vital to him. Still, he went to the university as a loyal son of the church and only there, about halfway through the course, began to experience confusion and doubt. In describing his conversion to a fully secular view of life, unfortunately he left no record of his earlier religious views. But the fact is that his intellectual defense of the faith crumbled quickly, and much of the crisis he experienced came from a reluctance to break away from church ritual and to accept the implications of an atheistic position. As early as August 1848, for example, he claimed that he maintained religious ties only out of habit and that religion appeared to contradict all his other views. Yet he was troubled by Plato's suggestion that without religion, society could not exist (I, 66).

Some sense of Chernyshevskii's approach to the problem of religion, as well as of the vagueness and confusion of his convictions, may be gained from a diary entry just a month after his claim to maintain religious ties only out of habit. This time he wrote that he accepted the basic tenets of Christ's divinity, suffering, and resurrection, but that Christianity had to improve with the times. Critics like the neologists, the rationalists, and even Pierre Leroux were not attacking Christianity in essence, but merely the existing interpretation of it. He praised the recognition by these critics that the church, in its relation to society, had to meet the needs of the day. For his own part, he accepted the fundamental concept of Christian love, but believed that this love must be developed and applied. He had more difficulty affirming God's divine help to man. How was this done? Was it limited to man's inner moral sphere, or could there be supernatural interference in the external order of this world? He could not answer from his own experience, except to report that some of his own actions seemed explainable only through faith in the supernatural help of God (I, 132–133).

Of the diverse intellectual challenges to religion available to

Chernyshevskii in late 1848 and early 1849, he considered two of the most likely alternatives: Hegel's system of philosophical idealism, which he quickly rejected, and Feuerbach's materialism, which gave him the basic assumptions of his later world view. In the fall of 1848, Chernyshevskii first read the *Geschichte der letzten Systeme der Philosophie in Deutschland von Kant bis Hegel,* by the German Hegelian Karl Ludwig Michelet. At first glance, he was impressed by Michelet's recognition of universal progress and his respect for Hegel. Chernyshevskii wrote that he too felt himself to be a partisan of Hegel, but then quickly admitted that he knew little about him (I, 147). At this point, Chernyshevskii's understanding of Hegel probably went not much beyond the idea of progress in history and the view of significant personalities as manifestations of a developing purpose. In diary entries of November and December 1848, he referred briefly, but with apparent approval, to Hegel's concept of the development of the Idea, though there is still no clear evidence of his having yet read any of Hegel's own works (I, 166, 193–194).

Early in 1849, Chernyshevskii began Hegel's *Rechtsphilosophie,* with the intention of making notes for his new acquaintance A. V. Khanykov. Contact with Hegel in the original sobered his enthusiasm. At first, he claimed not to see Hegel's genius, but then admitted that the problem was his own lack of understanding (I, 230–231). Yet the very next day, while reading the section on morality, he arrived at the view that became the basis for his rejection of idealistic philosophy. Again he assumed a depreciating tone: "It appears to me that he [Hegel] is a slave of the existing order of things, the existing structure of society, so that he does not even renounce capital punishment, and so on" (I, 231–232). He did not complete the book, deciding that it would be better to prepare a translation from the section on Hegel in Michelet's book on German philosophy than to continue his synopsis from the original work. Years later, writing of himself in the third person, Chernyshevskii gave a version of this episode that stressed the weakness of Hegel's system.

In the original, Hegel pleased him much less than he had expected [from his reading of] the Russian expositions. The reason for this was that the Russian followers presented his system in the spirit of the left-wing Hegelian school. In the original, Hegel seemed more like the philosophers of the seventeenth century and even the scholastics, than that Hegel who appeared in the Russian exposition of his system. Reading him was tiresome because of his obvious uselessness for forming a scientific mode of thought (II, 121).

In sum, unless more evidence can be found to credit young Chernyshevskii with a deeper insight into Hegel's system, he cannot be said to have moved through the school of Hegel to the position of Feuerbach.[24] In the fall of 1848, Chernyshevskii had no more than a superficial, second-hand knowledge of Hegelianism. Early in 1849, when he went directly to Hegel's writings, he admitted difficulty in understanding them and, without penetrating deeply into the works, concluded that Hegel's conservative social and political views were directly opposed to his own desire for change and reform. After this disappointment, he sought truth elsewhere. In later years, any further reading he might have done in Hegel was undertaken from a totally antithetical position.

If Hegel did not provide an acceptable alternative to Chernyshevskii's Christian cosmology and anthropology, the teachings of Feuerbach proved more fruitful. P. V. Annenkov noted that when Feuerbach's *Das Wesen des Christenthums* had first appeared, it caused a tremor of excitement among the "Westerners."[25] By 1848 and 1849, the book still aroused animated discussion in student groups. After his disappointment with Hegel, Chernyshevskii borrowed Feuerbach's book from Khanykov. He must have known the book by reputation, because in his diary he wondered whether he would accept Feuerbach's thesis and concluded that he would probably continue to believe in a personal God and in the reality of Revelation, though not according to the current church interpretation (I, 248).

At first, Feuerbach's argument—that man had created God in human image and assigned to Him the best qualities of human nature—did not appeal to Chernyshevskii. He admired Feuerbach's style and integrity but could not agree that man's tendency to think of God in human images proved anything about God's actual character or existence (I, 248). Despite favorable comments from his friend Lobodovskii, who apparently was also reading Feuerbach for the first time, Chernyshevskii continued to express doubts. In mid-March 1849, he noted that he was reading Feuerbach "without very much attention or willingness, but as if from obligation" (I, 255).

This inauspicious beginning led to a year of distressed confusion. Chernyshevskii first began to doubt the existence of a personal God, writing that he leaned toward the explanations of "the pantheists, or Hegel, or better Feuerbach" (I, 297). Early in 1850, he linked his confusion to his own character: "Concerning religion I don't know what to say. I don't know whether I believe in the existence of God, in immortality of the soul, and so on. In theory I am rather inclined not to believe, but in practice I lack the firmness and decisiveness to break with my former thoughts on this. But, if I had the daring, then, in negation, I would be a follower of Feuerbach and, in contention, I don't know whose [follower I would be], it would seem his also" (I, 358). By September 1850, he could be more definite and say that his skepticism had reached a point where he was given over almost completely to the teachings of Feuerbach (I, 391). Certainly Chernyshevskii's alienation from religion was completed not long after his graduation from the university. On his return trip to Saratov in March 1851, he argued religion in "the spirit of Strauss and Feuerbach" (I, 402). Soon after that, a contemporary noted his inclination to look upon Christianity as having only historical interest, and during his courtship in 1853, Chernyshevskii felt obliged to tell his future bride about his disbelief in religion (I, 424).[26]

Unfortunately, there are few other references to Feuerbach in Chernyshevskii's later diary. He is known to have read other materialists, like Claude Helvétius, at the same time (I, 385). According to his later statement, during this period he read and reread Feuerbach, and he even claimed to know whole pages by heart (II, 121; XV, 23). However, exactly which works he read is not known. E. A. Liatskii has argued from internal evidence that Chernyshevskii must have read the *Vorläufigen Thesen zur Reform der Philosophie* (1842) and *Grundsätze der Philosophie der Zukunft* (1843).[27] These books would have given him an understanding of Feuerbach's belief in the need for a radical break with all existing philosophy as well as with religion.[28] Further, they would have reinforced his own tendency to seek the theoretical basis for radical social and political action in a new philosophy closely allied with natural science. Conversely, he either did not read or consciously ignored Feuerbach's earlier criticism of absolute or metaphysical materialism, which might have helped to make his own position less extreme.[29]

Many parts of Chernyshevskii's writings cannot be explained merely as derivations from Feuerbach, but the fundamental insight upon which he built his world view did come from *Das Wesen des Christenthums*. Simply stated, it was that a dualistic opposition between man and God, or any other supernatural power or essence, did not exist. Man was matter alone, and he lived in a material universe. Chernyshevskii believed that recognition of this truth was the first step toward the liberation of humanity. Materialistic monism thus provided a weapon against all philosophy and religion which in the past had given comfort and support to political and social conservatism. Furthermore, materialism, considered by Chernyshevskii to be synonymous with natural science, could serve as basis for a new formulation of human knowledge.

Questions of political economy and social theory also held an important place in Chernyshevskii's thought during these years, but changes in this area cannot be described with precision. Although Chernyshevskii made frequent reference to his sympathy for western socialism in his student diary, and at one time even identified himself as an "ultrasocialist," neither the diary nor his contemporary letters give a clear picture of what he understood the word socialism to mean (XIV, 198).

A sympathy for victims of social injustice probably stimulated his early appreciation of Western novelists like Eugene Sue, George Sand, and Charles Dickens. In 1846, for example, he praised Sue's *Mysteries of Paris* and spoke of the author's "sacred" love of humanity (XIV, 45). But not until 1848, with news of the political and social convulsions in France, did he show evidence of giving the question of socialism serious consideration.

He learned of events in France largely from the *Journal des débats,* which transcribed speeches representing different political and economic points of view. Many of these views were new to him, and in 1848 at least, his knowledge of a given position often went little beyond what these speeches contained. Characteristically, his spotty knowledge of the original works of French socialists did not prevent his taking a strong partisan position in their favor.[30]

During 1848, the speeches of Louis Blanc before the Luxembourg Commission provided the strongest socialist influence on Chernyshevskii (I, 358). In July of that year, he attributed the program "from each according to his abilities, to each according to his needs" to Blanc and accepted it as his own long-range goal. By mid-summer, he was calling himself a partisan of the extreme party in France and giving special praise to Blanc and Pierre Leroux (I, 61, 66). A month later, Chernyshevskii added an appreciative comment on Alexandre Ledru-Rollin and formulated more specifically one of the building blocks of his future world view: the idea that political freedom alone could not guarantee social and economic well-being. He wrote in reaction to the speeches of French liberals:

I have no love for these gentlemen who speak the word freedom, freedom—and then limit this freedom to saying the word and writing it into laws, but do not introduce [freedom] into life. [I have no love for men who] abolish laws that speak of inequality but do not abolish a social order in which nine-tenths of the people are slaves or proletarians. It is not a question of whether or not there is a tsar, or a constitution, but whether in social relationships one class can suck the blood of another (I, 110).

Near the end of November 1848, at his first meeting with A. V. Khanykov, Chernyshevskii was urged to consider the teachings of Fourier.[31] In the following months, Chernyshevskii read the Fourierist journal *La phalange,* as well as parts of Fourier's writings on the subjects of free will and universal unity.

Although Chernyshevskii drew heavily on Fourier a decade later when outlining plans for a utopian community, in this first reading he did not seem overly impressed. He showed sympathy for Fourier's general ideas on associations and on the need to harmonize human passions, but he seems to have responded to Fourier as much for his challenge to religious convictions as for his teachings on socialism (I, 178–179, 183, 189, 194–195).

In July 1849, Chernyshevskii outlined his views in a number of areas. He described himself as a "red republican and socialist" and a partisan of Louis Blanc. However, in speculating about what he would do if power were in his hands, he mentioned only separate reform measures: liberation of the serfs, discharge of over half the army, limitation of administrative power, aid to education, and political rights for women (I, 297). It is impossible, from statements like this, to determine exactly what Chernyshevskii regarded as a positive socialist program. More than likely, he used the word *socialist* loosely, to cover many varieties of liberal and radical reform.

But if his socialist program remained poorly defined during these school years, there is no question about his general sympathies. His interest in the events of 1848 had helped to transform vague concern for the oppressed and underprivileged into a firm conviction that the emphasis on political freedom by European liberals offered no solution to the pressing social problems of the day. Almost a decade passed before he found the chance to elaborate his program.

In the area of political power and revolution, Chernyshevskii found it more difficult to make a direct step to a radical position. Here again, the news of unrest in Europe in 1848 served as a catalyst to help transform him into a professed revolutionary. But his general concern for social justice at first overshadowed any specifically democratic political program, and initially, he tended to think of Russia as a case apart.

In the summer of 1848, alongside his strong statements of support for Louis Blanc and Pierre Leroux, Chernyshevskii expressed the view that Russia could not be compared with the West: "They are men, we are children; our history has developed out of different beginnings. We have not yet had class struggle or it is only starting, and their political understanding is not applicable to our Empire" (I, 66). Probably this distinction allowed him to formulate the surprising solution to the problem of political power recorded in his diary in September of that year, which reflected the theory, but not the practice, of Nicholas I's "official nationality." He stated his approval of the principles of a republic and majority rule, but noted that there could be no true political equality between rich and poor. The poor or, as he called them, the weak members of society would be defeated in any conflict of interests, which would confront them with a new form of slavery.

Therefore I think that the only and possibly best form of rule is a dictatorship, or better a hereditary absolute monarchy, but one which understands its duty. [This monarchy should realize] that it must stand above all classes and that it is created especially for the protection of the oppressed. But these oppressed are the lower class, the peasants and workers, and therefore the monarchy must truly stand in support of them, place itself at their head, and protect their interests (I, 121).

Chernyshevskii thus conceived of an ideal monarchy, working to create the conditions in which its own existence would no longer be necessary.

Perhaps it was this hope that stimulated his generally favorable comments on N. M. Karamzin's *Memoir on Ancient and Modern Russia*. Appreciation of a strong defender of traditional autocratic power seems out of place in the diary of a partisan of the extreme party in France. Yet even when listing Karamzin's weaknesses, Chernyshevskii did not trouble over the basic question of the locus of sovereignty (I, 146). Furthermore, in other remarks on France, he hesitated to cope with the question of full popular sovereignty, and several times admitted that perhaps the time was not yet ripe for universal suffrage (I, 162, 194).

Such doubts, as well as his vision of a benevolent monarchy, faded with the increasingly depressing news coming from Europe in late 1848 and 1849. Chernyshevskii is known to have heard both Khanykov and Lobodovskii talk about the possibility of revolution in Russia, and later the topic was discussed in the Vvedenskii circle. It is not possible to follow him through all the steps of his transformation, but as early as June 1849 he claimed to have tried to suggest revolutionary ideas to a peasant. Although he admitted that he had acted foolishly, he maintained that the principle behind his attempt was sound (I, 291).[32]

Early in 1850, Chernyshevskii took occasion to review his earlier hope that an absolute monarchy would be able to protect the interests of the oppressed. He now realized that an absolute monarchy represented the crowning peak of an aristocratic hierarchy, so that it could never work against the privileges of that hierarchy. No other solution remained except the destruction of the monarchy, and the sooner the better. The people needed no time to prepare, as they would soon prepare themselves in battle. Chernyshevskii therefore looked with eagerness toward the coming revolution in Russia, even though it might bring initial hardship. He justified his expectation with the often-quoted statement, "I know that without convulsions there cannot be one step forward in history" (I, 356–357).[33]

Such strong words expressed Chernyshevskii's point of view on finishing his university work late in the spring. In a diary entry for May, he considered the possibility of someday setting up his own printing press, to publish clandestine revolutionary appeals. Such appeals, he wrote, need not contain lies but should describe the existing situation in demagogic language (I, 372–373). Steklov has called this day a significant turning point in Chernyshevskii's life, indicating a change from youth to the maturity of a conscious revolutionary.[34] Chernyshevskii did, in fact, write that he no longer felt like a person nourished by newspaper opinion and merely inclined toward socialism. He now regarded himself as a conspirator, or a general about to do battle, who was capable of daring, even foolhardy action (I, 373).

With respect to the intellectual stance the young man had achieved, Steklov was right in stressing the importance of Chernyshevskii's full admission to himself of his radicalism. By the time of graduation his ideas on religion had brought him to the verge of full acceptance of atheism, and these claims to be a revolutionary socialist showed that now the major lines of his life's thought had also been established. But however daring this statement of ideas, Chernyshevskii was still far from attempting to translate his complete alienation from established order into revolutionary action. His immediate plans included not the planning of a revolutionary underground, but continued education to prepare for a life of scholarship.

Moreover, in recording this transformation of his world view, Chernyshevskii revealed aspects of his character and personality that add a different dimension to the boldness of his intellectual position. In his student diary and in some of his early letters appears a detailed self-analysis, which alternates between boundless ambition and a crippling lack of self-assurance. Aware of his own intellectual ability, he dreamed of contributing to the progress of humanity and, in moments of elation, compared himself to Hegel, Plato, and Copernicus (I, 127–128, 193). For several years he hoped to discover the basic principle of a perpetual motion machine that would supply unlimited energy. In June 1849, besides imagining that someday he might become a leading left-wing journalist, he dreamed of relieving the material needs of the proletariat with such a machine, so that everyone might live as if he possessed a 15,000- or 20,000-ruble income (I, 298).

Despite these soaring flights of fancy and ambition, Chernyshevskii spent considerable time acting as his severest critic. Clearly, he went beyond the bounds of healthy self-questioning when, after noting the strain of pessimism in his character stemming from timidity, he said he expected to achieve only failure and disappointment. After wrestling with the problem of accepting the views of Western socialists, he added a strange qualification to his approval: "But all told, I am attached to this teaching with all my soul, insofar as I may be attached, with my abject, apathetic, timid, indecisive character" (I, 357–358). Even on a day that Steklov called a significant turning point in his life, Chernyshevskii made the bleak statement: "We will see what will come from me with my timidity of character and so on" (I, 373). If, by the time of his graduation, Chernyshevskii had already established the basis of his mature thought, it also seems fair to say that he still had considerable growing to do.

This was accomplished only during the next phase of his career as a teacher.

Given Chernyshevskii's family background, education, and personal preferences, few careers lay open to him on completing his undergraduate course. By his own choice, he recoiled from state service, and the only likely alternative seemed to be a teaching job and further work on a master's degree (I, 377; XIV, 181). One other possibility, that of writing for monthly journals, he had attempted several times during his final years at the university but with no success.

Late in 1847, in a letter to the Pypins, Chernyshevskii suggested that he might try his hand in the "literary field." If the assumption E. A. Liatskii makes about the dating of an incomplete manuscript is correct, his first attempt may have been a condensed translation of part of L. C. de B. de Sainte-Aulaire's *Histoire de la Fronde,* which was rejected by *Notes of the Fatherland* in June of 1848.[35] In January 1849, he wrote of already having two pieces rejected by *Notes of the Fatherland,* the second of which was probably the imaginative literary piece on Goethe entitled "Understanding" that he had worked on the previous fall (I, 166, 222).[36] Early in 1849 he wrote "The Story of Josephine," a didactic tale about the education of children, but again failed in his attempt to have it printed in *The Contemporary* (I, 222, 243; XI, 738–739). His final composition during his undergraduate years, the story "Theory and Practice," has been more fully preserved than any of the others, although it met with no greater success. He intended to try *Notes of the Fatherland* once more, but apparently never did. His literature teacher, A. V. Nikitenko, to whom he had given a first draft, demanded a more legible copy, but sometime in 1850, after transcribing and correcting the manuscript in part, Chernyshevskii seems to have let the matter drop (I, 338, 343).[37] After this unimpressive beginning as a writer, teaching and further study seemed his only remaining choice.

Although the general direction of his career was soon to be decided, the year 1850 proved to be one of vacillation and indecision. Chernyshevskii knew of his parents' desire to have him safely back under their protection in Saratov, and as a dutiful son, he felt a strong obligation. "Whatever seems best to you is best for me," he wrote at one point; indeed, he even appeared ready to enter state service had they pushed this choice (XIV, 181). But the attractions of St. Petersburg were powerful, and he could not easily envisage a life's career in a small provincial city. When he received their permission to stay in the capital, he felt profoundly grateful, for he knew how difficult the decision had been (XIV, 199). At the same time, the choice did not rest lightly on his conscience, as revealed on a visit home in the early summer of 1850. When the time came to depart, a tearful scene with his mother led him to regret his selfishness and almost caused him to turn back (I, 387). Perhaps to quiet this remorse, he made a point of stopping in Kazan on the return trip to inquire about a position in the Saratov Gymnasium.

Back in St. Petersburg, Chernyshevskii faced the difficulty of finding a job. He lost the position of tutor in the Voronin family, apparently because of the children's lack of success, for which he blamed himself. Two other job possibilities fell through, which he later attributed to his youth (I, 391, 397). In what might have become a desperate situation, Chernyshevskii was aided by Vvedenskii, whose discussion group he now regularly attended. Vvedenskii encouraged him and helped to arrange a trial lecture for a position at the Second Cadet Corps. The tryout took place in September 1850, at which Chernyshevskii felt he had done reasonably well (I, 393–395; XIV, 205–207). He showed surprise and disappointment the next day, therefore, when he was offered no more than a job as coach or drillmaster until an opening for a teacher could be found. He hesitated for some time before finally accepting the offer, and very soon he was given his own classes to teach. During the time he was weighing the choice, however, he received encouraging news of an opening as a teacher of literature in Saratov, for which he agreed to apply if the position were adequate and he could receive a definite answer without leaving St. Petersburg (I, 396). Perhaps he half expected these terms to be refused, but by the end of November, when a definite offer came, he decided to accept.

A number of considerations led to this decision to return to Saratov, despite his conviction that his future lay in St. Petersburg. Most important was a lingering sense of responsibility toward his parents. In addition, although far less is known about Chernyshevskii's several months at the Cadet Corps than about his longer experience as a teacher in Saratov, there are indications that his first attempt at teaching there fell far short of success. In his diary he expressed despair at the nastiness of the job, for which he appeared to blame the response of the cadets themselves. From the first day of class he found the cadets noisy, and he lamented his own youthfulness, which made him seem no older than those he taught. Perhaps, he wrote, if he spent a year or two in Saratov, it might help him to mature, and he could then return to the capital a more "sedate" man. Clearly this initial experience proved that he had much to learn about teaching. But that he was capable of learning from his own mistakes is shown by his comments on a failure at another tutoring position, where he realized that he had lectured his pupil too much, as if he were in the university, rather than developing the boy's capacity by asking questions (I, 397–398).

A final factor in his decision to return to Saratov was time. At this point, Chernyshevskii viewed his teaching as no more than a means to the goal of a higher university degree. Yet he found to his dismay that teaching and his growing number of acquaintances in the capital left him little time to prepare for the master's degree examinations. This fact, he claimed in a letter to Mikhailov, really forced his decision (XIV, 215–216). On March 12, 1851, he left for Saratov, fully intending that his stay there should be no more than an interlude of a year or two.

# III. The Teacher
## (1851–1853)

Chernyshevskii arrived in Saratov in April 1851, and very soon was longing for the exciting intellectual life he had known in St. Petersburg. "I find even more dullness in Saratov than you found in Nizhni," he wrote to his friend Mikhailov. His only consolation was that, with so few distractions, he would be able to conclude his work sooner and return to the capital (XIV, 217).

At first, Chernyshevskii saw little in the Saratov Gymnasium to relieve this dismal impression. The students seemed reasonably mature, and he spoke of wanting to help those who had not yet made appropriate progress, but the other teachers aroused him to "laughter and sadness." They would have been lost at a university, having forgotten everything except what was in their school notebooks, assuming they had ever possessed any understanding at all (XIV, 218).

For a young man of advanced convictions, the gymnasium held slight attraction, as it reflected the society Chernyshevskii had come to look upon with distaste. Judged in its time and place, however, something may be said in the school's favor.[1] It was considered one of the best secondary schools in the Kazan area, and the university at Kazan accepted its graduates without further examination. One of the teachers, who in time became Chernyshevskii's friend, described the school director,

A. A. Meier, as "an unselfish man who desired the good of the school and did a great deal for it."[2] But Meier's concept of education was narrow, suitable to the closing years of Nicholas I's reign. He saw his job, and that of the school, as training young men to take their places in the various hierarchies of state service, where competence meant particular skills and willing conformity, rather than bold and imaginative speculation. In practice, this meant that Meier concentrated on meeting the formal requirements of course content and school organization. Along with an inclination toward dry pedantry and formalism, Meier also apparently had a personality that made him few friends, either among the students or the faculty, over whom he kept constant surveillance.

In the matter of discovering the relevance of learning to the students, some of the teachers added obstacles of their own to the difficulties created by Meier. Neither of Chernyshevskii's two predecessors in the literature department, for example, gave the slightest attention to the works of recent Russian writers.[3] One can imagine that, by 1851, pseudoclassical forms and the poetry of G. R. Derzhavin no longer aroused much enthusiasm. It is no discredit to Chernyshevskii's achievement in the Saratov Gymnasium to say that the stage was set for the appearance of a new type of teacher.

At first sight, Chernyshevskii must have seemed an unlikely choice to teach in a school where young men, who tend to be unruly, had to be kept in line with strict rules and harsh discipline. One description of him reads: "His pale face, his quiet squeaking voice, his near-sightedness, his very fair hair, round shoulders, big steps and awkward manners—in general, all his outward appearance seemed very funny to the students. Therefore, among themselves, they began to laugh at him."[4] But laughter soon turned to respect and, in time, to deep affection. Chernyshevskii neither believed in authoritarian education nor had the personality and bearing to use that approach. Instead, he tried to stimulate in his students the same curiosity and thirst for learning that had freed his own study from a need for external compulsion.[5]

To their surprise and delight, Chernyshevskii's students found that he showed respect for their opinions and gave them opportunity to express themselves. Rather than concentrating on textbook requirements, he encouraged them to emulate his own wide reading. Modern literature, virtually forbidden under his predecessors, became the mainstay of his approach, which also stressed the relevance of learning to the students' own lives and society. Outside of class, Chernyshevskii treated his young charges with tact and in a spirit of equality that was foreign to the traditions of the school. He invited students to his home to continue discussions and helped to transform the school's monthly literary meetings from dry, formal affairs into sessions that brought excitement and a sense of involvement to the students, at the same time that they troubled some of the school's officials.[6]

The question of classroom order, which may have been a problem in the Cadet Corps in St. Petersburg, here proved to be no problem at all. Chernyshevskii's approach was simply to ask offenders to remove themselves, if they were not interested, because they disturbed the rest of the class.[7] Apparently his appeal to reason, rather than harsh authority, worked, and according to one very enthusiastic memoir, he even had a restraining influence on others in authority, who felt ashamed to apply their long-established forceful methods when the new teacher found them unnecessary.[8]

There is only one jarring note in the almost uniform praise for his teaching found in the memoirs of contemporaries. Although many of Chernyshevskii's students were well received when entering the university, official concern was expressed in Kazan that his students were not adequately prepared in the fundamentals of composition. One Kazan professor found the students from Saratov to be more involved in their subject and more inclined to independent thought than others, but less able to express themselves with correct grammar. Steklov further noted in some of Chernyshevskii's students an attitude of superiority toward the university, since they already knew what was taught there.[9] Given the official suspicion of Chernyshevskii's principles of education, it is difficult to evaluate these charges. They may have been exaggerated, or they may simply have been the reverse side of his positive achievement, in that he possibly sacrificed detail and accuracy for enthusiasm. For Chernyshevskii's part, in achieving his goal of arousing the curiosity and interest of his students, he made his first success in influencing those around him. Appropriately, he succeeded with members of the younger generation, who in the following years became his most avid readers and supporters.[10]

In 1866, a decade and a half after Chernyshevskii had begun work at the gymnasium, and just after the assassination attempt on the life of the tsar, the new Minister of Education, Count D. A. Tolstoi, spoke in Saratov on the subject of teachers who misused their position to spread dangerous and destructive propaganda. Although not mentioned by name, Chernyshevskii was clearly the target of this attack. Since that time there has been a dispute over the question of how much Chernyshevskii used his position in the classroom for revolutionary agitation.[11]

Two statements, frequently brought into the discussion, seem to indicate that the young teacher in fact took daring risks. During his courtship in early 1853, Chernyshevskii felt obliged to tell his future wife of his dangerous views and to warn her, perhaps overdramatically, that at any moment the gendarmes might appear. "I do things here which smell of hard labor— such things do I say in class" (I, 418). Moreover, it would appear that the school director, Meier, seconded Chernyshevskii's apprehension and was troubled by it. "What liberties Chernyshevskii takes with me," Meier is reported to have exclaimed once in desperation, "He speaks to the students about the evils of serfdom . . . They will send me to Kamchatka because of him." [12]

Yet one cannot accept the idea that Chernyshevskii openly advocated revolution. One contemporary, M. A. Liakomte, denied that Chernyshevskii was tendentious or that he agitated among the students.[13] Moreover, it is difficult to disagree with Steklov's view that the young teacher could scarcely have lasted for two years, under Meier's close observation, and then have left unmolested, if he had turned his classroom into a revolutionary forum.[14]

Further evidence that Chernyshevskii was not an outright revolutionary comes from his outside contacts. Chernyshevskii apparently felt free to share his deepest convictions with a small number of friends who met for weekly discussions at the home of another teacher, E. A. Belov. Belov knew that Chernyshevskii was a partisan of Feuerbach and Fourier, and heard him speak in defense of European revolutions. But Belov also felt that there were perhaps no more than five or six people with whom Chernyshevskii conversed about "social systems." [15] Another acquaintance, the exiled Ukrainian historian N. I. Kostomarov, knew enough of Chernyshevskii's thought to describe him as a violent apostle of godlessness and materialism and a hater of all authority. [16] But neither of these statements, from the two men who knew him best in Saratov, indicate that they suspected the serious commitment to a revolutionary position he claimed for himself in his diary. And it seems unlikely that Chernyshevskii would have spoken as openly in class as he did to a trusted group of friends.

Probably the stir Chernyshevskii caused in class should be called "revolutionary" only in a special, more subtle sense. For some time, Chernyshevskii had been fascinated by the relationship of literature to the society that produced it, and which it in turn described. Dealing as he did with recent Russian literature, he necessarily confronted his students with a consideration of various aspects of Russian society, which need not have been conscious revolutionary propaganda to make an impact on his young charges. One memoir noted that serfdom, the courts, education, religion, and political and natural science were all subjects of classroom discussion. [17] Even to treat these subjects openly, or to ask about their relation to literature, in the context of a provincial gymnasium in the Russia of Nicholas I was cause enough for Meier to be suspicious and fearful.

In the course of his two years in Saratov, Chernyshevskii brushed with Meier a number of times, in an uneasy relationship. One source of friction stemmed from the monthly literary meetings for students and faculty. According to one report, Chernyshevskii occasionally found it necessary to defend students from the harsh attacks of Meier, who confused his knowledge of philology with an understanding of literature and tended to be vituperative.[18] Furthermore, Chernyshevskii resented Meier's concern for petty details and his interference in the classroom. He tried in every way to discourage Meier's inspection visits to the classroom, either by purposely changing the subject when the director entered, or by making the students laugh, which offended Meier's sense of decorum. To a demand by Meier on one occasion that he question the class, Chernyshevskii refused, claiming not to have completed his explanation. On another occasion, when told to continue the discussion, Chernyshevskii excused himself on the grounds that both he and the class were too tired and needed a rest. Finally, and perhaps most serious of all, he disputed with Meier on the method of grading the students.[19]

Against this background of disagreement, ignoring any consideration of Chernyshevskii's "dangerous ideas," one would expect him to be under strong pressure either to conform or to resign. Steklov gives evidence to suggest that reports were made to the local bishop, charging Chernyshevskii with free thought. Because of these reports, pressure was brought on Meier to dismiss him, and in the spring of 1853 Chernyshevskii decided to quit Saratov, just before he would have been forced out of the position.[20] However, Meier had no direct evidence against him, and Chernyshevskii's diary, which was especially full for his final few months of teaching, gives no indication that fear of losing his job was an important reason for his resignation. Indeed, in March 1853, scarcely two months before returning to St. Petersburg, he wrote that only marriage could make him leave Saratov. Several days later, he even noted a certain mellowing in his relationship to Meier, who had refused to report him to Kazan. Chernyshevskii seemed pleased with himself for showing a new confidence in place of his earlier cowardice and faintheartedness (I, 481–482, 553–554).

A more important reason for leaving should have been concern for his future. For some time he had realized his error in expecting to make great progress either in compiling the lexicon for the Ipat'evskaia Chronicle or in preparing for his master's degree while in Saratov. After an initial flutter of activity he evidently let the work slide until shortly before returning to the capital. After one year in Saratov he went so far as to inquire about another teaching position in St. Petersburg, but he seemed unable to make the break, even though realizing that to stay meant to sacrifice his career (XIV, 222). In March 1853 he lamented that nothing had come of his earlier intention to leave, for which he blamed his "apathy" (a strange word for a conscious revolutionary) and his desire to spare his mother, who clearly enjoyed her son's presence (I, 481).[21]

It was not easy to find intellectual companionship in provincial Saratov. Chernyshevskii's initial impression of the dullness of most of the other teachers changed little during his stay.[22] Generally, he found them narrowly educated and untouched by the exciting new ideas that had transformed his own world view. Nor could his unorthodox technique of teaching have endeared him to many of his colleagues, because, in effect, he was denying what most of them stood for. Two notable exceptions to this estrangement were E. A. Belov, who at that time taught geography, and the history teacher, E. I. Lomtev.[23] During his second year in Saratov, a Tuesday evening discussion circle offered the kind of stimulation he had known at Vvedenskii's in St. Petersburg. Here, in an apparently liberal atmosphere, conversation ranged over a wide spectrum of scholarly and current topics. Unfortunately, Chernyshevskii recorded no significant comments on these discussions, but Belov's recollections of Chernyshevskii's views indicate that the talks were unguarded. In addition to identifying a number of Chernyshevskii's more radical opinions, Belov noted his characteristic tendency to go to the heart of the matter and also to generalize, without interest in particulars.[24]

A considerably less flattering picture of young Chernyshevskii emerges from the memoirs of N. I. Kostomarov, who at the time provided him with another source of intellectual companionship. On the advice of his teacher Sreznevskii, Chernyshevskii had sought the acquaintance of Kostomarov shortly after his arrival in Saratov and, in the course of two years, probably spent as much time with him as with anyone else.[25] Though different in personality and ideas, the two men shared a common delight in chess, reading, and scholarly discussion. Their paths crossed again in the early 1860's, when they took opposite sides on the student unrest in St. Petersburg, which left bitter feelings on both sides. But to the end of his life, Chernyshevskii respected Kostomarov's work as an historian (I, 777). During these years in Saratov, he visited Kostomarov often and described him to Belov as a "very good man." [26]

Two versions of Kostomarov's memoirs, recorded in 1869–1870 and 1885 and expressing his distaste for many of Chernyshevskii's ideas, no doubt show scars of the disagreement of the early 1860's. Still, there is no reason to accept the suggestion made by Chernyshevskii, who read and commented upon the first version, that Kostomarov was "sick of mind" when he dictated his autobiography (I, 775–777). Despite value-loaded criticism, Kostomarov showed insight when he wrote:

Chernyshevskii was an extraordinarily gifted man who had the supreme ability to fascinate and attract with his simple, obvious kindheartedness, modesty, many-sided learning and exceptional cleverness. He was otherwise void of what is called poetry, though he was energetic to the point of fanaticism and true to his convictions in all his life and actions. He was an ardent apostle of godlessness, materialism, and hatred of all authority. This was a man of extremes who always strove to carry his tendencies to their furthest limits.[27]

Despite subsequent distortions in Kostomarov's account, he did express something about Chernyshevskii that opponents noted throughout his life: the bewildering contrast between his mildness of manner and appearance and the hard inflexibility and extremity of his opinions. In time, Chernyshevskii came to enjoy playing the role of oracle to those who accepted his intellectual authority. During these Saratov years, however, another factor than pride was involved. In diary accounts of his confrontations with Meier, Chernyshevskii himself suggested that he was most strident and inflexible when least sure of himself (I, 554). Obviously, the commitment to one vision of truth may lead a person to strong statements and a desire to spread the influence of that truth; but those who are personally insecure may also require the props of militant certainty and intellectual victory. The excessively humble may thus resort to their own form of arrogance.

Except for a brief diary entry in November 1852, Chernyshevskii kept a record of his daily life only during the last four months of his stay in Saratov. It is no doubt true that during the preceding twenty-two months his own reading, teaching, and discussions took up the greater part of his time. However, F. V. Dukhovnikov's study of the memoirs of contemporaries who knew Chernyshevskii in Saratov leads to the conclusion that perhaps at no other stage did he lead such an active social life as well.[28] He often felt ill at ease in large gatherings, and found much that was uncongenial to his values and ideas in the ways of Saratov society. Still, Chernyshevskii's family position and his own reputation for being well read occasionally opened doors, including those of the governor of Saratov and the local bishop. He also tutored the son of a highly placed finance official, N. M. Kobylin, so that during his second year in Saratov he could look forward to invitations from this quarter. Chernyshevskii's parents, who apparently entered society very little themselves, urged their son to attend the social evenings of their friends and relatives. Despite reports that Chernyshevskii often appeared bashful and quiet at these gatherings, he offered little resistance to his parents' wishes. Indeed, at the home of one distant relative he met Olga Sokratovna Vasil'eva, his future bride. Before examining Chernyshevskii's courtship and marriage, it will be useful to examine both his earlier experience with women and his earlier views on the place of women in society. How was the young man prepared for what E. Lampert has called "one of the most remarkable love-stories of all times"?[29]

As a young seminary student, Chernyshevskii had led a very sheltered existence. He once remarked to Lobodovskii that, outside of his close family, not only did he have no female acquaintances, but until he was given glasses for nearsightedness (the date is not clear), he could not even distinguish the features of a female face at more than a yard away (I, 259). As one of his earliest letters home from the university explained, the character thus formed granted him immunity from some of the dangers young people might face in St. Petersburg (XIV, 123).

Although his relationship with women thus proved no problem for Chernyshevskii during his first two years away from home, he still became interested in the theoretical question of how men and women ought to relate to each other. One of his favorite authors during this time was George Sand, in whose novels he found persuasive objections to family relationships based on social convention and domestic tyranny, rather than on mutual love and respect.[30] Wide reading in literature, as well as his expanded opportunity to see family relationships other than those he had known at home, led him to become a strong defender of women's rights and a truly passionate sympathizer with the fate of women who, as wives and daughters, endured the despotic control of husbands and parents. By the middle of 1849 he described his position as "ultra George Sand" (I, 288). At the time these were daring words, and depending on who used them, they might have suggested an opening toward sexual license. In Chernyshevskii's case, nothing could have been further from his mind. Earlier he had written that the mutual affection of husband and wife was one of the chief sources of human happiness and had declared his own desire to remain pure "in body and spirit" so that someday he might say to his wife that she was his first love (I, 211; XIV, 111–112).

Young Chernyshevskii could continue to view the position of women as a purely theoretical problem for only so long, and early in 1848 he discovered a new dimension to his concern. After serving as best man at the wedding of his friend Lobodovskii, he found himself a frequent visitor in the newlyweds' home. It is clear from Chernyshevskii's diary that he experienced a short-lived infatuation for Lobodovskii's wife Nadezhda and was troubled by feelings that were new to him and could not easily be rationalized (I, 35–36, 156). The fact that Nadezhda was the wife of a friend was one obstacle, but he also felt embarrassment, even shame, over his own emotional involvement (I, 67, 300–301). While the infatuation lasted, the most that Chernyshevskii would admit to himself was that he sympathized with many aspects of her life situation and desired to help her, at almost any cost to himself. Thus, he translated personal attraction into sympathy and a desire for self-sacrifice, to which he claimed to be duty-bound (I, 156–158).

Chernyshevskii showed a similar pattern of rationalizing his emotions when he experienced a flutter of interest in the daughter of a family friend, at whose home in Moscow he stopped, whenever he traveled between St. Petersburg and Saratov.[31] In the summer of 1850, he thought with new enthusiasm about Aleksandra Grigor'evna Klientova, but when he considered the possibility of marrying her, he felt obliged to interpret the move as a means of relieving the girl from the distress of an unhappy home situation (I, 382–383).[32] In this case, his enthusiasm was also stimulated by Aleksandra's remark that she had once been a friend of Natalie Herzen's. This claim instantly put her in the special category of one with whom Chernyshevskii could share ideas and values, and therefore also admit being fond of. Although nothing came of this episode, it shows again how important was Chernyshevskii's need to have intellectual compatibility as the basis for closeness to another person, and how difficult it was for him to think of a relationship with a woman without casting himself in the role of self-sacrificing benefactor.

On the one occasion when Chernyshevskii risked a relationship of a different sort and openly sought gratification, the affair took a tragicomic turn and brought him only embarrassment and disappointment.[33] The episode began sometime around Easter 1852, when he was invited to spend an evening with the socially prominent Kobylin family, whose son he tutored. Although, as he admitted, he did not know how to conduct himself and was "as usual bashful as a sheep," he thoroughly enjoyed meeting and playing whist with his student's sister Katerina. Strange to say, this young man of radical views was thrilled not only by her appearance but also by the social position of the company (I, 406). He waited painfully for several months before receiving another invitation, after which his diary account temporarily breaks off.

By early January 1853, however, he was ready to declare his

love. When he contemplated what to say, some admittedly strange thoughts turned round in his head. One was that, because she was not well read, he might give her lessons, "naturally without fee," and thereby have the satisfaction of making her obliged to him. Even the words of his intended declaration were awkward: "The time has come for you to love, but perhaps you are in danger of choosing [someone] unworthy. Choose me, because I love you sincerely and [because] in any case this love would not be dangerous for you" (I, 408). To play the gallant lover was clearly not his forte. As it happened, these words were never spoken, for poor Chernyshevskii could not find enough time alone with Katerina to say his piece. He tried during one dance, but after making appropriate introductory remarks about the seriousness of what he intended to say, he noticed that she was not paying any attention. After an attempt that bordered on the pathetic and the comic, he had to admit to himself that she realized what was on his mind and simply did not want to hear it (I, 409). Thus, on the eve of his great romance, Chernyshevskii was still a painfully naive and socially inexperienced young man, who could easily play the fool when trying to assert himself socially. His noble sentiments favoring intellectual compatibility between the sexes and aid for suffering womankind were also a form of evasion from direct personal contact and therefore a shield for his own insecurity.

The external facts of Chernyshevskii's courtship and marriage, which many in Saratov saw as an unlikely match, are brief.[34] Olga Sokratovna Vasil'eva was the oldest of several children in the family of a somewhat unconventional Saratov doctor. Although her father, Sokrat Evgen'evich, enjoyed a good medical reputation, he attracted less favorable attention with his constant bustling, forgetfulness, coarseness of speech, and generally disordered way of life. Unlike his wife, who tended to be withdrawn and stern, Vasil'ev showed his children great affection, perhaps even spoiled them, and allowed them a great deal of freedom. To outsiders it appeared that permissive anarchy reigned in the home; the children were sometimes referred to as "children of nature." Olga enjoyed her father's special attention and indulgence. With few restraints to inhibit her, she became accustomed to the companionship of her brothers and their friends. As a young girl, she modeled her conduct so closely on theirs that some people referred to her as a "hussar in skirts."

By her twentieth year, Olga had developed into an attractive, playful coquette who felt unconstrained by many of the customs then prevailing among young women of her social background. Both her charm and habits attracted a good deal of male attention, which she enjoyed and perhaps exploited. At the same time, her conduct gave rise to rumors whose fairness at this distance is hard to judge. In any event, it is clear that by the time she met young Chernyshevskii, Olga bore a reputation, among the more fastidious in Saratov society, that few could envy.[35]

Chernyshevskii met Olga on January 26, 1853, only twenty days after his farcical attempt to declare his love to Katerina. He was swept off his feet and soon caught up in a passion such as he had never known before. In order to see more of her, he entered into a young people's society that sponsored dances and parties and with surprising haste began to press his suit. Although Olga apparently continued to play the coquette, she was more responsive than he at first dared hope. Within a month, Chernyshevskii was able to declare his love, and Olga accepted his proposal soon after. The prospect of marriage, with the need to support a household, revived Chernyshevskii's ambition to complete a higher university degree and to write for journals, with the result that he laid plans to return to St. Petersburg. Initially he thought of establishing himself there before assuming the responsibility of marriage, but Olga was more inclined to an early wedding and departure for the capital together (I, 514, 529–530, 542–543, 560–564).[36]

Chernyshevskii made his formal proposal to Olga's parents on March 30, and shortly afterward overcame the opposition of his own parents. Events thereafter moved quickly. Wedding plans were set for April 29, but early that month, after a very brief illness, Chernyshevskii's mother died. More than likely at Olga's insistence, the young couple refused to delay their own plans; they married on the scheduled date and left for St. Petersburg early in May. The town gossips now had opportunity to complain that they should have waited longer to show proper respect.[37]

So bare an outline leaves out the more complex and important question of how Chernyshevskii experienced these events and what part the episode played in his maturation. One could not ask for better evidence to deal with this question, for during the two and a half months of his courtship he again kept a detailed diary, which in printed form amounts to one hundred and fifty closely spaced pages. *The Diary of My Relationship with the One Who Now Comprises My Happiness* is an immensely revealing document, which tells more about his inner being during this brief period than is known about any other part of his life. Often the diary is so intimate that one cannot read it without a sense of intrusion. Yet within its pages is evidence of the emotional crisis through which Chernyshevskii passed in order to reach a personal maturity that matched his newly formed world view.

The first revelation of the diary is that this period in Chernyshevskii's life was marked not only by elation but also by confusion, self-torment, and doubt. He needed to rationalize the rapidly developing relationship in his own mind and to find some explanation for his feelings and justification for his proposed actions. At the same time, he was rarely sure of these feelings and never sure how to interpret Olga's actions and remarks. As a result, these few months were among the most difficult in his life, as well as the happiest.

One thing is certain: from the start he felt the pressure of the passage of time without his ever having achieved a successful relationship with a woman. He experienced an apprehensive sense of isolation. A few weeks after meeting Olga, he wrote, "I feel that were I to let this opportunity to marry pass, then with my personality, another chance might not come soon, and I would spend my youth in dry loneliness" (I, 414). But in drawing closer to Olga, Chernyshevskii found a number of obstacles he had to surmount. For one thing, he could scarcely fit comfortably into the frivolous world of fun and games that Olga presided over (I, 454–456).[38] He played his part, perhaps even with fascination, but it was totally out of character for him. Also, his early visits to Olga's home, with its disorder and lack of cleanliness, left the fastidious lover shocked. Even Olga's own actions at times seemed less worthy than he might have hoped. He could not adjust easily to her aggressive freedom with other men, although he rarely dared speak to her about it. At one point, he suspected her of being overly ambitious for the status she would enjoy as his wife, were he to become a professor (I, 433, 464).

That such obstacles did not prove insuperable is shown by an encounter on March 6 between Chernyshevskii and F. U. Palimpsestov, a young bureaucrat, who tried to warn his friend against becoming involved with Olga because, as he put it, she had already exhausted her feelings and was no longer capable of love. By this time, Chernyshevskii was able to claim that she was above reproach in his eyes, and he likened those who would criticize her to those who would speak ill of Voltaire, Louis Blanc, Proudhon, "Iskander," and Gogol (I, 489–491). His praise could go no higher.

Had this view held, Chernyshevskii's course would have been clear. But in fact, every assertion of certainty in his own mind was preceded or followed by some kind of troublesome doubt. There seem to have been two sources for this confusion, both of which reveal a great deal about Chernyshevskii. The first was simply his inability to understand Olga. Confronted by a suitor whose serious ideas she could not follow, she continued to play her familiar role of coquette, which baffled the inexperienced Chernyshevskii. For example, only with difficulty did he realize that perhaps there was no truth in her claim to have two other wealthy suitors, one the possessor of a thousand souls (I, 491). Even as Chernyshevskii declared his deepest love, she responded with words that seemed calculated to frustrate and yet provoke his ardor. In Chernyshevskii's word-by-word accounts of these exchanges, it appears as if a veil fell between Chernyshevskii and his surroundings, preventing clear insight. Again and again, until shortly before his marriage, he found himself tormented by the questions: Was she really being open with him? Was she being sly? Was she playing the coquette? (I, 462, 486, 488, 505, 512).

If Olga's manner and Chernyshevskii's own lack of worldliness explain in part his indecision, another difficulty went much deeper and was related to his adolescent lack of confidence. In one moment of brutally revealing self-analysis, he wrote about his doubts concerning Olga:

From where do my doubts arise? From my own character first of all. I have need of *too* clear proof that [people] don't reject me, that I don't weary or disgust [them]. It always seems to me, for example, when I am with someone, or someone is with me, that he is bored with me, that I came at the wrong time, and so on. It is difficult for me to convince myself that I am in the right place, that I am in the right relationship with someone. But this reason will soon be overcome if she really will be bound to me (I, 489).

What happened to Chernyshevskii during these few months, and what made his courtship especially trying, was that the success of his advance became a measure of his self-image. Caught up in a powerful passion, his ability to seize the moment and act with vigor became the test of his decisiveness in his own eyes, just as Olga's acceptance of him became the test of his worth. Amidst rigorous soul-searching, on March 4 he described what it would mean to him if he hesitated in reaching a decision, as so often in the past:

Then I really would be a Hamlet in my own eyes, a thought which even without this has always tormented me. Then I would never free myself from it. Now [because of his decision] I am calm. Now I feel myself a man, who in case of need may decide and act, and not a creature from among those rats who gather to tie a bell on the neck of a cat.

O, how I have been tormented by the thought that I am a Hamlet. Now I see that I am not. I see that I am a man like others, not those many who have a character as [I] would have wanted to have; but all the same a man not completely without will. In a word a man and not entirely dirt (I, 480).

Obviously, a great deal more was at stake here than simply seeking a marriage partner. The very next day Chernyshevskii wrote, "I must marry, also because in that way from a child, as I am now, I will become a man. Then my timidity, shyness, etc., will disappear" (I, 483).

As the marriage plans evolved from confusion and self-doubt, Chernyshevskii felt a reinforced sense of his own worth. From the day Olga first gave encouragement to his declaration of affection, he felt he had become a completely different person. "I have become decisive, daring, my doubts, my hesitation have vanished. Now I have will, now I have character, now I have energy" (I, 500). Despite later relapses from this apparent certainty, ultimately he found the courage to face the financial insecurity of a return to St. Petersburg, which his marriage necessitated.

For the relationship to grow, however, Chernyshevskii had first to assert himself and risk the pain of possible rejection. After his recent failure with Katerina, one wonders if he would have been so quick to try again if he had not been able to resort to the pattern, established earlier, of regarding another person within the framework of his own preconceived categories. In the case of Olga, this took two forms. The first was to try to make her views compatible to his own. At the very beginning, the rumor that she had once "toasted democracy" ignited his interest. To hear such words, which may have been made up by mutual friends, or to learn that Olga was not particularly religious, gave him the positive image he needed and allowed him to shut his eyes to counterevidence (I, 410–411).[39] An amusing example of the possible consequences of this self-deception was his unfortunate comment that she should live in Paris, which he intended as a compliment to her alleged democratic ideas, but which gave offense because Olga thought he meant to call her "light-minded" (I, 412).

The other form of what may have been a necessary self-delusion appeared in his strenuous effort to force her into the category of a troubled woman, who desperately needed to be saved from an unhappy home situation. Olga, in fact, had cool relations with her mother, but Chernyshevskii seriously exaggerated these so that he could interpret his feelings of love as representing the duty of a humane person. Olga thus had to play an assigned role. Chernyshevskii wrote: "But I am more interested in her than ever, because all unhappiness, all sorrow compels me to be more interested in a person and strengthens my disposition toward him. If a person is joyful, I rejoice with him. But if [that person] is in sorrow, I share more of the sorrow than the joy and love him much more" (I, 523–524). He could not rest content until he got her to say she wanted to marry *because* of her difficult situation at home.[40] In this way, by feeling both needed and morally bound, he found that self-assertion came more easily. At the same time, he had to pay for this spur to action with a blurred vision of reality.

Chernyshevskii's name has long been identified with the movement in modern Russian history to break the ancient tradition of female subordination in family and society. The claim is fully justified, but a reading of his diary shows that his position on the question of women's rights was not simply a matter of intellectual conviction. Though the elevation of women to a position of equality was an important part of his concept of the just society, inextricably involved with this was his personal need to place Olga in a commanding position and thereby abase himself. It is not easy to tell where conviction left off and a desire for subjection began.

Within a month of meeting Olga, Chernyshevskii recorded an often quoted statement about women's rights which may serve as an example of his mixed motives. Assuming the basic equality of women, he wrote that since the rod had long been bent in one direction, it must henceforth be bent in the opposite direction to straighten it. Respectable men must place their wives above themselves for the very reason that women were currently considered beneath them. A temporary advantage to women was necessary for future equality. But then Chernyshevskii went on to say, in words that are too often omitted from references to this paragraph, "Besides I have the kind of character which was made to be subordinate" (I, 444). Apparently he made no secret of this to others in their circle. In one account, when Olga's friends tried to warn him that marriage with her would bring unhappiness because she would treat him like a child, he replied that he needed just that kind of wife, one who would "govern" him.[41]

Similarly, in discussing future plans with Olga, or in contemplating their future life together, he was more than simply considerate or obliging; he actually sought disadvantage. In their early discussions, when it appeared that he might go to St. Petersburg alone for a time, he insisted that any engagement should be one-sided. That is, he would consider himself bound to her, but she should feel free of obligation to him. As an extension of this one-sidedness, he wrote of his desire to give her complete freedom after marriage, although he, of course, would remain faithful. Realizing that his own passion exceeded hers, he imagined his reactions if a more serious love appeared in her life. Not only would he give her up, but if the man were worthy, he would be happy for her (I, 489, 513).

Most revealing were his comments on their future life together. Because of his character, which was ready to agree and concede in all things, she was to be the head of the home, and his role that of the humble servant (I, 435, 464). Instead of the male obtaining the usual commanding position, in their marriage the stances would be reversed. Safe in her separate room, she would decide when she wanted to be with him. So much of their future days together did he contemplate sitting by her side that he momentarily wondered what time would remain for scholarly work, and concluded that three hours a day for his work would be enough, "because even now I almost never work more than that, and, in any case, I already have such learning that few can match." As for their relationship in what Chernyshevskii called a "social sense," he envisaged unequal forms of address. He would prefer to call her the more formal you (Vy), even though she used the thou (ty) form for him. In short, he proposed that their relationship "on the outside have the most official and cold character." But beneath the surface, on his part there would be the "fullest and deepest tenderness" (I, 534–535).

One other indication of the confusion and hesitancy created in Chernyshevskii by courtship appears in his concept of his revolutionary role. By the time he returned to Saratov in 1851, he had already arrived at an intellectual position of opposition to Russia's social and political order. Yet once in Saratov, except perhaps for exploring some forbidden questions in the class-room, he followed a strictly legal, almost conventional, course. Nothing came of his plans to be a radical journalist, or of his impulse to do battle against the system. In conversations with Olga the question of his involvement in the revolutionary cause arose again, which showed that at times he could display his earlier zeal. But it is quite probable that playing the suitor and then assuming the responsibilities of marriage had a tempo-rarily dampening effect on his vision of himself as a revolu-tionary leader. There is no reason to suspect any weakening in his ideas and convictions; rather, he seems to have reconsid-ered the active role he might play. The point would merit little attention were it not for the extensive but questionable use made of Chernyshevskii's quotations from this period by bi-ographers who would show an unbroken line of revolutionary intent from his student days to his arrest.

Not long after meeting Olga, Chernyshevskii revealed to her his revolutionary views and the dangerous consequences they might have for him and those close to him. The context of this discussion was his explanation for not being able to live in Sara-tov and his listing of obstacles to his marriage. He spoke to Olga of having the kind of views which made it likely that the gen-darmes would appear at any moment. In his enthusiasm, Cher-nyshevskii likened himself to the Christian martyrs awaiting their fate, and even predicted an imminent revolution in Russia in which he would surely take part (I, 418). Olga seemed singu-larly unimpressed. Could he not change his views? she asked, and she almost laughed when he spoke of a revolution. When he explained why a revolution was inevitable, she wondered if his friend N. I. Kostomarov would also take part, and thereby evoked Chernyshevskii's famous retort that Kostomarov was too "noble and poetic," unlike himself, who "feared neither mire, drunken peasants with cudgels, nor slaughter." To this came Olga's playful reply that she did not fear these things either. Chernyshevskii soon realized that she was bored by the whole conversation, and he ended simply by telling her how "Iskander's" family had suffered because of his views (I, 419). He believed he must expect a similar fate.

Chernyshevskii spoke in a comparable vein at other times; once when he linked the possibility of his having a voice in Russian literature with a relaxation of the censorship, and again when explaining why he could not marry, fearing that he might not be able to avoid prison much longer. Again Olga apparently failed to give the expected response. He noted, "I do not know whether she believed this—it would appear not very much, because she is little accustomed to such things" (I, 434, 466). With respect to the question of whether Chernyshevskii underwent a shift in attitude toward his active participation in a revolutionary movement, the date of the second reference is important. Although the dates in the diary are confusing, because Chernyshevskii occasionally returned later to deal in greater detail with an event mentioned earlier, it appears from a careful reading that the remark about his fear of prison was indeed written in early March 1853, where Steklov placed it, but that it refers back to events of the previous month.[42] Thus, the reference is to a conversation that took place on February 13. In view of this date, and of the timing of his references to the momentary appearance of the gendarmes and to his refusal to shrink from the violence of revolution, made on February 19 or 21, it becomes obvious that Chernyshevskii raised this whole issue relatively early in his courtship. Most significantly, this was a time when he seemed to be seeking reasons why he ought not to become further involved.

In the course of the following weeks Chernyshevskii's tune seemed to change, especially as his personal confidence grew and he cast about for reasons why he ought to marry. On March 5, for example, he wrote with an apparent cooling of his revolutionary ardor: "Finally, I ought to marry to become cautious. Because if I continue as I have begun, I really might be caught. I should have the idea that I do not belong to myself, that I do not have the right to risk myself. How else could I know? How else could I not risk? There must be some kind of protection against democratic and revolutionary tendencies, and this protection can be nothing else but thoughts about a wife" (I, 483–484). A list of reasons why he ought to marry gave further evidence that marriage plans did not fit easily into his earlier statements of intention to take part in the coming revolution in Russia. At the conclusion of the list, as if reaffirming his ideological commitment in the face of overwhelming personal concerns, he wrote, "I must somehow keep myself on the road to 'Iskander.'" [43]

As marriage plans were being made and he faced the problems of establishing a reasonably comfortable household, there is no evidence to suggest any wavering of his convictions, but it is probable that the revolutionary implications of these convictions, as they might affect his personal life, were pushed from the center of his concern. Responsibilities of family life brought added caution on his part, which he overcame only in the revolutionary unrest of the late fifties and early sixties. Perhaps his new attitude found best expression in his answers to a series of questions posed by Olga's mother concerning his plans. Although in these answers Chernyshevskii openly lied, as when he claimed to be a Christian, the following words probably express his mood on the verge of family life and during the early years of his marriage in St. Petersburg. He reiterated the familiar theme of his general inclination to make concessions and avoid dispute, but added: "There are things about which I am inflexible, but these things in no way concern relationships in life; they are my convictions on various theoretical questions. These I would not change for anyone because that is not in my power. But either these would not be of interest to my wife (which I would not wish or expect from Olga Sokratovna with her curiosity and her mind) or Olga Sokratovna would agree with me in these convictions" (I, 564). This sounds very little like a general about to do battle.

Most of the difficulties Chernyshevskii experienced during his courtship were essentially reflections of some aspect of his personality. The same cannot be said for the final obstacle he had to surmount, namely, his parents' dislike of the match. On his return to Saratov in 1851, he already lived in an intellectual world far removed from that of his parents, and yet strong ties of deference and dependence remained. Having returned partly because of his mother's wish, he knew that as long as he remained in Saratov, even if married, he would remain dependent on her (I, 481). As his passion for Olga grew, he had to face the problem of securing his parents' approval of his choice. Though he tried at first to convince himself otherwise, he soon realized there would be difficulty.

From the beginning, he understood that this kind of decision allowed for no outside interference: "There are things in which one must not ask for council." But in a rare moment of romantic weakness, he contemplated suicide if his parents should refuse to accept his choice, for it seemed better to die than to be refused happiness (I, 479). Delaying his statement of intention as long as possible, he sensed what the source of their reluctance would be and tried to build up his courage for independent action. "It may be," he wrote in early March, "that her bad reputation is too well known to them and they will not agree" (I, 479, 492).

It proved easier to write about the problem than to face the impending showdown. Chernyshevskii did not really fear his parents, for they were loving, not authoritarian, but he suffered bad conscience at the thought of hurting them (I, 493). Parental overprotection and overconcern, in its own way, can be the worst form of tyranny. Olga's inability to return his love in full measure only increased his feelings of guilt: "Mother loves me with all the strength of her soul, and here a stranger appears who has not even said that she loves me, and I love her so much that my attachment to my mother is completely insignificant before my love of her. What right have I to love her more than mother? Where is the justice in that? There is none. What can be done? You love more, not those you ought to love, but those you do love" (I, 495, 512).

After Chernyshevskii had gone through so much inner turmoil in making up his mind, the response of his parents to his announcement on March 28 must have been especially painful for him. His father appeared somewhat accepting, but this meant simply that in twenty minutes of discussion he had taken no note of Olga's bad reputation. His mother proved more difficult. She first tried to avoid a definite answer, and finally agreed only with reluctance and bad grace (I, 538–539).

The first painful meeting of Olga and Chernyshevskii's parents came as an even crueler trial, which may well have been the episode needed to turn him toward his new life with few apparent regrets. His mother behaved with affectation, which appeared to Olga as severity and dissatisfaction. Olga's grief at her reception brought Chernyshevskii to tears, and he was further saddened to hear her say that she "feared" his mother. Another blow came later that night when, to the question of how he liked his future daughter-in-law, his father replied that she was too "playful" (I, 544).

The unhappy Chernyshevskii, having tried to balance his new love with continued devotion to his parents, was forced by them to make a choice. But at least his course was clear: "It is all the same to me, and soon (immediately after the wedding) she will not care what relation my parents have to her, because she will see that for me it doesn't matter. Whoever does not love her may not interfere in my relationship to her" (I, 544). Thus, the lines of youthful dependence were cut. Scarcely more than two weeks later, Chernyshevskii's mother had died, but wedding plans went on apace. There could be no turning back.

During these critical months, Chernyshevskii completed his progress from boyhood to manhood, which his earlier intellectual transformation had merely begun. He had regretted his tendency to be a Hamlet and to postpone decisions ever since student days, when he had both felt the attraction of new ideas and yet found that bold, radical thought did not fit easily with what he described as his "abject, apathetic, timid, and indecisive character." Perhaps as a result of this tendency, he alternated between glorious dreams of future greatness and crippling doubts about whether he would amount to anything at all. By the time that he left St. Petersburg in 1851, most of his intellectual confusion was behind him, and he had developed confidence in his convictions, which, though becoming increasingly sophisticated, in fact varied surprisingly little throughout his life. But as for his emotional development, he was still a very immature young man, uncertain in personal dealings with others and not yet free from dependence on his parents. He could be assertive in discussion but, behind this intellectual facade, suffered doubts about his worth and indecision about his life course. He may have overstated the case when claiming to need an external circumstance to force him to leave the family nest in Saratov, but he had knowingly remained longer than was good for his career, and he had apparently made little direct progress in preparation for a higher degree.

Chernyshevskii's courtship and marriage served as a catalyst to hasten the maturing of his personality. Driven by a strong passion, he gradually worked his way through convoluted rationalizations about the wisdom of his marrying and finally reinterpreted his desire as an abstract obligation. Then, almost despite himself, he came to realize that Olga found him a worthy mate, even though she clearly did not return the full measure of his love, and this acceptance gave him desperately needed support. Convinced he was now like other men on this level of personal relations—a doubt that had long tormented him—he found the strength to differ decisively from other men in matters of conviction.

# IV. The Journalist and Editor (1853–1862)

Chernyshevskii returned to St. Petersburg with his young bride in the middle of May 1853 and plunged immediately into a furious round of activity. He needed to put his shaky financial affairs in order and, at the same time, make a definite choice of career. Neither proved easy to do, although circumstances beyond his control partially determined his choice. At first, intending to pursue a higher university degree, he turned to lower school teaching as a temporary expedient, to be supplemented by whatever he could earn by writing for journals.

Although he had left his job in Saratov suddenly, without completing the spring term, he apparently expected no difficulties with the St. Petersburg school authorities. It took about nine months to receive official approval for his transfer to the St. Petersburg school district, which arrived in January 1854, but he had actually begun work the previous September.[1] The income from this job, which he estimated at about one hundred rubles a month, was his main support until he found a market for his reviews and articles (XIV, 257). In spite of optimistic letters to his family telling of improvements in his financial situation, Chernyshevskii must have known dark moments in trying to make ends meet. Near the end of 1853 he asked Olga's mother, a woman he thoroughly disliked, to lend him a thousand rubles until he could increase his own income (XIV, 252–253).

He proposed to publish a multivolume history of universal literature, which he had not yet written, and assured his prospective benefactress that the venture would be profitable (XIV, 257–258). Nothing came of either his request for help or his ambitious plan.

Little is known about Chernyshevskii's return to teaching at the Second Cadet Corps, except that he remained there only about a year. The most prevalent account of his departure is that, having given offense to the officer of the day, who wanted to quiet a noisy class before the beginning of a lecture, Chernyshevskii left his job rather than apologize.[2] If true, the episode reflected Chernyshevskii's conviction by the latter part of 1854 that he could in fact support himself by writing. In November of that year he wrote to his father that it was not in his character to enter government service, either as a teacher or in any other capacity. Out of respect for his father's preference, he claimed that he would still be interested in a university professorship or a job as a public librarian (XIV, 277). By this time, however, he already felt a strong attraction to journalism as a full-time occupation.

Chernyshevskii's abandonment of his long-established plans for a scholarly career was not primarily his own choice, even though he seemed to be moving in that direction. Soon after his return to the capital, he registered for the master's degree examinations. As further evidence of his scholarly intent, he finally concluded his lexicon to the Ipat'evskaia Chronicle, a task that had dragged on since his student days. In a letter to his father, he described the lexicon as the driest, most unreadable, if not the most laborious, scholarly work ever to appear in Russia (XIV, 228). The lexicon was published in December 1853 as a supplement to the *News of the Imperial Academy of Science: Division of Russian Language and Literature*. But by that time Chernyshevskii had already lost interest in philology and had changed his field to literature, under Professor A. V. Nikitenko. In the winter of 1853–1854 he passed a series of examinations for his degree, so that it only remained to complete and defend his thesis. He did all this work at the university in addition to teaching at the Cadet Corps and writing.

Chernyshevskii's decision to switch from philology to literature occurred during the summer of 1853. In July, he told his father of his intention to write something on aesthetics, though it would appear that he was referring to an article he hoped to publish in *Notes of the Fatherland,* as his thesis plans still included work in philology (XIV, 235, 795). Two months later, however, he announced that he had already completed over half of his dissertation. Its subject was clearly identified as a critique of Hegelian aesthetics. In another letter, he gave a gloomy estimate of the level of his professors' understanding of philosophy, and wondered if they would be able to understand the relation of his own thought to the prevailing concepts of aesthetics (XIV, 240–242).

He had reason to be concerned, because the next twenty months brought seemingly endless delay and finally disappointment. Nikitenko long withheld his approval of the thesis, which in turn put off the public defense until May 1855. By the time that Chernyshevskii finally presented his thesis, *The Aesthetic Relation of Art to Reality,* some of his ideas had aroused bitter argument in the St. Petersburg journals. He had already made enemies and won supporters. This fact gave the defense a greater public significance than it would otherwise have had and led one enthusiastic follower of Chernyshevskii, N. V. Shelgunov, to describe it as a "humanistic sermon," which gave initial expression to the new tendencies of the sixties.[3] Chernyshevskii's own description of the event, in a letter to his father, was far more modest. He felt that only Nikitenko, among the examiners, had done a decent job in questioning him. The discussion, although superficially lively, had not really gotten to the core of the subject. In any case, he expressed no doubt that he would receive his degree and said that he intended to work for a doctorate, as time permitted (XIV, 298–300).

One cannot know if Chernyshevskii would ever have fulfilled this intention, even if the Minister of Public Education, A. S. Norov, had confirmed his degree. In light of the success he had achieved in journalism by 1855, and the new possibilities opened up in that field by the death of Nicholas I, it seems unlikely that he would have been willing to return to a career in education. As it happened, Norov's refusal left Chernyshevskii no choice. When the ministry finally granted his degree three years later, in 1858, he hardly even considered reentering the teaching profession.[4]

Chernyshevskii's career in journalism began unobtrusively in 1853 with a few reviews, but the following year developed into what most men would have considered a full-time occupation. Almost from the start, his work showed a characteristic polemical tendency, so that the fact that he contributed to both *Notes of the Fatherland* and its competitor, *The Contemporary,* placed him in an awkward situation. A number of his articles in *The Contemporary,* dealing with the meaning of art and its function in society, met opposition from writers for *Notes of the Fatherland.* By the middle of 1854, Chernyshevskii found himself in the unusual position of contributing regularly to one journal that was editorially at war with his articles in a competing journal. The ambiguous situation lasted until 1855, when A. A. Kraevskii, editor of *Notes of the Fatherland,* forced him to choose between the journals. According to Chernyshevskii's later account, in reaching a decision, he had to consider a warning by N. A. Nekrasov that the financial situation of *The Contemporary* was uncertain, but in fact Chernyshevskii scarcely hesitated (I, 714–722). By April 1855, he had made his choice in favor of *The Contemporary.*

In retrospect, the association of Chernyshevskii with *The Contemporary* seems natural, but his early years on the journal were precarious.[5] Several times he came close to being forced from his job, and finally he secured his position only with the departure of many of the well-known writers who were contributing to the journal when he began. Since 1846, *The Contemporary* had been edited by I. I. Panaev and N. A. Nekrasov. Panaev took legal responsibility, while Nekrasov carried the burden of finding copy and dealing with financial matters and the censorship. In the first two years of their editorship, circulation grew from two thousand to slightly over three thousand, approximately where it remained until the mid-fifties.[6] Relative to the standards of that time, *The Contemporary* was therefore one of the most popular journals. Its pages carried articles, reviews, and literature of many of Russia's most renowned men of letters. After 1848, during the heaviest censorship period of Nicholas I's reign, *The Contemporary* lacked a clearly defined ideological tendency.[7] Though generally progressive and possessing Western sympathies, its contributors did not follow a narrowly defined line, which would have been impossible at the time. Yet more was involved than censorship restrictions. The passionate call for political and social commitment in literature issued by Belinskii in the pages of *The Contemporary* shortly before his death had in effect gone unanswered, for none of the leading writers really agreed with his extreme position. It was significant that, after Belinskii's death, the main burden of literary criticism on *The Contemporary* fell to A. V. Druzhinin, a man of generally conservative social views, who feared that conscious moralizing in art would undercut the aesthetic values he considered more important. His concern for the integrity of art, as art, served as a strong bond among the literary contributors to the journal. A writer like Turgenev, for example, whose moving story "Mumu" condemning the cruelties of serfdom appeared in 1854, was more sensitive than Druzhinin to the desirability of social change in Russia, but he found common ground with Druzhinin in his interest in the integrity of literary craft.[8]

To many of the regular contributors to the journal, Chernyshevskii's initial reviews calling for a socially committed art came as an unpleasant shock. Nekrasov once had to evade a pointed question of the publicist V. P. Botkin, who asked whether he had dug up this new critic from a seminary.[9] Dissatisfaction increased the following year with the publication of Chernyshevskii's dissertation. Turgenev felt that Chernyshevskii's attacks on idealistic aesthetics were "stupid" and his thesis "false and injurious," an evaluation that Botkin seconded.[10] When Chernyshevskii began to devote full attention to *The Contemporary*, Druzhinin so disliked working with him that he transferred most of his efforts to *Notes of the Fatherland* and then to *The Library for Reading*. Such dissatisfaction and the prospect of losing valued contributors led Nekrasov to approach Druzhinin in August 1855 with the request that he renew his close collaboration with *The Contemporary*. Nekrasov made no offer to sacrifice Chernyshevskii, however, as he had long maintained hope that different points of view might find expression in his journal. But Charles Corbet is right in saying that this was a most dangerous period for Chernyshevskii, for if Druzhinin had chosen to fight for influence on the journal, he would have found strong support in many of the older contributors, and Nekrasov at this time might well have parted with his protégé.[11]

The danger of Chernyshevskii's losing his position on *The Contemporary* lessened with time, because he rapidly made a name for himself and attracted attention to the journal. By April 1856, he proved much less vulnerable when his enemies mounted another attack and sought to replace him in the criticism section with A. A. Grigor'ev. This time Nekrasov stood more firmly in Chernyshevskii's defense, as he did again in the summer of 1856 against the scurrilous personal attacks of L. N. Tolstoi.[12] It is probable that a temporary lessening of Turgenev's hostility at this time also helped Chernyshevskii.[13]

Thus, it required two years for Chernyshevskii to win a secure role in *The Contemporary*, which proved to be only the first stage in a larger struggle for influence.[14] Toward the end of 1856, he had assured his position as a contributor, but a more important role in the editorship was yet to be gained. In this next stage, one incident, which he could never have anticipated, worked greatly to his advantage. Nekrasov had long planned a trip abroad, and before his departure, in August 1856, he laid plans to ensure the smooth functioning of the journal during his absence. That spring, he had concluded an agreement with four leading writers—D. V. Grigorovich, A. N. Ostrovskii, I. S. Turgenev, and L. N. Tolstoi—granting them two-thirds of the net profits of *The Contemporary* in return for their promise to submit all they had written for exclusive publication.[15] Nekrasov hoped thereby to ensure a flow of high-quality contributions, to what he still considered essentially a literary journal. Nekrasov also wanted to provide for dependable editing while he was away. Evidently Panaev could not be relied on for sustained work, and Nekrasov's other choice, Turgenev, also planned to be absent. Nekrasov must have realized that, despite the controversy Chernyshevskii aroused among the staff, he was the most zealous contributor and the one who could be relied on to see that the hard editorial work got done. Thus, Nekrasov left to Chernyshevskii most of the editorial functions he usually performed himself.[16] This by no means automatically meant even temporary control of the journal, because Chernyshevskii, who was only a paid employee, stood against the four contributors who were profit-sharers in the enterprise. The editor, for example, could not block anything written by one of the four; as long as the other three agreed, the work had to be printed. Much of Chernyshevskii's freedom of movement and decision, therefore, depended on the relative willingness of the older writers to exert themselves.

From all indications, Chernyshevskii behaved prudently toward the major co-workers and tried in every way to encourage their contributions. Had they responded cooperatively, Chernyshevskii's influence on *The Contemporary* would have been balanced by a strong literature section, written by major writers who did not generally agree with him. But as it happened, the leading writers viewed Chernyshevskii's efforts with suspicion. Turgenev probably expressed the feelings of the three other writers when he wrote to Tolstoi in December 1856 that the editorship was in "bad hands." [17] The other writers showed their dissatisfaction by slowing down their contributions. This worked in Chernyshevskii's favor, for he not only enjoyed a greater opportunity than otherwise to select articles, but Nekrasov got the impression that the other writers, who put personal feelings above obligations, could not be relied on. By contrast, Chernyshevskii appeared to identify his whole career with the success of the journal.[18]

It was fortunate for Chernyshevskii that he could impress Nekrasov by his zeal, because in November 1856 he made a foolish editorial decision that might once again have upset his position. With Panaev's agreement, he reprinted in *The Contemporary* three selections from a recent volume of Nekrasov's poetry: "The Poet and the Citizen," "The Forgotten Village," and "Fragments from the Travel Notes of Count Garanskii."

All three poems included politically dangerous ideas, which had been overlooked when the book itself passed censorship (I, 752). As a direct consequence of Chernyshevskii's action, the censorship forbade a second edition of Nekrasov's poems and placed *The Contemporary* under stricter surveillance. Thus injured personally, Nekrasov had an additional reason to heed the complaints of the older writers against Chernyshevskii, but despite the temporary annoyance, he continued his support.

In time, Chernyshevskii's work on *The Contemporary* brought the journal unprecedented success, which proved that ideological commitment could be combined with profit. But this could not have been anticipated in the years 1855 and 1856, when Nekrasov's support literally saved Chernyshevskii's career. Nekrasov's motives were doubtless as complex and self-contradictory as his character, which combined self-seeking hedonism and opportunism with sensitivity and powerful social concern. From the start he recognized a vitality and partial validity in Chernyshevskii's ideas, although he admitted Chernyshevskii's "one-sidedness" to those who opposed him.[19] It is also possible that Nekrasov was moved by Chernyshevskii's efforts to help him define his own image as man and as poet—efforts which bolstered the poet's self-esteem and gave direction to his work. The evidence for Chernyshevskii's attempts to encourage Nekrasov appears in a series of letters written to the poet during his trip abroad, in the fall and winter of 1856–1857. Chernyshevskii may have exaggerated his praise in order to curry favor, but he also had a sincere appreciation of Nekrasov's poetry, and his honest concern for the proper use of the poet's talent is beyond question. Chernyshevskii sensed a crisis of spirit and despondency in Nekrasov, which he tried to overcome. Nekrasov's poetry, Chernyshevskii wrote in one letter, ranked with that of Pushkin, Lermontov, and Kol'tsov; his influence on the public was greater than anyone since Gogol, even than Turgenev or Tolstoi (XIV, 315). In another letter Chernyshevskii called Nekrasov the poet of his age and the only hope of Russian literature (XIV, 321–325). None of Nekrasov's older colleagues would have written such lines, and it is difficult to think that even the worldly Nekrasov was immune to the influence of such disarming faith in his ability and mission.[20]

In the course of 1857, and especially by 1858, two other factors worked in Chernyshevskii's favor. One factor was historical, since the debacle of the Crimean War, the accession of Alexander II, and the prospect of reform all encouraged hope for a greater role of public opinion in national life and offered new fields of attention for Russian journalism. As primary interest shifted from literary to social questions, Chernyshevskii's breadth of interest and knowledge allowed him to move with the trend and outpace his opponents on the journal. The announcement late in 1857 that in the following year *The Contemporary* would be primarily a "social-political" journal reflected Chernyshevskii's strengthened position. The other factor had to do with profits, a consideration never far from the center of Nekrasov's concern. As Chernyshevskii's influence on the journal grew, and economic, social, and political questions received more attention, sales increased. From 1854 to 1856, subscriptions averaged about 3,000. Thereafter they rose almost 1,000 a year, to reach just over 6,500 by 1860. The following year brought a leveling off, with an increase of only 60, but by that time *The Contemporary* had outstripped all competitors and become the most widely read monthly in Russia.[21] As early as 1858, a letter of Nekrasov's to Turgenev revealed that he attributed much of the journal's success to Chernyshevskii.[22]

Even with Chernyshevskii's participation in editorial decisions after Nekrasov's return in 1857, *The Contemporary* did not at once become an organ of his exclusive views. The struggle for influence on the journal lasted for several years, ending only with Turgenev's withdrawal and his final break with Nekrasov in 1860. But from 1857 on, the movement toward an extreme left position was unrelenting and irreversible, so long as it won the journal such considerable public approval. When older writers left in anger and despair, new contributors, who agreed basically with Chernyshevskii, took their places, until the journal resembled its former self in name only.[23] Among the new men, N. A. Dobroliubov stood out, not only for the quality

of his work but for his closeness to Chernyshevskii and his significant role in hastening the break between Nekrasov and his
former friends.

Dobroliubov's tie with Chernyshevskii and *The Contemporary* began in 1856, while he was still a student at the Peda-
gogical Institute in St. Petersburg. He contributed occasionally
to the journal until his graduation in 1857, and then joined the
staff full time.[24] Dobroliubov soon reached a leading position in
the criticism section, which relieved Chernyshevskii to devote
more time to other areas. Before long, he was contributing as
much to the journal's popularity as was Chernyshevskii himself.[25] The bedrock of their association was an unqualified ideological agreement, which both men seemed to require before
they could commit themselves in friendship. Clearly the older
man's ideas guided the younger man's development, a fact
recognized by Dobroliubov in a letter of August 1856, which
described an entire night spent discussing literature and philosophy with Chernyshevskii. The experience, he wrote, reminded him of how N. V. Stankevich and Herzen had taught
Belinskii, and how Belinskii had taught Nekrasov.[26] Chernyshevskii, in turn, found in Dobroliubov someone who reflected
and developed his own ideas, and in whom he could place complete trust. Years later, in the semiautobiographical novel *Prologue,* he described the importance of his young friend's work
on *The Contemporary.* The overworked hero in the novel, Volgin (Chernyshevskii), at last comes upon a worthy colleague,
Levitskii (Dobroliubov), who combines talent with a "correct"
view of things and can thus be relied on to take over part of the
work (XIII, 44–45).

During the five feverish years of Dobroliubov's career, Chernyshevskii gave him much more than intellectual guidance.
He showed an unfailing support of Dobroliubov's work and an
acceptance of his worth as a person, which Dobroliubov himself
sometimes doubted. Often this encouragement took a characteristically exaggerated form, as when he insisted on Dobroliubov's superior ability and minimized his own contribution to
Dobroliubov's thought.[27] But more important, Chernyshevskii
refused to pass judgment on his friend's behavior—the kind of

behavior he would never have tolerated in himself. One such case was Dobroliubov's love affair with Terese Karlovne Grinwal'd, a woman Chernyshevskii considered unworthy of him.[28] In a letter of August 1858, Chernyshevskii tried to discourage his friend from feeling obliged to marry the girl by means of a comforting, if improbable, comparison:

After your account, dear friend Nikolai Aleksandrovich, I can only be surprised at the similarity of the basic feature of our characters. It is as if I see my brother in you, the only difference being that the side of your character which seems bad to you, which really brings you grief, involving you in burdensome and ill-defined relationships—this side is even more strongly developed in me than in you. Thus were I your judge, I could feel only one thing: all the bad which you have done, I would have done (and continually do something like it). On the other hand, for the great good which you also have done, I have not the character. And if, as I said to you, I am not without a certain self-esteem, then all the less may I see grounds for your self-contempt. This is a temporary burst of feeling which will give way in you to a more just view of your moral worth.

You and I, insofar as I now know you, are people in whom generosity, or nobility, or heroism, or something like it, is much greater than nature demands. Therefore we assume roles that are higher than the natural strength of man, to become like angels, like Christs, etc. Of course this unnatural role cannot be borne, and we always stray from it and [then] again climb up. . . .

If I wanted to confess to you, I would tell you acts of mine more abominable than all that which you told about yourself. Take my word, or read Rousseau's *Confessions*, much is said about my life in that, but far from all. And all the same I am a good man and you are better than I am. I am as sure of this as that $2 \times 2 = 4$. To the devil with abjectness—we are people, we cannot be like the mythical beings of our martyrology, without weaknesses. But all the same we are very good people. We will take ourselves as we are, and believe me we are better than ninety-nine out of a hundred people (XIV, 359–360).[29]

Beyond intellectual guidance and this kind of moral support, Chernyshevskii did all he could to win recognition and financial reward for Dobroliubov's contribution to *The Contempo-*

*rary.* During Dobroliubov's long illness from tuberculosis in 1860 and 1861, Chernyshevskii tried in every way to ease his friend's distress (XIV, 428–429). Three months after Dobroliubov's death in November 1861, Chernyshevskii wrote that he could rarely pass a day without tears; it would have been better, he thought, if he had died instead of Dobroliubov, who was the best defender of the Russian people (XIV, 449).

Yet the relationship benefited Chernyshevskii as well, although in ways that are less easy to document. So close was the compatibility of values and ideas of the two men that Dobroliubov's contribution to the journal seemed like a doubling of Chernyshevskii's own effort. Other staff members regarded their voices as one in determining editorial policy. But Dobroliubov added something of his own, which was not so much a different point of view as an attitude that scorned accommodation and was more combative.[30] Chernyshevskii, for all his opposition to the older generation of literary men, did not engage so easily in the aggressive rudeness and contempt shown by Dobroliubov. This difference may have been related to the variation in social sensitivity of the two men, noted by A. Ia. Panaeva. Whereas Chernyshevskii was unobservant, Dobroliubov let nothing pass and readily took offense, because he detected at once any falseness in those about him.[31] In addition, though Dobroliubov adhered to his convictions with a passion and enthusiasm no more profound than that of Chernyshevskii, he was less controlled and less conscious of consequences. He more naturally maintained a position of uncompromising militancy, which served as a reinforcement for Chernyshevskii's increasingly bold expression of the radical position. In a memoir giving his own version of Turgenev's final break with *The Contemporary*, written long after the event, Chernyshevskii recognized this difference. He admitted agreeing with Dobroliubov about Turgenev but claimed that he would not have let these feelings be the basis of a personal break: "It seemed to me useful for literature that writers, more or less capable of sympathizing with something honorable, try not to have personal quarrels among themselves. Dobroliubov was of another opinion. It seemed to him that bad allies are no allies" (I, 729).

If Chernyshevskii did in fact differ from Dobroliubov in this attitude, he nonetheless never failed to back up his young colleague.

The shattering of Turgenev's relationship with *The Contemporary* demonstrated Dobroliubov's important contribution to the leftward movement of the journal, as well as his role in amplifying and reinforcing Chernyshevskii's essential ideas. Of all the older contributors to the journal, Turgenev stood the best chance of reaching an accommodation with the younger generation. He was not fundamentally opposed to social change, although he was much concerned with the degree of change and how it came about. Moreover, for some time he had maintained close personal ties with Nekrasov, which the younger men could never fully replace.[32]

It would also appear that, early in 1857, Chernyshevskii entertained hopes that he might win Turgenev over to his point of view and thereby influence the direction of Turgenev's art. Unfortunately, it is unknown whether Chernyshevskii was aware of earlier attempts to have him removed from the staff, but he could hardly have been ignorant of the hostile reactions to some of his early reviews and his dissertation, and Turgenev had shared in this hostility. However, his dislike softened somewhat during the course of 1856, under the impact of Chernyshevskii's "Essays on the Gogol Period of Russian Literature" with its glorification of Belinskii, whose memory Turgenev cherished.[33] Sensing the opportunity, Chernyshevskii made an oblique overture to Turgenev. Perhaps hoping that his words would be repeated, he wrote to Nekrasov late in 1856 that Turgenev seemed to him the most honorable and noblest of literary men. Turgenev's weakness consisted only in an excess of kindness (XIV, 330).

Early the following year, Chernyshevskii turned directly to Turgenev with two letters that clearly went beyond their ostensible purpose of appealing for copy. Chernyshevskii wrote: "By the nature of your talent and other qualities, you *cannot help* but write things which will be higher than everything written by others, not excluding your protégé Tolstoi." Against those who would criticize Turgenev, Chernyshevskii saw the need of an iron dictatorship in literature, "before which all would tremble, as before the dictatorship of Belinskii" (XIV, 332). In the other letter, he added: "At the present time, beside you and Nekrasov, Russian literature has no one. Every worthwhile person says this, I challenge you to believe it" (XIV, 345).

It is possible, of course, to attribute these letters to calculated self-interest on Chernyshevskii's part, as his participation in the editorship had just begun, and he wanted to encourage contributions and protect his own writers. If such was his motive, one must wonder at his easy ability to turn on his apparently sincere enthusiasm and appreciation. It seems more likely, however, that Chernyshevskii found much to appreciate in Turgenev's writing and wanted to influence its direction, just as he had tried to influence the writing of Nekrasov. He saw the tremendous power of works like *Sportsman's Sketches* and "Mumu" and hoped to elicit more of them.

A year later, when Turgenev showed no sign of responding to the friendly overtures contained in these letters, Chernyshevskii sought to exert influence by an open attack. In May 1858 he placed a review criticizing the frivolousness of Turgenev's romantic story "Asia" in the pages of another journal, an action that infuriated Turgenev (V, 156–174). Over the next two years Dobroliubov's articles in *The Contemporary* expressed a politically-inspired literary criticism that further offended Turgenev, not only by its content but by what Turgenev considered its inquisitorial and irresponsible style. Moreover, throughout this period of growing disagreement between moderate and radical opinion, personal animosity played a role. Reflecting back over these events in 1884, Chernyshevskii noted that Turgenev once expressed his special dislike of Dobroliubov with the comment that although Chernyshevskii was a "common snake," his young colleague was a "cobra" (I, 737). These words from the lips of the man whose weakness Chernyshevskii had identified, just a few years before, as "an excess of kindness" are a measure of the bitterness generated. Certainly the tendency of *The Contemporary*, under Chernyshevskii's influence, had become increasingly uncongenial to Turgenev, who by 1860 no longer contributed exclusively to the journal. Yet Turgenev did allow his speech "Hamlet and Don Quixote" to be printed in the January 1860 issue, and it required a final move by Dobroliubov to cause a complete break. In March 1860, apparently over Turgenev's protest, *The Contemporary* published Dobroliubov's angry political attack "When Will the Real Day Come?" based on Turgenev's novel *On the Eve*. With this blow, Turgenev severed all ties with the journal.

With Turgenev's withdrawal, there was no longer any question about either the direction of *The Contemporary* or its leadership. Nekrasov, for all his vacillation and claims of wanting to keep writers of different views, had in effect presided over the death of one journal and the birth of another.[34] Newly refashioned, *The Contemporary* consistently expressed a radical point of view. Chernyshevskii and Dobroliubov, while his health permitted, found their voices in editorial policy unopposed. Early in 1862, at the peak of his influence on what was now Russia's leading journal, Chernyshevskii claimed that he was as much a proprietor of *The Contemporary* as Nekrasov, with an equal voice even in financial matters (XIV, 445). This position brought him a considerable income, which he claimed reached 12,000 rubles in 1861 (XIV, 463).

At this point, Chernyshevskii might well have reflected on the brilliant success of his career. Nine years before he had returned to St. Petersburg experienced only as a secondary school teacher, still unsure of his proper vocation, and desperately in need of money to support his bride. He had only his wits and an extraordinary capacity for sustained work, but after a shaky beginning, these proved enough to establish him as a public figure, comfortably situated financially, and with a widespread influence on public opinion. And he had won his position essentially without compromise. Instead of sacrificing his convictions to achieve success, Chernyshevskii had literally made a success of his convictions. Six months later, he was in prison.

Chernyshevskii's achievement as Russia's leading journalist had required a tremendous effort and complete dedication to *The Contemporary*. After giving up his alternate plans for a higher university degree, the affairs of the journal consumed almost all his time and energy. On one occasion, however, he undertook to edit another journal. In January 1858 a professor of military tactics, General A. P. Kartsev, asked Chernyshevskii to edit the *Military Compendium,* a new journal dedicated to raising the general level of education in the officer corps. He accepted quickly, hoping thereby to add two or three thousand rubles a year to his income (XIV, 352). A year later he wrote home that he had refused reappointment to the job, though in fact he had been forced to leave the editorship, near the end of 1858, because of objection to the critical tendency of the articles he selected for publication (XIV, 370).[35] As much as he may have valued this expanded area of influence, it is difficult to understand how he managed the extra responsibility, even for several months.

Yet Chernyshevskii seemed willing to pay a very high price in his personal life for his career success and the success of the journal. His days became an endless round of work, all but devoid of diversion, and with little time for his wife and family. More often than not, he labored into the early morning hours. Many times he did not even emerge from his study when Olga entertained guests.[36] Still, it would be too simple to say that he sacrificed family life to achieve higher goals of social and political change. To a considerable extent, the causal relation between his marriage and his achievement worked the other way. That is, the peculiar character of his marriage probably helped to sustain the pace of his work.

A great deal has been written in evaluation of Chernyshevskii's marriage with Olga. Much of this writing is controversial, with the main points of issue being the degree of Olga's understanding of Chernyshevskii's work, her sympathy with his social objectives, and her worthiness to be the wife of so adoring yet dedicated a man. The strongest negative criticism of Olga is expressed by V. A. Pypina, who wrote from the general feeling of the Pypin family that their cousin's marriage had not been successful.[37] At the other extreme, recent Soviet historians have tried to reverse this condemnation with portrayals of Olga as a dedicated fighter for social justice in Russia, working side by side with her husband.[38] Were the problem simply one of describing Olga as a person, then allowing for family prejudices and the limitations of her evidence, Pypina's description would be the fairer of the two. But the most important and more difficult question is the significance of this marriage for Chernyshevskii's career.

Compared to her generous, self-effacing husband, who seemed totally devoid of concern for material advantage and personal gratification, Olga was not a sympathetic or attractive person. With little education and still less intellectual curiosity, she could find in Chernyshevskii's work no real meaning. She preferred a life that was self-centered and essentially frivolous, where gaiety ruled and she could be the center of flirtatious attention. She cared less for what her husband did than for the fact that her status and affluence grew with his fame as a journalist.[39] If Chernyshevskii seemed more than willing to oblige and serve, Olga seemed more than willing to demand and exploit.

Although definite evidence is sparse, it is possible to speculate about the difficulty faced by this couple, one so unlike the other, in establishing a relationship in the early years of their marriage. One recalls the conspicuous lack of realism with which Chernyshevskii had anticipated married life. He had dreamed of spending hours a day by his wife's side, whereas in reality he faced the oppressive time demands of teaching, studying for a degree, and writing. Nor did he at first possess the means to indulge Olga's whims and desire for entertainment. After a year and a half in St. Petersburg, he wrote to his father about Olga's loneliness and the fact that they could rarely go out (XIV, 272–273). With his success in writing, their financial situation improved, as did the social opportunities for Olga. It appears, however, that a deeper problem existed. Chernyshevskii was not the man to theorize in one way and act in another. He believed that a wife ought to relate to her husband in friendship, as the result of free choice and not obligation. Their separate rooms symbolized his respect for Olga's freedom (XIV, 307).[40] But for a person so unsure of himself and unperceptive in personal relationships as Chernyshevskii, living this kind of ideal must not have been easy. Many years later, in 1878, he revealed something of his difficulty in a letter to his cousin A. N. Pypin. He wrote that for several years at the beginning of marriage he had not really been sure of Olga's disposition toward him. He had married completely convinced that no woman, especially his bride, could ever love him, a man who found it wearisome to engage in any kind of amusement. He had tried to be a "friend" to her, but because of her "fiery" character, he could never be sure where he stood in her regard. As a result, it was only at the birth of their third son, in 1858, after living together for five years, that he knew her feelings for sure. Fearing for her life, Olga took leave of her husband with words which, as he put it, showed she did not dislike him (XV, 138–140).

Some exaggeration may be present in this account, because the letter to Pypin had the purpose of comforting Chernyshevskii's cousin, who was currently troubled by his own unhappy relation with Olga. But it seems unlikely that Chernyshevskii would have invented the entire story. Two letters written to Nekrasov in the winter of 1856–1857 offer further evidence on the same problem. In these letters, Chernyshevskii referred to a personal crisis that for some months had kept him from doing his best work and, indeed, had led him to drink and to thoughts of suicide. The second of these letters, written on February 7, 1857, claimed that his concern had all along been fear for Olga's health in the delivery of their second son, born January 20, because they had been warned that there might be danger to her life in a second pregnancy, and he had therefore intended to limit their family to one child (XIV, 336). In itself, this explanation is plausible, but as Lampert and others have noted, the earlier letter, dated November 5, 1856, hinted at a different source of Chernyshevskii's distress.[41] In it he took a position which he usually opposed, namely, that one's personal feelings ought to take precedence over political or worldly questions. It was not for the latter that men took their lives or resorted to drink (XIV, 322). He then praised four poems of Nekrasov that lacked a political tendency and yet had made a greater impression on him than any of his others. Their themes were loneliness, alienation from a loved one, frustration, and despair. Later in the letter, he again mentioned his torment:

If you had known what I lived through in the past month and a half, you would have been surprised that I could have written even a line during that time. I say only that the longer I live on this earth, the more I am convinced that people, thoughtlessly it is true, do absurd and stupid things—but all the same there is more good than evil in them. To put you at rest, I must say that this unpleasantness does not have its source in literature and concerns me alone, no one else. Even more than before I convinced myself that all institutions that now exist are stupid and harmful; however good their appearance, all this is stupid; love, friendship, enmity—all this if not nonsense, then has traces of nonsense. But man, all the same, is good and noble. All the same one cannot but respect and love people, at least many people (XIV, 327).

Without further evidence, one cannot speak with certainty about the meaning of this passage. If his story about the danger to Olga was true, he may have intended to condemn himself for risking her life, or to reproach Olga for behaving foolishly and risking her own life.[42] Or it may have been simply a temporary outburst of emotion by a man who bore the terrible burden of a love that was not returned in equal measure, and who, after speaking out once, could only bury and disguise his feelings. According to a pathetic note in a letter to A. N. Pypin in 1878, Chernyshevskii had never during their nine years together heard Olga speak of her love (XV, 146).

Despite the torment, Chernyshevskii did make an adjustment to the reality of his marriage, and this adjustment was successful, although in a manner peculiar to himself. He had chosen as partner a woman who could not understand him and whose world he could not enter, without giving up his own values and the most essential part of his personality. For most men this would have been an impossible dilemma. But Chernyshevskii was saved by his own convictions and unselfishness. He believed passionately in her right to be what she wanted, and he honestly found satisfaction in working to support her in a way of life he could not possibly share. Thus, while they lived in separate worlds, he could still, by supporting her entertainments and extravagance, express his own form of devotion, which may have been more important to him than the usual need of fully reciprocated love and understanding. From this perspective, one cannot say that he sacrificed his family life for his intensive work. He could not give up what in any case he did not have. His true sacrifice came only when he allowed his expression of radical opinion to undercut his own safety and thereby prevent him from continuing to express his devotion in the way he knew best.

Finally, one must recognize the important role that the relationship with Olga played in Chernyshevskii's career, regardless of any qualitative judgment on the nature of their life together. Throughout Chernyshevskii's life, Olga was the center of one important part of his being. Without her, he would never have been able to function as he did, because his concern for her comfort and happiness provided a source of energy and inspiration for his work. Steklov was right in stressing this aspect of the problem.[43] As Chernyshevskii wrote to Olga in 1888:

If I had never met you, my dear, and if you had not found that you could rely on my devotion to you, my life would have been dull and inactive as it was before I met you. If I did something useful, then all the benefit that Russian society received from my activity it owes to you. Without your friendship, I would not have published a single line, I would only have reclined and read, not putting on paper that which was considered honorable and useful. Your nature supported my faith in the reasonableness and nobility of people. Not strengthened by your personal reasonableness and honesty, I would not have considered people capable of conducting themselves as reason and honor demands, and would therefore not have been willing to write what was useful for them (as I did not write before my acquaintance with you) (XV, 700–701).

The circle cannot be squared. It is impossible to reconcile this revelation of the inner significance of the marriage for Chernyshevskii with the picture of Olga provided by outside observers and by Olga's own self-characterization. But there need not be consistency between the two. Chernyshevskii may well have profoundly misunderstood her and, in his mind's eye, placed her in a category of being that was in some way necessary for his own personality. The most important factor is what he derived from the relationship, and this he symbolized at the beginning of his most popular work, *What Is To Be Done?* where the dedication read, "To my dear O. S. Ch____" (XI, 5).

During this crucial period, information on Chernyshevskii's personal life is limited, since he no longer kept a diary, and his letters, with few exceptions, either dwelt on business affairs or, as in the case of letters to his family in Saratov, concealed as much, if not more, than they told. None of those who should have known him best—Olga, Dobroliubov, Nekrasov, or A. N. Pypin—left portrayals that tell very much about the man. Nor is the problem solely one of the scarcity of evidence. Other contemporaries, including those who were sympathetic and who worked closely with him, found it difficult to comprehend the man, apart from his ideas.[44]

Many years later, when writing about his working years with Nekrasov, Chernyshevskii himself referred to his problems in relating to people. He noted that Nekrasov had seemed more willing to discuss personal matters at the beginning of their acquaintance than later, when they should have known each other better. Chernyshevskii admitted that Nekrasov may have been put off by his appearance of not listening with serious, sympathetic attention and by his frequently absent-minded responses. In one example, Chernyshevskii reported that he had repeatedly angered Nekrasov because he could not remember that a particular offhand comment was being interpreted by Nekrasov as a personal affront (I, 729–730). It seems that Chernyshevskii was insensitive to the impact of his words on another person in direct conversation. Thus, he readily served mankind as an abstraction, and often showed kindness to those in need, especially to young writers, but few could speak of a genuinely close friendship with him.[45] He was most often a man apart. His partisans respected his views, admired his capacity to work, and appreciated his kindness and dedication. Yet, even when they followed him as a leader, they could not claim to know him as an intimate.

Among those who came to respect Chernyshevskii and worked

closely with him, he sometimes left an ambivalent or even unfavorable first impression. The same contrast between his forceful views and his unimpressive appearance and bearing that A. P. Miliukov noticed in the earlier days of the Vvedenskii circle again came into play. He seemed timid and modest in conversation, looking down when he spoke and smiling nervously. He had the habit of adding a final *s* to words like *da* and *net,* as if always to say "yes sir" and "no sir," in a servile way or in mock humility. Unless he knew someone well enough to trust him, he often simply refused serious conversation or spoke jokingly, with irony and double meanings, so that the person might be left not really knowing what had been said, or indeed whether Chernyshevskii had intended to make fun of him.[46] M. A. Antonovich, who became the leading critic for *The Contemporary* after Dobroliubov's death, left the following account:

Usually his speech was sprinkled with jokes, puns, sallies, anecdotes, and all the while accompanied by smiles and even laughter. People close to him knew this mannerism, became used to it, and waited patiently for that moment when, seriously and as if in passing, he would reply, usually in a very few words, to that which had been asked him, or that which he wanted to say. But on new acquaintances this manner produced a strange, unpleasant impression; they did not expect such behavior from Chernyshevskii. At that time interviewing was not yet much in vogue—but people who approached N. G., desiring to interview him, to know his thoughts and feelings on some occasion or event, were greatly disappointed. Sometimes very serious people appeared before him, with very serious questions or propositions. But even in these cases, he softened and embellished his manner just enough so that it would not appear impolite and offensive. This was some kind of strange caprice, the unwillingness to go at once to a serious tone.[47]

Antonovich's word "caprice" seems out of place here, because Chernyshevskii had reason to be circumspect concerning those with whom he would openly share his views. However, Antonovich probably realized this fact and merely wanted to describe an aspect of Chernyshevskii's personality that went deeper than his understandable caution. In whatever way the mannerism is explained, it must nevertheless have thrown people off balance.

If Chernyshevskii thus sometimes confounded his supporters, he more often infuriated his enemies. In the late 1850's and early 1860's, he became embroiled in polemics about issues of great and immediate social import, as opposed to his earlier concern with theories of literature or philosophical abstractions. These issues involved challenges to established interests and varying proposals to effect social and political change. As the stakes rose, so did the bitterness of the debate. Disagreement about the desirability of change and methods to be used was translated into personal hatred and invective.[48] In this context, extreme statements of hostility were common. However, some of the negative comments leveled against Chernyshevskii were not simply blind hostility; they showed a certain understanding of the man.

A. V. Nikitenko, who earlier had been Chernyshevskii's teacher of literature, and who throughout this period served as a government censor, mentioned his former pupil several times in his extensive diary. Once he wrote, with no little disdain, that Chernyshevskii combined a gifted mind with intolerance, and that he thought himself to be "the leading wit and publicist in Europe." Elsewhere he wrote that Chernyshevskii played the demagogue in order to attract "thoughtless youth."[49] In a similar vein, K. D. Kavelin, who at one time had reasonably friendly relations with Chernyshevskii, wrote of him at the time of his arrest, "For Chernyshevskii I have a very great affection, but a more crude, tactless, and conceited man I have never met."[50] And even Herzen, who unlike Kavelin, had social objectives that corresponded with those of Chernyshevskii, objected to the style and manner of the new men of *The Contemporary*. Although Herzen had Dobroliubov primarily in mind when, in 1860, he wrote the article "The Superfluous Men and the Bilious Ones," he would not have excluded Chernyshevskii from among those "Daniels of the Neva" whom he attacked for arousing melancholy and gloomily reproaching people because they ate without gnashing their teeth and could be carried away by a painting or music while forgetting all about the misfortunes of the world.[51]

One is impressed by the huge gap between these accusations of conceit and arrogance in Chernyshevskii and the picture of him obtained from more sympathetic sources, especially those having closer acquaintance with him. The distance between these conflicting views, however, is less a matter of different opinions than a reflection of two aspects of the same man: one his personality in relating directly to other people, and the other the stance he assumed in writing. Chernyshevskii clearly had both a private and a public image, which did not readily correspond. Since he rarely engaged in public action, his public image was essentially the impression left by his writing. Apart from the content and direction of his articles, certain characteristics of his writing made him either friends or enemies.

The first characteristic is related to Chernyshevskii's intellectual transformation at the university, which, though it occurred over the course of several years, still resembled a "conversion." In other words, he went from one set of absolute truths to another and, once having arrived at the new truth, strayed very little from it during the whole course of his lifetime. Consequently, when Chernyshevskii wrote, he rarely showed doubt or hesitation, and even more rarely admitted that there might be any validity in what opponents believed. Alternate views had little claim to be taken seriously. His writings were saturated with an unquestioned intellectual certainty, revealing a man who believed that the major lines of a great new set of truths had already been discovered and needed only to be elaborated and disseminated. It was the degree and absolutist character of this certainty that aroused greatest resentment. Chernyshevskii, to be sure, argued in an arena of tough journalistic polemic, where few holds were barred; but important as this context may have been in influencing the tone of his writing, his own cast of mind proved at least as important. Chernyshevskii's opponent was viewed as either a fool, who did not yet realize that many of the old ideas and values had been discredited and forced to give way before more convincing new truths, or a knave, who manipulated old ideas because in some

*Chernyshevskii in 1853*

way they served his narrow self-interest. Between such unattractive alternatives, Chernyshevskii allowed his opponents little room for honorable differences of opinion.[52]

A second characteristic of Chernyshevskii's writing had its origin in problems he encountered with the censorship. The ineptness of the government's censorship defies belief. All the articles that won Chernyshevskii his reputation as a dangerous threat to traditional society passed the censorship prior to publication. Crippled by an unimaginative literalness, the censors carefully deleted sentences and paragraphs, without really affecting the basic message. In articles carrying the official imprimatur, he managed to state the case for philosophical materialism and socialism, and strongly hinted at the need of political revolution. Occasionally he was able to state his position openly, as if no repressive machinery existed, but most of the time he could not. He was limited especially when other writers challenged his ideas, because he could not elaborate his position. The composition of each month's journal and its passage through censorship came as a recurring crisis, which at any time might have brought harm to *The Contemporary* and to Chernyshevskii himself.[53]

In this situation, he necessarily resorted to indirection and to the so-called "language of Aesop," that is, a language that referred to one thing in terms of another. Forced to use calculated deception to circumvent the censorship, he also made mocking humor and insinuation an important part of his writing style. Such techniques, in part necessary, proved useful as well. When he chose not to meet an opposing argument head on, he could discredit that view effectively with journalistic ridicule, a technique he employed with consummate skill. To those of contrary opinion, this technique, used especially against opposing schools of political economy and philosophy, seemed irresponsible and almost calculated to appeal to the immature faith of youth, rather than to the minds of serious readers. In a few reviews, for instance, Chernyshevskii spent most of his effort making fun of the opening pages of the book, and suggested that he had not even bothered to read through to the end because the author's main argument was not worth considering.[54] It is true that most of the criticism of this technique came from those who were writing from the privileged sanctuary of beliefs less threatened by the censors. Still, the techniques of journalistic polemic Chernyshevskii employed, by necessity or by choice, did affect the impression he made on the public and help to explain the exaggerated charges of arrogance and conceit that seem so incompatible with what else is known about his personality.

The public had one brief opportunity to compare their impression of Chernyshevskii the writer with the man himself. On March 2, 1862, he appeared on the program of a literary evening, set up to raise funds for indigent students and, secretly, to help M. I. Mikhailov and V. A. Obruchev, who had recently been arrested. The resulting impressions were a very mixed bag, which may have reflected the prejudices and preconceptions of the listeners, but which also showed that Chernyshevskii the man did not fulfill the expectations of those who knew only the writer.

Following a speech by Professor P. V. Pavlov, which was delivered in a provocative way and soon after led to his exile, several writers read from their own works, and then Chernyshevskii sought to describe his association with the recently deceased Dobroliubov. His inept manner of delivery confused his friends almost as much as it annoyed his enemies. He spoke in a quiet, matter-of-fact way, without preparation, without animation, and without a sense of contact with his audience. He evidently held himself awkwardly, played nervously with his watch chain, and made a few slips of expression which caused some in the audience to take offense.[55] One otherwise friendly witness contrasted the ovation when Chernyshevskii rose to speak, with the sigh of disappointment when he concluded.[56] There may have been calculated caution in Chernyshevskii's performance, after the daring speech of Pavlov, but one suspects that the main source of disappointment was his nervousness and lack of presence. He was apparently the kind of man who, in one context, would not shrink from challenging God and the powers of a coercive autocracy, and yet could feel threatened by having to speak in public, and, as a consequence, overreact with exaggerated indifference.

It is extremely difficult to measure the extent of Chernyshevskii's influence. One limitation, built into the Russian society of his day, was simply the geographic distribution of a literate population that could possibly be aware of intellectual issues and keep pace with what was, after all, a very high level of debate. The first issue of *The Contemporary* in 1862 published figures on the distribution of subscriptions for the previous three years, which are very revealing. In 1861, subscriptions totaled 6,658, and of these, St. Petersburg claimed 1,681 and Moscow 477. The next largest subscription concentration was Odessa, with 97; only five other cities had 50 or more. Another interesting fact about these figures, which is difficult to explain, is that while the overall number of subscriptions rose about 1,158 during these years, those for the city of Moscow actually fell from 622 to 477 (X, 454–479).

Matching the geographic concentration of Chernyshevskii's readers, which probably would have been roughly the same for any journal of the time, there was a further concentration according to generation. The newness and increasingly radical character of his message appealed most to younger readers in the schools, seminaries, and universities, and in the junior ranks of civil and military service. These readers had less stake in the existing order of society, as well as less experience and responsibility for the consequences of their views. Conservatives, or even moderates like A. V. Nikitenko, might call them "thoughtless youth," and to some the label might have applied, but they also composed a group that was willing to risk itself to fulfill its ideals of a better society. Nor can one say that they had nothing to lose: some of them denied privileged family backgrounds and endangered their prospects of a comfortable career; others gave up their freedom and their lives.

The number of young people who followed the radical position consistently, to the extent of committing themselves wholly to it, were few, but those who did owed much of their inspiration to Chernyshevskii. For others, who were simply living through a radical phase in their lives under the influence of the general mood of the times, he was a strong, if temporary, guide. In his *Reminiscences*, L. F. Panteleev recorded the great excitement caused by Chernyshevskii's articles among the young readers of the early 1860's. They would try to identify the source of his ideas, and a few young enthusiasts, carried away by the fad of partisanship, tried to model themselves on their master by imitating what they knew of his manner of speaking.[57] Other sympathetic memoirists support this impression of Chernyshevskii's special appeal to youth. N. V. Shelgunov stressed the contrast between Belinskii, who seemed to work out his thoughts before the eyes of his readers, and Chernyshevskii, who gave out the fully formed ideas that his youthful readers needed. Shelgunov also noted that students took delight in reading between the lines of Chernyshevskii's and Dobroliubov's articles, when these articles challenged some kind of authority and shook idols from their pedestals. The more daring and extreme the articles were, the better.[58] Among young readers who felt alienated from their own society and therefore receptive to radical views, the influence of Chernyshevskii's articles was limited only by their technical difficulty. Some young readers found themselves ill prepared to follow scholarly articles and preferred those that were clearly polemical.[59]

Chernyshevskii's popularity and the success of *The Contemporary* both reflected and helped to cause a deep cleavage in Russian journalism in the early 1860's. Though differences of view had existed from the beginning, *The Contemporary's* isolation increased as its position became more overtly radical. By 1861 and the first half of 1862, Chernyshevskii had led the journal into a vicious polemic with almost the whole spectrum of conservative and moderate journals, in a situation that scarcely offered a fair arena for argument. Because he attempted to state and defend positions that the entire censorship apparatus had been established to repress, arguments against him easily became denunciations, whether the writer intended them so or not.[60]

The ideological isolation of *The Contemporary* did not, however, mean that Chernyshevskii and like-minded writers stood totally apart from others in the intellectual community who disagreed with them. Even in the heat of argument, a few areas of meeting and joint action remained. In the spring of 1861,

Chernyshevskii joined a broad front of journalists concerned with improving censorship conditions, and he continually met men of varied persuasion through his involvement with the Literary Fund, an organization to help indigent writers (XIV, 425–426). After student unrest led to a closing of the university in St. Petersburg, and plans were made in January 1862 for a number of scholars to give free public lectures, Chernyshevskii found himself in a group with K. D. Kavelin and N. I. Kostomarov, two ideologically unlikely colleagues.[61] As late as February 1862, despite journalistic attacks and counterattacks, he could still request A. A. Kraevskii to join with him in a deputation of literary men to A. V. Golovnin, the Minister of Education (XIV, 448).

Although such contacts continued, Chernyshevskii's name was so frequently associated with radical ideas and social unrest that, during the last year of his active career, he became in effect a marked man. In September 1861, Nikitenko noted in his diary the rumor that Chernyshevskii had been arrested. Nikitenko apparently felt no need to speculate on the crime that had been committed; he simply assumed that the offense consisted in Chernyshevskii's writings.[62] Other persons, with no more evidence than rumor, suspected him of more serious involvement in the disorders of the day. In May 1862, shortly after the fires that destroyed St. Petersburg's Tolkuchii market, Chernyshevskii received a visit from F. M. Dostoevskii, who believed that the beleaguered editor not only knew who had begun the fires but actually exercised some control over the culprits. Dostoevskii pleaded with him to prevent a repetition of the tragedy (I, 777–779).[63] At about the same time, Chernyshevskii was subjected to anonymous threats, and denunciations were sent to the police. The growth of so dangerous a reputation naturally affected those who sought association with him. M. A. Antonovich noted a fall-off in attendance at the *jour fixe* at the Chernyshevskii home, a fact confirmed by police reports. The faint-hearted thought it wise to stay away.[64]

There is clear evidence of the government's recognition of Chernyshevskii's influence and the danger it posed, but dealing with him proved a ticklish dilemma. Since inefficient censorship had allowed him to state his position, it was difficult for the government to silence him now without losing face. It proved impossible to save the government's reputation, but beginning in 1861, a ring was built around Chernyshevskii that would be tightened to destroy him the following year.

In November 1861, an extensive report of the Main Censorship Authority noted the several reprimands already given to *The Russian Word* and *The Contemporary,* and remarked the need to warn them to change their direction or run the risk of being closed. The report stated specifically about *The Contemporary:* "Just as before, its articles in regard to religion are void of any Christian doctrine, in regard to legislation they are opposed to the existing structure, in regard to philosophy they are imbued with coarse materialism, in regard to politics they approve of revolution, denying even moderate liberalism, in regard to society they show contempt for the higher social classes, a peculiar idealization of woman, and an extreme devotion to the lower class of people." [65] With such a characterization representing official attitude, *The Contemporary* was clearly living on borrowed time.

From the end of October 1861, Chernyshevskii was placed under constant surveillance by police agents of the Third Section. They watched his home, noted where he went, and listed the visitors he received.[66] Later in November, the Minister of Internal Affairs issued secret orders to deny him a passport for travel abroad.[67] The hope, apparently, was to gather evidence of his participation in some revolutionary or illegal activity, which could be used to silence the voice they had allowed to speak for so long. Eventually, when sound evidence could not be obtained, the government resorted to less savory means.

Before it came to that point, however, the government tried one alternate way out of its dilemma, and failed. There is evidence that it made an attempt to silence Chernyshevskii by offering him personal safety in exchange for a cessation of his work on *The Contemporary.* Knowledge of the offer comes from two sources, which do not entirely agree. One version was provided by Chernyshevskii during his later years of prison and exile, in which he claimed that the Governor General of St.

Petersburg, A. A. Suvorov himself, had offered him a passport to leave Russia just before his arrest.[68] A more likely version comes from one of Chernyshevskii's own letters to Suvorov in 1862, in which he argued his innocence by referring to an official offer by A. V. Golovnin, the Minister of Education, to take a post abroad (XIV, 463). Chernyshevskii, of course, may not have been as innocent as he claimed, but it seems unlikely that he would have made up a story that Suvorov could so easily have checked.

Whatever the details, it seems likely that the authorities made some offer, in an attempt to find an easy way out of their difficulty. If so, by rejecting the possibility of trading his ideals for his freedom, Chernyshevskii dramatically underscored a decision he had already made when he refused, under obvious pressure, to alter the tendency of *The Contemporary* and chose instead to say as much as he could for as long as he was permitted to speak. It required tremendous courage to make this decision, because he knowingly chose a path that could lead to his destruction. Furthermore, he felt too great a responsibility to his wife and children to permit a light-minded choice. If he stayed and continued his work, their lives might be ruined, as well as his own. But his choice was either to sacrifice himself and those dearest to him, or to betray the ideas he believed could bring happiness to all men. In comparable situations, many men have broken. Chernyshevskii, with almost fatalistic resignation, chose a quiet heroism.[69]

After this decision, it was only a question of time before the government could find the best occasion for his arrest. His name appeared at the top of a list of suspected persons sent as part of a report to Alexander II by the chief of the Third Section, V. A. Dolgorukov, on April 27, 1862. By late spring, unrest in Poland, the fires in St. Petersburg, and the startling appearance of the inflammatory revolutionary leaflet "Young Russia," all helped the government stimulate public fear and indignation at the conduct of the radicals. Early in June, after many months of hesitation, the government finally acted. On June 7 it decided to suspend *The Contemporary* and *The Russian Word* for eight months.[70] A week later, both journals were closed.

There is no evidence as to what Chernyshevskii really thought would happen next, but he acted as if the repressive acts would eventually blow over. General A. L. Potapov of the Third Section told him in mid-June that the government had no further charge or suspicion against him.[71] On the 19th of June, Chernyshevskii told Nekrasov that he would sever all connections with *The Contemporary* in the unlikely possibility that this would help to remove the restriction on the journal (XIV, 453–455). Early in July, Olga set out on a visit to Saratov, and Chernyshevskii apparently intended to follow as soon as possible. He gave no indication in his letters to the Pypins that he expected a further blow (XIV, 455, 834).

It is difficult to think that the matter would have rested there in any case, but through a foolish mistake, Herzen made the government's task easier. He let word leak out in London that he was sending a letter to Chernyshevskii's associate, N. A. Serno-Solov'evich, offering to publish *The Contemporary* abroad. News of the communication reached the Russian police, and they picked up the courier as soon as he entered Russia on July 6. Herzen's offer could be construed as "proof" of Chernyshevskii's illegal complicity with the émigré group in London.[72] Chernyshevskii and N. A. Serno-Solov'evich were arrested the following day.

With the one notable exception of the writing and publication of Chernyshevskii's novel *What Is To Be Done?* which occurred during his first year in prison, the government had succeeded in one of its objectives. Chernyshevskii's strong voice of criticism was removed from Russian journalism, and no one of comparable stature came forward to replace him. In retrospect, his achievement during the brief years of his career was staggering. His ranging interests and knowledge of Western languages permitted him to write articles on almost all the vital social and intellectual questions in the Russia of his day. As his concerns were too widespread and his time too short to permit original scholarship in all fields, at times he simply reworked borrowed materials from his own point of view. But even articles based on extensive translations became, by his selection and accompanying comments, essentially his own. The hurried pace of his life rarely allowed him to give a subject exhaustive and fully systematic treatment. Nor, as a man wanting to change the world as well as to study it, could he claim dispassionate fairness. He wrote as a dedicated partisan of unorthodox views, in a context of censorship restriction and often bitter opposition from other journals. Despite these difficulties, he succeeded in establishing a relatively clear and coherent position in the fields of philosophy, aesthetics, literary criticism, economics, and politics. Furthermore, the views he expressed stood at the core of the protest movement of the 1860's.

Chernyshevskii did not give these different fields uniform attention during his career. His own interests and estimation of Russia's needs varied, as did the particular nature of censorship regulation. Perhaps the key to his willingness to shift the emphasis of his work may be found in an idealized portrait he once drew of Gotthold Ephraim Lessing (IV, 5–221). In a series of essays that appeared in *The Contemporary* in 1856 and 1857, Chernyshevskii credited Lessing with revolutionizing literary criticism, giving new direction to German grammar, contributing a strong plea for religious toleration, and preparing the soil for a reform in theology. But he appreciated most the fact that the German enlightener thought more about how he could aid the development of his people than about any particular branch of learning. Lessing had worked on whatever the times demanded. In his own career, Chernyshevskii fulfilled a similar goal.

# V. Philosophy

As a counterpart to the profound social changes wrought by the advance of science and machine technology, the nineteenth century gave rise to a wealth of rival theories and ideological systems that attacked long-established ideas and assumptions. In Western Europe, repeated assaults were made on the prevailing Christian view of man and nature, as well as on the rationale behind traditional social and political institutions. Secular rationalism and naturalism, which had developed in the eighteenth century Enlightenment, especially in France and England, largely as a response to earlier scientific breakthrough, suffered no more than a temporary eclipse by romanticism and German idealistic philosophy. Thus, by the middle years of the nineteenth century, a "new Enlightenment" renewed the challenge to the institutions and thought of the *ancien régime*.

There were many aspects to this "new Enlightenment," but two elements seem to have been central, and both had a great impact in Russia. The first was the "left" or "young" Hegelians' opposition to the conservative implications of orthodox Hegelianism. The second element, related to the growing acceptance of the methods and assumptions of natural science, was a resurgence of philosophical materialism, supported by the rapidly accumulating achievements of the laboratory, which proved to be a more potent weapon of criticism than it had ever been in

121

the eighteenth century. In Russia's version of the "new Enlightenment," which assumed an especially extreme character
because the old order remained so firmly intact, Chernyshevskii
played a leading part.

By the early 1850's, Chernyshevskii had adopted a position
of materialistic monism, which he identified with the name of
Ludwig Feuerbach. His last two years at the university had witnessed a collapse of his earlier religious convictions and, after
a brief attempt to understand Hegel, his rejection of philosophical idealism. Significantly, the basis for his rejection of Hegel
had been the philosopher's difficulty, which the young Chernyshevskii readily admitted, and his feeling that Hegel was a
"slave of the existing order of things, the existing structure of
society." By contrast, he believed that Feuerbach had spoken a
truth that would free man from oppressive intellectual and social traditions. Unfortunately, in this early period Chernyshevskii left very little evidence on his precise understanding of
Feuerbach, beyond the fundamental assertion that man lived
in a material universe and that a dualistic opposition between
man and God, or any other supernatural power or essence, simply did not exist.

Almost a decade passed between the time of Chernyshevskii's
conversion to these new beliefs and the first opportunity he
found to state his position openly.[1] During that period, however,
his articles clearly revealed his conviction that the latest advances in European and Russian thought had outstripped Hegel
and all other schools of idealistic philosophy. Unable to mention the name of Feuerbach, he resorted to thinly veiled suggestion. For example, in 1856 he wrote that Hegel's teachings,
having served as an important transitional stage in the development of philosophy, had been corrected by a new philosophical school. This new school had been able to throw off Hegel's
"scholastic forms of mystical transcendentalism" and acknowl-
edge a basic similarity between philosophy and natural science
(III, 179). Although useful in its time, Hegelianism was now
seen as no more than an unwanted legacy from a past era. During the 1850's, Chernyshevskii made a few other references to
separate aspects of Hegel's system, which have clouded the

issue. Consequently, most writers on Chernyshevskii have claimed a lingering influence of Hegel on him, and there has been a tendency, especially among Soviet writers, to exaggerate the role of dialectical thinking in his philosophical position.[2]

It is quite possible that Chernyshevskii owed something of his view of progress to Hegel, but a direct line of influence is difficult to establish in the absence of specific acknowledgment in Chernyshevskii's own writings. The early, unspecified reading he claimed later to have done in Russian writers who followed a left-wing Hegelianism may have contributed to his view of progress and historical change. Prior to his attempt to read Hegel's original writings, which led to his disillusionment, he also recorded in a student notebook, "Hegel great idea of development, eternal conflict, eternal movement forward."[3] As interesting as such hints are, they scarcely provide an argument that Chernyshevskii's view of progress was inspired by Hegel. Awareness of change and the desire to see purposeful development were widespread in the nineteenth century, feeding on many sources, including French social theory, which Chernyshevskii read with much greater sympathy than he ever did Hegel. If Chernyshevskii's sense of movement and progress thus reflected a general tendency of his times, the key questions are: What particular rationality did he see in historical change? How exactly did changes come about? Where were they heading? Since Chernyshevskii worked out his own answers to these questions, quite apart from Hegel's theories of development and change, his debt to Hegel, in this regard, shrinks in significance.

As for method of thought, however, twice during the 1850's Chernyshevskii referred sympathetically to specific parts of the Hegelian system, over and above his usual general comments that Hegelianism was a useful step to higher truth. In his "Essays on the Gogol Period of Russian Literature," published in 1856, he discussed the evolution of Belinskii's ideas, which had included a Hegelian phase. Later, in 1858, he wrote his "Critique of Philosophical Prejudices Against Communal Ownership," in which he tried to establish a relationship between the Russian village commune and a future social order based on socialism. Both of these instances have been referred to incorrectly by writers who assert that the study of Hegel left an appreciation of the dialectical method in Chernyshevskii's philosophical views.[4]

In "Essays on the Gogol Period of Russian Literature," Chernyshevskii confronted a serious problem in trying to describe Belinskii's Hegelian period. He wanted to condemn the position that Belinskii later rejected (and which Chernyshevskii himself had never really experienced), yet he did not want Belinskii's temporary infatuation with Hegel to appear ridiculous or useless. Thus, he described the error of Belinskii and his like-minded friends on the *Moscow Observer* as being a failure to see the contradiction between Hegel's principles and the deductions he drew from them. Whereas Hegel's principles were powerful and broad, his deductions were narrow and weak (III, 205).[5] On the surface, these remarks resemble the later comment of Friedrich Engels that Hegel's dynamic dialectical method contradicted his conservative system.[6] Upon closer examination of Chernyshevskii's essay, however, it becomes obvious that the two criticisms of Hegel should not be equated.

Chernyshevskii's comments on Hegel in this essay were far from clear. In the same paragraph that described Hegel as a thinker of genius, who lacked only the strength to adhere to his powerful principles, Chernyshevskii seemed actually to reverse himself, when he questioned whether Hegel was altogether clear about his own principles—whether they were not rather nebulous, vague, one-sided, and abstractly expressed. Chernyshevskii attempted to define Hegel's "principles" in a discussion of the philosopher's ability to rise above the rationalization of personal prejudice in his pursuit of truth. According to Hegel, a thinker must be prepared to sacrifice his most cherished opinions; he must never retreat before the results of his thought. In this context, Hegel's famous "dialectical method of thinking" was praised by Chernyshevskii as essentially a guarantee of open-mindedness: "The essence of [the dialectical method] consists in the fact that the thinker must never be satisfied with positive deductions but must inquire whether, in the subject about which he thinks, there are not qualities and forces that are contradictory to those which appeared at first sight. In this way the thinker is obliged to observe a subject from all sides, and truth emerges as the consequence of a struggle between all possible conflicting opinions" (III, 207). This dialectical method, Chernyshevskii felt, helped a thinker to overcome the one-sided understanding of a subject and to achieve a living understanding of all its real qualities. Indirectly, it also led philosophy to concentrate on the task of explaining reality; and since, in reality, everything depended on circumstances, on conditions of time and place, Chernyshevskii underscored Hegel's assertion that general, abstract statements about good and evil were unsatisfactory. "There is no abstract truth; truth is concrete." One can make a definite judgment about a definite fact only by considering all the circumstances on which it depends. To demonstrate what he meant by the concreteness of truth, Chernyshevskii referred to the problem of determining whether rain was good or bad, and in effect, he merely showed that value judgments were relative (III, 208).

In this very limited way, Chernyshevskii summarized some of the principles of Hegelianism that had once appealed to Russians like Belinskii. He then tried to account for the "astounding impression" made by the "great philosopher," noting that Hegel brought all areas of being under his authority by uncovering, in each sphere of life, the laws of nature and life corresponding to his own law of dialectical development, thereby explaining the facts from many fields in a systematic unity (III, 208). One cannot be sure what Chernyshevskii meant by this phrase "law of dialectical development," because he did not elaborate further. Nor is it clear what relationship he intended to suggest between dialectical development and the "dialectical method of thinking" he had just described as one of Hegel's broad principles. Unless he equated, or at least recognized, a close tie between the two, there is nothing here to suggest an approval of dialectical development. If Chernyshevskii did mean to include dialectical development among the admirable principles of Hegel, he confounded the reader even more in the next paragraph, when he claimed that Belinskii, and a few others, not only rejected the deductions from Hegel's principles but also came to realize the inadequacy of the principles themselves (III, 209).

Throughout these references to Hegel, Chernyshevskii seemed to give qualified approval with one hand, only to take it back with the other. Muddle and confusion dominated, although it is fair to add that exposition of the philosophy was not his foremost consideration. He sought rather to explain sympathetically Belinskii's temporary infatuation with what he called Hegel's "ingenious dialectics." Without better supporting evidence, this essay does not prove that dialectics of whatever character figured in Chernyshevskii's own philosophy, or that he embraced the idea of a dialectical process of historical development.

Among writers who stress Hegel's influence on Chernyshevskii, more frequent reference is given to the second article, "Critique of Philosophical Prejudices Against Communal Ownership." Here Chernyshevskii argued against the claims of liberal critics that the commune was an outmoded institution. As a socialist, he saw the similarity between the old communal organization and his own dream of a new social order, and he tried to take advantage of it in debate. Though he expressly denied being a partisan of either Hegel or Schelling, he suggested that their systems had established the general forms for the process of evolutionary development (V, 363). He defined this development as a three-stage movement (or sometimes more), with the first stage resembling the third. This proposition provided background for his further suggestion that, under favorable circumstances, the middle stage (or stages) might be shortened and a quick transition made from the first to the final stage (V, 389). Chernyshevskii meant to hint that Russia need not experience a prolonged period of private ownership, but might pass quickly from communal ownership to socialism.

No one would dispute the importance of this article in the later development of theories of Russian agrarian socialism, but whether any serious attention should be given to Chernyshevskii's claim that he accepted the idea of a three-stage pattern of development, based on the theories of idealistic philosophers, is quite another matter. He never really argued the point seriously, but rather asserted the proposition dogmatically, as if it were self-evident truth, and then buttressed his assertion with carefully chosen analogies, any one of which might have been matched by other examples where the given three-stage pattern would not hold. He not only offered no explanation of why development should take place according to a general three-stage pattern, but he could not seriously have insisted on this pattern without contradicting most of his other writings on historical development. It seems probable, therefore, that despite all the attention given this article as evidence of Hegelian influence, Chernyshevskii simply toyed with Hegelian phraseology as a convenient device to make more striking his expression of hopes for the future.[7] He doubtless enjoyed the irony of entering an argument with a page borrowed from the writings of one group of opponents.

Despite his frequent reminders that advanced scholars had already rejected "transcendental philosophy," Chernyshevskii wrote little to make his own philosophical views known until his article "The Anthropological Principle in Philosophy," which appeared in the April and May issues of *The Contemporary* for 1860 (VII, 222–295).[8] The article initiated a dispute and, as much as any other work, underscored in the minds of some of his opponents his danger to the existing order.[9]

By 1860, the Russian left wing had found further support for Feuerbach's basic position in the writings of other German popularizers of science and materialism. Ludwig Büchner's *Kraft und Stoff* appeared in 1855. Three years later, Dobroliubov wrote an abusive attack on Professor Wilhelm Bervi, of the University of Kazan, and noted that young people no longer stood in awe of old authorities but instead looked to the works of Jacob Moleschott, Emil Du Bois-Reymond, and Karl Vogt.[10] Traces of this new influence may be found in Chernyshevskii's article "The Anthropological Principle in Philosophy." Though hastily written and poorly organized, this long essay typified the exuberant confidence of the "scientism" of the mid-nineteenth century. "Chemistry," Chernyshevskii wrote, "is perhaps the greatest glory of our age" (VII, 248). Making a direct identification of older theories of materialistic monism and the latest teachings of natural science, he sought to define nature and man according to an "anthropological principle."

Chernyshevskii founded his system on an unshakable affirmation of the fundamental unity of man and nature. From the outset, he rejected any explanation of man's uniqueness that posited a spirit-matter dualism. Whatever existed was matter and, therefore, subject to the universal laws of nature. Man, he admitted, did not yet fully understand these universal laws, but nonetheless they were knowable and, in time, they would all be understood. He scoffed at the suggestion that some aspects of nature, which had remained a mystery, might belong to a basically different category of being. That idea preserved "certain aspects of the fantastic world view" (VII, 249). Exit the soul!

Chernyshevskii's description of the world of nature displayed the insights and many of the limitations of mid-nineteenth century chemistry. All variation in nature depended on two factors: the different qualities of the elemental forms of matter, and the specific combination of the elements making up a compound. Extending this basic view, he believed that the distinctions between inorganic and organic matter, plant and animal, and finally animal and human merely indicated the relative complexity of the compound in question. A higher, more complex compound contained characteristics not found in lower, simpler ones (VII, 242–245).

When Chernyshevskii applied this analysis to man, he encountered the most difficult problems and found himself making statements that understandably aroused the most vigorous opposition. Any attempt to define man's place in nature must confront the problem of explaining human consciousness and thought. In addition, any definition of man requires some statement on how man should act. Chernyshevskii faced both questions boldly, if not always without ambiguity.

At one point in his study, he defined the human organism as "an extremely complex chemical combination, which goes through an extremely complex process that we call life." In the same vein, he equated consciousness with sensation and defined sensation simply as one of the functions of the human organism, along with respiration, nutrition, and circulation of the blood. In fact, he echoed Feuerbach's assertion "Man is what he eats," and noted that nutrition and sensation were so closely related that one determined the character of the other (VII, 268–270). Taken alone, Chernyshevskii's equation of consciousness and sensation and his classification of sensation with other bodily functions were rigorous and consistent deductions from his definition of life as a complex chemical process. Earlier in his article, however, he had made a qualifying and perhaps even contradictory statement when recognizing that man's unified nature included two types of phenomena. One type, which he called a "material order," included activities like eating and walking. The other, a "moral order," included thinking, feeling, and wishing (VII, 241–242).[11] Yet he in no way intended this distinction to challenge the basic idea of man's total unity with nature. No object in nature possessed only one quality, and man merely happened to possess these two types. Chernyshevskii admitted that man was better informed about human motion (the material order) than about sensation (the moral order). Nevertheless, man already knew enough to make what he called the "negative deduction," namely, that the unexplained elements of sensation could not be used as proof of a fundamental dualism in human nature.[12]

In an elaboration of his views on human thought, Chernyshevskii returned to his insistence that plant, animal, and human differed in complexity but were not essentially different in type. He did not hesitate to ascribe "mental facilities" to animals, who in his view had memory, imagination, and the power to think. He noted that the young of all animals amused themselves by playing with external objects, which could not be used for such games if the young animals did not regard them in the nature of dolls. Therefore, animals must possess imagination! (VII, 277). The comparisons Chernyshevskii made between the thoughts of man and animal seemed calculated to shock those who held other views. Stressing differences of complexity and magnitude, rather than differences of essential type, he placed the functioning of Isaac Newton's nervous system during his discovery of the laws of gravity on the same continuum with the functioning of the nervous system of a chicken, finding bits of oats in a dung heap. Man had to be seen as a part of nature, and in no other way (VII, 278).

When Chernyshevskii tried to expand his definition of human thought, he in fact underscored his contention that the subject needed further study, because he could define one unknown only in terms of other unknowns. He wrote that thought occurred when a human organism chose, from within its memory, varying combinations of past sensations and conceptions in order to achieve a desired result. He saw the same process involved in both abstract thought and thought about mundane objects. For example, Newton developed his theory about the motion of celestial bodies from the sense perception of formulas and astronomical data. He combined these sensations to produce a new formula. But, one might ask, what was behind this particular combination? How did this particular process of formulation take place? Chernyshevskii pointed weakly to the "aim" of the nervous system, and thus left his reader with no explanation at all (VII, 277).

Although questions clearly were left unanswered, Chernyshevskii had at least suggested the outlines of a sensationalist theory of knowledge, and his later writings indicate that he held to such a position. In 1885, just four years before his death, writing under a pseudonym, he again defended a sensationalist epistemology. This defense, if not a part of his known legacy to Russian intellectual life in the 1860's, does show what he probably had in mind at that earlier time. In "The Character of Human Knowledge," he defended his position against questions raised by such natural scientists as Du Bois-Reymond and Rudolph Virchow concerning the natural limitations on man's ability to know. Chernyshevskii asserted not only the absolute reality of the noumenal world, but also man's ability to comprehend reality directly and accurately. He made no fine distinctions among those who disagreed with his position, classifying those who merely questioned the direct validity of human sensation with those who claimed that reality included only the phenomenal world, that is, the world of appearances. All were included under his reproachful label "illusionists" and criticized both for betraying the scientific advances of modern thought and for denying the existence of the human organism itself (X, 722–724).[13]

Because he viewed the functioning of the human organism in terms of materialistic monism, Chernyshevskii inevitably came to a mechanical explanation of human behavior. He frequently emphasized the influence of environment on men's actions and, with few exceptions, denied the existence of innate human qualities of goodness or badness (VII, 264–265). If followed consistently, this position presents a dilemma to the materialist who is also a social reformer, because he must explain how some men can rise above an environment to challenge and correct it. Marx solved the dilemma by positing a necessary, objective course of historical development, which in turn altered human consciousness. Although Chernyshevskii spoke of environmental influence, he at no time worked out an overall theory of determinism. His appeal for social change was always an appeal to the minds of men. Still, he gave considerable attention to the formulation of an ethic consistent with his materialism.

Chernyshevskii looked with suspicion on concepts like pity, altruism, and self-sacrifice, because of their association with the old "fantastic" world view. In an effort to show that even man's moral life could be considered in the light of the scientific method, he proposed an ethical system of rational egoism. He claimed that moral problems would soon be solved with the same certainty as problems in natural science. He wrote:

The natural sciences have already developed sufficiently to provide a great deal of material for the exact solution of moral problems. Among thinkers who are concerned with moral science, all progressive people have begun to work out [these problems] with the aid of exact methods, like those used to work out [problems] in the natural sciences . . . In their present form, the moral sciences are distinct from the so-called natural sciences only in that they began to be developed in a truly scientific way later and therefore have not reached the same level of perfection (VII, 258–259).

Chernyshevskii acknowledged no sources for his theory of rational egoism, but his explanation of what he called the latest scientific approach to ethics displayed a debt to earlier thinkers like Claude Helvétius and Jeremy Bentham.[14]

Chernyshevskii argued that the innate desire and need of the human organism for pleasure prompted men's actions, be they good or bad, heroic or cowardly, by traditional standards. Man chose the action that promised a larger gain or pleasure, rather than a smaller pleasure or pain (VII, 285). With words that were totally out of harmony with his own student diary or his touching letters written to loved ones, he tried to explain away the generally revered human virtues: "If a husband and wife have lived happily together, the wife will very sincerely and very deeply grieve over the death of her husband. But note the words with which she expresses her grief: 'To whom have you abandoned me? What will I do without you? Without you it is loathsome to go on living!' Underline the words 'me, I, for me.' In them is the meaning of her lamentation, they show the basis of her grief" (VII, 283). So, too, Chernyshevskii called egoism the basis of a mother's love for a child, or of the tenderest friendship. He noted that when children reached adulthood, they were less devoted to their parents than their parents were to them. He explained this by saying that parents saw their children as products of themselves (VII, 281).

Chernyshevskii also interpreted heroism and self-sacrifice as the choice of pleasure over pain. For example, in the case of the man who spent weeks of his life at the bedside of a sick friend and thereby gave up his own time and freedom, Chernyshevskii insisted that the primary consideration was gratification of the man's own feeling of friendship, which, of course, was egoism (VII, 284–285). No further quest into the meaning of friendship seemed necessary.

It is true that at times Chernyshevskii's argument led him to a mere juggling of words, and at other times he openly contradicted himself. The heroic "new people" of his later novel, *What Is To Be Done?* insisted on goodness and justice so long as the words were not used.[15] Many years later, in speculating on the course of human history, Chernyshevskii also backed off significantly from an ethic based on calculation. He wrote of man's innate inclination toward mutual good will and of man's ability to enter relationships founded on human kindness rather than calculation. Maternal love and the love between man and woman need not be reduced to egoism (X, 923). From all that is known of Chernyshevskii's own personality, such words were more congenial to him, but during his active career the message he gave to his generation was that love and self-sacrifice in fact represented calculated self-interest.

Personal egoism could by no means be an end in itself, and one suspects that Chernyshevskii raised the whole issue of personal motivation not only to deflate high-sounding words that too often were used to cover ignoble action, but also to provide a springboard for discussing social ethics and social action. As he made the transition to these larger problems, his human concern, with its natural tendency toward value judgments, constantly threatened the strictness of his logic. But generally he held firm:

A man likes what is pleasant and dislikes what is unpleasant. There seems no doubt of this because the predicate merely repeats the subject: A is A, what is pleasant for man is pleasant for man, what is unpleasant for man is unpleasant for man. A person is good if he does good to others and bad if he harms others. That also seems simple and clear. If we combine these simple truths we get the following conclusion. A man is good if he gets pleasure for himself by giving pleasure to others. He is bad if, to derive pleasure for himself, he must cause unpleasantness for others (VII, 264).

Chernyshevskii was not using the terms "good" and "bad" as judgments of personal praise or condemnation; rather, he used these words as measures of social utility. Goodness implied maximum utility. Both the good and the bad man sought personal pleasure, and the concept each had of pleasure was determined largely by his education (VII, 288–289).

Personal egoism became rational egoism when a person could find self-interest in actions of the greatest possible utility. To stress this point, Chernyshevskii established a hierarchy of importance for acts of utility, according to the number of persons involved. Concern for the individual was subordinate to concern for class, class to nation, and most important, nation to mankind. Chernyshevskii envisaged a generation of "new people," who would be enlightened enough to see their own best interests in the well-being of mankind. He believed that history had shown the opposite position—a narrow, irrational, personal egoism—to be ultimately self-destructive (VII, 286–288).

Throughout his argument on morality, Chernyshevskii implied that a good society was one in which an individual could pursue his own best interests and, at the same time, serve the interests of the community. Individual virtues could not hope to overcome the inherent evils of an irrationally organized society. Even the well-intentioned rich man usually spoiled his own son, not to mention causing injustice to the rest of society less dear to his heart (VII, 291–292). Of course, no society had yet reached this high level of rationality, but all of Chernyshevskii's writings of the early 1860's expressed promise for the future if only the rational egoism of communal association could replace the selfish egoism of private ownership. Chernyshevskii left his readers with the impression that the "old moral science" was hopelessly out of date, because it dealt with individual salvation instead of social well-being.

To support his philosophical views, Chernyshevskii claimed the absolute authority of science and the scientific method:

As a basis for its theories [modern learning] looks to the truths discovered by the natural sciences, using the most exact analysis of facts. [It looks to] truths as credible as the earth's revolution around the sun, the law of gravity, [and] the action of chemical affinity. From these principles, which are beyond all dispute or doubt, modern learning arrives at its conclusions with the same care as that used to reach the [principles themselves]. It accepts nothing without the strictest, most inclusive proof, and concludes nothing from what it accepts except that which necessarily follows from facts and laws that cannot be logically refuted. With such a character, the new ideas offer to a man who has accepted them no road of retreat, nor any kind of compromise with the fantastic errors of former times... Thus the basic character of present-day philosophical views is their unshakable validity, which precludes all vacillation of opinion.[16]

It is interesting to compare this claim of an absolute scientific validity for his own philosophical position with comments he made about past thinkers. Quite clearly, from his position as a political and social critic, he found it difficult to discuss a subject apart from its relation to the causes he espoused. Yet when the same held true for thinkers of the past—not only for writers like Hobbes and Locke, who paid special attention to political questions, but even for those whom he considered primarily as builders of metaphysical systems, like Kant, Fichte, Schelling, and Hegel—he accused them of letting their political party affiliation influence their philosophical work. "Everybody," he admitted, "who has reached intellectual independence, has political convictions and judges everything from the standpoint of those convictions" (VII, 224). Nevertheless, by basing his own views so firmly on the absolute and universal validity of natural science, he implied that his ideas transcended this kind of partisan limitation. He felt himself to be the exponent of ideas that were universally true in their own right, even though he also believed that his new views affected the larger struggle for the rights and well-being of the common people (prostoliudi).[17] His own position represented the only possible conclusion from properly applied rationality, and the same rationality required a new ordering of society. Anyone who remained shackled by old philosophical traditions—Proudhon, for example—could not be an effective leader in the struggle for a better society (VII, 239). Writing about Western Europe, but referring to Russia as well, Chernyshevskii insisted that in time the common people would realize that these new ideas corresponded to their needs. Once those who were trying to reform life in Western Europe embraced a sound philosophical position, the triumph of new principles of social life would quickly follow

(VII, 254). Naturally the new truth had to spread out from the more developed strata of society to those still in ignorance, and he considered his own work as a journalist to be part of this process. Chernyshevskii wanted his articles in *The Contemporary* to influence the broadest possible reading audience, and one of his unfulfilled dreams was to write vast compendiums of human knowledge, which would include works of popularization. To this extent, he was an "enlightener," as Plekhanov claimed, even though that label describes only a part of his contribution.[18]

L. F. Panteleev, whose student years coincided with the publication of "The Anthropological Principle in Philosophy," noted in his memoirs that this article created more of a stir among Chernyshevskii's opponents than it did among the radical youth, who went directly to the writings of Ludwig Büchner, Feuerbach, and Jacob Moleschott.[19] Since 1859, for example, a group in Moscow, led by P. G. Zaichnevskii and P. E. Argiropulo, had reproduced Russian translations of these writers and had circulated them among university students. But whatever the positive achievement of Chernyshevskii's article in winning new adherents, its appearance in Russia's most widely-read journal made it a prime target for hostile attacks. The most vocal criticism came from a diametrically opposed position, and the ensuing argument quickly became a statement of opposite basic assumptions, between which little communication proved possible.

The first serious attack on "The Anthropological Principle in Philosophy" might have received little attention had it not been for the journalistic debate that followed. Near the end of 1860, Professor P. D. Iurkevich published in the *Works of the Kievan Theological Academy* a long critique of Chernyshevskii's materialism, entitled "From the Science of the Human Spirit."[20] Iurkevich directed his most serious criticism against Chernyshevskii's description of human thought. While admitting the value of philosophical realism or materialism in the analysis of certain natural phenomena, Iurkevich made a careful distinction between the physiological and psychological aspect of human sensation and argued that materialism could explain only the former. Apart from external (vneshnii) sensations, which consisted of the mechanical functioning of the nerves and organs of the body, man experienced inner (vnutrennii) sensations, which were strictly psychical phenomena and beyond the ability of the physiologist to explain. Thus, an unbridgeable gap existed between nerve movement in the eye and man's experience of vision. To speak of the unity of the two, as Iurkevich accused Chernyshevskii of doing, was to introduce a metaphysical concept into the argument, a concept capable of neither scientific proof nor disproof. Iurkevich was further affronted by Chernyshevskii's insistence on the similarity between the mental processes of men and animals. Finally, he objected to Chernyshevskii's view of egoism as the sole drive behind human action, comparing that argument to the music of a violin with only one note.[21]

Iurkevich rounded off his critique with a condemnation of the general level of Chernyshevskii's writing. He accused Chernyshevskii of misapplying ideas he had not fully grasped and of confusing bits of knowledge with statements of faith. He also noted Chernyshevskii's attitude of condescension toward others who faced the difficulties of establishing a philosophical position.[22]

Chernyshevskii ignored this challenge, and early in 1861, *The Contemporary* printed another article on philosophy by M. A. Antonovich, who shared Chernyshevskii's basic beliefs and antipathies.[23] But direct confrontation could not be avoided. In February 1861, M. N. Katkov's article "Old Gods and New Gods" appeared in *The Russian Messenger*, in which he attacked the philosophical views of *The Contemporary* and of Chernyshevskii. He referred to materialism as a German illness, or its symptom, which he hoped would someday be healed. He objected even more strenuously to the way this doctrine had been adopted by its Russian followers, who were guilty of uncritical, fanatical acceptance of the new gods and priests of materialism. The Russian votaries of the new cult used the name of freedom to conceal their ignorance, and slandered those who asked for explanations. Katkov did not limit his antagonism to Chernyshevskii's philosophy. He remarked that Chernyshevskii spoke of opposing schools of economic theory with a tone of "charlatanic irony." Quoting Chernyshevskii's famous remark that the path of history differed from the sidewalks of Nevskii Prospect, and that men who engaged in public activity must expect to get soiled, Katkov suggested that Chernyshevskii imagined himself to be making just that kind of sacrifice. Instead of being a hero, however, Katkov believed Chernyshevskii to be playing the part of a clown.[24] Two months later Katkov reprinted in his journal sections from Iurkevich's criticism of Chernyshevskii's philosophy.[25] He shrewdly chose sections which attacked Chernyshevskii at his most vulnerable point, the technical problem of explaining human thought and self-awareness.

Chernyshevskii's reply to these attacks, "Polemical Gems," which appeared in the June and July 1861 issues of *The Contemporary,* displayed its author's potent ability at journalistic wrangling. In much of the article he merely repaid Katkov in kind, but Chernyshevskii hurt his own reputation when he spoke of Iurkevich, for he refused to consider Iurkevich's argument seriously and instead employed ridicule. As a former seminarist, Chernyshevskii said that he could not laugh at Iurkevich, because he knew the limitations of a theological professor's education and how hard it must be for him to get decent books. Claiming that he had not read Iurkevich's work, nor even all of the excerpts from it in *The Russian Messenger,* Chernyshevskii dismissed his opponent with mocking sympathy for having written the same thing as could be found in the exercise books of seminary students (VII, 725–726).

These comments added to the bitterness of the discussion and evoked a direct attack on Chernyshevskii by S. S. Dudyshkin in the July issue of *Notes of the Fatherland.* Dudyshkin took the position that Chernyshevskii erred, not only in his philosophical views, but also in his lack of seriousness and his refusal to defend his assertions. In this respect, Dudyshkin compared Chernyshevskii to Baron Brambeus (O. I. Senkovskii), one of Belinskii's journalistic opponents who never gave serious consideration to criticism leveled against him. With unconcealed malice, Dudyshkin charged that Chernyshevskii's philoso-

138

phy combined errors of logic with metaphysical confusion.[26]

Chernyshevskii could scarcely ignore this direct attack, but his rebuttal disappointed many who were not already his uncritical partisans.[27] In a second installment of "Polemical Gems," published later in July 1861, Chernyshevskii enlarged on his view that Iurkevich was out of date. "I look upon the school to which Mr. Iurkevich belongs in the same way as you view a scholar who embraces alchemy or cabalism" (VII, 762). He claimed to be so far beyond thinkers of Iurkevich's school that he did not care what they thought of him. They were "routine" thinkers, who considered him to be ignorant merely because he represented a new doctrine. A similar fate had befallen Hegel, Kant, and Descartes in their day, when they introduced new views. The arguments used against him were the stock arguments used against all "nonidealists," among whom Chernyshevskii listed Aristotle, Bacon, Pierre Gassendi, and Locke (VII, 769–770). Now that natural science had proven them right, there was no further need for argument.

Once again Chernyshevskii identified his doctrine as the latest link in a chain of philosophical systems. His theory had "emerged" from Hegel's theory and then had taken the place of Hegelianism. Still unable to mention Feuerbach's name in print, Chernyshevskii hinted playfully at the source of his inspiration: "But, after all, perhaps the matter is still not clear to you. You want to know who the teacher is, of whom I speak. To help you in your search, if you wish, I will say that he is not a Russian, not a Frenchman, not an Englishman; he is not Büchner, not Max Stirner, not Bruno Bauer, not Moleschott, and not Vogt. Who then is he? You start to guess after reading the paper of Mr. Lavrov. 'It must be Schopenhauer,' you cry. The very man, you guessed it" (VII, 771–772).

Clearly, then, Chernyshevskii used the two "Polemical Gems" to repeat his statement of faith in materialistic monism, but he refused to give serious attention to sophisticated criticism, and he reduced a number of very complicated questions to an oversimplified either-or choice. Among one segment of his audience, his technique of ridicule proved effective. When Iurkevich took up a new post at the University of Moscow, he received an anonymous letter from a student, threatening him with hisses and whistling if he did not give up his "cynicism" and treat materialism with more respect.[28] However, Chernyshevskii risked his reputation among readers whose approbation he had tried to win with serious argument in other areas. Exactly why he did this is difficult to say with certainty. The general climate of 1861, when the radicals were more openly and angrily proclaiming their differences with moderates as well as conservatives, had something to do with it. Chernyshevskii also wrote under an imposing pressure of time, which forced painful decisions of priority. And he wrote from a precarious position, limited by the censorship and threatened by the suggestion of Katkov and others that his views were dangerous to the state. However, it would be wrong to accept uncritically the suggestion of many writers that censorship conditions alone prevented a more respectable defense.[29] Chernyshevskii was not in fact exercising necessary prudence when he belittled and scorned everything Iurkevich stood for, instead of arguing specific technical points, which Iurkevich's original article had invited him to do. It was probably true that Chernyshevskii's sweeping condemnations made him more, rather than less, liable to repressive action by the state. In any case, further explanation for Chernyshevskii's actions must be sought in a general evaluation of his whole approach to philosophy.

Were Chernyshevskii's philosophical writings to be judged from the point of view of technical philosophy alone, there would be little to recommend them. In his total life's work, he devoted relatively few pages specifically to philosophical questions, and even these were generally mere paraphrasings of views he had adopted from others and wanted to popularize. His own contribution often consisted of little more than the addition of crude examples and the insistence that the truth he represented could not possibly be open to question. If he was thus disinclined to come to grips with technical problems of philosophy, and more willing to apply the truth than to examine it, one must also recognize that he did not claim an original contribution in this field. In the "Polemical Gems," for example, he described himself as a "well-read man," rather than a specialist in the field, and admitted he simply wanted to popularize the conclusions of others who were specialists (VII, 764–765).

Even if judged as a popularizer, Chernyshevskii is liable to criticism, if one takes seriously his claim to be a follower of Feuerbach. There is no question of the importance of Feuerbach for the development of his philosophical views; many of his most important assertions can be traced back directly to his "teacher," even if Chernyshevskii himself left few direct references. The idea that God in traditional terms was dead, the criticism of Hegelian idealism as a last refuge of theology, the attempt to find a new basis for philosophy in natural science, the belief that a new philosophy was a prerequisite for political and social change, and even the appreciation of some of the blatant assertions of writers like Moleschott—all have a solid place in different parts of Feuerbach's writings. Yet between teacher and self-proclaimed student there were also differences, which reflected both the dissimilar contexts in which they wrote and the significant variation in their approaches to philosophy. Feuerbach, even as he rejected Hegelianism and denied the traditional God, whom he defined as the negation of man, by his own admission remained true to his central theme of religion and theology.[30] He sought a "religion of humanity" in a context of left Hegelianism, and he, like Marx, worked out his new position with the aid of a style of thought—Hegelianism—whose overall conclusions he rejected. By contrast, Chernyshevskii's quest was not primarily for a new religion but, more directly, for social and political change, and he approached philosophy without the weighty heritage of a significant engagement with Hegel. In asserting his rejection of the God of European tradition and German idealism, the two negative points he shared most strongly with Feuerbach, Chernyshevskii, in fact, more readily adopted the older position of materialistic monism, buttressed by the scientific popularizers of his own day.[31]

One can thus see a paradox in Chernyshevskii's approach to technical philosophy, which he viewed both as a source of inspiration for many other areas of his thought and yet as an area of secondary importance in its own right. In the heat of argument, he would not allow demands for technical consistency in philosophy to stand in the way of a needed, or useful, assertion. But neither did he simply manipulate ideas as weapons in his fight for social justice. The truth of materialism, in denying religion and idealism, appeared totally beyond question to him. If partial objections proved embarrassing and had to be pushed aside, to avoid challenge to his main point, Chernyshevskii could do so, firm in the conviction that further progress in human thought would prove him right.

In many ways, his attitude typified the "new Enlightenment" in Russia after the Crimean War. This movement faced the tremendous task of discrediting the institutions and traditions of the past. From the radical point of view, negative criticism and destruction had to prepare the ground for a careful working out of new truths. Some of the very weaknesses of Chernyshevskii as a technical philosopher comprised his strength as a leader in a movement that scorned traditional philosophy in the name of social progress.[32] Refined speculation had been associated with inaction for too long.

Chernyshevskii's particular version of materialism did not provide him with automatic answers to many of the questions he faced in other areas of concern, but it helped him to discredit older views and often gave him guidelines for the direction of his own thought. To whatever degree he achieved a system of thought, his philosophical beliefs must be seen as the core of that achievement.

Concerning his philosophical legacy to the radical movement, Chernyshevskii's work was most valuable in its negation. In the name of natural science, he, as much as any other writer of the 1860's, discredited past religious and metaphysical alternatives and made thoroughgoing secularism and naturalism a permanent part of the radical tradition. The least permanent part of his teaching was his uncompromising statement of rational egoism as the basis for a new ethic—an assertion which had never in any case rested comfortably with the way he lived his own life. Within a decade after Chernyshevskii's imprisonment, a reaction set in with the writings of P. L. Lavrov and N. K. Mikhailovskii, who, although they shared many of Chernyshevskii's antimetaphysical views, sought to consider questions of morality and the individual's responsibility for action in history on a plane of subjective choice, not easily explained by the techniques of the laboratory or the materialist's references to "matter in motion."

# VI. *Aesthetics and Literary Criticism*

In the course of the eighteenth century, the prevailing neo-classical tradition in European art and aesthetics gave way to a jumble of rival theories and assumptions, which up to the present have withstood incorporation into a coherent whole. Succeeding generations of artists, philosophers, and critics sought to define taste and aesthetic value in theories that would be related to other concerns of their age. By the time Cherny-shevskii turned to these questions, in the 1850's, two approaches, often mutually exclusive, commanded greatest attention. Neither approach allowed the realm of art to exist in its own right, and thus both contributed to the countermovement of art for art's sake that developed later in the century.

In one approach, beginning perhaps with Alexander Gottlieb Baumgartner in the eighteenth century and involving German writers in particular, aesthetic theories were developed as part of an all-inclusive system of philosophy. Post-Kantian German idealism showed this tendency most clearly. Philosophers, like Schelling and Hegel, whose systems described the organic unity of the universe and sought to define man's relation to nature and transcendent Being, necessarily involved art in considerations far removed from simple concern with canons of beauty and taste. Schelling believed that artistic perception was superior to ordinary perception as a means of penetrating the essence of the universe. Thus art, as a special kind of intellectual intuition, became a pathway to more profound philosophical insight, and the artist assumed a unique role in man's intellectual life. In a similar fashion, Hegel pronounced what René Wellek calls an anti-aesthetic "funeral oration on art" when he defined art as representing the initial stage of human perception of Absolute Spirit, a stage to be surpassed by religion and philosophy.[1] In view of this involvement with philosophy, the definitions and assumptions concerning art and aesthetics in German idealism could not easily be separated from metaphysical concepts.

An alternate approach stressed the relation of art to human society. The period of the French Revolution had seen attempts to regiment artists as a means of legitimizing newly gained political authority. In the nineteenth century, as diverse social critics argued the need of reform, they saw the advantage of using art for didactic purposes. Painters were to sit beside scientists, writers, and composers in Saint-Simon's proposed "Council of Newton," which would guide society from above. Later, Auguste Comte, going beyond the recognition of art's dependence on the state of society, advanced the view that art could help bring about a more perfect social order. Proudhon, in turn, recognized the subservience of art to a higher moral purpose and its power over human thought and emotion.[2]

These same questions about aesthetic standards and the meaning and function of art troubled mid-nineteenth century Russian intellectuals, for whom they may even have had greater import. During the reign of Nicholas I, opposition sentiment found its best chance of expression in literature and criticism, where the censor's crude measurements for determining danger to the state proved least effective. Chernyshevskii once expressed his recognition of this special role played by literature among the Russians, in contrast to those peoples he called more "enlightened." More of Russia's intellectual life was concentrated in its literature, which was therefore like an "encyclopedia" for Russian readers (III, 303–304).

In part because of his belief in the special role of literature, and in part because he had little other choice, Chernyshevskii devoted the largest part of his early writings from 1854 to 1857, when the censorship was most limiting, to an attempt to define the nature and function of art. He necessarily confronted the basic questions of establishing an aesthetic theory in the larger, overall context of a philosophical world view and of defining the relation of art to social development. He worked toward a theory that would encompass both concerns.

On principle, Chernyshevskii denied serious attention to any theory of art or criticism that confined discussion to the relative merits of works of art and avoided more fundamental questions. Within this restriction, he found the school of aesthetics based on German idealism a convenient target for attack (II, 127–128). As so often in his career, he developed his own position in the heat of a good fight. From Chernyshevskii's point of view, many midcentury aestheticians were in a strange and hopeless impasse. Although the latest advances in human understanding had demonstrated, beyond any reasonable doubt, the fallacies of Hegelianism and had reached a new level of truth in the teaching of Feuerbach, the influence of outmoded Hegelianism lingered on in separate fields of study, such as aesthetics. Here the battle had yet to be fought, and Chernyshevskii entered the lists as champion of a new truth, which though expressed in separate articles written in 1854, 1855, and 1856, as well as in his master's thesis *The Aesthetic Relation of Art to Reality*, is considered here as a single statement of theory.

Near the end of his life, writing a new introduction to his master's thesis, Chernyshevskii described his first approach to the problem of aesthetics so as to minimize its originality:

Six years after his [Chernyshevskii's] first acquaintance with Feuerbach, he faced the mundane necessity of writing a scholarly treatise. It seemed to him that he might apply the basic ideas of Feuerbach to the solution of some questions in branches of learning that did not come within his teacher's investigations . . . The author [Chernyshevskii] had not the least pretense of saying anything new of his own. He wished merely to be the interpreter of Feuerbach's ideas in their application to aesthetics (II, 121).

It is important to consider the extent to which this statement can be taken at face value. He was right in saying that his "teacher" gave little attention to these questions. But with regard to the "application to aesthetics" of Feuerbach's ideas, Chernyshevskii's work shows but a pale reflection of the complex subtlety of Feuerbach's writing, which even while pronouncing a new humanism, always retained a theological orientation. It would appear that Chernyshevskii's debt to Feuerbach consisted in little more than his own incorporation of the one great truth he always attributed to Feuerbach, namely, that only the material realm had real existence. He may also have received from Feuerbach a heightened appreciation of man's life in nature, but beyond that, his method of analysis and his conclusions were his own, or from other sources that are difficult to identify.[3]

The object of Chernyshevskii's attack was what he called the "prevailing view," which requires elaboration. His master's thesis criticized passages taken from the early volumes of a ponderous work by the Hegelian F. T. Vischer, *Aesthetik, oder Wissenschaft des Schönen* (1846–1857), the only scholarly study to which he made reference.[4] Chernyshevskii later made the improbable claim that he was not allowed to mention Hegel's name, even though he intended his thesis to be a polemic against Hegel's theory of aesthetics. He also insisted that he had quoted passages from Vischer only if they presented Hegel's ideas without modification (II, 122). However, Chernyshevskii's thesis adviser, A. V. Nikitenko, had objected to his identifying ideas from Vischer as "Hegelian philosophy." Nikitenko advised Chernyshevskii either to omit his discussion of Hegelianism or to revise it.[5] Since Chernyshevskii preferred to retain most of the basic definitions taken from Vischer, he adopted the term "prevailing view" to suggest a connection with Hegel and yet avoid the responsibility for giving a coherent picture of Hegel's views or quoting him directly.

Chernyshevskii began his analysis with a definition of aesthetics as the "science of the beautiful," and as his primary concern, he posed the question of whether the prevailing view of the beautiful could remain valid after the metaphysical system which had produced that definition had fallen (II, 127–128).

First he summarized the idealistic understanding of the beautiful, in nature and in art; then he offered his own contrasting view, based on a philosophy of materialism. As he argued his position, he stressed the question of whether art or reality was "higher" in each system.[6]

Idealistic or Hegelian philosophy, Chernyshevskii wrote, related beauty in nature to the realization of the Absolute Idea. Since the Absolute could not endure the confinement of time and space that is unavoidable in a single object, it had to be divided into a chain of definite ideas, which in turn found expression in an infinite number of objects. It was an illusion to think that the Absolute Idea could ever find perfect expression in a particular object. In fact, the Absolute expressed itself only to a degree in any definite idea, and only to a degree in any separate object. Nonetheless, it was this illusion of perfect expression that man considered beautiful (II, 6–7).

Chernyshevskii defined the idealistic position as also holding that beauty is created by man's fantasy, because in reality or nature there is no true beauty (II, 14). He quoted Vischer to show the many flaws that mar beauty in nature (II, 32–35). In the search for ideal beauty, man was forced to turn from inadequate nature to art, where human imagination could alter the character of reality. Art achieved this by stressing only superficial externals, apart from the material substance of the object and other limiting conditions (II, 140). Herein Chernyshevskii saw the essence of what he called "transcendental aesthetics," which he viewed as no more than an act of selection and decoration, intended to produce a dreamlike distortion of reality. Thus, in idealistic aesthetics, he argued, art was higher than reality, or rather an attempt to escape from reality into a more beautiful realm. As a student of Feuerbach, caught up in the social and political concerns of his day, Chernyshevskii could hardly allow such a theory to go unchallenged.

Admitting the advantage of destructive criticism over efforts to construct a system, Chernyshevskii proposed a bold new definition of beauty, in accordance with his own philosophical assumptions. He argued that, since beauty in nature aroused sensations in man much like the sensations he feels in the presence of a loved one, there must be something in beauty that is near and dear to his heart. This quality had to be general and yet capable of producing diverse forms, because there are diverse examples of beauty. The low level of sophistication with which Chernyshevskii explained his position may be gauged by his own words:

> The most general thing that pleases man, and the dearest thing in the world to him, is *life*. Most dear is the life that he would like to lead, the life he loves, and then any life, because all considered it is better to be alive than dead. All living things by their very nature fear annihilation, nonexistence, and love life. And it appears that the definition:
>
> "beauty is life";
>
> "beauty is that being in which we see life as it should be according to our understanding; beautiful is the object which expresses life, or reminds us of life"—it appears that this definition explains to our satisfaction all cases which arouse in us a sense of beauty (II, 10).

Here, surely, was a definition that cut through philosophical complexity with a vengeance. Chernyshevskii argued further that if one identified beauty as "life as it should be according to our understanding," a definition must be given of "understanding," lest it imply an unexpected reintroduction of the very concept of the ideal he was trying to get rid of. Chernyshevskii's definition rested on the relativity of class attitudes, claiming, in effect, that such understanding depended on a person's life situation. He noted that common people defined the "good life" by sufficient food and shelter, adequate sleep, and hard but not exhausting work. Translated into the terms of feminine peasant beauty, this way of life prized the attributes of "physical robustness and a balanced constitution." Beauties of fashionable society were a far cry from this rosy-cheeked ideal, since the world of idleness exalted other characteristics, delighting in small hands and feet, pallid cheeks, and even sickliness. In associating diverse standards of beauty with different classes of society, Chernyshevskii used every opportunity to show his preference for an alleged freshness, vigor, and health in the ideal life of the common people and to protest against the idleness of others (II, 142–144).[7]

To identify beauty in nature, apart from human life, Chernyshevskii used as a criterion the degree to which a natural object resembled man. In the absence of external likeness, qualities such as freshness, roundness of form, and fullness indicated the similarity of natural objects to man. According to this line of reasoning, Chernyshevskii evaluated a landscape more highly if it also contained some kind of animation (II, 12–13).

In this way, Chernyshevskii proclaimed a definition of beauty that he believed to be free from any suggestion of transcendentalism. Still, he had to answer the claim of idealistic aesthetic theory that art sought a more perfect beauty than could be found in nature. He did this first by questioning whether the realm of art was truly an improvement.

In one of his least felicitous lines of argument, Chernyshevskii wrote that it was fantastic to think that man must have perfection. "When you have enough, you don't seek more." It was only the poor fellow lying on bare boards who dreamed of a luxurious bed of precious woods and Brabant lace. Abnormal desires for perfection stemmed from abnormally poor conditions of life. In addition, desires for perfection went beyond what the human organism could stand, because human senses became tired and satiated. Man's aesthetic sense could not be called insatiable or infinite when he would tire even of a work by Raphael, if seen everyday for a month (II, 35–38).[8] Thus, Chernyshevskii called into question the very idea of the human pursuit of ideal beauty.

His defense of beauty in reality and his questioning of beauty in art produced some rather bizarre arguments. For example, although he admitted that beauty in nature was unpremeditated, in contrast to the conscious creations of art, he assured his reader that the inequality of creative forces guaranteed nature's superiority. "It must be admitted that our art has been unable, to this day, to produce anything like an orange or an apple, let alone the luxurious fruit of tropical lands" (II, 38).

Chernyshevskii gave more serious attention to defending the proposition that beauty in nature was neither so rare as the German aestheticians asserted, nor less beautiful for being temporary and inconsistent. He argued further that beauty in nature was not dependent on only one point of view but, unlike art, was beautiful from all angles. He could not avoid the objection that nature's beauty had imperfections, but he minimized them, and traced the source of the objection back to the "unsound" idealistic view that beauty was only surface form and not the object itself (II, 39–47).

He used many of the same charges against beauty in art that the idealists had leveled against beauty in nature. Artistic creation could also be unpremeditated, and certainly beauty was rare in art. Many tragic and dramatic events occurred each day, in comparison to the few truly beautiful tragedies and dramas. Art could be called transient, since it was subject to damage. Furthermore, art had its own imperfections: Sir Walter Scott's novels were too long and drawn out, and those of Dickens often sickly and sentimental (II, 48–52).

But Chernyshevskii might have spared himself much of this tired, commonplace argument. From the moment he made his basic definition, "beauty is life," he left no further room for discussion. His definition had reduced the debate to a question of whether there was more life in life itself than in art. He asked, in effect, whether the original or the copy was more original.

The definition "beauty is life" affected Chernyshevskii's appreciation of the various arts, all of which, he believed, achieved beauty by imitating the beauty in life. Architecture proved to be a stumbling block, because it could not be said to copy life. He admitted that architecture might have grace, elegance, and a beauty of sorts, but its productions could in no way be considered works of art. Architecture, therefore, became a "practical activity," different from furniture making, not in its essential character, but in the size of its undertaking. The other arts fell more readily into place. Sculpture sought to reproduce human beauty, although St. Petersburg alone had many people more beautiful than the finest statues (II, 55). Painting received much the same treatment. Even in music, he found imitation: "Thus instrumental music is an imitation of singing, its accompaniment or substitute; [and] singing as a work of art is only an imitation and substitute for singing as a work of nature.

After this, we have the right to say that, in music, art is only a weak reproduction of the phenomena of life that are independent of our strivings for art" (II, 63). Chernyshevskii was primarily concerned with literature, which he placed above the other arts, but for its content alone. Were the comparison limited to the strength of impression made by the different arts, he felt that literature would fall behind the other arts, because it approached only man's imagination, whereas painting and sculpture directly affected man's visual sense. Nor was the creative process in literature any more exalted than the copying of nature done by the painter and the sculptor. Denying the creation of literary characters in an ideal sense, Chernyshevskii described the writer as a historian or a memoirist. Though the creative writer had special techniques of selection, in essence he could only strive to reproduce that which he had experienced in reality (II, 65–68).

From this analysis, Chernyshevskii was able to answer his own question about the proper relation of art to reality. Despite the difficulty of artistic execution, the credit it reflects on its maker, and its pampering of man's artificial tastes, he believed that, if thinking was free from idealistic fantasy, it must admit the superiority of reality over art. The assertion that reality was higher than art became the main point of Chernyshevskii's work on aesthetics and the touchstone of all his new definitions.

He devoted considerable attention to redefining the concepts of the sublime and the tragic in order to cleanse them of all traces of transcendentalism. Concerning the sublime, Chernyshevskii opposed the view that it was a "manifestation of the idea of the infinite," which he took to be the essence of the Hegelian position (II, 16–17). Chernyshevskii felt the introduction of words like "absolute" and "infinite" merely confused the issue, founding a philosophical definition on empty, meaningless concepts. In his own definition, he preferred to stress qualities and quantities that could be measured. He defined the sublime primarily in terms of magnitude: "The sublime is that which is much greater than anything to which we compare it— A sublime object is one whose dimensions far exceed those of objects to which we compare it. A sublime object is one that is far more powerful than other phenomena to which we compare it" (II, 19). Chernyshevskii went to the extreme of suggesting that it might be better to substitute the word "great" for sublime. If the word "sublime" were kept, it should be used to describe something existing in nature, not something introduced by man's imagination.

If Chernyshevskii's definition of the sublime denied the idea of the infinite, his definition of the tragic challenged the idea that man was in conflict with fate, or with a law of necessity that governed the external world. He had little sympathy with the concept of fate, which he called a fantasy of the semisavage, having no place in modern thought (II, 24, 177–178). Primitive man used the word "fate" to explain occurrences that Chernyshevskii recognized only as contingency. Though human plans were not always realized, this resulted from chance misfortune, not irrevocable fate, and certainly did not imply a tragic flaw in the character of the person suffering. Man indeed had to struggle, but he struggled with nature and other men, not with fate. Nor did the person suffering have to be an extraordinary personality or a hero. A farmer in misfortune might suffer just as much as Oedipus. In this way, Chernyshevskii laid the groundwork for his all-embracing definition, "the tragic is that which is horrible in man's life" (II, 30). Again, this definition cleansed a concept in aesthetics from all the transcendental implications of prevailing theory, which linked the tragic to a concept of fate, whose intrinsic hollowness he believed had been proved by science (II, 115).

By way of contrast, Chernyshevskii had little objection to the prevailing theory of the comic. He referred to Vischer's definition of the comic as the preponderance of form (obraz, das Bild) over idea. Surprisingly, he accepted the term "idea" here without any suspicion of transcendentalism, even in reference to its use by German aestheticians (II, 185–195).[9]

Had Chernyshevskii's analysis of aesthetics ended with these new definitions, he would have achieved a view of art fully consistent with his philosophy of materialism. He could claim, by definition, that true beauty existed in nature, especially in its highest form of human life. The artist, in such a conception, could imitate the beauty of nature but could in no way improve on it, because reality was "higher" than art. So stated, his position would have been a useful weapon against escapist art, but it would not necessarily have served a particular social tendency. Chernyshevskii, therefore, asked further questions about the function and purpose of art, and when he answered them, not all of the initial definitions in his new aesthetics stood without modification or even contradiction.[10]

Although Chernyshevskii criticized existing theories of aesthetics, he had no intention of questioning the right of art to exist (II, 90). Indeed, he believed that art had a splendid mission, which one writer has recently summarized as the need to reproduce, to explain, to judge, and to teach.[11]

Chernyshevskii insisted that art must reproduce reality, not because of reality's inadequacies, but because certain worthwhile experiences were available to a limited number of persons. Few people lived by the sea; hence seascapes, which allowed people who lacked the opportunity of enjoying beauty in reality to acquaint themselves with it, or remind themselves of it, at least in some degree (II, 77). But Chernyshevskii did not rest content with art as simple imitation or second-best substitute. He allowed that some aspects of reality might not be worthy of attention, so long as the decision was made according to what ordinary men found to be of interest and not according to artificially imposed limitations. He felt that idealist aestheticians had frequently gone beyond a legitimate concern with beauty of form, to an improper concentration on objects of beauty as the most suitable content for art. Properly speaking, he wanted all aspects of reality, in nature and in life, to be considered fair game. He even made a special point of not excluding the world of man's imagination from art. If man at times lived in a dream and that dream had an objective significance for him, it too might justifiably be reproduced by art.[12]

Chernyshevskii sought to give a more precise definition to the word "reproduce" in order to avoid the objection that he sought the photographic copying of reality. The artist, in reproducing reality, had to have understanding and the ability to distinguish essential from unessential features. Both in his dissertation

154

and in a review of a new Russian translation of Aristotle's *Poetics*, Chernyshevskii tried to distinguish between "reproduction" (vosproizvedenie), which he considered closer to the original Greek concept of mimesis, and "imitation" (podrazhanie), which he felt implied only surface similarity. Reproduction did not mean "crude and vulgar copies"; it might even include a form of idealization, if this meant the omission of details not essential for obtaining a full picture (II, 80, 278–280).[13]

Chernyshevskii moved further from the idea of art as mere imitation when he discussed the function of art to explain. To some extent, merely calling attention to an object helped to explain its significance and forced people to understand life better. Though art might resemble a learned statement, it would more easily be absorbed and comprehended. Thus, the novels of James Fenimore Cooper had done more than ethnographic descriptions to acquaint society with the way of life of savages. While all arts performed this function of pointing to new and interesting objects, they did so in different ways. Unlike the painter and the sculptor, who reproduced objects in all their detail, the poet had to leave out a great deal in his description, which necessarily pointed up sharply and clearly the features retained. For the writer, a well-chosen word often had to take the place of unessential description, and as a result, the object or event might be more intelligible in a prose or poetic work than in reality. In this way, art helped to explain reality, not by false idealization, but by a clearer or more vivid allusion to reality. The artist helped to reveal the essence of reality to the inexperienced eye (II, 85–86).

When Chernyshevskii wrote on the necessity of art to judge, he began to develop his theory of art's social mission.[14] He felt that if a writer were intellectually alive, then consciously or not, his works pronounced judgments on the aspects of life that interested him. In this way, the writer's work resembled an essay on subjects presented by life. "In such a case," Chernyshevskii wrote, "the artist becomes a thinker, and works of art, while remaining in the sphere of art, acquire a scientific significance" (II, 86).[15]

155

This reference to science, or learning, was not a casual one. With admittedly different methods, both art and science engaged in the same process of explaining the axioms of life and deducing maxims. Chernyshevskii saw art and science as "handbooks for those who are beginning to study life; their purpose is to prepare the student for reading the original sources and later to serve as references from time to time" (II, 87). Unfortunately, the prevailing school of idealistic aesthetics had turned its back on this mission of art.

Idealistic aestheticians too often expressed the idea that art must exist only for its own sake, and that it degraded art to make it serve a human need. Chernyshevskii agreed that such ideas might once have been valid as a protest against the pressure on an artist to write pompous odes, or to distort reality for the sake of arbitrary, sentimental maxims. But this freedom had long since been won, and it was now time to think how art could be useful. Any human activity had to serve mankind, if it were not to remain a useless and idle occupation. There could no more be art for art's sake than wealth for wealth's sake, or science for science's sake (II, 271). In his theoretical writings, when he spoke of using art to serve mankind, he meant simply that life had serious concerns, and that the thinking artist must deal with them. Art as a mere pleasure-producing pastime was inadequate. Later on, driven in practice by his own impatience at the slow progress of social reform, he went beyond his theoretical position to demand a more specific partisanship of the artist.

When Chernyshevskii wrote of the need for art to teach, he again stressed the relation of art to science and learning, whose latest discoveries had to be popularized. The learned experience and reflection of the human race often proved too difficult for many to grasp, even at the existing level of popularization. Yet all readers found pleasure in novels and stories, which, without being consciously didactic, could spread information to the reading public, much as conversation with an educated person helped to instruct one of little education (II, 273–274).

Chernyshevskii's writings on aesthetic theory were not free from ambiguity with regard to the artist's creative process and the function of the artist in society.[16] He appeared anxious to avoid the charge of didacticism, but at the same time, he wanted to gain for art the benefit of having a purpose and direction. When he defined art's function as reproduction, he reduced the creative process in art to an act of separating the essential parts of life's experience from the unessential parts. But the question remained how even a selective reproduction of life could aid the social concerns of the present and future. Chernyshevskii's best answer to this question came with his attempt to place art, the artist, and the critic in a context of historical development.

He revealed many of his values and concerns when he assumed history to be a dynamic, progressive process. The implied upward movement reflected his faith that man's reason could master the natural environment and develop new social forms, which approximated ever more closely an ultimate truth. Not all members of society participated equally in this triumphant march; some indeed barely understood what others achieved. The artist, with his uncommon talent, belonged rightfully to the elite that led the way.

Chernyshevskii sadly admitted that not all artists accepted their rightful roles. He distinguished among artists according to the degree to which each was attuned to his age. Every age, representing a different stage of historical development, had its own unique problems, and every thinking member of society necessarily had views on these problems. Such views were manifest in a writer's work, even when he did not consciously try to propagate an ideology. Up to this point, Chernyshevskii's argument did not violate what many of his opponents would have called art's right of free expression.[17] But he went on to deny the right of an artist to consider his artistic work apart from the problems of the age. From Chernyshevskii's point of view, art could not be removed from life. As all literature served some interest, it was merely a question of which one. Those who insisted on "pure art," isolated from life's concerns, really supported existing social injustice, because they favored epicureanism, which in fact served the status quo by distracting attention from the more important strivings of the age. In his own day, he described the main strivings as "humaneness and concern for the betterment of human life." Other activities, including enlightenment and separate branches of learning, were necessarily linked to these two basic ideas (III, 302).[18]

In a number of references defining artistic form and the relationship between form and content, Chernyshevskii made more explicit his belief that art must not be allowed to expend itself in unworthy pursuits. Briefly, he defined form as the means by which the artist carried out his intention; it indicated his talent or technique. Beauty of form, an essential quality of every work of art, required a harmony between the idea and the image, but this consideration was limited to the formal aspect of art and did not necessarily refer to its content. Form described how something was done; it did not specify what was done (II, 82). This distinction displayed Chernyshevskii's respect for form, and he occasionally gave some attention to form for its own sake (II, 514–516).[19] More often, however, especially in his reviews, he concentrated on the ways that the artist chose to direct his talent. The overall evaluation of an artistic production had to consider the degree to which its form corresponded to its content, and also the truth of the idea that served as the basis of the work. This idea, or content, reflected the willingness of the artist to confront important questions. Chernyshevskii thus could make a rapid transition from a discussion of aesthetics, in the narrow sense, to praise or blame of a writer's point of view. He wrote: "Artistry consists in the correspondence of form with idea; therefore to discern the artistic value of a work, one must, as strictly as possible, inquire into the truth of the idea which lies at the base of the work. If the idea is false, there can be no talk about artistry, because the form will also be false and the execution incongruous. Only a work which manifests a true idea will be artistic, if the form corresponds to the idea" (III, 663). Given a "correct" idea, or content, the merit of a writer might still be questioned, but no hope existed for a writer whose works were "empty" or "without sense," who viewed literature as a mere plaything. Against a straw man opponent who objected in the name of artistic freedom, Chernyshevskii gave mocking replies:

"This is the caprice of talent"—who needs caprice?

"This is the freedom of creativity"—does freedom really consist in idle talk?

"This pleases me"—a pity if you cannot find another source of pleasure besides trifles which are not worthy of attention.

"I have no need of your attention"—then why do you ask for it by placing your book in the window of the bookstore? (IV, 520–521).

This reasoning, couched in the same scornful attitude, stood at the core of many of Chernyshevskii's critiques of writers whose views differed from his own. Its usefulness in journalistic polemic and its ability to arouse irritation were marked.

Chernyshevskii's theory of aesthetics led him to comment on the history of Russian intellectual life and literature. Since evaluation of an artist's merit depended, in part, on the correctness of his content, and correct content meant that the artist's concerns and views were compatible with the needs of his time, it was necessary to establish clearly just what the times demanded. In 1855 and 1856 Chernyshevskii attempted to do this in his "Essays on the Gogol Period of Russian Literature," in which he identified himself as the heir and champion of Belinskii and displayed all the one-sided sympathies of a devoted disciple (III, 135–136). Having undergone several years of the most severe censorship at the end of Nicholas I's reign, when it was forbidden even to mention Belinskii's name, Chernyshevskii believed that a reacquaintance with his idol's views would be of value to the Russian public. As a result, he often did no more than quote or paraphrase judgments of Belinskii on earlier figures in Russian literature and criticism. But he also went beyond the restatement of older opinions to place Belinskii in historical perspective.[20]

In surveying Russian literature, Chernyshevskii made use of views and judgments taken from articles written in different periods of Belinskii's kaleidoscopic career. This meant that some insights had their origin in articles whose overall direction differed fundamentally from Chernyshevskii's own theory of aesthetics. But Chernyshevskii knew and understood the evolution of Belinskii's thought well enough to make a careful selection and to avoid self-contradiction. In the main, he selected from articles written near the end of Belinskii's life: "The Works of Alexander Pushkin" (1843–1846), "Thoughts and Notes on Russian Literature" (1846), and Belinskii's last two surveys of Russian literature for the years 1846 and 1847.

Chernyshevskii based his review of earlier literature on the assumption that the current natural school represented the highest point in a line of historical development; he therefore judged writers of the past according to the contribution they made to the natural school. But changes in literature along with general intellectual and social development were to continue. In time, with changed conditions, the natural school would also be replaced by something "higher" (III, 191–192).

For the period prior to Pushkin, Chernyshevskii made no systematic analysis. In the manner of a Westerner, he praised Peter I's reforms for bringing the seeds of enlightenment and learning to Russian soil. Minimizing the contributions of A. D. Kantemir and V. K. Trediakovskii, he called M. V. Lomonosov the real founder of Russian literature. But Lomonosov left an ambiguous legacy. Although he made a beginning and wrote works that commanded attention, the very style and content of his writing plagued Russian literature up to the time of Pushkin. Lomonosov's style, imitative of European and classical models, remained bookish and artificial. Furthermore, he directed the attention of writers to ideal, sublime themes, far removed from the life concerns of the people. Thus, though Lomonosov served as a catalyst, he left impurities which could be corrected only by several generations of Russian writers (III, 247–249).

Chernyshevskii paid little specific attention to the writers between Lomonosov and Pushkin, though he noted that they strove to achieve an original, natural art. Pushkin, in turn, rose on their shoulders to become Russia's first national poet. Because of them, Pushkin could produce works of more sophisticated literary significance than would have been possible if Russian writers had merely developed the traditions of native folk literature. A temporary schooling in foreign forms had been necessary, but equally necessary was the achievement of a virile and mature art, which could overcome imitation and bookishness to become national and realistic.[21]

Following the example of Belinskii, Chernyshevskii devoted one of his major series of articles to Pushkin (II, 424–516).[22] Chernyshevskii expressed the highest regard for Pushkin's ability and his contribution to Russian literary development, while warning that the poet's "colossal" talent ought not to obscure the fact that he belonged to a bygone period in Russian literature (II, 468–469; III, 200). Pushkin's greatest service was to acquaint the Russian public with truly artistic poetry and to outmode forever the artificial, rhetorical attempts of his predecessors. His work began a new epoch because of its effect on the Russian public. By awakening a sympathy for poetry, he greatly increased the number of people interested in literature and thus laid the groundwork for a higher level of moral development. Once the public had mastered a sense of poetic form, it could go further and seek content in that form, as in the ensuing period of Lermontov and Gogol (II, 474, 516).

However, that Pushkin never achieved significant content, as Chernyshevskii used the word, was clearly stated:

Of all the circumstances that influenced Pushkin's habit of devoting so much attention and effort to reworking the form of his verse, the most important was that Pushkin was predominantly a poet of form. By this we do not mean to imply that his essential significance in the history of Russian literature was the fashioning of verse; that would be too narrow a view of the significance of literature in society. But really, the essential significance of the works of Pushkin was that they were beautiful or, as they like to say now, artistic. Pushkin was not a poet of any defined view of life, like Byron. [He] was not even a poet of thought in general, like Goethe or Schiller. The artistic forms of *Faust*, *Wallenstein*, and *Childe Harold* arose so that in them might be expressed deep convictions about life. In the works of Pushkin, we do not find this. With him, artistry was not merely the covering, but the kernel and the covering together (II, 473).

Even in his works based on historical themes, with the exception of *The Captain's Daughter*, Pushkin merely expressed the views of Karamzin, while remaining uninvolved himself. Chernyshevskii softened his judgment only slightly when adding that, because Pushkin was a man of outstanding mind and education, his works could still benefit the reader.

In order to emphasize his point that the Pushkin era had passed, Chernyshevskii devoted considerable attention to the public's reception of Pushkin's later works. Starting around 1830, public approval of Pushkin had diminished. Pushkin himself had not changed, having matured in a way that was true to the nature of his earlier works. Rather, there had been a basic shift in public opinion, which Chernyshevskii described by quoting directly from Belinskii:

> Our age honors only the artist whose life is the best commentary on his works and [whose] works are the best justification for his life. The personality of Pushkin was high and noble, but his view of the artist's role nevertheless was the cause of the gradual cooling of the enthusiasm aroused by his first works. It is true that the most immoderate enthusiasm had greeted his plays which were weakest in an artistic sense; but in them a strong personality was evident, animated by subjective strivings. And the more perfect Pushkin became as an artist, the more his personality was concealed and hidden behind the marvelous, luxurious world of his own poetic vision. The public, on the one hand, was unable to evaluate the artistic merit of his later works (this naturally was not his fault); on the other hand [the public] rightly sought more moral and philosophical questions than they found in Pushkin's poetry (and this naturally was not its fault). Meanwhile the path chosen by Pushkin was justified by his own nature and calling. He did not succumb, but remained true to himself. Unfortunately [he did so] at a time that was unreceptive to a tendency which favored art but gained little for society (II, 511–512).

As society could no longer find complete satisfaction in a literature of pure form, Pushkin's day was past. However, he left the legacy of a larger reading public, better schooled in aesthetic taste and thus ready for the literature of the Gogol period.

Chernyshevskii linked the natural school in Russian literature indissolubly with the name of Gogol. He had the highest respect for Lermontov, whom he called "the most original of our poets up to his time, not excluding Pushkin." But even though Lermontov approached a new social awareness, an early death cut off his career before its full growth, leaving him no real following (II, 501–502; III, 20, 110).

Chernyshevskii credited Gogol with combining an artistic talent comparable to Pushkin's with an outlook more attuned to the needs of the day. Any view of Gogol that considered only his artistic talents risked misunderstanding him completely, because Gogol had perfected a "satirical" or, as Chernyshevskii preferred to call it, a "critical" tendency in Russian literature. Though Gogol had predecessors in the use of satire—A. D. Kantemir, A. P. Sumarokov, D. I. Fonvizin, I. A. Krylov, A. S. Griboiedov, and even Pushkin himself—it remained for Gogol to raise the critical element from its secondary role. Chernyshevskii affirmed Belinskii's emphasis on Gogol's works as social analysis and protest against existing conditions. He defined criticism broadly as making judgments on the phenomena of life, according to the level of understanding reached by humanity and the demands of reason. Chernyshevskii contrasted a "critical" direction in literature to an "analytic" direction. The analytic direction also studied life, but from almost any point of view, or even entirely without thought or sense. Only the critical direction held up life's phenomena to the norms of reason and noble sentiments (III, 17–18).

According to Chernyshevskii, it required no special character or turn of mind to appreciate Pushkin, but for Gogol the case differed. Chernyshevskii looked upon the works of Gogol as vivid protests against the ignorance and injustice of serf-bound Russia. Because the author of *Dead Souls* denied the evil and vulgarity of his day, he could not have been other than a controversial figure. The reader's enjoyment of his work required a similar way of thinking, because he wrote in the service of a "definite direction of moral striving" (III, 21).

The stumbling block in Chernyshevskii's interpretation was the need to reconcile this view of Gogol as a social critic with the position of religious conservatism taken by Gogol in his *Selected Passages from Correspondence with Friends*, against which Belinskii himself had raged so magnificently. Belinskii's accusation that Gogol betrayed his earlier tendency had been difficult for Chernyshevskii to accept during his student years; now he offered an explanation that was more ingenious than convincing. In effect, Chernyshevskii blamed Gogol's relapse on an unfavorable environment. He pictured Gogol as a genius born into a society which, instead of firm convictions, provided him with outworn ascetic traditions, no longer vital to the society itself. Neither his early education, nor life in St. Petersburg, helped Gogol develop a deep and consistent view of life. Thus, he wrote about subjects which aroused his noble nature, and he unmasked evils without being able to explain them. In later years, when Gogol sensed the need of a more general theory, he knew only the religious traditions of his childhood. To Gogol's credit, he could not toy with ideas, and he strove passionately to make the most of the little he had to work with. In this way, Chernyshevskii excused the pathetic confusion of Gogol's later life, as if the writer never really had a chance (IV, 662–665). Very few Russian writers who strayed as far from Chernyshevskii's conception of the true path were treated so generously.

Still, since the main impression made by Gogol's works was one of forceful protest, making the public aware of unpleasant truths about Russian society, Chernyshevskii felt justified in applying the terms "natural school" and "realism" to the imaginative world of his creation, which appeared, at first glance, a far cry from what is usually understood to be realistic. Ought the grotesque caricatures of *Dead Souls* to be accepted as true pictures of provincial life? Were the characters of *The Inspector General* fair examples? To these questions, Chernyshevskii would have answered both no and yes. He refused to be held responsible for the verisimilitude of all of Gogol's characters. To do so would have meant the denial of satire and caricature, two of the most effective forms of criticism (III, 18n). But Chernyshevskii insisted that mendacity, cruelty, and absurd pretensions were true to life in the society Gogol depicted. Consequently, the essence of realism in literature consisted in the honest facing of life's problems, not in the literary techniques employed to achieve the goal, which were of secondary importance. Chernyshevskii supported his position with a quotation from Belinskii: "Our literature . . . constantly strove to change from a rhetorical literature into a natural literature . . . And we do not hesitate to say that in no other Russian writer was this striving so successful as in Gogol. This could be achieved only by the exclusive attention of art to reality, eschewing all ideals" (III, 228).[23] This passage implied a definition of rhetorical literature as distorting reality, consciously or unconsciously, and giving a false idealization of life. Unfortunately, the definition may lead to confusion, because one usually considers writing to be rhetorical when it employs a stilted, unnatural form of expression. But from Chernyshevskii's point of view, if a writer produced an idyll based on the life conditions of serf-bound Russia, the work deserved to be called rhetorical, despite superficially accurate details of reproduction. Conversely, Gogol wrote caricatures, but by virtue of their critical tendency, he in fact dealt realistically with Russian life (III, 244–245). Thus, within Chernyshevskii's definition, content, or the concerns and strivings that motivated the author, not only towered above form in evaluating a work, but also determined its classification according to type. The crudest restatement of this position would be that all literature either exposed or tried to cover up the needs of society, and that only the former deserved to be called realistic and part of the natural school. Such a reformulation would not be too unfair to Chernyshevskii, as he avoided subtleties, in the firm conviction that history justified his view alone.

Thus interpreted, Gogol and the natural school represented the highest achievement of Russian literature. Gogol earned his leading position by influencing young authors to write prose. Though Chernyshevskii recognized Pushkin's similar influence, Pushkin had in fact left no school behind him. Only Gogol's combination of prose style with realistic content had inspired young writers to become independent and seek themes of native importance and thereby achieve national self-awareness (III, 16–20). He always maintained the likelihood that the future would bring a change to a higher type of literature. But during the years 1854–1857, when Chernyshevskii was devoting most of his attention to aesthetics, literary history, and criticism, his view of Gogol provided a yardstick to measure the efforts of other writers.

In addition to considering the development of Russian literature, Chernyshevskii discussed the development of literary criticism. In this critical tradition, Belinskii held the foremost rank, as a counterpart to Gogol in literature. Until the time when Chernyshevskii could mention Belinskii's name in print, he referred to his hero as "the critic of the Gogol period."

Chernyshevskii gave no systematic treatment of the development of Russian literary criticism. In his "Essays on the Gogol Period of Russian Literature," he wrote extensively on a number of critics and grouped them primarily according to their appreciation of Gogol. Again he reflected many of the judgments of Belinskii. But appreciation of Gogol was not the sole criterion. Indeed, one position that commanded consistent respect from both Belinskii and Chernyshevskii was their joint rejection of lightheaded, undirected, and uninvolved literary criticism. The possession of a consistent, ideological point of view thus became the second criterion by which Chernyshevskii judged earlier critics.

He used both criteria in his evaluation of N. A. Polevoi. Much in Polevoi's career could not have appealed to Chernyshevskii. Polevoi had been a negative critic of Gogol and, later, an associate of the reactionaries F. V. Bulgarin and N. I. Grech. Nevertheless, there was a lingering aura of martyrdom surrounding his early career, because the government had closed his journal, *The Moscow Telegraph,* in 1834. Furthermore, Belinskii had once praised Polevoi's role in the establishment of Russian journalism. In Chernyshevskii's estimation, Polevoi's judgments suffered from his adherence to the tenets of French romantic criticism, and his excessive concern with form prevented him from appreciating the new departure in Russian literature represented by Gogol. He could only see *The Inspector General* as a farce and *Dead Souls* as a caricature. But the saving grace of Polevoi was that he had a point of view, even if the wrong one. In fact, Chernyshevskii generally treated Polevoi with sympathy because of his attempt to apply the standards of French romanticism. Any systematic criticism appeared at least as a step in the proper direction (III, 22–43). Conversely, Chernyshevskii viewed the criticism of another opponent of Gogol, O. I. Senkovskii (Baron Brambeus) as a colossal waste of time. Without a guiding direction or ideology, Senkovskii harped on engaging details, at the expense of making significant points. His negative view of Gogol was based on his personal fear of being outdone as a humorist (III, 44–47).

When Chernyshevskii turned to critics who appreciated Gogol, he still asked whether they did so for the right reasons. For example, Pushkin, his friend Prince P. A. Viazemskii, and P. A. Pletnev were among the first to recognize the worth of Gogol as a man and a writer (III, 131–132). Yet for the most part Chernyshevskii showed little patience with these critics, whom he viewed as esoteric dilettantes because they lacked a clearly defined system to support their evaluations. He preferred to concentrate on the correct understanding of criticism from N. I. Nadezhdin to Belinskii.

As an iconoclastic critic, much of Nadezhdin's life was clouded by controversy, but Chernyshevskii felt that Nadezhdin did for the Pushkin period of Russian literature what members of the French romantic school of critics, like Polevoi, had done for the preceding period. That is, by subjecting literature to severe criticism, he cleared the way for further development (III, 146–147). In this undertaking, Nadezhdin used the weapon of German philosophy, notably Schelling, and also some ideas that approached those of Hegel's *Aesthetics* (III, 159). In view of Chernyshevskii's own aesthetic theory, his endorsement of a criticism that relied on Schelling appears contradictory. But Chernyshevskii believed that the phase introduced by Nadezhdin had been one of necessary transition:

Nadezhdin was the first firmly to introduce a deep philosophical view into our thought. He gave our critics the profound universal principles, uncovered for aesthetics by German learning. He was the first to explain to our critics the meaning of poetry and artistic creation. From him they learned that poetry is the embodiment of an idea; that the idea is the kernel from which the artistic creation grows, the spirit which animates it.

167

[They learned] that beauty of form consists in its correspondence with the idea. He first began strictly and truly to examine: Is the idea expressed in the work understandable and [presented with] sympathy? Is there artistic unity in the work? Are the characters of the protagonists sustained and true to human nature and the conditions of time and nationality? Do the details of the work stem from the idea? Does the whole course of events develop naturally according to the laws of poetic necessity? Do the given characters and situations fulfill the idea of the author?—in a word, he was the first to give to Russian criticism the aesthetic basis on which it had to develop, and [he] gave examples of the application of these principles to the judgment of poetic creation (III, 163–164).

Thus, by considering the question of how well the artist gave expression to the idea at the core of his work, German idealistic philosophy actually helped introduce a greater awareness of content into Russian literary criticism. However else Chernyshevskii objected to those "mystical teachings," he could always find praise for a denial that literature consisted merely in the play of the writer's personal fancy. If, as idealistic philosophy claimed, literature expressed national self-awareness and helped a people along the path of historical development, then literature had to express a significant idea (III, 177–178). The next point at issue remained the nature of this significant idea which had to await the arrival of Belinskii, but Nadezhdin had at least left the necessary stepping-stone to a higher level of understanding.

In his discussion of the transition from Nadezhdin to Belinskii, Chernyshevskii offered an explanation of how such changes in the character and content of criticism came about. They depended on two fundamental elements: a "scientific understanding," which served as the basis for criticism, and the nature of the national literature itself. In the years after the forced termination of Nadezhdin's career in 1836, Chernyshevskii noted important changes in both of these elements. He had only to mention Gogol's *Dead Souls*, Herzen's *Who Is To Blame?*, Dostoevskii's *Poor Folk*, Turgenev's *Sportsman's Sketches*, and Goncharov's *A Common Story* to make his point that, by 1847, when Belinskii achieved his fullest insight, Russian literature appeared as little like the literature of 1835, as the literature of Pushkin's era resembled that of Karamzin's time. In the same way, a change had occurred in Western Europe, as the novels of George Sand and Charles Dickens replaced those of Victor Hugo and Sir Walter Scott (III, 181–182).

Variation in the other element, the so-called scientific understanding, presented a different and more complicated story. But to discuss Belinskii was to deal with this variation, because Belinskii had passed through the main phases of Russian intellectual life during the 1830's and 1840's. According to Chernyshevskii, Belinskii appeared on the literary scene as a student of Nadezhdin, and, in the manner of his teacher, made a sweeping condemnation of romanticism in his "Literary Reveries: An Elegy in Prose," in 1834. Later, when Belinskii wrote for *Notes of the Fatherland,* he continued this struggle but on a significantly different basis. Nadezhdin, who had remained essentially a follower of Schelling, had criticized French romanticism largely from an abstract point of view, claiming that modern romanticism was no more than a pseudoromanticism, that is, a pitiful imitation of the true romanticism of the Middle Ages. By contrast, Belinskii came to a wider understanding of the question, which suggested that romanticism had a false and affected view of life (III, 183–188). Belinskii's temporary adherence to Hegelianism explained the difference.

Chernyshevskii's view of the influence of Hegelianism was essential to his understanding of the whole development of Russian criticism. Hegel's influence, as he presented it through the career of Belinskii, proved to be a temporary but necessary preparation for something higher, namely, the influence of Feuerbach. It was Chernyshevskii's belief that only in this higher, post-Hegelian stage did German philosophy cast off its "scholastic form of mystical transcendentalism" and merge its theories with natural science and anthropology. He saw in Belinskii's later writings a combination of the latest philosophical teachings and the more practical questions raised by the French socialists about the material side of life. This combination stood as the only true scientific understanding, but Hegelianism had helped to achieve it, by serving as a bridge

169

from "abstract science" to the "science of life" (III, 179, 208–209).

As an example of the contribution of Hegelianism, Chernyshevskii pointed to the enthusiasm for this philosophy that animated Belinskii and his friends on the short-lived *Moscow Observer* in 1838. For the first time all the contributors to the literary section of a Russian journal sought to bring the meaning of their works into harmony with ideas they believed to be correct. Hegelianism not only filled these young writers with a deep desire for truth and goodness, it also turned their attention to a fresh appreciation of the joys of real life. Concerned as they were with a system that tried to explain and reconcile all aspects of reality, they found it necessary to pay extraordinary attention to areas of reality that had earlier been ignored or distorted. In Chernyshevskii's faithful attempt to follow Belinskii consistently, he thus credited the initial impetus toward naturalism to the very philosophy whose aesthetic theory he regarded as having attempted to distort reality (III, 200–202, 207–208).

Chernyshevskii stood on surer ground when he traced Belinskii's subsequent rejection of Hegelianism. He believed that the staff of *Notes of the Fatherland* reached a new stage in Russian intellectual life when they became able to consider "alien authorities" without necessarily submitting to them (III, 224). In Belinskii's case the irrationality of Russian reality finally forced him to make a dramatic break with Hegel. But Belinskii's new position did not bring an immediate change in his literary criticism; he required a good part of the 1840's to purge his criticism of all abstract elements and readjust to a new concept of reality. Belinskii's annual reviews of Russian literature and his essays on Pushkin (1843–1846) were cited as a progression toward a final position allowing severe criticism of Gogol, who had long been the object of Belinskii's praise. In this way, Chernyshevskii could insist that Belinskii showed logical development rather than contradiction, even if comparing two articles as far apart as his "Sketches of the Battle of Borodino" and his review of Gogol's *Selected Passages from Correspondence with Friends*. One had only to read through his intermediate writings to see the logic behind Belinskii's gradual changes. Perhaps, since Belinskii faced the task of instructing his readers in the basic facts of literature and criticism, this slow progression was beneficial. Chernyshevskii likened it to teaching the alphabet before reading (III, 219–221, 248–249).

The question remains as to what Chernyshevskii meant when he said that Belinskii moved from the abstract toward the positive and reality. In the early 1840's, Belinskii, still saturated with the vocabulary and assumptions of Russian Hegelianism, often used the word "reality." According to Chernyshevskii, however, he used the word in an abstract way, meaning only man's spiritual life, because he considered the material side of life illusory. For his own part, Chernyshevskii believed that the word "reality" could only refer to the life known through man's physical senses, and he described the later years of Belinskii's career as the gradual acceptance of this position. If, initially, Belinskii's abstract, idealistic view of reality permitted a purely aesthetic criticism, his final position, based on the materialist's view of reality, focused the critic's attention on social issues. Thus, in 1840 Belinskii considered only the artistry of Gogol's *The Inspector General;* three years later, though he still spoke mainly of Gogol's art, he remarked of another writer that a poet achieved significance only if he had a lively, urgent sympathy with the contemporary world (III, 240, 253–254). Chernyshevskii described Belinskii by 1845 as being possessed by a Faustian passion for life, by which Chernyshevskii meant that Belinskii could no longer view a work of art apart from life's problems. This change was reflected in the increasingly profound content of Belinskii's articles on Pushkin, written between 1843 and 1846 (III, 256–258, 274–275). In his final two annual reviews of Russian literature for 1846 and 1847, Belinskii did not change his views. He had arrived at the position that Chernyshevskii considered to be his own point of departure.

At the conclusion of his "Essays on the Gogol Period," Chernyshevskii explicitly condemned the weakness and empty concern with trifles that dominated Russian criticism following Belinskii's death. He also clarified his position on the critic's proper role. If writers remained insensitive to the greatest concern of their time—the search for human well-being—the critic should work against their influence. If writers had misguided humane sympathies, the critic must show them the way. Only a successful combination of talent, sympathy, and correct social tendency deserved the critic's full support (III, 303, 309). In his own career as a critic, Chernyshevskii put these ideas into practice.

Chernyshevskii wrote most of his literary reviews before Dobroliubov's full-time work on *The Contemporary* and before he had secured his own position on the journal. In applying his standards to the literary scene, he made a number of enemies. A few examples will provide an indication of the challenge Chernyshevskii presented to the writers of his day, a challenge that evoked protest from other journals and from among his early associates.

Chernyshevskii's review of M. V. Avdeev's *Novels and Stories* in 1854 was a classic example of an attack on an art that lacked a proper content of ideas. He admitted Avdeev's talent, but after the accusation that Avdeev had borrowed from Lermontov, Pushkin, and Druzhinin, he made his main point that the short stories did not fit the present age, "which is prepared to adjust rather to inadequate form than to inadequate content or the absence of thought." He called one story, "Serene Days," a sentimental idyll, beside which Karamzin's *Poor Liza* would seem like a work by Gogol in its naturalness. There was too much in life which could not be made lovely for Avdeev's approach to fit the times. A writer could produce real beauty only if he understood the life of real people in contemporary society (II, 210, 220).

Chernyshevskii showed his strong desire to correct wayward talent in his reviews of the plays of A. N. Ostrovskii. When he wrote a review of *Poverty Is No Crime* in 1854, Ostrovskii had for several years been associated with the Slavophile editors of *The Muscovite*. The Slavophiles valued this work for its sympathetic treatment of authentic Russian customs, whereas Chernyshevskii preferred to emphasize Ostrovskii's ability to portray cruel patriarchal family relationships and the grasping life of the Moscow merchants. He felt that the characters and situations in *Poverty Is No Crime,* however, were not believable. As a resolute feminist, he objected to the storybook ending in which a father, who was about to sentence his daughter to a grim but profitable marriage, suddenly realized the error of his ways, endured public humiliation by a ne'er-do-well brother, and came to see the virtue of a true love marriage. Such an unlikely plot toyed with serious matters and transformed bitter into sweet, in an imagined world of sentimentality. Chernyshevskii thus called the play a terrible blow to Ostrovskii's literary reputation and tried to wean him from his Slavophile admirers: "In our opinion [this play] has harmed his literary reputation but he has not yet destroyed his excellent talent. Mr. Ostrovskii may still appear as fresh and strong as before if he leaves the muddy path that led him to *Poverty Is No Crime* ... Talent finds strength in truth; a false direction destroys the strongest talent. Works which are false in their basic thought are weak even in purely artistic terms" (II, 240). In 1857, Chernyshevskii showed greater sympathy for Ostrovskii's play, *A Lucrative Post,* because it exposed self-seeking officials (IV, 731–735). It is unlikely that the playwright was governed by the critic's demand for a certain kind of content, but in the following years, while Chernyshevskii's journalistic influence was approaching its peak, Ostrovskii wrote two of his most powerful indictments of household despotism, *The Pet of the Mistress* (1859) and *The Thunderstorm* (1860).

Although he usually neglected form in order to concentrate on an author's content, Chernyshevskii occasionally applied his theories with a better balance. In 1857, in a review of a book of poetry by N. F. Shcherbina, he argued that, even with significant content, care had to be taken to find an appropriate form of expression. Chernyshevskii respected Shcherbina's talent, but objected to the poet's inability to find simple, contemporary modes of expression when he shifted from themes of antiquity to a content more attuned to the modern world, in particular to Russian society. Whenever Shcherbina strayed from antique themes, he seemed cold and sententious. The article concluded with an appeal for artistic autonomy, which in the context of

Chernyshevskii's other reviews strikes one as an unintended irony. If the artist's concerns took a new direction, Chernyshevskii maintained, he should be fearless about using a new form of expression, regardless of his earlier work. But clearly, Chernyshevskii here referred to a limited freedom, for he assumed that "new direction" meant a content appropriate for the artist's times (IV, 528–544). Obsessed by a historical "ought to be," Chernyshevskii could scarcely consider a broader freedom of choice and point of view.

One notable exception to Chernyshevskii's general practice of literary criticism was an evaluation of Tolstoi's early works *Childhood, Boyhood,* and *War Stories.* This review is often cited to show that Chernyshevskii had the capacity to make sensitive, purely literary judgments, even if he did not often choose to do so.[24] In this favorable review, Chernyshevskii praised Tolstoi's unique ability to carry the reader's attention directly into the psychic life of his characters and to infuse his stories with a purity of moral feeling. Here, Chernyshevskii not only stressed his appreciation of Tolstoi's technique, rather than analyzing how well the content fitted the needs of the day, but he also made explicit the view that not every poetic idea allowed social questions to enter a work. If Tolstoi chose to portray the life of children, for instance, he could hardly be expected to do more than deal with their feelings and understandings. The poetic idea would be destroyed if foreign elements were introduced into such a work. Everything had its proper place, and Chernyshevskii even quoted approvingly a long passage from Tolstoi's *Two Hussars* that depicted a young woman gradually overcome by the premonition of love (III, 429–430).

Had Chernyshevskii consistently maintained this kind of respect for an artist's choice of subject, he would have made fewer enemies. But less than two years later, he wrote in a review of Turgenev's love story "Asia": "Take them away, these questions of love. They are not for the reader of our times, who is occupied with administration and improvement of the courts, financial reforms, and liberation of the peasants" (V, 166). His review of Tolstoi's stories, admittedly one of Chernyshevskii's most perceptive, must thus be considered the exception which tested the general tendency of his criticism. There is also reason to believe that, when he wrote the review late in 1856, he had ulterior motives in mind and was not being fully honest in expressing his feelings. During that November, when he was trying to prove his ability to carry the temporary responsibilities of editorship, he had written to Nekrasov of his desire to exert influence over Tolstoi. The next month, he wrote to Nekrasov that he had written the review in such a way as to please Tolstoi, "without doing too much violence to the truth." One month later, in a letter to Turgenev, he belittled Tolstoi's work, making especially cutting comments on Tolstoi's *Youth*, a work written in a fashion similar to *Childhood* and *Boyhood* (XIV, 328–330, 332).[25]

The reputation Chernyshevskii gained as the scourge of pure art did not rest solely on his criticisms of literary content, for he wrote other reviews that had little or no connection with literary criticism. These reviews merely used a piece of literature as an excuse to develop a point of view that belonged more properly to philosophy, economics, or politics. Since his view of art had always been involved with social concerns, to step outside the realm of aesthetics was not especially difficult. Such reviews did not necessarily imply adverse criticism. M. E. Saltykov, for example, had no reason to be offended by Chernyshevskii's review of his *Provincial Sketches* in 1857, which praised the work because of the truth it presented in satirical form, and this evaluation in no way suffered from the fact that most of the review dealt with the proposition that any improvement in provincial morality would have to be preceded by a basic change in the system of social organization and government (IV, 263–302).

At the other extreme, Turgenev fared less well in Chernyshevskii's attack on his love story "Asia." The review "A Russian Man at a Rendezvous" had the significant subtitle "Thoughts on Reading Turgenev's Story 'Asia'." Chernyshevskii's article was clearly not a review at all, but rather an attack on a type of man, represented by the indecisive hero of the story, who symbolized a sickness in Russian society. With thinly veiled references to Russian liberalism and the decaying aristocracy,

Chernyshevskii quickly moved from Turgenev's story to an indictment of those in society who either saw current problems in terms of outworn stereotypes or, if able to make correct evaluations, lacked the will to act (V, 156–174).

A review of Chernyshevskii's contribution to Russian aesthetic theory and literary criticism must emphasize his two guiding concerns, which were not always compatible and, at times, led inescapably to self-contradiction. He sought to define a theory of art that would be fully consistent with philosophical materialism. At the same time, he clearly wanted art in some way to help fashion a better future for mankind.

To stay within the framework of materialism, Chernyshevskii had to provide aesthetic theory with an essentially new set of definitions, which avoided any suggestion of transcendentalism. He offered new definitions with relative consistency, and these led him to the position that reality and the beauty of reality stood above art. Art itself was no more than the attempt to reproduce reality; it was a surrogate for life. Lesser definitions fell into place. "Beauty" was defined as that which reminds man of life according to his own understanding, which suggested that a person's idea of beauty would vary according to his way of life. The word "sublime" expressed magnitude, and any serious misfortune in human existence was called "tragedy." Nor could the domain of art be limited to objects of beauty. All human experience had to be considered worthy of attention.

Chernyshevskii contended that beauty in art had to be inferior to the beauty of reality, because the image in the artist's mind could not transcend what he had experienced in life. This would suggest that art merely reproduced or copied life and nature. Had his argument rested here, Chernyshevskii could have offered no suggestions as to which segments of human experience or nature ought to be used as subject matter or content. The artist would have had no basis for a critical attitude toward his subject matter, and the art or literary critic could have done no more than evaluate the artist's fidelity of reproduction. Chernyshevskii could not rest content with such a view.[26] Concerned as he was with economic, social, and political questions, he extended the goal of art beyond the limits of reproduction and described the mission of the artist, and indirectly the critic, as to explain, judge, and teach. Thus, Chernyshevskii found himself in the difficult position of trying to explain how art could pronounce judgments over a reality to which, according to his own definitions, it was inferior.

In his theoretical writings and in some of his reviews, Chernyshevskii tried to bridge the gap between his revised definition of aesthetics and his insistence that art could not and should not exist for its own sake. He wanted art to be free creation, rather than calculated didacticism. Yet he insisted that the artist, as a thinker and a citizen, had the responsibility of being attuned to the needs and strivings of the epoch, which Chernyshevskii identified in his own time as humaneness and concern for the betterment of human life. Only then could the artist select the aspects of reality that were worthy of reproduction and comment truthfully on the reality he reproduced. An artist who did not stand in harmony with his times, by definition produced bad art because of faulty content. Chernyshevskii thus demanded that the artist be the right kind of thinker, so that his free creation would in fact serve the needs of the day. In practice, he often reduced his theory to a demand that artists change their subjects, or indeed, that they alter their points of view.

Although he spoke of humaneness and the betterment of human life, Chernyshevskii left unsolved in any systematic way the question of how to arrive at these criteria and values. He frequently wrote about the "needs of the day" without explaining how to formulate those needs. If Chernyshevskii could have joined his views on art with an objective theory of historical development, also based on materialism, he would at least have offered a self-contained theory. Instead, as Charles Corbet has noted, he frequently used the expressions "all cultivated people understand," and "everyone today sees," without an accompanying system to explain why his own position should be labeled the sole locus of truth.[27] Chernyshevskii used an appeal to science, or the latest learning, as an argument from authority to support his own preferences in social, political, and moral imperatives.

In short, Chernyshevskii's attempt to use materialism as the basis of a new theory of art led him to some strikingly new definitions and gave him a useful weapon against older theories of aesthetics. However, his own definitions, if strictly applied, would have allowed art merely to copy various aspects of reality. Dissatisfied with that prospect, Chernyshevskii also tended toward a utilitarian view of art's role in the progress of mankind. Clearly a utilitarian tendency suited the needs of a reforming or revolutionary journalist, but one seeks in vain for any necessary connection between his utilitarian view of art and his fundamental reformulation of aesthetics, based on a philosophy of materialism.[28]

For his time, Chernyshevskii's ideas were sufficiently extreme to invite disagreement. Beyond that, several factors combined to make his works the center of an angry controversy. He frequently wrote with the tone and manner of a dogmatic iconoclast, and he claimed to be the sole interpreter of Belinskii, even among older men who had known and respected Belinskii during his lifetime. Furthermore, Chernyshevskii wrote as an unknown upstart, against men of established reputation. There was also an element of personal rivalry in the case of one opponent, A. V. Druzhinin, whose place Chernyshevskii had taken as literary critic on *The Contemporary*.[29] Even the mundane struggle for subscribers affected the controversy, for in the middle of the 1850's, *The Contemporary* and *Notes of the Fatherland* competed for the same general group of readers.[30] A final consideration was antagonism between Chernyshevskii and others based on class differences and conflicting social beliefs, although this factor has frequently been overemphasized or used in a crudely simplified way.[31] Chernyshevskii had indeed issued a strong challenge when he wrote that all art served some social tendency and that artists who tried to avoid social issues really supported the status quo. But in the early years of his career, from 1854 to 1856, when he met strong opposition to his views on art, his general position on economic and social questions was not yet widely known. Nor were those who opposed him united in their acceptance of existing conditions in

Russia. On many questions these opponents agreed only in regarding Chernyshevskii's aesthetic theory and criticism as a misunderstanding of the meaning of art, or as a threat to art's integrity.

Except for Chernyshevskii's own review of his master's dissertation, *The Aesthetic Relation of Art to Reality,* which he placed in *The Contemporary* as a safe form of self-advertisement, the general reaction to its appearance in 1855 was negative.[32] One reviewer, in *Notes of the Fatherland,* took special pains to make fun of the idea that the function of art was to serve as a surrogate for reality, "the way the potato in Ireland serves as a surrogate for bread." He called it a "horrible theory," which would give offense to anyone with the least bit of taste. As for the derivation of Chernyshevskii's ideas, the reviewer called the dialectical process by which they had been derived from German aesthetics "completely false." The *Library for Reading* greeted the dissertation with the acid comment that the only thing new in Chernyshevskii's theory was the absurdity of its conclusions.[33]

Turgenev agreed with these negative evaluations. He wrote to A. A. Kraevskii, editor of *Notes of the Fatherland,* to thank him for the critical review of Chernyshevskii's work, which had disturbed him more than anything he had read in a long time. Elsewhere Turgenev called the dissertation "false and harmful" and comforted himself with the fact that the work was too "lifeless and dry" to cause much damage.[34] Turgenev softened this judgment only slightly the following year in a letter to A. V. Druzhinin, who had taken one of the strongest stands against Chernyshevskii. Turgenev admitted that he took offense at Chernyshevskii's dryness, crude taste, and manner of dealing with people, but he would not allow Druzhinin's claim that Chernyshevskii was like "carrion." Even if Chernyshevskii understood poesy badly, he comprehended the needs of real life.[35] Some years later, Turgenev expressed the opinion that critics like Chernyshevskii and his followers had the wrong idea of what took place in the mind of an author. They refused to believe that to reproduce truth and the reality of life correctly and powerfully was the greatest happiness for an author, even if the truth did not coincide with his own sympathies.[36] Turgenev cited an example from his own work, *A Nest of Gentlefolk,* wherein one of his characters, a Slavophile, won out in argument with a Westerner. Turgenev himself favored the Westerner's position, but in this case he felt that his presentation best showed life as it was. There was much in this statement that Chernyshevskii could have agreed with, because he too, in theory, favored fidelity to life. But Turgenev hit close to the mark when he implied that Chernyshevskii could not long maintain respect for true artistic detachment.

On at least one occasion, in 1855, Chernyshevskii was the victim of a tasteless attack that lacked any statement of theory or principle and sought simply to lampoon his person. In the September issue of *The Library for Reading,* D. V. Grigorovich published a farcical short story, "A School for Hospitality," in which one unpleasant character, Chernushkin, a self-indulgent sponger who babbled constantly and set people against each other, bore many of the physical attributes of Chernyshevskii. Few who knew Chernyshevskii could have missed Grigorovich's intention, and Chernyshevskii himself recognized the point of the crude attack (XIV, 462). Grigorovich may have thought he was replying in kind for Chernyshevskii's earlier parody of Grigorovich's stories about peasants (II, 655–662). However, Chernyshevskii's parody at least had a serious point, while Grigorovich's lampoon simply displayed ill-humor; it represented a low point in a journalistic arena that was hardly known for gentle manners.[37]

The publication of "Essays on the Gogol Period of Russian Literature" in 1855 and 1856 drew clearer battle lines between Chernyshevskii and opponents like V. P. Botkin, P. V. Annenkov, and A. V. Druzhinin, all of whom held to more traditional views of aesthetics and criticism.[38] Near the end of 1856, Druzhinin, then editor of *The Library for Reading,* formulated many of the objections to Chernyshevskii's evaluation of Belinskii and Gogol in an article, "The Critics of the Gogol Period of Russian Literature and Our Relation to Them." Druzhinin couched much of his article in general terms, but he directed specific attention to Belinskii, and one senses that in speaking of the criticism of the Gogol period he never had Belinskii far from his mind. That he intended the article as an attack on Chernyshevskii was obvious from the opening pages, where he declared that the critic ought to express his own times and not make a fetish of past achievement. New understandings and the expanded horizons of the present made it wrong to set up a figure of the past as an idol who could be copied, but not challenged.[39]

As so often happens in heated debate, many of Druzhinin's statements showed that he and Chernyshevskii were talking past each other. Chernyshevskii had set up the alternatives of frivolous, self-indulgent art as against art that dealt responsibly with life and was attuned to the needs of an epoch. Druzhinin, by contrast, set up the alternatives of true art, which pursued the eternal ideals of beauty, goodness, and truth, or consciously didactic art, which sought an advantage in the present. Druzhinin did not dismiss didacticism out of hand. It had a contribution to make, as shown by Thomas Hood's "Song of the Shirt." But clearly, something of value was lost if didactic purpose overshadowed art. In Druzhinin's view, didactic art was ephemeral, whereas the great artists—Homer, Shakespeare, and Goethe—left a legacy of lasting value, which could always edify man.[40]

Despite the frequent failure of their arguments to meet, the debate between Chernyshevskii and Druzhinin established significantly different positions for them. Part of Chernyshevskii's theory was that the artist should not feel obliged to concentrate solely on objects of beauty, because such a restriction would distort reality. Conversely, Druzhinin believed that concentration by the natural school on negative aspects of Russian life also produced a distortion of reality and a restriction on artistic freedom. As an antidote to the high and one-sided appreciation of Gogol by Chernyshevskii, the aesthetic critics gave special praise to the works of Pushkin. Druzhinin could not accept Chernyshevskii's view that Pushkin belonged to a bygone epoch. Rather, he saw Pushkin's view of art, a view that placed art above partisan schools, as the only hope of combating the unfair concentration on satire in Russian literature.[41]

The arguments of the civic and aesthetic critics in the 1850's did injustice to both great Russian writers, when they attached the labels "Pushkin tendency" and "Gogol tendency" to antipodal literary positions.[42] Moreover, argument led naturally to overstatement. In 1858, Tolstoi complained of hearing the opinions that literature was only a weapon for the civic development of society, and that the time was coming when Pushkin would no longer be read.[43]

By 1858, Dobroliubov had taken over the main burden of literary criticism on *The Contemporary*. Chernyshevskii directed his efforts toward economic and political questions, and his literary influence continued primarily in the work of his talented protégé. Though there was continued development and variation among writers who favored the civic mission of art, those who followed Chernyshevskii found the main battle lines already established, the product of an almost single-handed effort in the first four years of Chernyshevskii's career.

Chernyshevskii's writings on aesthetic theory and criticism formed a vital link in the tradition of civic or utilitarian art which extends, with many shifts of method and emphasis, from Belinskii to the present day. For several decades in the nineteenth century, long before the Soviet state established its own version of civic art as literary dogma, pressure for a socially useful art helped direct the work of Russia's writers and artists. Chernyshevskii's part in the development of this doctrine may be seen in a comparison of his views with those of Belinskii, Dobroliubov, and Pisarev. Chernyshevskii proudly recognized Belinskii as his teacher. In different ways, he might have recognized Dobroliubov and Pisarev as his pupils.

Paradoxically, the views of Belinskii in his later years and those of Chernyshevskii were similar, and yet widely disparate. Except for his own unique attempt to refashion the basic definitions and categories in aesthetics, there is no question that Chernyshevskii's views on the role of art and the artist relied heavily on earlier statements by Belinskii. The idea of art as the expression of national cultural life, the rejection of art as mere enjoyment, and even the ambiguous claim that the artist, though free to create, was under obligation to help mold national culture—all came from Belinskii's writings. Similarly, Chernyshevskii made extensive use of Belinskii's evaluations of earlier writers. But even this common core of doctrine and value judgment cannot justify an equation of the two men or unqualified acceptance of the statement that Chernyshevskii merely continued his teacher's work.

Unlike the critics who followed him, Belinskii experienced every phase of influence from German idealistic philosophy, and the experience left an indelible mark. René Wellek noted that, through the entire course of his career, Belinskii used the same categories, concepts, and procedures, the same basic theoretical idiom in his criticism, whatever his shifting emphasis and political convictions.[44] Throughout his restless search to find the proper meaning of art, Belinskii kept a respect for the inviolability of the artist as a discoverer, as opposed to merely a conveyer, of truth. Chernyshevskii, for all his protestations, could not maintain this respect. Probably no man in nineteenth century Russia sensed the shortcomings of his native environment more profoundly than Belinskii, and surely his views of art were firmly joined to social protest and a rejection of idealism in the later years of his career. But when Belinskii turned the attention of literature to social questions, he did so with an unquestioned concern for the literature itself. Even in the face of social injustice, literature could not be simply a tool. In his final review of Russian literature for 1847, Belinskii wrote: "Without any doubt, art must first of all be art, and only then may it be an expression of the spirit and direction of society in a given epoch. Whatever the beautiful thoughts that fill a poem, however strongly it speaks about contemporary problems, if it has no poetry it can have neither beautiful thoughts, nor problems, and all one may note in it is good intention, badly fulfilled."[45]

Chernyshevskii also possessed a concern for literature, as well as a desire to influence the course of society, but in him the two factors were weighted in a significantly different way. He had no legacy from earlier intellectual commitments that might act as a limit on the temptation to use literature, especially as the changing times held out more possibility that his hopes might in fact be realized. His primary interests were not artistic or literary. More important to him was the fact that aesthetics and criticism could serve as a convenient battleground to argue a total point of view and a program of change.[46] This modification of emphasis by Chernyshevskii, who saw art more as a means of propagating truth than as an area of human experience in which truth might be found, was a necessary prelude to the crude exaggerations of utilitarian criticism in the decades following.

Dobroliubov, in turn, made his career as an effective advocate of Chernyshevskii's interpretation of Belinskii. He generally worked so closely with his teacher that it is difficult to tell where the influence of one man left off and the characteristics of the other began. Furthermore, Dobroliubov wrote the bulk of his criticism a few years later than Chernyshevskii, at a time when the radical wing of Russian public opinion had openly assumed on all fronts a more extreme or, indeed, revolutionary position.[47] Yet some distinction between the men can be made. Dobroliubov, like Chernyshevskii, remained ambivalent on the question of whether literature could be an active influence on social change, but in his extensive and forcefully written reviews, he went beyond Chernyshevskii in openly mixing politics and literary criticism.[48]

To accommodate his primary concern with social questions, Dobroliubov developed a type of critical review whose main function was to effect a rapid change of subject away from the literature under consideration to an analysis of society. The most explicit statement of this technique appeared in 1860 in the opening pages of "When Will the Real Day Come?" Dobroliubov's discussion of Turgenev's *On the Eve.* Dobroliubov rejected "aesthetic criticism" as having become the possession of sentimental young ladies. At the same time, he denied a desire to bind the author to his own ideas or to set up tasks for the author's talent. What the author wanted to say was not so important as what he in fact did say, even unintentionally, in the process of reproducing facts from life. Dobroliubov thus variously described his method of criticism as an attempt to interpret the phenomena of life on the basis of a literary production, or to explain those phenomena of reality that called forth a given artistic work.[49] Within this general approach, Dobroliubov's acceptance or rejection of literary characters, and his evaluations of the fidelity to life of a literary work, became direct comments on Russian society. In theory, his approach to criticism might have remained a tool of analysis to investigate the creative process and the relation of literature to society; in practice, it became a weapon in the hands of an angry social critic, who used it to underscore the weaknesses of the existing social order, to castigate his political opponents, and to demand that literature produce a hero, created in accordance with his own radical ideals.[50]

In their different ways and in different degrees, Belinskii, Chernyshevskii, and Dobroliubov all maintained a considerable respect for the unique contribution of the artist. They also shared the dubious hope that a truly spontaneous literature could somehow be coaxed into serving their visions of progress. A theoretical position that demanded no more than a crude utility from literature was reached only by Pisarev in the middle of the 1860's. In his most extreme statements, which admittedly obscured the complexity and sophistication of his other writings, Pisarev reduced art to the communication of socially useful ideas, and the role of the critic to a judgment of those ideas. Thus concerned with content, Pisarev viewed form as a mere vehicle of expression, totally separate from content and not worth considering for its own sake, as aestheticians were inclined to do. He declared himself completely indifferent to the traditional arts of music, sculpture, and painting, because they did not contribute directly to the moral and intellectual perfection of humanity. Such arts displayed only ornamental sensuousness, and in this regard, even poetry, seen as a dying art, was little better. Literature still had a social use, although its utility would diminish as mankind progressed to a higher age of science.[51]

Although Pisarev frequently found himself at odds with Chernyshevskii's direct heirs on *The Contemporary*, he defended his general onslaught against aesthetics with specific refer-

185

ences to Chernyshevskii's master's dissertation. Pisarev's article "The Destruction of Aesthetics" in 1865 claimed merely to continue a process that Chernyshevskii had begun. He argued that Chernyshevskii himself had wanted to destroy aesthetics, but that he had realized the need to speak to society in a familiar fashion that it could understand. Chernyshevskii had gone as far as he could at the time when he argued that there were no absolute standards of beauty, only the relative preference of each individual.[52]

There is no evidence in Chernyshevskii's writings that he ever made direct comment on these views of a man who claimed to be his pupil. It would appear that Pisarev took the element of conscious didacticism, which belonged more to Chernyshevskii's practice of criticism than to his theory of aesthetics, and carried it to its logical and ridiculous conclusion. But even if Chernyshevskii had rejected Pisarev's most extreme ideas, he also would have recognized them as a part of the tradition he had done as much as any man to establish.

# VII. Economics and Social Theory

By the mid-nineteenth century, one noticeable consequence of Russia's retarded economic development was that its climate for the discussion of political economy differed markedly from the economically advanced countries of Western Europe. In Europe, both the liberal economists and their socialist critics wrote primarily in response to the experience of capitalist industrialization. Their Russian counterparts wrote primarily in anticipation of it. Many of the unique characteristics of Russian socialist thought stemmed from this fact.

The lag in economic achievement did not prevent Russian thinkers from considering the most recent European experience and economic theory. By the 1850's, all but the most short-sighted defenders of personal privilege realized the connection between serfdom and Russia's economic difficulties. Humanitarian concern thus coincided with a desire to establish the necessary conditions for economic growth. Following the Crimean War, when change became an immediate possibility, the varying examples offered by the European experience divided those in Russia who sought to put the economy on a significantly different basis.[1] The capitalist economies of the West had already shown their dynamic potential for growth, but they had not yet demonstrated an ability to distribute the fruits of industrial advance throughout the population with any degree of fairness. Lacking the ameliorative influences of a strong labor union movement and government regulation of the economy in the name of social justice, the dream of some of the earlier classical economists that a free enterprise economy, as a self-regulating system, would produce general prosperity had been discredited.[2] Knowledge of the desperate condition of the working class in Western Europe made the capitalist model of development unacceptable to Russians whose concerns were primarily humanitarian. No purpose could be served by replacing the old oppression of serfdom with the new oppression of proletarian life in an industrial society.[3]

This negative view of the experience of Western Europe in large part reflected the acquaintance of Russian thinkers with the works of European socialists. In many cases, socialist theories, condemning the capitalist economic system, came to the attention of Russian thinkers along with, or even before, the theories of liberal economists. This juxtaposition of liberal and socialist theory, each posing a future alternative, provided the basis for the strain in Russian radical thought that endeavored to take advantage of Russia's economic backwardness by choosing a course that would avoid or minimize the experience of capitalism and lead Russia more directly to socialism.[4]

A number of Chernyshevskii's articles, devoted to economic questions, contributed significantly to this radical movement. At the same time, he wrote much more extensively on economic theory in general and on the immediate problems of the peasant commune and liberation of the serfs.

Prior to his work on *The Contemporary*, Chernyshevskii clearly identified himself as a socialist, but in his own writings at this time he left little to give precise definition to his position. His early desire to serve humanity had been reinforced by the social novels of Eugene Sue, George Sand, and Dickens, and his interest in socialism had been aroused by the events of 1848 in France. During his student years he followed the speeches of socialists like Louis Blanc in the *Journal des débats*. Through contact with A. V. Khanykov, he also read in the works of Fourier. But though contemporaries commented on the radical nature of his views, the strongest statement Chernyshevskii made in his diary was a bitter denunciation of the liberal concept of freedom, which he considered shallow and hypocritical because it did not include guarantees for social well-being.

Chernyshevskii's position on *The Contemporary* at last provided him with a forum, and the public discussion surrounding the preparation of the peasant reform gave him an opportunity to speak out on questions of economics and social theory. His emphasis varied with the situation. He wrote relatively little in this area until 1857, and thereafter for about two years dwelt most heavily on the peasant reform. In the last two years of his active career, he concentrated on general questions of theory. Taken together, his works in this area constitute one of his most impressive and original contributions.

There is a long-standing difference of opinion over the degree to which Chernyshevskii ever seriously hoped for amelioration of the peasants' condition through reform from above. One view would place Chernyshevskii firmly within the united front that opposed serfdom after the Crimean War and responded positively to the government's statement of intention to liberate the serfs.[5] According to this view, Chernyshevskii worked hopefully and constructively toward that end, and he took a revolutionary position only after the reform as it finally took shape proved totally unacceptable. At the other extreme is a point of view that would insist on Chernyshevskii's revolutionary purity and his complete rejection of what Soviet writers call "liberal illusions." In one study of Chernyshevskii's economic views, for example, V. N. Zamiatnin wrote: "Understanding the gentry class character of the tsarist autocracy, Chernyshevskii harbored no illusions about the possibility of introducing reforms that would consider the interests of the peasant masses. All his activity was directed toward proving the inevitability of revolution, heralding [this revolution], working out a revolutionary program and [working toward] practical preparation for the revolutionary appearance of the masses."[6] Support for this interpretation is often given by reference to a paragraph from Chernyshevskii's semiautobiographical novel *Prologue*, which he wrote in prison in the late 1860's, after the fact of the reform settlement. In the setting of this novel, Chernyshevskii's hero, Volgin, was clearly meant to represent Chernyshevskii himself in the late 1850's. In one fictional exchange, he took an extreme position against the liberal point of view, arguing that it mattered little whether the landlords kept all the land or gave it to the peasants and then made them pay for it. In fact, he continued, it might be better if the peasants received no land at all, which implied a position of "the worse the better." Here, it seems, Chernyshevskii was trying to suggest that since he currently saw no serious hope for reform, his earlier position had been to welcome anything that would infuriate the peasants and drive them to overthrow the existing order (XIII, 187–188).

There is no doubt that Chernyshevskii's early statements looked eagerly toward a revolution in Russia, although concern for his marriage may have cooled, at least temporarily, his zeal for active participation. However, were one to accept the idea that preparation for revolution was his sole motive during his years as a journalist, many of his most extensive and impressive articles would have little or no meaning. Thus, to appreciate the effort Chernyshevskii made in his writings on economic questions, it is necessary to avoid the oversimplifications of his work as either a thinly-veiled call to revolution, or a mistaken belief that Russia could be reformed from above. In the years before his imprisonment, Chernyshevskii preached socialist theories that could never have been adopted by the existing society. At the same time, on other issues of the day he chose to support, from among realistic alternatives, the ones he believed to be most beneficial under the circumstances. He certainly did not mean thereby to endorse the system in Russia that had set up those circumstances, nor did his actions necessarily indicate a high level of faith that improvement would come. Rather, on many occasions Chernyshevskii merely demonstrated his strong sense of responsibility toward the common people he wished to serve, by seeking partial improvements concurrently with proposing total solutions. His enormous effort to influence the conditions of land settlement for the liberated serfs is a prime example.[7]

Alexander II initially limited his action on the peasant question to an appeal to his nobility. In 1856, he told a gathering of

Moscow nobles that he did not intend to abolish serfdom at once, but that existing conditions could not continue, and liberation from above was preferable to liberation from below. He asked the nobles to think of ways to accomplish this end. When his appeal produced no response, Alexander established a secret committee of bureaucrats in January 1857 to consider the problem. At the same time, a strict censorship prevented direct mention of serfdom in the press.[8] Writers like Chernyshevskii, who wanted to encourage the reform impetus, necessarily relied on vague suggestion. In 1856, for example, he welcomed the appearance of a new Slavophile journal, *Russian Discourse*. Although Chernyshevskii insisted on his fundamental disagreement with the Slavophile point of view, he accepted the new journal as a partner in a larger struggle. In Aesopian language, he referred to the widespread opposition to serfdom and the hope of reform: "Really, what is it we all want? an increase in the number of those who teach and those who are taught, an increase in scientific and literary activity, an extension of the railroads, a rational allocation of economic forces and so on" (III, 652). The expression "rational allocation of economic forces" required no further explanation.

Near the end of 1857, this situation changed radically. Angered by the hesitation and obstructionism of his secret committee, as well as by the suggestion of some Lithuanian landlords that the serfs receive freedom but no land, Alexander published a rescript on the peasant question to V. I. Nazimov, the governor general of the Lithuanian provinces. In this rescript, and those that followed in the first half of 1858 to the other governors general, the tsar by his own example made his intention to abolish the existing bondage law a matter of public debate. Though censorship remained, in 1858 it eased sufficiently to permit the printing of articles that would have been unthinkable a year earlier. At the same time, the government set up new machinery to carry out the tsar's wishes: committees of nobility in all of the provinces and a Main Committee on Peasant Affairs, which took the place of the earlier secret committee. Furthermore, Alexander set up guidelines for discussion of the reform. The rescripts acknowledged the landlords' legal possession of all the land on their estates, but barred a landless settlement with the stipulation that liberated serfs could purchase their house plots (usad'ba) and other necessary land to support their way of life and ensure fulfillment of their obligations to both the landlords and the state.[9] The rescripts further specified the organization of the peasants into village communes, with the landlords maintaining certain police functions. Any settlement had to assure the peasants' payment of taxes and other financial obligations. Apparently, during most of 1858 the government hoped to avoid its own direct financial commitment in any redemption (vykup) of land by the peasants.

By referring the problem to provincial committees of nobility, the government, in effect, asked the landlords, within these general guidelines, to work out the details of a settlement suitable to themselves.[10] As Chernyshevskii later noted, the peasants had no part in these deliberations, although their vital interests were involved (V, 713). While the committees discussed questions of the land to be sold to the peasants, the price to be paid, and the means of payment to be used, Chernyshevskii tried desperately to influence public opinion in favor of the peasants, who, as he noted, had no other voice.

The publication of Alexander's rescripts evoked an almost unanimous response of approval from Russian journalism. Not all agreed on how the serfs should be liberated, but serfdom was seen from many points of view as both a symbol and a cause of Russia's economic, social, and political difficulties. The purely moral relief of erasing this blot on the national conscience was obvious, but equally important was the fact that any number of programs for Russia's future required some change in the bondage law. No other issue could have united, even temporarily, proponents of Russia's capitalistic economic development, Slavophiles, advocates of different varieties of socialism, bureaucrats concerned with state power, and even self-seeking landlords who found decreasing profit in the existing serf system.

In his first article about the rescript, "On the New Conditions of Village Life," published in February 1858, Chernyshevskii joined the paeans of praise to Alexander II. He began with a quotation from the Forty-fifth Psalm: "You love righteousness and hate wickedness. Therefore God, your God, has anointed you." Chernyshevskii went on to compare the significance of the proposed reform to the deeds of Peter the Great: "The history of Russia from this year on will be as much different from all which preceded it as the difference between Peter's era and earlier times. The new life, which now begins for us, will be as much more beautiful, prosperous, brilliant, and happy, in comparison to our former life, as the last one hundred and fifty years were superior to the seventeenth century in Russia" (V, 69–70).[11] Chernyshevskii's enthusiasm may be discounted in part as a calculated attempt to commit the government as fully as possible to the case of reform, but the remainder of this article and those that followed showed his desire to make a constructive contribution to the great debate. He sought to give his readers sufficient factual material to permit intelligent discussion of the issue. A long series of articles, "The Organization of the Way of Life of the Landlords' Peasants," which ran into 1859, reprinted the tsar's rescripts and also the detailed instructions given to the provincial committees by S. S. Lanskoi, the Minister of the Interior. Furthermore, the whole point of the review of A. G. Troinitskii's article, "On the Number of Serfs in Russia," from the *Journal of the Ministry of the Interior*, was to give his readers information to help them form their own opinions.[12]

Initially, Chernyshevskii seemed to support cooperation within a united front of opposition to serfdom. In 1858, his bibliographical surveys of articles on the peasant question showed a generous tolerance for points of view which, though not his own, at least looked in the proper direction.[13] Early in that year, he printed in *The Contemporary* a reform project of K. D. Kavelin that had already passed from hand to hand in manuscript form, with the knowledge of the government.[14] Chernyshevskii and Kavelin did not share a common vision of Russia's future, but Chernyshevskii supported Kavelin's plea that the peasants receive all the land they actually farmed and that the government take part in the redemption operation. The government, fearing bankruptcy in its precarious financial position after the

Crimean War, reacted violently to the second suggestion. Kavelin lost his position as tutor to the tsarevich, and for several months the censors placed more severe limitations on subjects allowed to appear in the press. The question of government participation in the redemption operation could not be mentioned again until 1859.

In his own articles, Chernyshevskii placed the problem of serfdom in the broadest possible perspective. He identified serfdom as the chief problem underlying all of the difficulties facing the Russian state. The impoverished condition of village life, the unfair legal system, and the low level of education all stemmed from serfdom. Even the nobility, Chernyshevskii added, because of their assured income derived from serf labor, had no stimulus to serious study (V, 65–68). Serfdom hindered many aspects of government in the same way. It affected the tariff policy, the national budget, the military organization, and the judiciary. Most specifically, serfdom hampered national productivity because bondsmen were less productive than free labor.[15] Whether the peasants' obligations were defined as money payments (obrok) or the performance of labor services (barshchina) made little difference. Obrok payments produced apathy in the peasants, because the size of the payments tended to rise according to what the traffic would bear. Barshchina had a worse effect on the peasants and hurt national productivity, because at the landlords' caprice the peasants had been forced to labor under such difficult conditions that their own land could not be worked rationally (V, 75–81, 102).

Had Chernyshevskii's intent been solely to agitate and arouse revolutionary sentiments, he might well have continued simply to dwell on the negative aspects of serfdom. But because Alexander's rescripts had stated a firm intention to alter the bondage law, with the next step awaiting the discussion of terms by the provincial committees, Chernyshevskii chose a different course. He emphasized in some of his articles during 1858 and 1859 that the landlords would actually be better off under new arrangements, without serfdom. His arguments combined an apparently sincere conviction with a moral concern for peasant well-being and a willingness to fight in their behalf by whatever means. Thus, he seemed to accept the prospect that much of the land would remain in the hands of the nobility, who would be compensated for any land they turned over to the peasants. However difficult this must have been for him to swallow, the apparent acceptance of the government's ground rules allowed him to enter an arena of public discussion where he could stress the need to keep the redemption payments as low as possible, and later, when censorship permitted, he could urge government aid in the redemption operation.[16]

In order to support his recurring assertion about the greater productivity of free labor, Chernyshevskii made use of a study by D. P. Zhuravskii on wage rates for hired labor and the actual income received by landlords in the province of Kiev. Working from Zhuravskii's figures, Chernyshevskii was able to show that Kievan landlords who used serf labor to work their fields received an income from this process that was less than the same amount of labor could have earned in the free labor market. According to Chernyshevskii, this showed the inefficiency of serf labor, and he insisted that such inefficiency hurt not only the state but the landowners themselves (V, 81–84).[17]

The task of reconciling the landlords' interests with low redemption payments may appear quixotic, but in one article Chernyshevskii made a manful attempt (V, 341–356). Indeed, at one point he argued that it would be preferable if the sum would be small enough to be paid all at once, which in view of the state of peasant savings, amounted to suggesting little or nothing. But from this he passed on to calculations having at least some chance of acceptance, however small. He outlined the three factors that should determine the nature of the redemption operation: the original price charged for the land, the interest charges on each year's unpaid balance, and the amount the peasants could possibly pay each year.[18] Chernyshevskii underscored the essential problem of the peasants' inability to pay more than a relatively small amount each year. Therefore, if either the original price of the land or the interest rate were high, the whole process would drag out interminably. Moreover, the total amount finally paid by the peasants, for each ruble's worth of land, would be unfairly inflated by accumulated interest payments. Chernyshevskii tried to drive home his compassionate plea that a small concession by the landlords would mean a great advantage to the peasants. At one point, as he calculated the effect of variations in the factors of cost and interest rate on the duration of the peasants' indebtedness, he described a final termination date of forty, fifty, or fifty-five years hence as "impossible," which helps to explain his later reaction to the emancipation (V, 352).[19]

But his words, however just, could not magically dissolve the antagonistic interests of buyer and seller. The best Chernyshevskii could do was to base an argument on the assumption that the landlord himself, rather than the state, would carry any unpaid balance of the redemption payments, as a loan to his former serfs. Were that condition to prevail, Chernyshevskii tried to make the point that a prolonged period for repayment would not be to the landlord's advantage. The landlord, unlike the moneylender who lived from interest alone, stood to gain by getting his capital back—even if in lesser amount—in order to use it for his own enterprise. But the marginal living standards of most peasants gave them little capacity to pay more than extremely small amounts each year, and this fact undercut any semblance of sense in Chernyshevskii's reasoning. Even if the landlords had been willing to accept a lower total payment, they could not have recovered that amount more quickly than the tragically low ability of the peasants to pay would allow. Thus, in effect, Chernyshevskii tried to convince the landlords that they would be better off receiving the same small payments for a shorter rather than longer period of time (V, 347–348).

It is also possible to interpret one of Chernyshevskii's articles in 1858 as an attempt to divide the ranks of the nobility over the question of redemption payments. He suggested a plan that treated large and small landowners in separate categories and proposed that the small landowners should have their claims for payment considered first (V, 349).

By the end of that year, Chernyshevskii already seemed inclined to express doubt that any reasonable settlement could be reached within the framework of the government's action. In an article dedicated to the peasant commune, he wrote that the preservation of the commune was only one aspect of the problem of peasant well-being. He added bitterly that two other conditions also had to be met: "First the people who make up the commune must receive its income. But this is still little. One must also realize that income only seriously deserves its name if the person who receives it is not overburdened with credit obligations that arise from its very receipt" (V, 360). But despite a perceptibly sharper tone, Chernyshevskii's articles during much of 1859 continued to point constructively toward a solution. In response to rumors of fantastically high redemption estimates under discussion in the provincial committees, he tried to make an exact calculation of what proper payments should be. Then, as soon as allowed to do so, he began to urge government participation in the financial settlement.

Chernyshevskii claimed throughout his writings that he gave the landlord the benefit of every doubt, yet he suggested redemption payments far lower than others being considered. In the article "Is Redemption of the Land Difficult?" in January 1859, he suggested an average redemption payment of 39 rubles 24 kopeks per male soul for barshchina peasants and of 68 rubles 67 kopeks per male soul for obrok peasants. The difference in the two figures reflects the assumption that owners of serfs paying obrok should receive compensation for the loss of these payments and not merely for the land they would give up. Though Chernyshevskii believed that this assumption was unjust and illegal, he went along with it in his calculations so that his voice would be heard in an overall plea for lower payments. He estimated that there were twice as many barshchina as obrok peasants, so that for the whole operation the proposed average redemption payment was 49 rubles 5 kopeks per male soul (V, 514–515). Chernyshevskii insisted that this figure was high, because he based his calculations on relatively rich areas of Russia. Actually, this figure probably represented the lowest amount he thought might be introduced into the discussion with any chance of being noticed. In other articles, discussing how the redemption should be financed, he at one time seemed to accept an average redemption payment of 75 rubles per male soul, and elsewhere he considered reasonable a figure between

70 and 90 rubles (V, 567, 733–734). If the average redemption payment were to be as high as 75 rubles, however, Chernyshevskii pointedly suggested that the landowners be made to pay taxes (V, 548).

Early in 1859, when Chernyshevskii was permitted to discuss the government's role in the redemption settlement, he wrote that ideally the state should carry the whole burden. He minimized the difficulties: certainly two-thirds of the nation could help the one-third actually affected. In this case, he argued, justice fully coincided with advantage. All would benefit from an economy based on free labor; therefore all should help pay (V, 503, 543, 565–566). But once again, rather than seeking absolute fairness, he sought whatever advantage could be found in compromise suggestions and made extensive calculations on the relative benefits of varying degrees of government help. Since he worked in the dark as to the government's financial situation, he used arguments of expediency rather than careful consideration. At one point in his discussion, for example, he endorsed the issuance of assignats to pay for the land given over to the peasants. His attempt to play down the inflationary dangers of adding more paper money to the economy displayed his determination to forward his main point in any way possible (V, 548–562).

By October 1859, the last of Chernyshevskii's major articles devoted specifically to the peasant reform began to show obvious scars of bitterness. Sarcastically, he praised the provincial committees for their refusal to allow liberation without land, a point that the government had insisted on at the time of the rescripts (V, 712–713). He further suggested the one major difficulty preventing the full success of these committees was that they "were made up exclusively of the representatives of only one side of those whose interests touched on the peasant question. It seems unnecessary to show that for a satisfactory solution, the thoughts and interests of the other side, the peasants themselves, should have been better known" (V, 713).

Perhaps because by this time the important activity of preparing the reform had shifted from the provincial committees back to editing commissions in the capital, Chernyshevskii saw little point in trying further to appeal to landlord self-interest. He seemed to shift tactics, seeking merely to limit the landlords' pretensions with the suggestion that they had no legal right to redemption payments at all. If they were to receive payments, he reasoned, it was only because the nation's welfare required that no one class (soslovie) be severely hurt (V, 731). Chernyshevskii examined barshchina and obrok estates separately and came to the same conclusion for both. He built his argument on the principle, established in the government's guidelines, that the landlords were to be paid only for their loss of land, not for their loss of peasant labor. On barshchina estates, Chernyshevskii insisted that all the land used by the peasants for their own support, and for which the peasants would have to pay redemption, had no real value to the landlord. Even though this land supported an otherwise unpaid labor force, bonded labor was so inefficient that the landlord could dispense with it entirely, pay the prevailing wages for more efficient free labor to work his land, and still be better off. Therefore, even without redemption payments, the owners of barshchina estates had nothing to lose. In answer to a possible objection that the gentry would have difficulty making the transition without capital, Chernyshevskii commented sharply that the landlord himself would have to worry about that. Nobody else need supply the landlord with capital from which he alone derived profit (V, 723–724).

Chernyshevskii made a more daring attack on the claims of obrok estate owners. Rather than the size of existing obrok payments, he insisted that the land value alone, which on most obrok estates was relatively low, should be used to calculate the redemption fee. Lest this be considered too great an injustice to the landowners, he attacked the whole practice of obrok as a violation of the bondage law, which the state had established originally only to ensure a supply of agricultural labor for the nobles' estates. If the landlord did not possess sufficient land to make such an arrangement profitable, it was his own misfortune (V, 729–730).

In his attempt to influence the course of reform, Chernyshevskii also urged that, in any settlement, the peasants not be moved from the land they currently farmed, nor suffer a reduction of the amount of land available for their support. He coupled this request with thinly veiled threats about the importance to the landlords of keeping good relations with the peasants after the reform (V, 714–721).[20] Chernyshevskii also opposed the suggestion that the peasants and the landlords be left to work out their own arrangements, as the two sides were not truly independent of each other (V, 735). In addition, he warned that obligatory labor must not be used as a way of paying off the redemption: "Thus, to maintain obligatory labor would be, in essence, to maintain the bondage law. The people could understand this in no other way and they would be right. There is no need to say what consequences would follow if the people were left with conviction that serfdom remained in tact" (V, 737).

Chernyshevskii reserved his strongest words for a final statement about keeping the redemption payments relatively low. Again insisting that the figures should really be much less, he proposed an average redemption payment of between 70 rubles and 90 rubles per male soul, as an amount that would neither offend the national feeling nor bring disorder to the state. With a figure in this range, he claimed, one-third of the landlords would lose nothing and two-thirds would actually be better off. He had already lost his point that low redemption fees would bring advantage to the landlords, but this restatement allowed him to append his most severe warning and threat:

But if a redemption of 150 rubles [per male soul] is demanded, the people will succumb under the heaviness of the burden, and then what will happen? What does the peasant expect now? He expects freedom. What does he expect from freedom? [He expects] an improvement of his fate. What kind of improvement will he feel and how will he understand freedom if he is forced to pay obrok no less and even more than he does at present, or is forced as before to offer barshchina? How will he understand such a liberation? He will not understand it. He will consider himself cheated—and then what? (V, 734).

In the latter part of 1859 and throughout most of 1860, the editing commissions, established by the Main Committee on

Peasant Affairs, worked to formulate a final reform settlement. The government, now seeing danger in continued public discussion of the question, again imposed the censorship ban. In August 1860, Chernyshevskii wrote to Dobroliubov that it was forbidden to write about serfdom at all (XIV, 401, 406). The closest he could come to the question was to reprint an article from the *Edinburgh Review,* which argued against the claim that the abolition of slavery in the British West Indies had resulted in a lowering of production (VII, 186–211).[21] Unable to write further on the peasant question, Chernyshevskii found more time to concentrate on general questions of political economy, philosophy, and politics. By this time, he had lost any shred of hope that the reform could bring even slight advantage to the peasants. With this conviction, he felt freer to express more openly his radical political position.[22]

From Chernyshevskii's point of view, the Great Reform of February 19, 1861, represented a betrayal of the interests of the many for the benefit of the few. He obviously could not comment adversely on the reform proclamation, but in contrast to the general reception in the press, he greeted the reform with telling silence. During the following year, he hinted in every possible way that the reform had done nothing more than alter the form of exploitation of the peasants, without altering its substance.[23] His hints were not difficult to grasp. In a satirical review in January 1862, for example, Chernyshevskii stated that Russian literature had not advanced a step in the preceding five years, and since literature reflected life, this meant that Russian life had not advanced either. A few lines later, in mock repentance, he added, "Really now, what foolish thoughtlessness [springs from] callous skepticism! How could I forget that in these five years the peasants were liberated!" (X, 71). Later in the same article, he equated the position of the liberal Dmitri Samarin with the position of Nikolai Bezobrazov, who believed, according to Chernyshevskii, that the peasant question could be solved merely by changing the names of the prereform relationships (X, 75).

Chernyshevskii made his most explicit condemnation of the reform in his "Letters Without Address," which were written in

February 1862 but never passed censorship. In these letters, Chernyshevskii repeated much of his earlier criticism, but in an almost recklessly brusque tone. He described the Russian government, which had originally created serfdom, as being dependent on serfdom for its rule. The old order had not really fallen after the defeat of the Crimean War. Therefore, when the government undertook the reform, it looked to principles that were foreign to its own character. Bureaucratic methods and a partiality toward the nobility blocked any satisfactory settlement of the serf problem. The liberation merely changed the form of relationship between the gentry and the peasantry, with an almost imperceptible change in the substance of that relationship (X, 98–99). And even this slight change was not necessarily an improvement. Chernyshevskii's final letter included a calculation to show that, in some cases under the reform settlement, the peasants had to pay one ruble and ten kopeks for every ruble they formerly paid as serfs (X, 114).

This hopeless view of the reform may at the same time be seen as a judgment on Chernyshevskii's own efforts to defend, as best he could, the interests of the peasantry during the reform preparations. Thus, the statement of Kornilov that Chernyshevskii's articles on the peasant question remained without real influence may well apply, at least in regard to the government and the nobility. Among the Russian radicals, however, his articles did have influence, because they showed the futility of trying for an improvement within the existing system. Chernyshevskii's failure reinforced the radical view that the tsarist system itself should be the prime target of attack.

In his role as a spokesman for the peasantry, Chernyshevskii also argued in defense of the Russian village commune. But his defense of the commune rested in large part on his overall evaluation of the economic life and theory of Western Europe.

Only at the end of 1859, when censorship prevented further discussion of the peasant question, did Chernyshevskii find time to attempt a systematic exposition of his views on political economy. During the preceding five years, however, in scattered book reviews and articles, he had managed to express a well-defined tendency and a set of values that clearly criticized the capitalist economy and liberal economic theory of Western Europe.[24]

Chernyshevskii's concern for Russia's economic life and the choice open to her in the future provided the focal point for his consideration of economic systems. Aware of the dynamic forces of economic change at work in Russia after the Crimean War, he asked where these forces were leading. If Russia was following a pattern of development already set by Europe, Chernyshevskii questioned whether this pattern was worth following, and he considered what could be done to direct Russia along a more beneficial path. He often spoke of patterns of development as if they were inevitable, but he merely intended to show what would happen if rational decision and action did not intervene.[25]

Chernyshevskii fully realized Russia's retarded economic position, in comparison to the more advanced nations of Western Europe. In 1857 he noted that many of Russia's methods of production were almost patriarchal. Not only her agriculture, but her internal trade and industry, reminded one of the seventeenth century more than the nineteenth. After the Crimean War, however, he saw a change in this situation, as Russia entered a period of economic development akin to the capitalism of Western countries (IV, 304). Insofar as this meant more modern methods and increased production, Chernyshevskii called the change progress. Indeed, he approved of the surge of railroad building after the war, and at one point even welcomed a government act lowering the interest rate from four to three percent, because it would help increase industrial capital (IV, 811–812). But more significantly, Chernyshevskii insisted on asking the further question of what these changes would mean to the masses of people who would have to live under them—whether they would in fact be better off. This question led him to examine the economic and social relationships of Western Europe, which in turn he came to deny as an adequate model for Russia. In this one area, as he developed a critical view of the consequences of an economic system based on competition, he admitted partial agreement with those he labeled the "better Slavophiles," because they rejected the program of the uncritical "liberal westerners" (IV, 737, 760).

Chernyshevskii's analysis of the system of unlimited competition repeated many of the strongly worded statements of Louis Blanc's *L'Organisation du travail.* Free competition, by creating a propertyless proletariat, had brought virtual ruin to the vast majority of workers. They were completely dependent on the caprice of the system and on the few rich capitalists who possessed most of the wealth. He wrote: "In this way there developed, in England and France, thousands of rich people on one hand and millions of poor on the other. According to the fatal law of unlimited competition, the wealth of the former must always increase and concentrate in an ever fewer number of hands, while the position of the poor must become worse and worse" (IV, 740). This dismal tendency reinforced Chernyshevskii's evaluation of the liberals' advocacy of political freedom, which he viewed as a hypocritical attempt to soothe their own consciences. The simple guarantee of legal rights was inadequate, so long as no thought was given to guaranteeing material life.

When Chernyshevskii considered agriculture, which seemed of more immediate concern to Russia, he found the Western example equally unacceptable. In Europe, the earlier feudal and communal forms had already given way to private ownership, which change would have to be expected in Russia if no steps were taken to prevent it. Chernyshevskii painted a depressing picture of Western landholding. Private land tenure had shown several tendencies, all equally baneful. In England, for example, land ownership had concentrated into fewer and fewer hands, which produced a proletariat cut off from the security once provided by private possession of the land. In other areas, which avoided these large units, an opposite tendency could be observed toward smaller and smaller holdings, as several generations divided an inheritance that might once have supported a family. In one form or the other, poverty thus resulted for the mass of the people. Nor did a tenant system provide the answer, because under this system one man had to work another man's land under ruinous conditions (IV, 419–433).[26]

Chernyshevskii did not restrict his condemnation of the private property system to its harmful effects on the masses. At one point, he tried to challenge the claim of economic liberals that private ownership provided an effective spur to increased output and to improving the land. He argued, with a clever mixture of selected statistics and abstract reasoning, that the private ownership system did not aid agricultural production at all. The large landowner had no need to improve methods of farming, since he already enjoyed an adequate income. If the landowner leased out his land, his interest probably went no further than the rent he received. Neither did the tenant have a real interest in land improvement, because at any time his contract might be terminated, and he might be forced to move or pay higher rent. Chernyshevskii noted further that little could be expected from the landless agricultural worker, whose only concern was to be paid, not to improve another man's land or make another man rich. Thus, Chernyshevskii believed that a sincere desire to improve the land could be assured only if the man who worked the land also received the full product of his labor. Of the small units that continued in family ownership, he acknowledged that their owners might desire land improvement, but they lacked capital, and in any case, small size obstructed the introduction of modern technological improvements.[27]

Upon this rather depressing estimate of the operation of the free enterprise economic system in industry and agriculture, Chernyshevskii based his critique of laissez-faire economic theory. Up to the end of 1859, he concentrated on the major point that laissez-faire theory stood in the way of rational direction of the economy, which would be needed if Russia were to avoid the mistakes of Europe.

Chernyshevskii considered the theory of laissez faire unrealistic, because it claimed to be the ultimate expression of freedom, and yet unlimited competition might lead to situations of monopoly in which freedom could not exist (V, 579–580). In effect, he accused the system of laissez faire of bringing about the very thing its proponents professed to oppose, namely, oppression of the individual. From this point of view, he felt justified in calling the followers of this doctrine "utopians" (V, 606).

Referring to proponents of the free-enterprise system, Chernyshevskii made the following plea for a rational consideration of economic relationships:

At times they fancy that by saying "price depends on the relationship of demand and supply" [or] "competition must in no way be restricted" they have already expressed complete truth and have given a prescription for the recovery of all economic illnesses. They often forget that unlimited competition (which is the modern form of the medieval law of the fist) leads to monopoly which they themselves oppose. [They forget] that man is not an economic machine, but a living being endowed on one hand with various needs and on the other with reason. They forget that in human society, over the blind, irrational, pitiless principles of the relationship of demand and supply, another principle should prevail—the law of the satisfaction of human needs and the rational organization of economic strength. Supposing that the best system is formed without the interference of rational intention, by some instinct of the manufacturers, they deny the necessity of theory and accept the inviolability of practice (IV, 713).

Chernyshevskii attacked the theory of laissez faire (or as he called it, the "prevailing" or "old" school) on the two points that he considered least defensible: its general optimism, and its claim to be natural or inevitable. He could not come to terms with a theory that cited "iron laws" to explain the depressed condition of the working class, and yet taught that self-adjustment of the economic system would lead to overall benefit. Furthermore, Chernyshevskii chided those writers he called "apologists," who were so optimistic about the general benefits of a free-enterprise economy that they were callously insensitive to the system's real failings. In one of his earliest articles, for example, Chernyshevskii defended the main outlines of David Ricardo's pessimistic theory of rent against the mitigating revision of A. L'vov (II, 395–397). He lost no opportunity to underscore the capitalist system's shortcomings.

In regard to the view that a free, competitive economy was the only natural one, Chernyshevskii insisted on the importance of distinguishing between man and external nature. An economic system ought to correspond, not to blind external forces, but to human desires and needs. Man surely existed as part of nature, but he had the power at least to try to rework that nature to suit himself (V, 621). Thus, human reason must do what the system working by itself could not do—provide man with a better way of life.

As for the question of how this could be done, Chernyshevskii had neither the time nor the freedom to give a full answer up through the end of 1859. In February of that year, however, his article "Economic Activity and Legislation" had suggested action by the state that could help bring rationality into the economy. He argued that, since any action the state took or refused to take affected the economy, the state had the moral obligation to control the economy wherever necessary (V, 576–626).[28] Chernyshevskii shifted the rightful concern of the state from merely providing a secure context within which the economy could work, to participating actively in the economy to ensure national well-being. Elsewhere he defined national well-being as the greatest good for the greatest number (V, 583–589, 603–604).

In "Economic Activity and Legislation," Chernyshevskii's suggestions for state action fell generally within the limits of legislation in a modern welfare state. He proposed that the state correct gross inequalities of wealth, direct rather than operate the economy, and reconcile conflicts of interest. More specific references to socialism in industry had to await Chernyshevskii's writings in 1860, but in this article he did endorse the communal principle in agriculture and suggest that a "new school" of political economy was ready to replace the old school, based on private property and laissez faire. Earlier, he had hinted that the new school embodied the teachings of Robert Owen and Louis Blanc (V, 606, 615–620).

In several ways, Chernyshevskii's censure of laissez faire resembled his comments on the schools of Russian literature that had preceded the natural school of Gogol. Instead of condemning the doctrine in absolute terms, he admitted it had once been of value in combating the equally one-sided doctrine of mercantilism. Now, however, laissez faire had outlived its historic usefulness (V, 577–578). In Adam Smith's time, even England, not to mention the continental states, suffered from obsolete, medieval regimentation, which hindered the development of industry. At that time, the doctrine of laissez faire served a purpose. But in his own day, Chernyshevskii disapproved of the "old school" or "routine" economists, who continued to advocate laissez faire when the system of free enterprise had shown its harmful effects and clearly needed regulation (V, 589–590). These economists had reduced themselves to apologists for those who stood to profit from the system, at the expense of the mass of the people.

By the end of 1859, then, in addition to extensive writings on the reform question, Chernyshevskii had already expressed a number of his most important economic views. He recognized that, after the Crimean War, Russia faced the prospect of undergoing basic changes in her economic structure. He asked what these changes would be if rational decision did not lead to counteraction, and what these changes should be if social justice were realized. Confronted with the example of the West, Chernyshevskii criticized both the practice of the free-enterprise economy and the laissez-faire theory that defended it. He looked hopefully to a new theory, better suited to the needs of the day. These views, along with his desire to protect the immediate interests of the peasants, formed the background for Chernyshevskii's vigorous defense of the Russian village commune (obshchina).

With the general examination of Russia's social and economic institutions after the Crimean War, the village commune became a central point of discussion and disagreement. Earlier, impetus to consideration of the commune had been given by a Prussian student of agricultural affairs, Baron August von Haxthausen, who in 1848 published a large work on Russian rural life, *Studien über die innern Zustände, das Volksleben und inbesondere die ländlichen Einrichtungen Russlands*. By emphasizing the importance of the commune in the lives of the

Russian peasants, Haxthausen had brought the institution to the attention of Russian thinkers. Then in the late 1850's, such questions as how the commune had come into existence, its value, and whether it should have a place in Russia's future engaged many writers and evoked the most varied response. Seen as a mark of innate Russian virtue by the Slavophiles, the commune stood as a depressing symbol of backwardness and obstruction to those who hoped that Russia would follow the course of European industrialization.[29] For several years, Chernyshevskii added his voice to the chorus of discordant opinions.

From the outset, Chernyshevskii concerned himself with the practical question of the commune's utility. He objected to the view of B. N. Chicherin that the original patriarchal commune had lost its significance between the thirteenth and the sixteenth centuries, and that later government legislation on serfdom and taxation had been necessary to create the commune in its modern form (III, 644–650). Chernyshevskii held that Russia had maintained the ancient communal institution, not because of state action, nor because of some mysterious Slavic or national characteristics, but because the commune appeared to the peasants to serve their interests (IV, 334). However, the commune's origins were not Chernyshevskii's primary interest. Instead, he asked whether the commune still had worth in the present, or potential worth for the future.

When Chernyshevskii considered his country's situation in comparison with Western Europe, he admitted that Russia would no doubt long remain a predominantly agricultural country, even though it might soon be "fully in the sway of the laws of competition" (IV, 743–746). However, Russia need not accept the evils of a system merely because others had experienced them; men possessed the resources of human reason and free choice. Thus, Chernyshevskii looked to the peasant commune as a possible means to mitigate the pernicious effects private ownership had brought to the West. Realizing that his defense of the commune, a relic of former times, might appear close to Slavophile fantasies, he made a careful distinction: "The view of the commune which we defend belongs to Western learning and not to the Slavophiles. We presume that the

Slavophiles share [this view], and we say that, in this case, they are right only insofar as they agree with the truths and testimony of Western learning, neither more nor less" (IV, 617).

Chernyshevskii implied, by this reference to Western learning, that his defense of the commune had a dual purpose, which looked both to the existing situation in Russia and to Russia's long-range economic future. In the short run, the commune could save Russia from the "ulcer" of a landless proletariat. In this regard, he once proposed a compromise plan to protect those peasants least able to protect themselves. He suggested that the population could be considered in two groups: those who were inclined to venture and those who preferred security. To satisfy both, he envisaged an agricultural economy made up partly of state-owned communal land and partly of land in private possession. The state-owned communal sector would always be ready to receive those who needed land, and thus, pauperism would be avoided (IV, 437–438). But this plan certainly did not represent Chernyshevskii's ideal solution. In his hopes for Russia's long-range economic future, he looked to the "new school" of political economy in Western Europe, which taught that a new stage of socialist ownership would soon replace the reign of private property (IV, 389–391). Before 1860, Chernyshevskii did not spell out this agrarian socialism, but he compared it to the early stage of communal land ownership once common to all agricultural peoples, before the spread of private land ownership (V, 389–390). Following this line of reasoning, Chernyshevskii found his second justification for the commune. Apart from its immediate advantage as a protection against pauperism, since the latest theories of "Western learning" indicated the necessity of restoring the communal principle, the Russian village commune, far from being a backward liability, as some Westerners claimed, became a positive model. In one of his early articles in 1857, he wrote with immoderate enthusiasm that what Russia knew in practice, Western Europe knew only in theory. Correspondingly, the Russian masses held one advantage over European workers, in that they had not yet been seized by the desire for private property (IV, 738–743). Here, in essence, was the main contention of Russian populist socialism, that the very backwardness of Russia's economic development might facilitate Russia's attainment of a socialist society.

Chernyshevskii could make no clear statement on exactly how this higher stage of socialism would come about in Russia. He did, however, come close to an open expression of his views on the relationship of European to Russian socialism in his article "Critique of the Philosophical Prejudices Against Communal Possession," published in December 1858 (V, 357–392).[30] This work should not be taken as an example of a serious commitment to dialectical thinking in Chernyshevskii's world view, because he simply borrowed convenient phrases from Schelling and especially Hegel, to give authority to his proposition that the evolutionary development of social institutions unfolded in three or more stages, with the initial and final stages having basic similarities of form, albeit different levels of complexity (V, 363–364). Relying on this generalization, he examined the changing forms of land tenure, from primitive communal ownership to private ownership and then to a more advanced communal ownership, by which he meant socialism. He asked whether, if the cycle had run full course in one area, it was necessary for the same cycle to be repeated elsewhere. Arguing from analogy, and using such examples as the adoption of a modern invention by less advanced peoples, Chernyshevskii claimed that the same cycle need not be repeated, and that a shortcut might be taken. In this way, he implied that Russia did not have to go through the full phase of private ownership but might shorten, if not bypass, this step on the path to socialism (V, 387–390).[31]

As early as 1857, Chernyshevskii made it clear that communal ownership alone did not represent his final goal. He clarified his conception of socialism by suggesting a progressive application of the communal principle, which, although increasingly difficult to effect, would bring ever more beneficial results. First, communal ownership had to be gained; but to be fully effective, it must gradually develop into communal production; and as a final stage, the most difficult to attain, Chernyshevskii placed the goal of communal consumption (IV, 415).

Because of the limited opportunity to refer in print to the socialist writers of Western Europe, Chernyshevskii faced a formidable task in trying to defend the commune. He wished to avoid close reliance on Slavophile arguments, so he tried to meet the objections to the commune by liberal political economists on other grounds. He reduced the criticisms of the Western "old school" economists and their Russian followers to two basic thoughts: the commune hindered land improvement, and communal ownership sapped human energy (IV, 756).

Chernyshevskii found it relatively easy to defend the commune's long-term potential. He argued that the commune could avoid both of the failings evidenced in the private ownership system in the West—namely, separation of the agricultural worker from ownership (by tenantry or agricultural wage labor) and inability of the small private owner to use modern methods. By contrast, the commune member would consider the land as his own and would receive all the fruits of his efforts. Furthermore, if the commune could advance from the stage of communal ownership to communal production, its size would put it in the best possible position to employ modern, large-scale farm machinery (IV, 345). This analysis assumed that the commune would have clear title to all its land, but Chernyshevskii took pains to stress the positive advantages of the commune even in its present form. Left to themselves, the peasants had developed a system of exemplary fairness. Complex legal disputes, which were inherent in a system of private property, found no place in the commune. When disagreements arose, the truth of the matter was known to all the other commune members, and a settlement was reached quickly and fairly. This saved the government the concern of administrative interference (V, 615–619). He argued further that the commune should not be considered rigid and inflexible. Expressing more a statement of faith than a provable point, he affirmed that changes could be introduced into the communal system. One needed only to show the advantages of change to the peasants, and they would look after their own best interests (IV, 327).

Chernyshevskii could not easily defend the commune against the charge that it was both a symbol and a cause of economic backwardness. He could give no evidence to prove that the existing communes were more productive than privately owned land. Instead, he noted the commune's more equitable distribution. With elaborate calculation, he showed that other systems in Western Europe brought advantage to so few that they could not stand comparison with communal ownership (IV, 373–381). In one example, he compared two units of land of equal size but unequal productivity. He found the less productive unit preferable, because its communal organization permitted the most equitable distribution of the produce, and thus more people benefited (IV, 751).

Chernyshevskii's best line of defense, however, simply denied any causal relationship between the existence of the commune and the retarded economic position of Russia. He developed this argument most thoroughly in one of the last articles he wrote specifically on the commune, "Superstition and the Rules of Logic," in October 1859 (V, 686–710). The logic of a cause-effect relationship, he insisted, demanded more than a simple observation that two events occurred. Such an observation could lead to an erroneous connection between facts or events, which had no intrinsic relation, and the result would be superstition, not logic. He accused the "old school" economists of precisely this error. Though the weak development of Russian agriculture had to be admitted, "could it have reached a high degree [of development] whatever the system of land ownership? Do we have, right up to the present, even one of those conditions upon which the higher development of agriculture depends?" (V, 688). Chernyshevskii answered his question with a forceful no. By blaming communal ownership for a condition whose causes went much deeper, the "old school" economists had violated one of the basic rules of logic; they had too quickly joined an effect to a cause, without considering all of the factors to which the effect might be attributed. Chernyshevskii enumerated the many unfavorable factors that hindered Russian agriculture: a weak intellectual development among the people, exhaustion of the people's energy, the condition of serfdom, insufficient working capital, poorly developed trade and industry, little urban development, and a relatively low population density. The commune alone could not be made the whipping boy for Russia's agricultural backwardness (V, 696). In presenting his view of the real cause of the difficulty, Chernyshevskii went about as far as he could go in open condemnation of the Russian government:

> But if we wish to see a country in Europe, where the circumstances of agricultural production are more similar to ours, we must look at Turkey. Here it cannot be said that communal ownership holds up the success of agriculture.
> The word Turkey arouses in us a new thought, which unfortunately did not occur to us until now, [or] otherwise all our previous discussion would have been unnecessary. European Turkey, up to this time, remains an Asiatic state, even though it lies in Europe. Isn't that so? Thus we find the key to all we have discussed in detail, but now seems completely superfluous. An Asiatic way of life, an Asiatic structure of society, an Asiatic system—with these words all is said and nothing need be added. Is it possible for agriculture to take on a European character with this Asiatic system? (V, 698).

Thus Turkey, and by implication Russia, suffered from "Asiatic" backwardness. Lest his readers not understand the epithet "Asiatic," he tried in a subsequent paragraph, rejected by the censor, to explain it by reference to Dobroliubov's article "The Realm of Darkness," which analyzed the tyrannical and obscurantist nature of Russian society as expressed in Ostrovskii's plays. Chernyshevskii thereby tried to show that, rather than the commune, the chief cause of Russia's backwardness was lawlessness and serfdom, both the result of what he euphemistically called "poor administration."

Chernyshevskii wrote little more in specific defense of the commune after the latter part of 1859. He shifted his position on the question of whether the commune could simply be left alone to develop in its own way or, as he suggested in 1861, the government would have to intervene to protect it (IV, 460; IX, 725).[32] On the whole, however, Chernyshevskii's reasons for defending the commune remained constant throughout his writings. He wanted protection against the impending "ulcer" of a landless proletariat, and he harbored the hope that, in the future, the existing commune might somehow facilitate Russia's transition to socialism.[33]

The government's prohibition in 1860 of articles relating directly to the peasant reform may have helped to turn Chernyshevskii into a more dangerous opponent. As long as any hope remained that good might result from his reform efforts, he would probably have continued to write on the question, despite his discouragement. Had he done so, his articles would necessarily have proposed solutions having at least a chance of realization within an economic system of private ownership. When the government prohibited such attempts, Chernyshevskii redirected his efforts toward expounding economic theory, which, from his point of view, meant openly to endorse socialism. Nor did the government's censor do much to prevent him. Although a comparison of his articles on economic theory, as they appeared in *The Contemporary,* and recent Soviet editions, based on Chernyshevskii's original manuscripts, shows considerable deletions, they merely moderated his tone without altering his basic message.

In his writings on economic theory, Chernyshevskii sought a replacement for the theory of laissez faire, which he regarded as outmoded and unfair. His article "Capital and Labor," which appeared in the January 1861 issue of *The Contemporary,* argued that the workers needed a new theory of political economy to replace the theory of the capitalists (VII, 5–63). The two privileged classes (soslovie) of modern society each had theories that served their own best interests, to the exclusion of consideration for the "common people." Although historically in Western Europe, the landowning nobility's monopoly of power had been challenged successfully by the middle class, these two classes now possessed a common interest in opposition to the people, whose actual labor produced value in society. Underlying Chernyshevskii's discussion of economic theory was always this belief that the major division in society existed between those who profited from the labor of others and those who did

215

not receive the full measure of reward for their efforts. From this point of view, both land rent and interest on invested capital appeared unjustified (VII, 31–37).

In order to support the demand for a new theory, Chernyshevskii appealed to science and modern learning. He insisted that the first requirement of any theory, according to these authorities, was that it benefit the greatest possible number of persons (VII, 46). This requirement, in turn, dictated his major emphasis on the question of what kind of system assured the most equitable distribution of wealth and the products of human industry:

In fact, the theory of those who work (this is what we will call the theory corresponding to the needs of modern times, in contrast to the old, prevailing theory, which we will call the theory of the capitalists) turns its main attention to the problem of the division of value [tsennost']. The principle of division which is most advantageous is a combination of the statement of Adam Smith, that all value is exclusively the product of labor, and the rule of common sense, that production should belong to the one who produces it. The task is merely to uncover the type of economic system in which this demand of common sense may be fulfilled (VII, 43–44).

Perhaps Marx's praise of Chernyshevskii as a "great Russian scholar and critic" rested on the similarity of this kind of reasoning to Marx's own theory of surplus value.[34] But Chernyshevskii's theories and hopes for a future economy based on socialism all emphasized what ought to be, rather than what would inevitably come as a result of objective laws inherent in the system. Chernyshevskii saw contradictions as well as injustice in the capitalist system, but his insistent appeals to men to alter the economic system, in the name of reason and morality, prevent the full acceptance of his views by any consistent economic determinist.

As an alternative to the many failings that Chernyshevskii considered to be necessary parts of the competitive system of private ownership and wage labor, he fashioned a new theory around the principle of association, that is, the organization of workers in cooperatives (tovarishchestvo). If the competitive, capitalist economy could only produce luxury for a few, while others remained in want, Chernyshevskii tried to show that another system, based on cooperation, could plan production and distribution for the benefit of all. In the course of his writings, he made several references to cooperative associations of quite varied character.

In "Capital and Labor," Chernyshevskii described in some detail the model organization of a cooperative association engaged in both agriculture and industry. His debt to Louis Blanc and Charles Fourier appeared throughout. As he described this form of planned economy, he insisted that his proposal in no way restricted individual freedom, but rather, for the first time, offered the individual a freedom that had meaning because it was founded on material prosperity. Were such an ideal association to be set up, it might initially receive financial aid from the government, but such aid was necessary only to speed its formation.[35] Chernyshevskii added that the government already gave similar aid, in the form of subsidies, for the building of railroads. The proposed association, of about 400 or 500 families, would consist of perhaps 1500 to 2000 persons. The entrance and departure of members would be entirely voluntary, except that care would have to be taken by the corporate association to balance the skills of its members, and the group must have the right to expel any who would not work. Within the organization, communal needs, such as church, school, and library, would be supported by the association's funds; other joint undertakings, such as communal eating, might be optional for the members. Those who used the communal kitchen would enjoy lower living costs; families could make their own choice. Chernyshevskii suggested that leadership could at first be provided by a director, but by the second year, the whole association might decide whether or not to retain his services, much in the manner of the choice of director for a joint-stock company. Members of the association would receive two kinds of income, in addition to the services provided for all: their regular wages, differentiated according to the value of their work to the group as a whole; and annual dividends, which would be apportioned according to the number of days they worked during the year, but apparently paid at the same rate per day for all (VII, 58–63). Chernyshevskii painted the advantages of such an association in glowing terms. Rational planning would replace the many inefficiencies and inequalities of the existing competitive system, and perhaps even more important, the members would feel that they worked for their own benefit and not for the profit of others. In conclusion, he noted the blind opposition to these "simple" and "easy" proposals by economists of the "backward" school (VII, 63).

Three years later, in his novel *What Is To Be Done?* the principle of the cooperative association appeared in two different guises. The first example remained relatively close to reality. His heroine, Vera Pavlovna, having been awakened to the liberating ideas of the "new people," organized a successful association of seamstresses. The association not only achieved collective business prosperity in an otherwise competitive private economy, but its members learned the joys and economies of communal consumption as well (XI, 126–135). Why, after all, should each person own an umbrella, when everyone did not leave the common dwelling at one time when it rained? In this instance Chernyshevskii suggested a more modest and, if the police would not interfere, even realizable undertaking, which required no more than a right-minded entrepreneur, who could see advantage in larger terms than his income ledger, and who would turn as a friend to employees, show them their own best interests, and return the profit of the enterprise to the rightful owners.

In contrast, Chernyshevskii's second example of association in *What Is To Be Done?* was truly fantastic. In Vera Pavlovna's fourth dream, she envisaged a glorious utopia based on the principle of association, in which the desert was transformed into a blossoming garden, and the land of milk and honey (translated into nineteenth-century images of aluminum and glass) finally achieved (XI, 269–284). Chernyshevskii's message was clearly that the competitive system of private ownership had produced luxury for the few and misery for the masses, whereas the new socialist society, based on cooperative association, promised abundance for all. Chernyshevskii's novel exhorted youth to love the dream of a better future and to work for its realization.[36]

Chernyshevskii scarcely intended these examples, as well as other scattered references to the basic ideas of socialism and cooperative association, to be exact blueprints for a future society. He wanted to popularize a principle, which he hoped and expected would become the basis of European and Russian life in the years to come. He would have needed more freedom than was available to speak in detail of when, or exactly how, these changes might take place. Quite possibly, he did not even think in more specific terms, because any hope of fulfillment seemed distant, especially in the case of Russia. In his "Anthropological Principle in Philosophy," Chernyshevskii referred to the possible triumph of "new principles" of social life in Western Europe by men of his own generation. But he admitted that, even in the West, probably little more could be achieved than to pave the way for the next generation (VII, 254).[37]

There is no evidence to indicate that Chernyshevskii ever credited his examples of the principle of association with great significance. In later years, when he looked back over his career, he saw his own achievement not in his utopian plans, but in his attempt to justify the principle of association by means of a scientific critique of bourgeois political economy.[38]

In the article "Capital and Labor," published early in 1860, Chernyshevskii had summarized the major conclusions of his new theory of political economy "for those who work." However, he did not develop his ideas fully or offer extensive argument until later that year and in 1861, in his comments on John Stuart Mill's *Principles of Political Economy*.[39] Initially, he intended to make a complete translation of the fourth edition of Mill's *Principles*, but after translating the first book and adding critical notes, Chernyshevskii presented the following four books in the form of selections and summary, mixed with his own comments.

Chernyshevskii's fundamental approach to questions of political economy suited well the needs of a social critic and publicist. He assumed the existence of what he called economic laws, which met the "scientific" demands of reason, and which could be used as standards to evaluate the capitalist system and the theory of the classical economists.[40] He wanted to show that the classical economists had accepted certain characteristics of the capitalist system, which were in fact unreasonable and therefore unscientific, as if they were immutable laws. The meaning Chernyshevskii actually gave to the words "unreasonable" and "unscientific" would have been more accurately expressed by the word "nonutilitarian." Equating reason and goodness, he wrote: "Science views all objects from the humanitarian or social point of view. It must therefore be evident that when it [science] speaks of benefit, the benefit to society is meant, otherwise the sense of the word would be limited by a definite restriction" (IX, 155). This basic message appeared throughout his comments on Mill, but nowhere more clearly than in his emphasis on equitable distribution when defining political economy. Lacking a more precise definition, he feared lest a description of political economy as the "investigation of the means and conditions for the increase of wealth" be taken as a concern to increase the number of wealthy persons or the amount of wealth possessed by each of them. This conclusion, in Chernyshevskii's view, would be tantamount to accepting the necessity, or inevitability, of huge differences in wealth among members of society. Consequently, he defined political economy as "the science of man's material well-being, inasmuch as it depends on objects and conditions produced by labor" (IX, 30–31). This definition paved the way for discrediting the competitive economy founded on private property.[41] It also fit in well with his statement, made elsewhere, that the theory of distribution constituted the main subject of political economy, and that production was considered by political economy only insofar as it prepared material for distribution (VII, 21).

Rarely in his career did Chernyshevskii waste kind words on writers who did not share his views. He called Mill "second rank" in comparison to scholars in general, and yet, in the particular field of political economy, he also called him a "remarkable thinker" (VII, 229). Perhaps Chernyshevskii sensed Mill's honest pursuit of truth, which he did not detect in those writers he called the "routine economists" or the "apologists" of his day, and he surely appreciated Mill's refusal to accept the inevitability of poverty for the working class (VII, 39–40). But he had another reason for basing his own analysis on Mill's *Principles*. He wrote, in the preface to his translation, that everyone recognized Mill's work as the best presentation of the "theory based on Adam Smith." Although Chernyshevskii could not accept this theory as his own, he hoped that part of the work done by the classical economists might serve as the basis for "further conclusions" (IX, 7).[42]

Chernyshevskii's favorite method of analysis—the hypothetical method—proved to be better as a technique of polemic than as a tool of investigation, and it has been a source of embarrassment to some of his warmest supporters.[43] He paid only lip service to the usual methods of the political economist: measurement and calculation. An example of his application of these techniques to specific problems is his analysis of the repeal of the Corn Laws in England, where he argued that since one could measure a larger per capita consumption of grain after the repeal, it could be judged advantageous. However, Chernyshevskii believed that many problems relating to the economy could not be solved in this way, because statistical evidence was often the result of so many variable factors that the meaning of the data could not be readily established. Rather than pursue empirical evidence and then undertake what seemed a hopeless task of separating significant factors from the complex whole, he resorted to the hypothetical method, whose main feature was deductive reasoning. He sought to evaluate a given factor in the economy by exploring its function in an abstract hypothetical model set up to suit the needs of the question. In his abstract model, he could trace the effect of variation in one factor while holding all other factors constant—a situation that never could exist in reality. Separated from the confusion of an actual situation, the truth, he claimed, would be more apparent. To explain his method, he gave as example the question of whether Great Britain had benefited from its conflict with France during the period of the Revolutionary and Napoleonic Wars. Chernyshevskii proposed that first a solution be found to the general hypothetical question of whether war could be beneficial to a large nation, and that then this answer be applied to the specific problem. He easily showed that in a hypothetical model, if one-fifth of the labor force went to war, the remaining workers had more people to support. Therefore, in general, war was harmful to the welfare of society, and thus the particular series of wars must also have been harmful. Chernyshevskii insisted that any counterevidence, such as in this case the growth of British industry and trade during the wars, must have another explanation. The conclusions reached by the hypothetical method remained valid (IX, 58–62).

It is no discredit to Chernyshevskii to note that the manner in which he used the hypothetical method placed a tremendous power of choice in the hands of the person making the analysis. The one setting up the conditions of the hypothetical case decided, in effect, what the truth would be. In many ways, this suited his purposes; it permitted him to criticize capitalism on the basis of his own deductive reasoning, rather than an exact, empirical study of conditions in the West.[44]

In his discussion of production, capital, and labor, Chernyshevskii emphasized and elaborated his basic affirmation that production came from the efforts of labor and, therefore, rightfully belonged to those who worked. He denied the dominance of capital over labor by redefining capital itself. His argument distinguished between useful labor and detrimental labor. Useful labor created products that increased socially desirable future production. These included new machinery and also the support and education of workers, who in turn created new production. Detrimental labor, by contrast, concentrated on the production of luxury items or anything harmful to the physical, intellectual, and moral strength of man. The wrong kind of social institutions would misdirect potentially useful labor, but if not misdirected, useful labor produced capital, since Chernyshevskii defined capital as the products of labor that served future production. He objected to the terminology of the school of Adam Smith, which described capital formation in terms of saving and thereby suggested that the person who saved should be rewarded. Instead, Chernyshevskii stressed the need to use the products of labor in a rational way. The "correct" laws of political economy required that the products of labor be used for the general social advantage. He clearly implied that the competitive bourgeois economy could never meet this demand (IX, 153–164).

Chernyshevskii further underscored the inadequacy of the competitive economy in his discussion of distribution. Despite agreement with Mill on the functioning of specific parts of the existing system, he attacked the whole principle of a three-part division of the economy's total product into rent, profits, and wages. What he called the "demands of economic theory" condemned this division as a harmful interplay of antagonistic interests:

Theory says that the success of labor depends on the quality of work, that is, on the quality of the worker. Theory takes as an axiom that the best possible qualities of man depend on [his] well-being. Consequently the success of labor depends on the well-being of the worker. With the three-part division [of the product] wages cannot be satisfactory, the worker cannot be good. Profits, in this type of division, leave the worker as small a share of the product as possible.

Theory says that profits should serve as the stimulation to activity and thriftiness. With the three-part division, profits always develop to an excessive degree, which plunges men into laziness and dissipation.

Theory is concerned with the removal of obstacles to industrial progress. A system that separates rent from workers' wages and profits creates, in rent, a force which is hostile to progress.

These characteristics are found in the very nature of the three-part division of the product. It is incompatible with the demands of economic theory, not in one of its chance parts, but in its very essence. The contradiction with science and with the conditions of human well-being rests not in details, which might be changed while preserving the principle, but in the principle of the three-part system of division itself (IX, 516–517).

Perhaps this passage, as much as any other in Chernyshevskii's work on Mill, shows his basic approach. He considered his work to be a scientific contribution because, from a utilitarian point of view, he had defined "correct" economic theory as that which offered maximum material advantage to the greatest number of persons, and he had shown how far the competitive economy fell short of this ideal.

Chernyshevskii extended the argument that the capitalist system did not satisfy human needs to many points of detail: the system's inability to use resources rationally, its reduction of the worker to the position of a commodity in the market, its waste of time and effort in trade transactions, and its production of luxury goods before necessities were availat 'e to all (IX, 420, 544, 596, 603). In each case, he insisted that these shortcomings could be overcome in a society based on the principle of association, rather than on private ownership and competition. At the same time, he tried to show certain self-destructive tendencies within the capitalist system. But his identification of such tendencies was not made part of a coherent theory propounding capitalism's necessary collapse from within.[45] Instead, his long-range hope for human betterment rested on a belief that the mass of people would not always remain content with a depressed condition. In some unpublished notes to Mill's *Principles*, written at the same time, Chernyshevskii wrote that neither socialism nor the more extreme communism would have an early or painless triumph, but history was moving in that direction. He pointed to the great procession of the Chartists and to the June Days on the streets of Paris as evidence of a movement that ultimately would triumph. The irresistible spread of enlightenment, he claimed, made this expectancy neither "fanatical nor utopian." To underscore his point, Chernyshevskii observed:

Literacy and education are increasing gradually among the people, [and] . . . because of this the people are coming to understand their own human worth, to distinguish favorable things and institutions from those unfavorable to them, and to think about their needs. How can this even be doubted? And if this indubitable historical law brings some inconvenience to our routine, or some disadvantageous consequences for our interests, then, however one tries to avoid it, the course of history will not be stayed (IX, 833).

224

An evaluation of the significance of Chernyshevskii's writings on economics must distinguish between articles devoted to immediate questions of reform and government policy, and articles arguing the case for socialism. In the reform articles, despite his fundamental opposition to the Russian system, Chernyshevskii generally proposed responsible, constructive solutions for specific issues, in line with his utilitarian position. He consistently favored the many over the few, and he refused to allow general considerations of economic growth to overshadow a humanitarian concern for the material condition of the common people. His proposals had little influence except among the radicals, who considered that the very failure of his constructive efforts was proof that no progress could be expected so long as the existing system remained intact. Chernyshevskii's other articles, however, which argued the case for socialism, left a lasting imprint on the whole tradition of Russian social thought.

As Marx used the term "utopian," Chernyshevskii must be considered a utopian socialist.[46] One of the most convincing points in Alexander Kucherov's study of Chernyshevskii's economic views is that Chernyshevskii never overcame his vacillating attitude toward the central problem of whether changes in economic systems depended on the necessity of an objective historical process or on the free choice of rational men. He varied his position according to the needs of his immediate argument. At times, he would stress historical necessity in explaining the origins of the Western system of private enterprise; elsewhere he seemed to view the system as a historical misfortune, the result of man's wickedness and foolishness.[47] So, too, he thought that the capitalist system necessarily brought disaster and was doomed to destruction, yet he pleaded with men to choose socialism, because of its rationality and ability to satisfy human needs. Chernyshevskii called the triumph of socialism a "historical law," essentially because he believed that the gradual spread of enlightenment would make the mass of people less willing to accept injustice. If this particular emphasis on the power of ideas to achieve historical change differed from one strain in Marxism, Chernyshevskii's desire to see Russia avoid, or mitigate, the capitalist phase of development differed from another. Lenin, for example, once classified Chernyshevskii as a utopian socialist, because he believed that Chernyshevskii charted a path to socialism through the "old semifeudal peasant commune," without realizing that the only path was through a full development of capitalism.[48]

Chernyshevskii would probably have objected to this classification, at least insofar as the term utopian implied that he placed his hopes in the goodness of men. In 1860 he criticized the socialism of the St. Simonians because they appealed to a brotherhood based on love rather than self-interest (VII, 168–170). Chernyshevskii fervently believed in the "scientific" significance of his doctrine of rational egoism, or enlightened self-interest, which he felt gave his projections of a socialist future a scientific validity not shared by the dreams of the utopians. But beyond his demonstration that only a socialist system could meet the requirements of rationality, and his assumption that when men realized their own best interests they would inevitably pursue them, Chernyshevskii developed no coherent theory to prove that his vision in fact represented the wave of the future.

Franco Venturi's recent study of the Russian revolutionary movement is organized around an expanded definition of the word populist, which includes not only the particular movement "to the people" in the 1870's, but the entire tradition of Russian writers who sought to establish socialism by means other than following the experience of the West.[49] Chernyshevskii may be said to belong to this larger populist tradition, but only with qualifications. Clearly he shared the central populist belief that subjective choice, rather than objective necessity, could direct Russia along the path to socialism. In his view, the grim experience of Western Europe warned against Russia's acceptance of an economic development based on private ownership and competition. He therefore urged an attempt to stave off dissolution of the peasant commune, because its underlying communal principle resembled the socialism that was his goal. To some extent he recognized the "advantage of backwardness," in that a desire for private ownership did not yet seem to be widespread among the Russian peasantry.

But against these points of agreement with what is generally taken as the tradition of populist socialism, one must place other views of Chernyshevskii that leave a somewhat different impression. He shared none of the illusions of some populists about the special character and worth of "the people," nor about Russia's unique ability to inspire the West with socialist ideas.[50] Indeed, he wrote one of his bitterest articles against Herzen on this very question. Under the guise of a review of Guizot's *Histoire de la civilisation en France,* published in 1861, Chernyshevskii argued that, far from being exhausted, Western Europe in the nineteenth century still possessed abundant creative forces and needed no revolutionary assistance from the Russian peasant. In much of Europe, the middle class had not yet secured its own power, and the mass of the population had only begun to enter historical life (VII, 663–666).

Both Russia and the West faced the same task of achieving a level of understanding in which socialism would be recognized as the only rational form of social organization. If Russia enjoyed the "advantage of backwardness" because the institution of the commune had survived so long, she nevertheless had the distinct disadvantage of a lower level of general enlightenment.[51] Although in practice, Chernyshevskii took part in the abortive revolutionary movement of the early 1860's, in his writings he never overcame one outstanding contradiction. Russia's opportunity to find a shortcut to socialism had its origins in the same conditions of general backwardness that prevented a sufficient number of Russians from appreciating the latest achievements of learning and recognizing rationality. This dilemma may help to explain the skepticism, noted by some of Chernyshevskii's acquaintances, in his view of the popular movement in Russia.[52]

# VIII. Politics and the Theory of Revolution

Insofar as the accession of Alexander II raised hope for progressive reform in Russia, after the humiliating defeat of the Crimean War, it also provided the setting for a more precise differentiation of political views. After the hopeless political stagnation of Nicholas I's reign, the possibility of change stimulated a consideration of alternatives by opponents of Russia's bureaucratic autocracy. Questions concerning the proper direction of reform, how quickly it might be achieved, and how it might be implemented no longer appeared as distant, unrealistic speculation. Furthermore, the growing expectation of change led to more serious consideration of ways of forcing improvement, should the government's attempts falter, and, as a consequence, produced the first appreciable signs of revolutionary thought and action since the days of the Decembrists.

The late 1850's and early 1860's witnessed the definition of points of view, rather than the formation of anything resembling political parties. Several decades were to pass before changes in the Russian economy and social structure provided the base for organized party activity, either liberal or socialist. But the development of a radical political point of view, and the abortive attempts to organize conspiratorial groups, did have undeniable significance during Alexander's reign, even though they were restricted to a relatively small segment of the intellectual elite. The best reform efforts of the tsar were inadequate to stave off the growth of an implacable revolutionary movement, which, however unsuccessful in its own time, became a constant source of inspiration and guidance to revolutionary socialists in the decades that followed. Attempts at open revolutionary action that were futile and often unrealistic, nonetheless helped to make more sophisticated the whole discussion of revolutionary tactics. At the same time, the revolutionary attempts of the 1860's helped to frustrate the hopes of moderate reformers and to influence the government toward a more reactionary policy. Behind the new revolutionary movement stood a set of radical assumptions and expectations, in whose formation Chernyshevskii's writings on politics played no small part.

Yet Chernyshevskii's writings present difficult problems in deciding exactly what he meant, for he could not state his opinions as openly and systematically in this area as he could in philosophy, aesthetics, and economics. The censorship was most sensitive and restrictive in areas that touched directly on royal power. To the end of expressing whatever he could of his political ideas, Chernyshevskii employed book reviews on historical subjects, essays on recent European history (extensive parts of which were translations or close copies of works that originally appeared in Western Europe), and, beginning in 1859, a monthly section in *The Contemporary* entitled "Politics" devoted primarily to analysis of political news from abroad.[1] The total impact of these writings gave support to the revolutionary movement of the early 1860's. However, it is important to determine whether he varied his tactics during the course of his career, and whether at times he considered something short of a complete revolutionary overturn as a realistic alternative to autocracy in the immediate future.[2]

The difficulty is that the answers to this kind of question are most often found between the lines of what he actually wrote. Certainly he used comments on political affairs abroad to pass specific judgment on the Russian scene.[3] Yet from another point of view, if one consistently assumes that his sole motive was revolutionary agitation, and that the revolutionary ardor ex-

pressed in his student diary remained at equal intensity throughout his career, it is possible to read too much into these works.
Hints may be found that go beyond Chernyshevskii's intention,
and certainly go beyond what contemporary readers could have
seen in his articles.[4]

One further consideration is that Chernyshevskii wrote these
articles with several purposes in mind. Without doubt, he often
sought specifically to criticize the Russian autocracy and what
he considered the ineffectual or hypocritical moderation of
Russian liberals. But he was also seriously concerned with the
general level of political sophistication among his readers. He
wanted to add to their general knowledge and their awareness
of the political changes that were rocking midcentury Europe.
He did so by means of generalized statements about the political
conduct of established authorities, opposition parties, and
classes. Exactly when Chernyshevskii intended the generalization to stand in its own right, as an aid to his reader's overall
understanding, and when he used the generalization as a mask
for a specific statement about the situation in Russia, is a question that must constantly be raised.

There is evidence to indicate that, as a result of limitations
placed on the full expression of his ideas, Chernyshevskii's
writings on politics occasionally left an impression other than
what he intended. One such example ties in with interpretations
of his work which suggest that, in his pursuit of material advantage for the underprivileged, he was relatively unconcerned
with institutional forms and political freedom.[5] In memoirs
describing his own Siberian imprisonment, S. G. Stakhevich
recorded part of a conversation he had with Chernyshevskii in
the late 1860's, when Stakhevich was surprised to hear Chernyshevskii take a theoretical position decidedly in favor of political
liberty. Stakhevich claimed that young people like himself,
whose political views had taken shape largely under the influence of *The Contemporary*, generally felt that political forms
by themselves were unimportant. They believed that a constitution and a republic did not necessarily guarantee the well-being
of people, any more than absolutism necessarily condemned
people to misery. To sentiments of this kind, Chernyshevskii

230

apparently responded heatedly: "You say, gentlemen, that political freedom cannot feed a hungry man. That is perfectly true. But really, can air, for example, feed a man? Naturally not. Yet without food man can live for several days, without air he cannot last even ten minutes. Just as air is necessary for the life of an individual man, so political liberty is necessary for the just life of a human society." [6] When Stakhevich asked Chernyshevskii directly why, in his articles, he had often written about political forms with scorn, Chernyshevskii replied evasively that it was sometimes necessary to write that way. He might better have said that, in the context of discussions in the late 1850's and early 1860's, he had wanted to show not that political liberty and democratic political forms were unimportant, but that alone they were inadequate, and that those who favored them might not really wish to serve the general good.

The source of confusion for young readers like Stakhevich may be seen in several of Chernyshevskii's articles. For example, in 1858 in the opening pages of "The Party Struggle in France," he defined his basic understanding of the liberal, democratic, and radical positions. He identified liberalism with the politics of Guizot, whom he called doctrinaire and out of date. Like the medieval scholastics, the liberals denied fact with their insistence on outworn formulas. Suited better to the time of the Bourbon restoration than the present day, the liberals added confusion and absurdity to political life and brought hardship to the mass of people, for whose welfare they insincerely claimed concern. The liberals, according to Chernyshevskii, limited their demands to issues of free speech and constitutional organization, desiring no change in the class (soslovie) structure to allow the lower classes more benefits and political power. Liberals feared that true democratic control would be antithetical to the freedoms they valued so highly (V, 215–216).

In this fear, liberals differed from democrats, who wanted to destroy the mastery of the higher classes over the lower in society. Democrats, Chernyshevskii claimed, cared little about the means used to change society, so long as the strength and wealth of the lower classes was increased. The democrat placed

Siberia above England, for example, because in Siberia the common people enjoyed well-being, whereas in England most people endured severe want. Democrats categorically denied only one social form, that of aristocracy. By contrast, liberals often found some degree of aristocracy suitable to their needs (V, 216).

Chernyshevskii defined radicalism, not as attachment to one or another political form, but as a belief that the most important inadequacies of society could be corrected only by completely remaking its basis.[7] Radicalism was not concerned with the correction of trifling details. Its adherents were prepared to use force to achieve significant change and were even prepared to sacrifice freedom of speech and constitutional forms to achieve their ends. Thus, radicalism seemed least compatible with liberalism (V, 216–217).

Turning to the questions of parliaments and free speech, Chernyshevskii further showed his overriding and immediate concern for the material needs of people. He did not deny the principle of popular representation, but he objected to the parliaments of recent European history, particularly to that of France in the July Monarchy. Liberals, Chernyshevskii maintained, believed that the necessary conditions of political freedom were a free press and the existence of parliamentary rule. But in the current condition of Europe, since true freedom of expression would have been used for democratic and radical propaganda, the liberals restricted free expression. The same kind of limitation applied to parliaments. If parliaments had consisted of representatives of the nation in the broadest sense of the term, parliamentary debates would perforce have taken on a radical-democratic character. Fearing this, liberals limited representation to those who were well off in the present structure of society. In this light, the value of liberalism was relative to one's status in society.

From the theoretical side, liberalism may appear attractive for a person delivered by good fortune from material needs: liberty is a very agreeable thing. But liberalism understands liberty very narrowly, in a purely formal way. Liberty for him consists in abstract rights, resolutions on paper, in the absence of juridical prohibitions. He does not want to understand that legal resolutions have value for a man only if the man has the material means to make use of that resolution. Neither I, nor you, reader, are forbidden to dine on a golden service, but unfortunately neither you, nor I, really will ever have the means to satisfy this exquisite idea; therefore I say frankly that I value my right to have a golden service so little, that I am prepared to sell this right for a single silver ruble, or even less. All those rights that the liberals fuss over are the same way for the people. The people are ignorant and in almost all countries the majority of them are illiterate: not having the money to get education, not having the money to give education to their children, how can they value the right of free speech? Want and ignorance deprives the people of all opportunity to understand state affairs and to be engaged with them. Tell me, will they value, can they use the right of parliamentary debate? (V, 217).

With his emphasis on the material needs of all members of society, Chernyshevskii risked leaving the impression that he was unconcerned with the particular form of political institutions necessary to achieve his goals. In 1860, he noted in "The July Monarchy" that the common people (prostoliudi) in France had repeatedly switched allegiance when they realized that the various governments in power did nothing to aid their situation. He argued that these governments could have had mass support if they had acted differently, because in essence the masses were indifferent to political forms (VII, 153). But it would be wrong to conclude that Chernyshevskii himself shared this indifference. He tried also to show that no political group could profit long from policies that were contrary to the interests of the whole society. Moreover, the general tenor of his writings suggested that no small ruling group had ever learned this lesson, nor probably ever would. Even if the masses had not yet shown a well-developed political sense, they would have to develop one in the future. Help could be expected from no other quarter; the masses would have to learn to look out for their own best interests, just as smaller groups in the past had looked out only for themselves. Thus, although Chernyshevskii, by necessity or by choice, never wrote in detail about the political forms that someday would be created to suit the needs of the people, his writings clearly implied the need for broad-based democracy.[8]

Consistent with this belief in the long-range necessity of mass participation in the control of government, Chernyshevskii throughout his career on *The Contemporary* maintained a critical attitude toward autocratic, monarchical rule. Though the opportunity to state his position varied with censorship conditions and his own choice of emphasis in his work, he never returned to the hope expressed in his student diary that the monarchy might rise above class interests and use its authority to serve the weaker members of society. He employed every conceivable technique to discredit the institution of monarchy, both in general and in its specific manifestation in Russia. It would be an exaggeration to claim that he thereby cut himself off entirely from tactical maneuvers or statements that might look to partial improvement within the overall framework of the existing system.[9] Yet no contemporary reader who looked at his writings with any degree of regularity and attention could have drawn any other conclusion from Chernyshevskii's political works than the ultimate need to destroy traditional autocratic power.

Up to the end of 1857, Chernyshevskii's comments on the institution of monarchy were quantitatively few and qualitatively less daring than in the years that followed.[10] In works like his study of Lessing or his review of V. P. Botkin's *Letters on Spain* in 1856 and 1857, Chernyshevskii tried to point out how autocratic governments stood in the way of national prosperity. These governments oppressed the population with heavy taxation and needless expenditures, and seemed unable to rule except in a corrupt, arbitrary way.[11] Probably not all readers made an immediate connection between his negative comments on an institution abroad and the comparable institution in Russia, but in retrospect, it is difficult to think that Chernyshevskii did not have that association in mind. Occasionally, he gave what seem now to have been hints, although these were of a decidedly cautious character, and they might easily have been missed by his readers.[12] On one occasion, in a letter to Nekrasov, he described his intention to write on subjects in pre-Petrine

Russia "which had a relationship to the present day" (XIV, 340). The article in question, however, described aspects of Russian life in the seventeenth century as seen by foreign writers, and although much of what they noticed was backward and obscurantist, the article was not simply an attack on autocracy. Chernyshevskii described Peter the Great, who was certainly no less an autocrat than the tsars of the seventeenth century, as a progressive force of change (IV, 246–262).

Chernyshevskii made one of his strongest points of condemnation in what purported to be a literary review of M. E. Saltykov's *Provincial Sketches,* published in 1857 (IV, 263–302). Pursuing the question of the low level of provincial morality as raised by Saltykov's stories, he argued that one could not rightfully blame an individual for misconduct because the given setting in which he found himself colored all his decisions. To the degree that Chernyshevskii succeeded in relieving the individual of guilt, he by implication blamed the system or, as he preferred to call it, the "false situation" in which the individual found himself. One suspects that it did not take an unusually perceptive reader to realize that he was arguing for a fundamental change in the Russian social organization and government.

Around the time of Alexander's rescripts on the peasant question in late 1857 and early 1858, Chernyshevskii employed a temporary tactic of constructive encouragement to the government's move toward serf reform.[13] He gave a warm reception to the publication of the rescripts, and his series of articles on the serf question was apparently directed toward a positive improvement within the system. Further evidence of this conciliatory tactic may be found in an article that is sometimes referred to as proof of a completely opposite intent. In October 1857, on the eve of Alexander's first rescript, Chernyshevskii published a commentary on a speech by I. K. Babst on the means of increasing national capital or prosperity. With the aid of quotations from Babst, he stressed the point that the greatest obstacle to the growth of national wealth was inadequate civic institutions (IV, 492). By his use of Babst's references to "poor administration," "arbitrary extortion," and "despotic and arbitrary rule," Chernyshevskii implied a severe attack on the Russian government. But in the following pages, he quoted with apparent approval from the writings of Jeremy Bentham to the effect that intelligent action by the state to improve its basic laws could ward off change by "historical events," a euphemism Chernyshevskii used here in place of revolution. He took special pains to stress the advantage to the state of peaceful change, as well as the fact that Bentham's advice could be followed by states regardless of their forms of government (IV, 495). If one considers that the contemporary reader did not know of Chernyshevskii's student diary, nor of the more daring expressions of a revolutionary position that he would make in the next few years, it is difficult to think that Chernyshevskii intended these words to fall within an unbroken line of revolutionary agitation, as some writers have claimed.[14] The reference to Bentham may be described more accurately as part of his temporary tactic of encouraging any immediate improvement in the people's condition.

The course of the reform preparation, which Chernyshevskii viewed as nothing short of disastrous, did not alter his fundamental opinion of absolute monarchy, because there is no evidence that in these years he considered the monarchy with anything but contempt. By 1859, however, he was taking risks he had not taken earlier, and in the expectation of a violent outburst by the peasants, he was engaging in what increasing numbers of his contemporaries could recognize as barely disguised revolutionary agitation. The low opinion of Austria in Russia, because of her refusal to give support during the Crimean War, probably facilitated Chernyshevskii's use of the Hapsburg monarchy as an example of the evils of absolutism.[15] Almost everything he wrote about Austria applied equally well to Russia, and yet his articles passed censorship. He dwelt on the point that the very nature of absolutism prevented reform. In the fall of 1859, Chernyshevskii chided the Austrian liberals for their belief in their government's promises to eliminate corruption and create a more enlightened administration. Playing on the parallel to Russia after the Crimean War, he called the Austrian government's promises "meaningless phrases," spoken in the embarrassment of military failure in Italy. But Austria, he asserted, had suffered no setbacks severe enough to force serious reforms from the government. Perhaps if Austria had lost the Tyrol or Bohemia, or if the enemy had reached the gates of Vienna, those in power might have felt stronger pressure for change. As it turned out, the government pacified its critics with a few minor changes, while it remained basically "obscurantist." The Austrian government continued to rely on armed force to support its despotism and persecution of free thought. It ruled through a bureaucracy, overburdened its people with taxes, and squandered the nation's wealth on the army and court luxury (VI, 406–409).

Early in 1861, in an article on the proper role of credit in state finances, Chernyshevskii made the parallel between Austria and Russia even more obvious. He contrasted England, a financially sound state that could use credit for economic expansion, with Austria, whose many worthless expenditures forced it to live off borrowed money. Chernyshevskii pointed to two of Austria's most wasteful institutions: the unproductive standing army, used largely to maintain internal order, and the equally unproductive bureaucracy. He charged that the bureaucracy constituted Austria's main problem and demonstrated the need of a basic change (VII, 525–536). Several pages later, this time openly discussing Russia's credit situation, Chernyshevskii suggested the radical reforms of taxing all land and luxury items, as well as taxing according to ability to pay. At the same time, he noted that real savings could be made, with no consequent disadvantage, in expenses for the army and the bureaucracy (VII, 552). Since Chernyshevskii's censors, unlike many of his readers, were unable to connect hints placed several pages apart, they let pass criticism of Russia's bureaucratic government and its worthless expenditures that were no more disguised than these.

It is possible, of course, for even the most severe criticism and condemnation to take diverse forms. One can gauge the full measure of Chernyshevskii's revolutionary position only by examining the critical comments he made on the actions of

European liberals and, by implication and sometimes direct statement, on the actions of those in Russia who placed hope in moderate and peaceful reform. In this examination, it is important to distinguish between his overall evaluation of liberalism, and his comments on specific liberal tactics in opposing autocracy.

At no time did Chernyshevskii soften the criticism inherent in his definition of liberalism given in "The Party Struggle in France." Yet it is also true that this condemnation pointed to the deficiencies of liberalism as a complete solution to the needs of the majority of any nation; it did not deny a relative advantage of liberalism over autocracy. One can find ample evidence in Chernyshevskii's other writings on political affairs that if it were a choice between the liberal alternative of constitutional rule, with relative civil liberties, and the arbitrary rule of bureaucratic autocracy, his preference was liberalism. For example, he realized the limitation of representation in the English parliament, which prevented that institution from dealing fairly with the relations between factory owners and workers because only one side enjoyed political representation (IV, 800). But in relative terms, he also showed clear preference for the English form of rule over that of continental powers, and in one direct comparison of Queen Victoria to Napoleon III, he explained that parliamentary approval made Victoria's commands the more likely to be fulfilled (VI, 172–173). Chernyshevskii made similar statements of relative preference when he discussed Italian affairs. His own political views were far removed from those of Cavour, whose tactics he also frequently criticized, but he preferred Cavour to other ministers who would have been further to the right (VI, 426). In one statement of his preference, the word Russia may be readily substituted for Austria.

We have no doubt that the Sardinian principle of government, with all of its imperfections, with all of its present evasions of concern for bettering the material share of the people, all the same, is a million times better than the Austrian. [The Austrian principle of government] by its very nature combines oppression of the people in a material sense with oppression of the people in a moral and intellectual sense, while the Sardinian principle is essentially obliged to turn toward a betterment of the people's way of life, even though it temporarily evades this responsibility because of chance circumstances (VI, 366–367).

Perhaps the closest Chernyshevskii came to a theoretical statement on the relationships among defenders and opponents of the existing order appeared in his "Politics" for August 1859 (VI, 337–340). This analysis began with the assertion, so often found in his writings on economic questions, that the main division in European society was between those who lived off the labor of others and those who lived off their own labor. The first group prospered; the second lived in want.[16] This division according to material interests, which was the most important concern of man, also found expression in politics. Chernyshevskii's description of the political arena, however, did not suggest a simple confrontation between haves and have nots. Among those who were currently active in European and, by implication, Russian political life, he drew a fundamental distinction between defenders of the existing order and reformers. Defenders of the present order, realizing that it would be dangerous to allow reformers to create an alliance with the masses of people, whose needs had for so long been neglected, took measures to prevent such an alliance, which earned them the title of obscurantists or, as Chernyshevskii called them, reactionaries. The reactionaries thus fought for their material interests. The reformers were defined only as people who had a strong intellectual and moral development, were tormented by the sight of injustice and illegality, and therefore wanted change. Although the reformers understood change in a different way from the masses, whose concerns were material, Chernyshevskii seemed to grant that reformers wanted changes that were to the people's benefit.

Because they were few in number and not strong in themselves, the reformers tried to find support among the people. When reactionaries sought to prevent this, the reformers divided into two groups, according to the tactics to be employed. One group, in ordinary times the largest, tried to argue with the reactionaries and make them understand the value of progressive change. This group Chernyshevskii called the moderates. Other reformers, finding that rhetoric and justice would not convince reactionaries to accept progress, took a stance of uncompromising hostility and thereby earned the name revolutionaries. Chernyshevskii thus defined the three main groups: reactionaries, moderates, and revolutionaries. He lamented the belief of the moderates that reactionaries opposed reform because of the hostility of revolutionaries; the true reason was simply their desire to protect their own material interests.

With an extraordinary show of boldness, Chernyshevskii went on to identify his own revolutionary position. He did so by means of the unsubtle technique of denying the moderate view and claiming, in mockery, that he was himself a reactionary. No one but the even more unsubtle censor could have been fooled (VI, 338).

Considering the relationship among these three groups, Chernyshevskii also touched on the question of proper political tactics. He urged that once people had accepted a principle, they ought not to shrink from its consequence. They must also show judgment in evaluating the strivings and actions of other men to avoid being duped; misplaced confidence could ruin a worthy undertaking. Chernyshevskii offered this general advice as background for his specific recommendations on cooperation and conflict among the contending parties: "We said there are three parties. But conflict requires only two camps: only two of the three parties can fight their own battle most strenuously with each other. The third must join one of these, until that time when, together, they [the two allied parties] overcome the other, only then to separate themselves" (VI, 339).

If, in this tripartite political arena, two parties must oppose the third, Chernyshevskii asked which temporary alliance would be the most logical until time for a final showdown. His answer, "in the sphere of abstract ideas," was unequivocal: reactionaries on the one side, moderates and revolutionaries on the other. This division was logical because it reflected an essential difference in goals. Reactionaries wanted stagnation; moderates and revolutionaries wanted progressive reform. For the sake of his immediate argument, Chernyshevskii seemed to play down the differences between the final goals of moderates and revolutionaries, which elsewhere he insisted on strongly. Thus, according to the "essence of their strivings," the only "natural" relationship of parties was an alliance between moderates and revolutionaries, an alliance that could be satisfactory to both sides (VI, 340). If either of these two parties helped the reactionaries, however, it would lead to disappointment and a shattering of their illusions. Clearly in this advice Chernyshevskii referred only to the needs of the moderates. In the closing paragraph of the article, he issued a final warning to "liberals," a term he used at that point interchangeably with moderates. Claiming facetiously to be referring only to Italy, he reminded liberals of their own lack of strength and their need to find support in the mass of people if they hoped for any success. If liberals were not sympathetic to the needs of the people, and if they were unwilling to arouse the people (as presumably the revolutionaries were eager to do), then the liberals or moderates had better sit still and be quiet. Nothing would come of their efforts, and their movement would be destroyed by a triumphant, vengeful reaction (VI, 374–375).

As Chernyshevskii here defined the tactical positions of defenders and opponents of the existing political and social order, he gave no support to the idea that in his own mind he was wavering between a liberal-moderate and a revolutionary position. Throughout his writings, he maintained a consistent criticism of both the theoretical limitations of the liberal-moderate preoccupation with political forms, and the actions of these parties —actions he viewed as showing their basic fear of the people. But this criticism left unanswered a vital question, which continued to trouble revolutionary socialists in Russia as long as the old order remained essentially intact. The question was: what kind of encouragement, if any, should be given by the revolutionaries to moderate opponents, or reformers, of autocracy? Were they to be dismissed out of hand? Might they be useful as temporary allies? Almost everything Chernyshevskii wrote showed his profound contempt for the liberal-moderate approach. Yet in 1859, a year that saw *The Contemporary* take an especially strong stand against moderation, Chernyshevskii could still write of an alliance of moderates and revolutionaries as the only "natural" one. Rather than blame Chernyshevskii for inconsistency, one must recognize the difficult tactical decision he had to make. Within his own set of definitions and values, he granted the relatively progressive character of European liberalism and moderate reform in contrast to autocracy. Had there been no other immediate alternative, and had liberals and moderates acted significantly and resolutely against autocracy, he could have given them temporary encouragement and perhaps even limited support, resembling the united front tactics used by revolutionaries of a later day. In Chernyshevskii's eyes, however, both the Russian moderates and many European liberals of his day were failing to meet their historic responsibility in the struggle against autocracy. At the same time, in Russia, he witnessed the preparation of a serf reform whose terms, as they became known, seemed destined to drive the peasants into open rebellion. The only response his situation seemed to permit was to accept and even encourage the polarization of views in Russian public opinion and try to prepare a generation of revolutionary leaders.

Chernyshevskii's writings did not show this intention with equal clarity from the start, and in this sense his tactics, rather than his basic beliefs, may have been influenced by the course of the reform preparation. One example is his article "Cavaignac," written at the end of 1857 and printed in the January and March 1858 issues of *The Contemporary,* at just the time that serious work on the reform began in the recently established provincial committees. Chernyshevskii's description of Cavaignac and his party, the "moderate republicans," included all his standard complaints against European liberals and moderates. Because such parties were not concerned with the true needs of the people, the alliance made by the Parisian workers with the moderate republicans to overthrow the July Monarchy was "unnatural." The alliance would never have been made if the workers and republicans had understood each other. The workers paid for their terrible political mistake in the bloody "June Days" (V, 37). However, Chernyshevskii added quite a different thought in his extensive criticism of the moderate republicans themselves, who did not have enough strength to rule in their own right and who in time lost out to Napoleon III. As Cavaignac's party desperately needed more support, Chernyshevskii suggested that, even after the "June Days," the moderate republicans might have made efforts to win support from the left rather than from the reactionaries (V, 43, 50, 54).

Not entering into alliance with the parties that had many members, the moderate republicans should not have hoped for help from people who led those parties. But the masses never have firm and clear political convictions. They follow impressions that are produced by separate events and separate measures of importance. The moderate republicans might have drawn the masses to themselves if they had taken care that their rule produced a favorable impression on the masses and satisfied those desires [of the masses] which they could have fulfilled without changing their own manner of thought (V, 44).

The final impression left by Chernyshevskii's article is not free of ambiguity. Beyond his surface intention of giving readers an opinionated version of revolutionary events in another country, he tried to convey a number of lessons that might apply to Russia as well. Having condemned the moderate republicans with greatest severity for turning on the workers and doing nothing to ameliorate their condition, he suggested the necessary conclusion to be drawn was that only a strong independent radical movement, which did not trust moderate reformers, could serve the needs of the oppressed.[17] But countering, without entirely balancing, this view was Chernyshevskii's additional suggestion that the moderate republicans need not and, for their own good, ought not to have acted as they did. In other words, he seemed to hold out the possibility of an alternative if men, who were clearly inclined to act in one way, instead acted in a different way. This possibility of alternative action coincides with what he called a year and a half later, in theoretical terms, the "natural" or "logical" temporary alliance of moderates and revolutionaries.

To note a shift in emphasis in Chernyshevskii's writing from late 1857 to 1862 is not, therefore, to suggest that in those years he developed a radical or revolutionary point of view that was in any way new for him. The change in his writing consisted rather in a growing insistence that the theoretical possibility of a temporary moderate-revolutionary alliance against autocracy had no possibility in reality. Chernyshevskii assumed this tactical position because the best efforts by moderate reformers that he could see fell far short of what he believed to be immediately necessary. Moreover, it seemed useless to encourage small deeds that could easily detract from the major task at hand. Consequently, by 1859, Chernyshevskii was in the midst of an angry campaign that criticized liberal or moderate half-measures about as strongly as it attacked autocracy.[18] With barely concealed militancy his political writings sought to discredit any compromise in politics; he insisted on an either-or choice.

Chernyshevskii had clearly assumed this position by the time he wrote "Mr. Chicherin as a Publicist," in October 1859. The main thrust of the article was an irate rebuttal to Chicherin's view that democracy, not unlike absolutism, showed a tendency toward bureaucracy. But Chernyshevskii made a special point of insisting on the importance of partisanship in journalism, and he bitterly attacked the indecisiveness of Chicherin's moderate and cautiously reformist political position. Here was no hint of the possibility of cooperative action, which might be of temporary advantage to different groups who opposed autocracy. Chernyshevskii described Chicherin's views as a confused mixture of honorable thoughts and theories of stagnation and reaction, which denied the living forces of progress. But Jehovah and Baal could not both be served at once. Chicherin thus must choose, either giving full support to Chernyshevskii's point of view or, in effect, supporting the forces of reaction. Only two possibilities existed. "To be a protector of the persecuted, or one of those who persecutes—the choice is not difficult for an honorable man" (V, 669).

Chernyshevskii's campaign to define the alternatives for Russia as a choice between two diametrically opposed extremes took several forms. Foremost among these was his repeated suggestion that, in general, attempts at reform within the system of autocracy could have no significant issue, and might indeed prove harmful. He directed this criticism against both progressive servants of a monarch and moderate opponents of absolute monarchy, who rested content with half-measures or empty promises. Concluding a review article in October 1858 on the ideas and unsuccessful progressive efforts of Turgot, Chernyshevskii listed what this reformer had hoped to accomplish until the court camarilla undermined his position, including a change in feudal rights, destruction of the nobility's privileges, reworking of the tax system, and introduction of a free press. His highest aspiration was to introduce into France a constitution. Chernyshevskii then commented on the sponsor of this program, which so closely paralleled the program of moderates in Russia:

May one not laugh at such a simpleton?

Of course, if he had succeeded in achieving all these transformations there would have been no revolution. But one may ask where could he have found the strength to do even a hundredth part of that which he wanted to do.

Is it not just as if you, receiving an invitation to a party to play preference, turn to your future partners with the hope to read them a lecture on astronomy?

People do have strange hopes!

Among my acquaintances—probably also among yours, reader —there are such strange people. It is impossible not to respect their pure intentions, their devotion to the general good, but, as you wish, hearing them one cannot help but smile (V, 317).

Chernyshevskii's references here to "pure intentions" and "devotion to the general good" may not have been intended with complete seriousness, but there is significance in the fact that, at this point in 1858, he could still find humor in those whose ambitions for reform so far outran the means of fulfillment at their disposal. Three years later his comments were sharper and more clearly showed his revolutionary intent. In October 1861, he turned daringly to Russian history to comment on the reform attempts of M. M. Speranskii. He called Speranskii a "dreamer" for not realizing the futility of his efforts. Yet such efforts, which

Chernyshevskii had ridiculed before, were no longer simply a source of amusement; in their own way, they were dangerous: "All such people are ridiculous with their alluring dreams, but they may be harmful when they delude themselves in serious matters. In their enthusiastic bustle on a false path, they seem to achieve some success, and with this lead many astray, who follow the same false path which leads to nothing but illusions. From this point of view, the activity of Speranskii may be called harmful" (VII, 827).[19]

Chernyshevskii's evaluation of those in European politics who feared the people and were satisfied with half-measures reached an angry peak of criticism in a review of de Tocqueville's *Democracy in America* in 1861. Again he stressed a polarized view of politics. After attacking de Tocqueville's association of democracy and centralization, which went against Chernyshevskii's preference for decentralized authority, he noted that a Frenchman would have had other grounds to attack the writer. De Tocqueville and liberals and democrats who thought like him had brought great harm to France, opposing all measures needed by the nation in critical times, bringing affairs to a head in the terrible slaughter of the June Days, and finally throwing themselves into the arms of reaction. Without these people, who staunchly claimed the reputation of liberals and democrats, the reactionaries would have been helpless (VII, 696–697). The obvious conclusion from Chernyshevskii's words was that the popular struggle against reaction would have to include opposition to any middle position, because those who held that position had proved so irresolute in their conduct that they in fact supported the main enemy.[20]

Another technique employed by Chernyshevskii to push Russian public opinion to an either-or choice was his ongoing ridicule of liberal tactics and the false hopes that stood behind them. The monthly article "Politics" proved a useful vehicle for this criticism. In March 1859, he wrote one such attack, which caused a considerable scandal among those of essentially progressive views. He refused to join the general chorus of sympathy for the liberal Carlo Poerio and his comrades, who had recently been released by the King of Naples from a long and cruel imprisonment for their part in the revolution of 1848. Chernyshevskii argued that Poerio's lack of political realism had brought about his punishment. The monarchy had merely followed the logic of survival, whereas Poerio had made the foolish mistake of trusting the liberal promises of a monarch who understood only absolutism. A month later, responding to criticism of his position, Chernyshevskii added that Poerio had imagined he could act like a minister in England, when really his position was in Naples. One's actions must correspond to the reality of the situation. If Poerio did not understand what had to be done in a given situation, or did not wish to take the necessary action, he should have left the field to those who realized what the times and situation demanded (VI, 149–154, 186–187).

If any of Chernyshevskii's readers missed the point of these remarks, he made it easier for them several months later by drawing on the same parallel between Austrian and Russian affairs that he had used to criticize the autocracy. In this case the object of his criticism was misplaced trust and the tendency of the liberals to rest content with small concessions:

Austrian liberals (there are liberals in Austria, even quite a few of them) are now basing great hopes on the plan of their government "to improve the inadequacies of legislation, to root out abuses, to introduce enlightened rule in administration" and so on. Perhaps the reader does not think such things can take place in Austria. He is mistaken; the hopes of the liberals rest on the most trustworthy proof—on the concluding words of the Austrian emperor's manifesto on the conclusion of the peace. Who can doubt an official promise? Show us such a skeptic— no you will not find him, at least among liberals, whose characteristic features in Austria, as everywhere, are two: to trust and to be enraptured (VI, 406).

After noting that only military failure had driven the Austrian government to think of its internal structure, he remarked that in any case the reforms in question were insignificant, designed to appeal to liberal gullibility. These reforms would have true significance only if they appeared as secondary features in a general reform of the state's whole system, which was permeated with a spirit of oppression (VI, 407).

Along with the moderate reformers' false hopes went irresolution, with which Chernyshevskii dealt most severely. He maintained a constant criticism of those who claimed to want change and yet hesitated to employ the means needed to achieve that change. Good and evil were always intertwined in any decision, but one had to weigh the matter, decide on the best course, and then act resolutely. Chernyshevskii decried the fact that a person would assume leadership in a political matter and then delude himself as to the necessary consequences of his decision. Vacillating leadership led only to the ruin of an undertaking. In offering this general advice, Chernyshevskii claimed that he did not mean to take sides on different issues. Thus, he could praise Napoleon I for realizing and undertaking what was necessary for military conquest, without meaning to praise Napoleon I for such conquest (VI, 415–417). However, he also gave as examples—whose intended reference to Russia in late 1859 seems especially clear in retrospect and probably passed by few of his readers—the liberal leaders of central Italy, who seemed not to realize the essence of their undertaking and who feared the means it required:

Their cause is revolutionary, but they think to give it the character of legality; the principle whose realization they wish—the principle of supreme power of the people—is mortally hostile to the principle of legitimacy, but they wish to obtain the help of continental diplomacy which maintains treaty rights and the dynastic principle; finally their goal is the goal of national aspiration, therefore, it must be attained with the enthusiasm of the masses, but they do not want the masses to be aroused. Perhaps the means required by this undertaking are bad, this we do not know; but if they are bad, then, in that case, the undertaking should not be begun. Whoever rejects the means should also deny the undertaking that cannot be achieved without these means. Whoever does not wish to arouse the people, who abhors scenes which are inseparably linked with the rousing of popular passions, that person should not take upon himself the conduct of affairs which can be maintained only with the rousing of the masses (VI, 418).

In the conditions of the time, Chernyshevskii could not have made his position clearer. During the following two years, he took every possible occasion to repeat the message: absolute monarchy could never be reformed from within, and moderate opposition, which feared disorder more than it hated injustice, offered no alternative worth considering.[21]

Chernyshevskii may have reached the peak of his denunciation of ineffectual moderation in the article "Introduction to Present-Day Austrian Affairs," which appeared in *The Contemporary* precisely at the time of the serf reform manifesto in February 1861. He made a special effort to establish the parallel between Austrian affairs in 1848 and the situation in Russia in his own day (VIII, 433–465).[22] This parallel extended to an evaluation of Metternich in terms that applied equally well to Alexander II. Chernyshevskii presented Metternich less as an evil genius than as a captive of a system he neither invented nor could alter. His power was unlimited only so long as he supported the system, yet the system itself was a century out of date and inevitably led to bad consequences. After noting that the normal result of repression was the intensification of human strivings, Chernyshevskii remarked that, in contrast, the people in the so-called liberal and even radical provinces of Austria in 1848 lacked trust in their own strength and in fact thought it necessary to support the government rather than weaken it. Such people did not need to be taken seriously; they did not even require repressive measures. Indeed, a shrewd leader could grant such people whatever constitutional rights they asked for and still remain master of the situation (VIII, 443–447).

For several years prior to his imprisonment, Chernyshevskii thus offered his readers a severely polarized view of political life in much of Europe and, by implication, in Russia. Since moderates and liberals hesitated in their opposition to autocracy and made compromises at the expense of the mass of the population, they deserved to be classified with the reactionaries. Only two conclusions could be drawn from this analysis. Either one could accept the situation in despair, or one could realize, as Chernyshevskii did, that if the masses wanted their interests served, they must act in their own behalf. To assume the second position was not to think that a mass movement could be called forth by articles in a monthly journal that circulated among a small literate elite. In the article "Introduction to Present-Day Austrian Affairs," for instance, Chernyshevskii showed his awareness of this fact by belittling the efforts of Austrian authorities to control the circulation of dangerous books. Words could not evoke unrest if the unrest would not have developed without words, and if the unrest necessarily arose from existing social relationships, no silence could arrest its course (VIII, 450). But writing in *The Contemporary* gave Chernyshevskii an opportunity to reach that portion of the educated elite who might sympathize with a mass movement and give it leadership and direction. Chernyshevskii was not a revolutionary adventurer. His nature knew none of Bakunin's blind impetuosity, and an element of skepticism tempered his hope for a peasant revolution.[23] Yet, his own estimation of the situation in Russia in the late 1850's and early 1860's forced his hand. Convinced that no significant change would result from the peasant reform and that the settlement would be a triumph of reaction, which the peasants likely would not accept, he tried to educate potential leaders for a mass movement.

Under conditions of censorship, Chernyshevskii communicated his revolutionary position primarily as a necessary, but unstated, corollary to remarks criticizing the other alternatives. On occasion, however, he risked more obvious hints to the effect that the downtrodden would only be helped when they helped themselves. Early in 1860, for example, he noted that the futility of peaceful acceptance had been demonstrated in France under the July Monarchy: "The poor class, far removed from participation in affairs, was oppressed by armed strength which was prepared to punish 'all criminal attempts to overthrow existing institutions.' Each may judge this as he wishes, but the fact is that no one need concern himself about those who have neither power nor arms. No one is concerned for another's benefit just for the joy of it" (VII, 99). Another hint, this time relating directly to the situation in Russia, appeared a year and a half later in November 1861, in Chernyshevskii's article "Has Not the Change Begun?" the review of a collection of stories on peasant life by N. V. Uspenskii (VII, 855–889). He praised in particular Uspenskii's truthfulness in writing about the people without adornment. The picture that emerged was unflattering, but Chernyshevskii preferred this realism to the false idealization or condescending pity of earlier writers. Their sympathy was of no use to the people, for it indicated that they viewed the people's position as hopeless. The fact that Uspenskii could be critical of aspects of peasant life showed that he wrote in a new situation, in which the misery a man endured might be removed if he himself wished it and those close to him in feeling helped (VII, 856–857, 884). In this way, Chernyshevskii transformed the characterizations in Uspenskii's stories into a hopeful sign of the times. One could now criticize the masses in tacit recognition that the fault was theirs in allowing the oppressed conditions to continue.[24]

Through his tactical decision to belittle ineffective attempts at partial reform, and to look for hope in the least sign of peasant unrest, Chernyshevskii led *The Contemporary* into a bitter dispute with Herzen, who shared many of the long-range goals of the radical left in Russia, but who retained hope for improvement by peaceful reform from above until 1861, when disheartened by publication of the reform manifesto.[25] At the time that Alexander first announced his intention to liberate the serfs, Herzen promised he would support "those who liberate as long as they liberate." In the following years he held firmly to this position, although he was vulnerable to criticism from all sides.[26] Radicals, fully committed to a revolutionary solution, criticized Herzen's false hopes, while moderate reformers, concerned with avoiding a total breakdown of order, rightfully worried over the conditional nature of his support for peaceful improvement. As early as August 1857, Herzen stated clearly that the one thing not to be accepted was a continuation of the existing situation. He wrote with general approval of the regeneration that had occurred in Piedmont during the previous decade, as the result of an unsuccessful war and a series of concessions to public opinion by the government. He acknowledged that the "artist-revolutionaries" did not like such a peaceful manner of change, but he could not agree with them. For his own part, although he felt deeply that the existing system was unjust, he preferred a path of peaceful human development to a bloody one. Yet he added just as sincerely that he "preferred the most stormy and unbridled development to the stagnation of Nicholas I's status quo." A year later, Herzen added: "The liberation of the peasants with land is one of the main and essential questions for Russia and for us. Whether it be liberation 'from above or from below' we will be for it." [27] This statement typified the brilliant campaign conducted by Herzen in London, in his journal *The Bell,* to support those in Russia who worked for a generous peasant settlement, and to denounce defenders of the old order. The same statement also contained the seeds of his conflict with those who had given up on half-measures.

Herzen's disagreement with *The Contemporary* in 1859 resulted from the tendency of Chernyshevskii and his followers to condemn moderation almost as severely as they fought reactionary opposition to change. Both Chernyshevskii's criticism of Carlo Poerio and the appearance of a new satirical section of *The Contemporary,* called "The Whistle," showed this tendency, but it was probably some literary reviews by Dobroliubov that aroused Herzen's greatest ire.[28] Dobroliubov's "Literary Trifles of the Past Year" and "What Is Oblomovism?" printed in 1859, not only criticized a position for which Herzen had sympathy, but in effect blamed the opposition members of the older generation for their concern with petty details and implied that the new generation of radicals alone knew how to serve humanity.[29] These intemperate accusations drew Herzen's stinging reply in the article "Very Dangerous!" which appeared in *The Bell* in June 1859.

Herzen argued that the uncompromising turn taken by *The Contemporary* played into the hands of the Russian reactionaries. The powerful weapon of ridicule, he wrote, should be used against the obscurantist censorship, not against those who worked for a better Russia. Herzen thus defended "accusatory" literature (directed at malfeasance rather than the system) against Dobroliubov's claim that such petty faultfinding had no value. Since any free criticism was of recent growth in Russia, it would require time to mature and find the proper direction. Herzen saw an end to the era of superfluous men in Russia, because a course of action was now open to everyone. The time had not yet come to give up hope for positive achievement, and certainly it made no sense to reject the liberals' progressive efforts. In conclusion, Herzen suggested that the present path of *The Contemporary* might lead to the type of police-inspired reactionary journalism once practiced by F. V. Bulgarin and N. I. Grech.[30]

This criticism, from the pen of another leader of the progressive movement, presented both a serious challenge to *The Contemporary* and a threat, because it would draw closer police attention to the journal. Nekrasov had reason to be worried for the fate of his journal. Dobroliubov expressed shock when he first heard about Herzen's attack, noting in his diary strong disbelief that the story was true. He also commented on the danger of letting Nekrasov meet with Herzen, for fear the affair would end in a duel.[31] According to M. A. Antonovich, after his initial anger, Chernyshevskii made a characteristic joke, remarking that now the censors might treat *The Contemporary* more kindly. But clearly, the matter could not be laughed off. Nekrasov, fearing that Dobroliubov's manner might too easily offend Herzen, pleaded with a reluctant Chernyshevskii to undertake a visit to London to try to set matters straight and, if possible, reconcile the position of the two journals.[32]

Little is known of the meeting between Herzen and Chernyshevskii in late June 1859, except that it did not achieve its purpose. The two men were profoundly unlike, if not in their social objectives, at least in their personalities and intellectual styles, and they represented different generations of the protest movement.[33] On his return trip, Chernyshevskii wrote a cryptic note to Dobroliubov hinting at these differences. He reported that he found it too "tedious" to remain longer in London, and he seemed in despair at the outcome of his conversations. Chernyshevskii did not refer to Herzen by name, mentioning only "those with whom he spoke," but he told Dobroliubov to accept Nekrasov's opinion of them, and Nekrasov's dislike of Herzen and his associate on *The Bell*, N. P. Ogarev, was common knowledge (XIV, 379).[34] One further statement, made by Chernyshevskii in a letter shortly before his death and claiming that Herzen behaved like a schoolboy with him, cannot be taken seriously (XV, 790). Neither Herzen, Dobroliubov, nor Nekrasov left any other direct evidence on the visit, and if Antonovich is correct, the leaders of *The Contemporary* talked little about the episode outside their immediate circle. Antonovich's impression from his conversations with Chernyshevskii was that the whole trip had been a painful experience for him, one of his acts of folly (glupost') that he wished to forget. He had, with a considerable show of emotion, opened his thoughts to Herzen, only to be humiliated by Herzen's comment, pronounced with an Olympian glance, that his view could be justified from a narrow party point of view alone.[35]

Perhaps the most likely account of the message that the editorship of *The Contemporary* tried to bring to Herzen is contained in S. G. Stakhevich's memoirs, which described a conversation he had with Chernyshevskii in prison, about a decade after the event. At that time, Chernyshevskii claimed that he had attacked Herzen for the "purely accusatory character" of *The Bell:*

> If ... our government had better sense, it would thank you for your accusations. These accusations help it to control its agents in the local areas, and at the same time leave the state structure undisturbed. But the essence of the matter is in the state structure, and not in the agents. It would follow for you to set forth a definite political program, let us say constitutional, or republican, or socialist, and then any accusation would appear as a support for the basic demands of your program. You would constantly repeat your: *ceterum censeo Carthaginem delendam esse.*[36]

If these were Chernyshevskii's words, there is no further indication how Herzen responded. All one can say for certain is that he was not overwhelmed, nor did he submit. In the August 1859 issue of *The Bell*, Herzen made a brief and inconspicuous qualification to "Very Dangerous!" He denied that the article was intended as a direct insult, asserting that his irony should not be misunderstood. This mild statement in no way brought his position closer to the views of Chernyshevskii and his friends on *The Contemporary*.[37]

Herzen's dispute with Chernyshevskii's revolutionary position came to the fore again in March 1860, when *The Bell* printed an angry call to mass action under the title "Letter from the Provinces," together with Herzen's more moderate reply. There is still an open question concerning the authorship of this letter.[38] Although Chernyshevskii probably did not write the letter himself, it nonetheless expressed the prevailing view of the radicals on *The Contemporary* that all alternatives to peasant rebellion had been exhausted. The "Letter from the Provinces" accused Herzen of having lost touch with peasant opinion in Russia. Lulled into false optimism by liberal talk of progress, Herzen sent hymns of praise for Alexander II from the banks of the Thames, instead of stern disclosures of injustice. The writer of the letter insisted that the peasants no longer believed in the tsar's benevolent concern for their interests, nor would they rest content with liberal moderation. With special bitterness they prepared to resort to their axes. The letter concluded on a desperate note. The Russian situation was so unbearable, only the axe could help (VII, 1001–1004).

In reply to this extremism, Herzen held firmly to his position that a peasant rebellion would be a great misfortune. It might come, because of the character of Russian landlords and the lack of character of the Russian government. In that case, each would have to act as his conscience and his love commanded.[39] However, if possible, the axe should be avoided, so long as there was work to do for the broom. At the same time, Herzen insisted that he shared common aspirations with the writer of the "Letter from the Provinces":

We differ from you *not in ideas* but in methods; *not in principles* but in ways of acting. You are only *the extreme* expression of *our* own position. We understand your one-sidedness. It is close to our hearts. Our indignation is as young as yours, and our love for the Russian people is as alive now as it was in the years of our youth.

But we will not call for the *axe*, for that oppressive *ultima ratio, so long as there remains one reasonable hope of a solution without the axe.*[40]

A few months later, in October 1860, Herzen resorted to more cutting words in his article "The Superfluous Men and the Bilious Ones," which was directed against the general attitude adopted by the angry writers on *The Contemporary*. He sensed a secret craving for admiration in the younger radical generation, a craving barely hidden under their masks of humility. Surely the world could not long endure their gloomy, one-sided lack of humor and sensitivity. Herzen defended the achievements of the "superfluous men" for their own time, and predicted that the "bilious ones" who followed on the historical stage would not themselves last long.[41] Here Herzen scarcely rose above the personal invective of Turgenev's comment to the effect that Chernyshevskii was an ordinary snake and Dobroliubov a cobra. But behind these personal reproaches stood Herzen's conviction that Chernyshevskii and his followers had given up too soon on the possibility that progressive change might stave off a peasant revolution.

In the final year of Chernyshevskii's active career, he crossed pens with Herzen on two other issues related to the fundamental questions of reform and revolution. Chernyshevskii's article "On the Causes of the Fall of Rome," printed in May 1861, took Herzen to task for belittling the revolutionary potential of Western Europe and for asserting a unique potential for social transformation in Russia (VII, 643–668). In his answer, "Repetitio est mater studiorum," in September 1861, Herzen made no attempt to deny this essential point of disagreement that continued to divide the Russian protest movement throughout its history. Whereas Chernyshevskii had stressed his conviction that Europe was far from exhausted in the search for a new social order, Herzen not only insisted on Russia's uniqueness, but saw the difference between Russia and the West as an indication of Russia's greater capacity to make the needed change.[42]

The other issue to cause disagreement had to do with the more practical and immediate question of the ability of revolutionary leaders to understand and respond to the people's needs. Herzen's article "Liberation Fodder" ("Miaso osvobozhdeniia") appeared in February 1862, shortly after Chernyshevskii's "Has Not the Change Begun?" to which it was in part an answer.[43] In defending himself against critics, from both the left and the right, who charged he did not have a sufficiently defined program, Herzen argued that those who proposed specific solutions too often viewed the people as an inert material that could be molded to suit their own abstract schemes. They were convinced that it was better to instruct the people, than themselves to learn from the people of their true needs and aspirations. In this way, both Peter I and the leaders of the reign of terror in the French Revolution had made the same error. Moving rapidly ahead with their own ideas, it was easy for cabinet thinkers to lose needed contact with the people. For example, Herzen cited socialists who taught before they knew, and who constructed phalanxes without locating the people who would wish to live in the workers' homes.[44] In this extreme form, Herzen's criticism could not have been directed against Chernyshevskii with any degree of fairness, because Chernyshevskii sought more to popularize the principle of cooperation than to make definite prescriptions. Yet the concluding part of "Has Not the Change Begun?" was, in effect, an appeal to an educated elite to work with the people to develop their revolutionary consciousness, which they might not otherwise achieve (VII, 889). Although the variation was one of degree rather than kind, Herzen was correct in noting that his own understanding of the relationship between the people and the educated potential leaders differed from that of Chernyshevskii and many of his followers.

Finally, Chernyshevskii's political ideas were influenced by his general understanding of historical change. He never achieved his goal of writing a major work on history, and occasionally when making historical statements in polemical articles, he sacrificed accuracy to gain a point. Thus, in his article "On the Causes of the Fall of Rome," when he wanted to discredit Herzen's suggestion that Western Europe, like Rome in its decline, showed signs of exhaustion, he painted an unreasonably optimistic picture of the internal strengths of the late Roman Empire (VII, 654–657). Yet all of Chernyshevskii's writings displayed a basic faith in historical progress and offered a reasonably coherent explanation of the process of historical change. Indeed, despite the claims of most Marxist commentators that Chernyshevskii's views of history contained an incorrect admixture of "idealism," he developed a theory in line with his own understanding of materialism.[45]

Chernyshevskii once called progress a "physical necessity," claiming that one could no more deny progress than deny the law of gravity. Elsewhere he likened history to the flow of a great river whose general direction could not be altered (IV, 70; VI, 11–13). However, Chernyshevskii did not view progress as an objective, mechanical process in which mankind merely played out an assigned role. He sometimes stressed the environmental influences on human behavior and, more often, spoke of the relation of men's ideas to the material interests of their class (IV, 479–481). But Chernyshevskii's optimism concerning progress in history rested essentially on his belief in the irresistible force of human development. Man possessed two innate qualities: a desire to improve the conditions of life, and a desire for knowledge. Both these qualities were inalienable to man's material being; they formed an integral part of any healthy nervous system and provided the initial impetus for progress (VII, 447; X, 920). The best minds of any generation sought new truths and gained new insights. Through their efforts and the gradual dissemination of their findings to the rest of mankind, the level of human knowledge improved. Guided by improved human knowledge, the natural, egoistical drives of man became more rational and thereby led to progress.[46] But those who tried to lead society could never succeed if they went so far beyond the understanding of the mass of people as to lose popular support (IV, 70–71). Ultimately, hope rested not only on the insights of the few, but on the acceptance of new truths by the many. In the nineteenth century, for example, Chernyshevskii believed a stage had been reached where the best minds saw the need of socialism. When the masses came to hold the same conviction, the achievement of a new society would not be long delayed (IX, 422–423).

In his view of historical change, Chernyshevskii assigned a decisive role to an intellectual elite.[47] He compared intellectual progress to the movement of an army. In times of rapid advance, the bulk of troops fell far behind those who marched with the colors. Only a small section of the original army fought the battle and made the conquest. Subsequently the gap closed, as the stragglers rejoined the victors. The truth, which had been won by the few, turned out to be simple and intelligible to all. The masses accepted the new truth readily, although they could not have discovered it themselves (VII, 431–433).

From this general understanding of historical change, Chernyshevskii drew support for his optimistic view of the future. New truths and new understanding must inevitably be realized in political and social change. Though the process of realization would likely be characterized by violence and occasional reversals, even the most disappointing political setbacks were bound to be temporary. Men would always seek their own betterment and, in time, would do so more rationally. Chernyshevskii believed that in the nineteenth century the common people had for the first time developed to a point where they could enter political life (VII, 666). As they attained a rational understanding of their position and potential strength, their demands would become irresistible.

Except for the few who knew Chernyshevskii's views from direct contact and conversation, readers of *The Contemporary*, in the late 1850's and early 1860's, had nothing more on which to judge his position on politics. Right up to the time of his arrest, his published writings showed no noticeable departure from a stark description of polarized alternatives: either stagnation, because the government could not reform itself, and moderate pressure for change was ineffective; or action by the people themselves, which in Russia could only mean a peasant revolution. Yet even as Chernyshevskii held to this position during 1861 and into 1862, perhaps with no more than a desperate hope, some of the assumptions on which the position was based altered, at least to the extent of allowing a change in tactics. Most significant was the fact that although the peasants did not everywhere accept the terms of their new freedom passively, their protests were disorganized and fell pathetically short of posing a real threat to government stability, or of forcing the government to alter its policy. At the same time, a movement of opposition from one segment of the nobility showed more vitality than Chernyshevskii could have anticipated in the preceding few years. Early in 1862, the assembly of the Tver nobility protested that the emancipation manifesto of February nineteenth had raised problems rather than solved them. The Tver nobles pressed for credit and court reforms and spoke of the need to educate the public in the functioning of the administration. They advanced the daring claim that the government, in its existing form, could not carry out the needed reforms, and should therefore call for an assembly of men elected by the whole nation without respect to class.[48]

Such demands barely approached what Chernyshevskii felt to be the needs of Russian society. In the situation of the spring of 1862, however, he apparently saw value in giving public support to this kind of progressive, nonrevolutionary movement. A year earlier he had scorned comparable efforts at progressive reform and even considered them harmful; now he wrote an article, "Letters Without Address," intended as an open appeal to Alexander II, which remained unknown to his own generation because it never passed censorship, but which came to light in 1874 in Lavrov's emigré journal *Forward.* In this article, Chernyshevskii described his change in tactics and surpassed himself in irony when commiserating with the tsar in that both of their hopes had suffered from the people's apathy (X, 91). Perhaps because he had come to realize the small likelihood that the peasants, aided by a few of the educated elite, would be able to act decisively on their own behalf against the established power of the state, he again seemed willing to try to force concessions from the government with the threat of opposition from many different sides. After several years of grouping into one hostile category all who opposed his own particular point of view, he now spoke of many classes of society united in their demand for further reforms from the autocracy. Chernyshevskii

even claimed to fear popular revolution for the sake of enlightenment, which he admitted was dearer to him than to the mass of
the people (X, 92). In a probable reference to the February 1862
conference and resolutions of the Tver nobility, he wrote that
the nobility acted as the representatives of all other classes.
They spoke most forcefully because they alone enjoyed the
opportunity to make their voices heard, though other classes
had more serious grievances (X, 101).

One could hardly describe these unpublished "Letters Without
Address" as a retreat to greater moderation on Chernyshevskii's
part. He wrote in a defiant tone, and he gave no quarter in his
scathing attacks on the Russian bureaucratic autocracy or on
the inadequate peasant reform, which he felt left some peasants worse off than before. Still, the "Letters" did reflect his
evaluation of the situation in Russia in 1862, and showed his
willingness to alter his tactics to meet the situation with at
least temporary support of a united front of opposition. The
"Letters" must therefore be considered in any overall evaluation of his writings on politics, even though they never reached
their intended readers, and even though one has no way of
knowing how consistently he might have followed the new
tactic. As it happened, the tsar quickly brought the Tver nobility to heel, and Chernyshevskii's own arrest a few months
later ended his writing on political questions.

In summary, the conditions under which he wrote and his
own order of priorities prevented Chernyshevskii from establishing as clear a theoretical position in politics as in the other
major areas of his thought. Yet it is also true that his political
writings had the most significant and immediate impact. In
his view, the specific forms of political life seemed less significant than the ability of a society to satisfy the material needs of
its members. From his reading on the political affairs of Europe
and his knowledge of conditions in Russia, however, Chernyshevskii became convinced that no government based on representation limited to a minority could truly act for the popular
well-being. Egoism dominated politics just as it directed personal morality. Consequently, the good society would be attained
only when the mass of people insisted on benefits for them-

selves and proved willing, as necessary, to support their demands with force.

With reference to this general approach, it is thus possible to classify Chernyshevskii both as an "enlightener" and a "revolutionary." A rational political structure required widespread acceptance of a "correct understanding of things," yet it seemed unlikely that fundamental change could ever be achieved without revolutionary pressure. In contrast to many who have written about his career, Chernyshevskii allowed neither enlightenment nor revolution to become an exclusive, doctrinaire approach.

In the context of Russian life, Chernyshevskii faced the difficult choice of immediate political tactics. Here he proved flexible, simply responding to the Russian situation in the way he believed would do the most direct good. Thus, at the time of Alexander's rescripts, without compromising his belief in the long-range necessity of revolution, he briefly joined the united support for the government's attempt to reform from above. Again, early in 1862 he made the decision to add his voice to a united movement of protest led by the Tver nobility. But these tactical moves in no way detracted from the force of his primary political message, which was less a theory than a decision based on his evaluation of Russian reality. For about three years, at the pinnacle of his influence, in barely disguised words that a reasonably attentive reader could understand, he preached an uncompromising antagonism between the government and moderate reformers, on the one hand, and the oppressed peasantry and those who gave full support to the peasantry, on the other. His decision to accept the necessary corollary of this position, a peasant revolution, despite any misgivings he may have had about the intellectual preparedness of the peasant masses, was his major contribution to Russian political thought and action. For those who were open to his message, he popularized the thought of revolution as no other writer had before him and thereby directly prepared the soil for the diverse attempts to translate protest into action in the 1860's and after.

# IX. *Chernyshevskii and the Revolutionary Movement (1860–1862)*

By almost any standard of measurement, the points of view Chernyshevskii expressed in legitimate journalism during the years 1853 to 1862 represented a revolutionary departure in the Russian intellectual tradition. On an abstract level, he challenged many of the religious and traditional assumptions that legitimized social and political power in the Russia of his day. On a more concrete level, he made suggestions and popularized values that could not have been incorporated into the existing order of society without altering it profoundly. Probably few of his contemporary readers had so systematic an understanding of his work as is available today. But even if some of the young men who came of age in the early 1860's could not know all he had written, or if others found some of his technical articles too long or too difficult, there is no doubt that, in general terms, his message got across to his readers. As a result, his extensive writing provided the substance of the radical world view of his day, and through them he made his most significant contribution to the Russian revolutionary movement.

However, his legitimate writing was not his only contribution. The question remains of Chernyshevskii's direct participation in underground activity and in the preparation of illegal, revolutionary propaganda. Any separation of Chernyshevskii the radical journalist from Chernyshevskii the conspirator and organizer is necessarily artificial. His activity in one area must have influenced his activity in the other. However, the problem is that the quality of evidence concerning his involvement in underground activity is so far below the quality of evidence for his journalism that it is risky to try to explain the one by the other. If the problem is approached from one side, one can readily admit the possibility that the man who wrote in *The Contemporary* could, without any contradiction, have been an underground revolutionary leader. But possibility is not necessity, and from the evidence of his journalism alone, Chernyshevskii could with equal consistency have been no more than a courageous radical writer who saw fit to limit his contribution to the cause to dueling with the censorship. The choice between the two possibilities must await more specific evidence. Even the zealous, painstaking work of recent Soviet scholarship remains generally within the realm of speculation and probability. For example, in a collection of articles describing the "revolutionary situation" in Russia between 1859 and 1861 and published in 1965, two essays appeared, side by side, each coming to a different conclusion on the question of Chernyshevskii's participation in the authorship of the illegal pamphlets entitled "The Great Russian." [1]

The probable reasons for the paucity of firm evidence on Chernyshevskii's role in the revolutionary movement are so convincing as to obviate any "argument from silence" to deny his involvement. Police observance had, after all, forced such activities underground, so that names and organizational plans were concealed. The authors of revolutionary propaganda, unless they enjoyed the sanctuary of a foreign land, necessarily hid their identity. Although the Russian authorities were not completely helpless in the face of conspiracy and made a number of key arrests, the full story on some of the underground organizations was never known to them. The conspirators were beginning to learn the value of silence in interrogation, and generally they tried to shield the identity of their comrades. The very failure of the underground opposition movement contributed to the problem of evidence.[2] Because state power remained intact, men who had been involved but had avoided detection

were sure to write in a way that would not incriminate themselves so long as a chance existed that they would be punished.
Later, when they felt free to write memoirs, frequently so much
time had elapsed since the events described that their accuracy
on points of detail is open to question. One extreme example is
that of A. A. Sleptsov, whose reminiscences touch on Chernyshevskii's illegal activity. Sleptsov wrote some forty years after
the event, apparently without the aid of his contemporary notes,
which had been destroyed much earlier, and even his own manuscript is known only through the transcription of others.[3] A
further difficulty may be traced to the nature of the underground
organizations themselves, particularly the first attempt to form
a nation-wide revolutionary organization, the "Land and
Liberty" group. One suspects that this organization was relatively loose and that distinct lines of authority were not defined
and respected. Probably few members had a clear picture of the
whole operation, so that a conflict of testimony was possible
among former participants who claimed intimate knowledge
but in fact knew only part of the truth.

At the core of this problem of evidence is the conduct of Chernyshevskii himself. From the time of his arrest in 1862 to his
death in 1889, he never varied his consistent denial of guilt,
nor gave any support to the charge that he had engaged in illegal
activity. Most probably he realized that it would discredit the
government if people believed him innocent, and in this he was
not mistaken. For those who accepted his version, it was as if
the government, not the man, had been placed on trial and
found guilty.[4] Even during the many years of his exile, Chernyshevskii did not reveal himself fully to anyone, at least to anyone
who wrote about it. Several memoirists came away from conversations with him with conflicting impressions, which were
obviously only guesses. Moreover, Chernyshevskii's silence, as
well as the fact that he remained in the hands of the authorities
for a quarter of a century, limited what anyone who had known
of his activity could write without risk of doing him further
harm. One example is the earliest public statement on the
activities of Land and Liberty by one who had worked within the
organization. In 1868 in Geneva, N. I. Utin, who considered

himself a partisan of Chernyshevskii, published the article "Propaganda and Organization," which analyzed the tactics of the earlier organization. Whatever Chernyshevskii's role had been, Utin was probably in a position to know, yet to write of it could only have hurt a man he greatly admired. And this may have been the reason that little of what he wrote is specific enough to be useful, except as a characterization of the overall movement.[5]

Apart from the problem of weak evidence on Chernyshevskii's illegal activity, there is also the question of determining which activities to consider. For several years he took part in the Literary Fund, and he was one of the founders of the St. Petersburg Chess Club, which opened in January 1862 and soon came under police suspicion as a center for dangerous political discussions. Similarly, he was interested in the Sunday School movement, and he joined with other writers in protest against both the censorship and the rumored intention of the government to punish professor A. P. Shchapov of Kazan for his speech in sympathy with the peasant victims of the suppression at Bezdna in 1861. But this "open activity," as Steklov described it, was not restricted to men of radical opinion.[6] Here Chernyshevskii joined not only with men who thought as he did, but with others who were progressive but considerably more moderate in their views. Whereas the radicals may have used an organization like the Chess Club for meetings or as a means of extending their influence, it was by no means their exclusive province or a front for a revolutionary organization.[7]

It would appear that the problem of Chernyshevskii's illegal revolutionary activity is best approached through a consideration of four areas of possible involvement: the student movement, the series of proclamations written in cooperation with M. I. Mikhailov and N. V. Shelgunov in the winter of 1860–1861, the organization and publication of "The Great Russian," and the first Land and Liberty organization. In each of these areas, there has been strong suspicion of Chernyshevskii's involvement, and the evidence deserves serious attention.

The student unrest of the 1860's had its origins in the long-overdue attempts of the government to relax the oppressive restrictions that had bound the universities and the students under Nicholas I.[8] Beginning in 1856 and 1857, more liberal regulations tempered the military discipline in student life, eliminated the requirement of uniforms, and allowed (in some cases even encouraged) new student organizations and publications. Reformed admission policies not only expanded total enrollment considerably, but also added a significant number of poor students who needed more financial help than the government was able or willing to provide. Coming so suddenly and in a general context of social awakening, these reforms soon whetted the students' appetites for further changes in the direction of corporate rights and self-government. Such aspirations found expression in student assemblies, which the school authorities could not control, and in the establishment of treasuries to help fellow-students who needed financial aid. These measures went beyond any moderate changes the authorities had in mind. After what seems, in retrospect, a long period of tolerance and doubtless confusion, in 1861 steps were suddenly taken, without careful plan, to control the situation. By this time, however, the proposed new regulations could only be seen by many students as an attempt to set back the clock and were, in turn, rejected as intolerable. In St. Petersburg, the ill-conceived attempt by the government to reverse what appeared to be a dangerous trend toward unruly student government led, in the fall of 1861, to demonstrations and disorders that would have been unthinkable when Chernyshevskii was a student there a dozen years before. By the end of the year, in an apparent impasse with the students over the new regulations, the government closed the university until its own version of order could be restored.

Defense by the students of their newly conceived corporate rights took place in an atmosphere of questioning of authority and tradition, which reflected, perhaps in exaggerated form, the more general intellectual and social ferment.[9] Just as Chernyshevskii in the 1840's had been tempted from academic work by his interest in Western European affairs, so now Russian students often found their course work dull and irrelevant when compared to the lively discussion of current issues in the periodicals. V. N. Lind, a university student in Moscow in 1861, described the situation as one in which the faculty had lost the trust of the students and thereby any influence over them. University learning seemed far removed from questions of the day.[10] In this mood, many students were receptive to the writings of the radical journalists. *The Contemporary, The Russian Word,* and *The Bell,* despite differences in approach, all found willing readers among the students, especially as each of these journals gave warm support to the students' demands of the authorities.[11]

Although there were small student circles which, even in the 1850's, had reached a revolutionary political position, they were scattered, with few if any mutual ties, and by no means did they characterize the student movement as a whole. In general, the students in St. Petersburg and Moscow made a connection only gradually between their own university concern about corporate rights and the larger questions of Russian social and political life, under pressure of frustration with the authorities, the events of 1861, and the influence of the radical journalists. Writing about the disturbances in Moscow, V. N. Lind noted that although the student demands were purely academic during 1861, some students were coming under the influence of revolutionary ideas. He mentioned especially the impact of Ogarev's appeals in *The Bell* and the program of "The Great Russian." [12] According to L. F. Panteleev, beginning in St. Petersburg in 1861, a change took place in the mood of progressive circles and the youth, from a vague love of freedom, with some enthusiasm for socialist ideas, to a more sharply defined political mood. He credited Chernyshevskii and the men around him—M. I. Mikhailov, N. V. Shelgunov, the brothers Serno-Solov'evich, and V. A. Obruchev—with preparing society for a revolutionary departure. They preached the message that only by its own efforts could society break from the past. With this encouragement from intellectuals, the students were more inclined to act. Had the new regulations, which brought on the St. Petersburg student disorders in the fall of 1861, appeared a year earlier, the issue might never have left the walls of the university.[13]

Contemporary suspicion of Chernyshevskii's involvement in the student disorders, however, went much deeper than his obvious journalistic influence. The reports of the police agents who kept Chernyshevskii under close observation after September 1861 were careful to point out any contact he had with student leaders. Although no evidence came from these investigations that could be used against him at his trial, and they could only guess at what he talked about with the students, this fact did not alter the official suspicion that he was directly involved in instigating the unrest.[14] This view was shared by some in society, as borne out by F. M. Dostoevskii's visit to Chernyshevskii in the spring of 1862, in the belief that Chernyshevskii had the power to control the radical students who were assumed to have been responsible for the outbreak of fires in St. Petersburg (I, 777).[15]

There can be no doubt that Chernyshevskii had contact with a number of St. Petersburg student leaders, either directly or through his co-workers on *The Contemporary*. E. P. Mikhaelis, who helped to distribute the pamphlet "To the Young Generation," was the brother-in-law of N. V. Shelgunov, and was said by one memoirist to have had free entry to Chernyshevskii.[16] In the spring of 1862, Chernyshevskii visited the quarters of N. I. Utin during a meeting of student leaders, although L. F. Panteleev, who recorded this visit, claimed that Chernyshevskii had not attended any of their earlier meetings, and claimed also that Utin was the only one who knew Chernyshevskii personally.[17] I. A. Piotrovskii, another student leader, actually contributed to *The Contemporary* before his tragic suicide in 1862.[18] Chernyshevskii's contacts also included the student leaders N. Ia. Nikoladze and M. P. Pokrovskii. Indeed, Pokrovskii once made the improbable claim that he had been approached by two writers on *The Contemporary*, G. Z. Eliseev and M. A. Antonovich, with a proposal to organize an attack on Tsarskoe Selo, to kidnap the heir to the throne.[19]

Through contacts such as these, Chernyshevskii kept abreast of student discussions. In April 1862, for example, he surprised L. F. Panteleev with a question about the stand Panteleev had taken some time earlier at a closed meeting of the student committee.[20] Yet this contact with students and his obvious concern for their struggle and well-being does not mean that he necessarily encouraged them to disorder, beyond his general ideological guidance and his insistence, in public and private, on the justness of their cause. Rather, it would appear that on this question, as on several others, he faced a dilemma in the contrast between his long-range aspirations and the short-run possibilities of the situation. He believed in the need for radical changes in Russian life, which he did not expect would be accomplished peaceably. Furthermore, he saw the hope of Russia's future in its youth. In the immediate situation, however, he must have questioned how much could be gained by encouraging students to unruly demonstrations over school regulations. Such a course led too easily to encounters by students with the authorities and to punishments that would cut off the young people from more important work. Chernyshevskii probably also realized the danger of the students going too far and losing public sympathy for their cause. This was a time, after all, when the police in Moscow could enlist the aid of townsmen to put down student disorders.[21] Despite Chernyshevskii's antipathy to the government and his full sympathy with the students' wish to be free of traditional regulation, one suspects he realized that perhaps the students had no one to hurt but themselves.

If this is true, then it is possible to explain several aspects of his position in the latter part of 1861 and up to his arrest in 1862. At no small risk to himself, he defended and justified student action on the pages of *The Contemporary* against any show of hostile public opinion. He also cooperated in efforts to organize financial aid for students. But at the same time, he spoke against needless and fruitless conflicts with the authorities. This divided attitude explains a statement of I. A. Piotrovskii to the effect that Chernyshevskii could not replace Dobroliubov in the students' eyes because he was "too cautious." [22] It also clarifies a remark made by Chernyshevskii sometime after the punishment of several students for their part in the fall 1861 demonstrations, charging that those who continued to flaunt their radicalism were like the Bourbons: they never learned or forgot anything; neither prison nor exile would teach them.[23]

Chernyshevskii's restraining support was also apparent in his relationship to an effort to aid students under the aegis of the Literary Fund, after the closing of the university in St. Petersburg. Earlier, he had urged that money from the fund be used to help imprisoned students (XIV, 444, 829). Now he approved the formation of a second section of the fund for students, but he refused to become a member of its committee, both because of the pressure of time, and because he did not want needlessly to attract the close attention of the authorities to the newly established section.[24]

Events in the spring of 1862 gave Chernyshevskii further opportunity to follow this ambivalent course. With the university remaining officially closed even after the release of student demonstrators from confinement, an attempt was made to organize a free university, with public lectures to help the students continue their education. A number of professors sympathetic to the students' plight volunteered their time. The government did not permit P. L. Lavrov or Chernyshevskii to accept invitations to lecture, although two other outsiders—I. M. Sechenov, the physiologist, and V. V. Bervi (Flerovskii), then in the Ministry of Justice—were allowed to do so.[25] The free university experiment, itself a veiled condemnation of the government's policy, proved short-lived. At a meeting on March 2 (the same one at which Chernyshevskii disappointed many of his followers with a poorly delivered talk on Dobroliubov) the highlight of the evening was Professor P. V. Pavlov's speech on "One Thousand Years of Russian History" implying criticism of the government. The speech led to Pavlov's arrest and exile. His popularity among the students assured a response, and a movement developed to suspend the free university public lectures in protest against his harsh treatment.[26] Not all of the participating professors agreed to the wisdom of this course, however, and when the historian N. I. Kostomarov, who had been close to Chernyshevskii in Saratov a decade before, chose to continue, he found himself confronted with unruly student behavior and insults, which might easily have led to new demonstrations and police intervention. Chernyshevskii intervened, trying to convince Kostomarov that he should discontinue his lectures; he even suggested that for Kostomarov to go on would be to play the role of an agent provocateur. Kostomarov objected to what he called "despotism from below" and refused outright.[27] Chernyshevskii, although he had insisted all along that the "public" rather than the students would be the cause of any demonstrations, in a further attempt to ward off an incident in which he knew the students would be hurt, approached the Minister of Education, A. V. Golovnin, only to discover that the free university had just been ordered closed (I, 763).

The incident with Kostomarov stimulated criticism of the students in the press and directly inspired an attack by A. V. Eval'd, "To Study or Not To Study," which appeared later in March in the *St. Petersburg Gazette*. Eval'd's censure of the students for being ill-bred and succumbing to agitators from outside the university implied that the students were to blame for their own difficulties. Because the students did not really want to study, they had themselves brought on the closing of the university and the public lectures.[28] In angry response, the April issue of *The Contemporary* contained Chernyshevskii's article "Have They Learned?" which came just as strongly to the students' defense (X, 168–180).

Chernyshevskii put the responsibility for the disorders directly on the new university regulations of 1861. In his view, these changes insulted the students by treating them like children. Furthermore, the rules seemed designed to take away from the poorer students the opportunity to study. He pointed both to the restriction on the ability of university officials to excuse needy students from fees, and to the limitation on student assemblies, which amounted to destroying the student treasury that was needed especially by the poorer students. Thus, the problem was not that the students did not want to study, but rather that these regulations took away from many the opportunity to study.

In reviewing the course of events that had resulted in the closing of the university and the public lectures, Chernyshevskii presented the students in the best possible light. He played down the student demonstrations and noted how unfairly the students had been treated by the authorities. The professors, he claimed, rather than the students, wanted to close the public lectures, a view directly contradicted by the memoirs of L. F. Panteleev, a member of the student committee at the time.[29] As for the unruly conduct at Kostomarov's lecture, here again the public, not the students, was to blame. Finally, Chernyshevskii denied outright that outside agitators controlled the students' actions. In conclusion, he asked whether those who decried the demonstrations had learned their lesson of handling the students more sensibly in the future (X, 180).

In this article, Chernyshevskii went beyond anything he had written earlier. It was not that he took such an extreme position, compared to views he had expressed on other social and political questions. But in this case, he discarded any attempt to speak indirectly with "Aesopian" language that might be taken in several ways. He identified a specific government policy and spoke forcefully against it.[30] In the Russia of the 1860's, it is difficult to see how such action could have gone on for long. In fact, the April 1862 issue of *The Contemporary* proved to be the last one to contain his writing before his arrest. If "Have They Learned?" was thus Chernyshevskii's swan song in Russian journalism, it was fitting that he wrote it in defense of the youth in whom he placed so much hope in *What Is To Be Done?*

The full story of Chernyshevskii's relationship to the student movement may never be known. So long as the content of private conversations with individual student leaders remains a mystery, some grounds for suspicion remain. Yet it appears highly unlikely that a convincing argument will ever be possible to show that he "organized" the student unrest. The student movement had an ample dynamic of its own, to which Chernyshevskii could add only his sympathy and his efforts to interpret the movement to the general public. The influence he exerted, however, was less on the movement as a whole than on individual students who came under his ideological guidance, and who thereby learned to see their parochial university concerns as part of a larger, more important struggle for the liberation of society. This influence was significant for the revolutionary movement because a number of these young men took an active part in the secret organizations of 1862 and the years following. A. A. Sleptsov recorded that recruitment among the youth was in full swing from the spring of 1862.[31] Thus, it was as an ideological leader that Chernyshevskii made his primary contribution to the student movement, rather than in the encouragement of disorders.

The most persuasive evidence of Chernyshevskii's direct involvement in illegal activity concerns an attempt to write and distribute a series of proclamations to potentially revolutionary groups within Russian society in the winter and spring of 1860–1861. One of these proclamations, "To the Landlords' Peasants," is generally attributed to Chernyshevskii and, indeed, figured as the main charge against him at his trial. Despite the attempts of some scholars, notably M. V. Nechkina, to find evidence of Chernyshevskii's participation in an earlier revolutionary organization dating back to 1859, it would appear that his work with M. I. Mikhailov and N. V. Shelgunov on these proclamations in 1860–1861 is the first genuine case of Chernyshevskii's attempt to transform word into deed.[32]

All of the later printed versions of "To the Landlords' Peasants" are based on a manuscript in the hand of M. I. Mikhailov, which came to the attention of the Third Section in August 1861, as part of a denunciation of V. D. Kostomarov by his own brother.[33] The document, important as an expression of a determined revolutionary position, is also fascinating as an early attempt to translate a revolutionary message into words and concepts that peasants could understand. The opening lines spoke directly against the peasants' belief in the tsar's goodwill: "You waited for the tsar to give you freedom (volia), and freedom came to you from the tsar. Is it a good freedom that the tsar gave you? Now you see for yourselves" (XVI, 947). The proclamation belittled the February nineteenth reform, denying that it had brought any significant improvement in the peasants' condition. It warned that the period of temporary obligation could last for a long time, perhaps up to thirty years, and that during this time the peasant would be defenseless against the landlord. The peasant would no more be able to complain of his plight than the goat could complain to the wolf. Even when the period of temporary obligation ended, the proclamation warned of severe hardships. Wanting to incite rather than explain, it charged that the landlords would always be able to drive the peasants from the land and, after warning of the grim life led by those who lived without land in other countries, that the tsar's manifesto thus meant eternal bondage (kabala) for the peasants—a bondage much worse than at present.

"To the Landlords' Peasants" further undercut the myth of the tsar's fatherly beneficence by explaining that he too had his bonded peasants and was, in fact, the landlord above all other landlords. This meant that he and they were all the same. The tsar took the landlords' side because "one dog would not eat another" (XVI, 950). As for the reform manifesto, which pretended to give freedom, the tsar had issued it merely because he was ashamed before the French and English who had no serfdom.

The proclamation went on to describe what it meant to be a free people, using France and England as examples. Without any reference to socialist ideals, it pointed with approval to France, where all who worked the land, rich or poor, owned the land themselves and were ruled by one administration and one set of laws. It noted that England had no forced recruitment, but rather voluntary military service, which existed in Russia only for the officers. Freedom consisted in both the absence of passports, so that people could go where they wished, and in just courts, which could not be bribed. To explain the difficult concept of popular sovereignty, the proclamation described lines of authority in a free state in terms appropriate to a peasant village. Thus, everyone, whether peasant, landlord, or general, stood under one authority (starosta), and this authority in turn was subject to control by the whole people (mir). While favoring a fully elected authority, the proclamation affirmed that a nation could live well under a tsar, provided the ruler were subject to a popular control he dared not oppose (XVI, 950–951).[34]

The proclamation next advised the peasants on what had to be done. The peasants should be of one mind on the need to act. They must recognize their friends, even among the officers, and they must learn what they could from the soldiers. But most important was the advice not to act too soon. At this point the proclamation promised a directing leadership which, in retrospect, can be seen as far beyond the capacity of any revolutionary group or organization that existed in Russia in the early 1860's:

This is the way things are: all the peasants must be in agreement among themselves in order to act as one, when the time comes. Until the time comes, it is necessary to conserve strength, not to bring on trouble in vain, that is to remain quiet and let on to no one. The proverb says that one in the field is not a warrior. What is the sense of revolting in one village if other villages are not ready? This would only mean spoiling the undertaking and destroying yourselves. But when everyone is ready, then the undertaking can begin. But up to that time make no move, remain quiet, and with your fellow peasant, you must explain and convince him so that he understands the undertaking as it really is. And when you are all agreed, then the call will come for all to begin together. We will see when the time will come and will announce it. You know we have our men everywhere, and news comes to us about the people and what they do. Thus we know that all is not yet prepared. But when all is ready, we will also see that. Then the declaration will be made that the time has arrived for the Russian people to begin the good undertaking, everywhere and at one time, because then everywhere the people will be prepared and in agreement, and one place will not lag behind another. Then it will be easy to win freedom. But until that time, prepare for the undertaking, but do not let on that preparations are going on among you (XVI, 952–953).

"To the Landlords' Peasants" seems clear enough as an early example of the attempt to reach out to the Russian countryside with direct revolutionary agitation from above. It is only when one tries to establish beyond question that Chernyshevskii wrote the proclamation as it stands that the issue becomes somewhat cloudy. The first consideration in determining the authorship must be whether to credit the testimony presented at Chernyshevskii's trial to support the specific charge that he wrote "To the Landlords' Peasants" and attempted, without success, to have it printed and distributed illegally in order to incite revolution.[35] Since M. K. Lemke published his first collection of trial documents in 1907, the general tendency has been to condemn Chernyshevskii's trial as a judicial farce and yet, paradoxically, on the basis of evidence unknown to the government, to insist just as strongly that he in fact wrote "To the Landlords' Peasants." According to this interpretation, the authorities, in an attempt to fabricate a case against him, unwittingly blundered onto the truth even though they could not recognize it as such. The explanation, which is clearly favorable to Chernyshevskii's reputation as a revolutionary conspirator and damning of the government's malfeasance and ineptness, is probably the closest approximation possible to what actually happened.

The story of Chernyshevskii's trial as it emerges from the document collections makes depressing reading. His arrest, on July 7, 1862, was occasioned by Herzen's carelessly sent letter to N. A. Serno-Solov'evich, offering to publish *The Contemporary* abroad. Intercepted by the police, the letter became an excuse to arrest some of the persons mentioned by Herzen, on suspicion of their complicity with dangerous emigrés.[36] At the time of Chernyshevskii's arrest, it is obvious that the government had no other clear evidence of his illegal activity besides this letter and the inconclusive reports of agents of the Third Section, who had kept watch on his activities and contacts since the previous fall. Almost four months passed before the initial interrogations of Chernyshevskii by the investigating commission, under Prince A. F. Golitsyn, on October 30 and November 1, 1862 (XIV, 722–724). The few questions asked showed that the government's concern was still to establish his relationship with Herzen and Ogarev in London, a charge that could not be given any substance and eventually played no part in his conviction. Again long months passed, with no apparent movement in the investigation, until on March 16, 1863, eight months after his arrest, Chernyshevskii was confronted with further questions on his relations with the London emigrés and, for the first time, questioned about his relations with V. D. Kostomarov, M. I. Mikhailov, and N. V. Shelgunov, and about the composition of revolutionary proclamations, including "To the Landlords' Peasants" (XIV, 724–728). Now, for the first time, Chernyshevskii had an inkling of the government's case, against which in the following months he would uselessly try to argue. After that, events moved relatively quickly. In May 1863, the investigating commission finished its work and the case went to the Senate for trial. Early the following year Chernyshevskii was sentenced.

Even at the time, before extensive documentation was published, it was not possible for the Russian government to convince all of the public that it had acted fairly. Among Chernyshevskii's partisans, his case became a cause célèbre, yet another example of the tyranny he had tried to oppose. But even some of those who disagreed with Chernyshevskii felt that the government had put reasons of state before regard for justice. A. V. Nikitenko, who readily criticized the actions of his former pupil, claimed that he had heard Senator M. N. Liuboshchinskii admit doubts about the validity of the juridical proof in the trial. Nikitenko himself feared that the government had injured its reputation by making Chernyshevskii a martyr.[37] In the twentieth century, with more information available, there has been only one serious attempt to defend the juridical validity of the trial. In 1913, M. V. Klochkov devoted two long articles to an analysis of the evidence used to convict Chernyshevskii as well as other evidence that had since come to light. He concluded not only that Chernyshevskii did write "To the Landlords' Peasants," but that the juridical case against him was valid, according to the legal system and rules of evidence in force at the time.[38] Klochkov's work, especially on the last point, carries some conviction, but only if one excludes the possibility of false witness and fabricated evidence. Yet it is just this possibility that makes the government's case most open to question.

Apart from the general suspicion aroused by sections of Chernyshevskii's diary, his published writings, and the inconclusive reports of police spies, the evidence used against him consisted of both eyewitness testimony and written documents.[39] V. D. Kostomarov claimed to have had direct dealings with Chernyshevskii concerning the printing of "To the Landlords'

Peasants" and also to have heard Chernyshevskii admit that he wrote it. A second witness, P. V. Iakovlev, testified that he overheard Kostomarov and Chernyshevskii discuss the printing of the proclamation during one of Chernyshevskii's visits to Moscow in the summer of 1861.[40] The written evidence consisted of a brief note, allegedly in Chernyshevskii's hand, which instructed Kostomarov to make a textual change in the proclamation before it was printed, and a longer letter to the poet A. N. Pleshcheev, again allegedly in Chernyshevskii's hand, which referred obliquely to secret printing and spoke of the need to take risks because no time could be lost.[41] Both pieces of written evidence were supplied to the police by Kostomarov, who claimed that he had been asked by Chernyshevskii to deliver the letter to Pleshcheev two years before. Kostomarov said that he had temporarily misplaced the letter and, when he found it, did not give it to Pleshcheev. Thus, conveniently, it was still in his possession.

There is no way of proving with absolute certainty that the case presented by the government was false, but on every point it is open to serious doubt, and when taken together, these doubts leave little ground for confidence. The main weight of the government's case fell on Kostomarov, both for his testimony and the documents he supplied, yet almost everything in Kostomarov's situation casts doubt on his reliability. V. D. Kostomarov himself was vulnerable to criminal prosecution after his arrest in August 1861, when his brother N. D. Kostomarov, to whom he owed money, informed on him. He could not deny his possession of an illegal printing press and his involvement in an attempt to print revolutionary proclamations, so to ease his own situation, he turned state's evidence, and his testimony figured significantly in the conviction of M. I. Mikhailov. For this service he received a lighter sentence, and there is record of payment made to his mother, presumably as a reward. In his testimony against Mikhailov no mention was made of Chernyshevskii, and indeed as late as January 1863, when he had begun to cooperate in the case against Chernyshevskii, Kostomarov still maintained that "To the Landlords' Peasants" was written by Mikhailov.[42] Furthermore, there is no question that Kostomarov received additional rewards for his testimony against Chernyshevskii, which need not automatically invalidate what he said, but makes it suspect. Within Kostomarov's testimony, there was also the highly dubious claim that Chernyshevskii continued to be concerned with the printing of "To the Landlords' Peasants" up to the summer of 1861. As Chernyshevskii pointed out during his own interrogation, it scarcely seemed likely that at that time one would make a revolutionary appeal to the peasants without referring to the uprising and suppression at Bezdna of the previous spring (XIV, 766). The same objection would apply to the corroborative testimony of P. V. Iakovlev, who claimed to have overheard incriminating conversations between Chernyshevskii and Kostomarov. In the instance of Iakovlev's testimony, however, a stronger objection would be the reputation of the witness himself. He was a drunkard and a notoriously unreliable character.[43]

As for the written evidence, since the brief note was signed "Ch.," and the letter to Pleshcheev signed "N. Chernysh.," the question was whether the writing was Chernyshevskii's. Six of the eight secretaries of the Senate initially felt that the brief note with instructions to alter the wording of "To the Landlords' Peasants" was not generally like Chernyshevskii's writing, which should have cast doubt on all of Kostomarov's testimony, of which the note was a part. Instead, the Senate agreed to find a general similarity between the note and Chernyshevskii's hand.[44] Both the secretaries and the Senators agreed that the letter to Pleshcheev was written by Chernyshevskii, but after 1917, according to Steklov, a new comparison by handwriting experts reversed that judgment with the claim that the document merely copied Chernyshevskii's hand. In any case, even after Chernyshevskii's death Pleshcheev denied any knowledge of revolutionary activity by Chernyshevskii that would have given credence to the content of the letter.[45]

In light of the manner in which the case was assembled, the doubts concerning the handwriting analysis, and the character and situation of those who gave oral testimony, the evidence presented at Chernyshevskii's trial cannot be taken on its own merit as proof of his composition of "To the Landlords' Peasants." More reliable evidence does exist, however, although it is sparse and less specific than one would wish. This evidence indicates that, in the winter of 1860–1861, Chernyshevskii took part in a plan to write a series of proclamations to different groups within Russia whose grievances against the government should have made them receptive to revolutionary agitation. The evidence in turn suggests a different interpretation of the trial itself. Rather than being a lucky guess on the part of the authorities, it may have come about because Kostomarov knew indirectly of Chernyshevskii's involvement but could not support his knowledge with eyewitness experience or authentic written evidence. Thus, he may have cooperated in the fabrication of a false case to support a charge that he knew to be true but could not otherwise prove.

Most valuable, but tantalizingly brief, are the comments in the memoirs of N. V. Shelgunov, who along with M. I. Mikhailov had apparently cooperated with Chernyshevskii in the undertaking. Shelgunov wrote these memoirs more than twenty years after the event, with the admitted desire to revive new interest in the protest movement of the 1860's in which he had taken part. Despite some lapses of memory and the limitations he may have placed on open expression, these memoirs remain one of the best sources for this problem. Shelgunov described the appearance of the revolutionary proclamations in 1861 as the response of a small group of people to the disappointing outcome of the peasant reform, and he said they caused undue panic in the government and unjustified hope among the youth.[46] After telling how the group in St. Petersburg had made the acquaintance of V. D. Kostomarov, an impoverished cavalryman who had a secret printing press in Moscow, Shelgunov referred directly to the proclamations:

That same winter, that is, in 1861, I wrote the proclamation "To the Soldiers" and Chernyshevskii [wrote] the proclamation "To the People" and [we] entrusted them to Kostomarov for printing. In general we talked little, and especially about the proclamations. I rewrote the proclamation in a disguised hand and since all discussions were conducted by Mikhailov, I gave the proclamation to him and he gave it to Kostomarov. Besides,

Kostomarov knew what I wrote. In midwinter, Kostomarov went to Moscow.

That same winter, I wrote the proclamation "To the Young Generation," but we decided to print it in London in the "Russian printing office." No one knew about this proclamation beside Mikhailov and myself. The contents of the proclamations "To the People" [and] "To the Soldiers" I have forgotten, but I remember "To the Young Generation." [47]

This is certainly meager information from one of the few men who in fact knew what was going on. Shelgunov forgot not only the contents but even the correct title of "To the Landlords' Peasants." Nor did he add much to support these words. He mentioned the authorship of an appeal to the peasants at only one other place in his memoirs, where, without further comment, he reported that in 1863 a distraught Kostomarov accused Chernyshevskii of the deed. [48]

Although Shelgunov's comments were disappointingly brief, his memoirs have definitely established Chernyshevskii's participation in the attempt to circulate these revolutionary proclamations. As Shelgunov was personally involved in the events he described, even though twenty years had passed since their occurrence, he would surely have remembered their main outlines. Nor can one think of any reason why he would have distorted the facts. However, his memoirs have left important questions unanswered, such as whether the document that fell into the hands of the authorities was the same one he claimed Chernyshevskii had written, and if it was, why it should have been transcribed by Mikhailov. One must also question the degree of cooperation among the three men, if Chernyshevskii was not included in the writing and printing of "To the Young Generation," the only one of this group of proclamations ever to be distributed. [49] In addition, "To the Young Generation," printed reluctantly by Herzen in London, contained statements about the possibilities for Russia's future that Chernyshevskii could not have accepted without contradicting his own published writing in *The Contemporary*. [50]

There is one other reference by a contemporary to support

Shelgunov's claim that Chernyshevskii wrote a revolutionary proclamation to the peasants. Unfortunately this reference is from the published extracts of A. A. Sleptsov's memoirs, a source generally less reliable and accurate than others of the period. Sleptsov's reminiscences are known primarily through the efforts of M. K. Lemke, who encouraged Sleptsov to write them forty years after the fact and who then published extensive extracts of the reminiscences in the notes to his own 1915–1925 edition of Herzen's works, as well as shorter extracts in his 1923 collection of documents on the political trials of the 1860's. Lemke based his extracts on a notebook of Sleptsov's, written apparently in 1905, which has not been preserved.[51] In one of the extracts, despite some confusion in dates, Sleptsov claimed to have heard about the proclamations directly from Chernyshevskii:

The plan was very well conceived, having in view, in a comparatively short time, to turn consecutively to all those groups which would have reacted to the February 19th reform that cheated the people. Peasants, soldiers [and] schismatics (upon whom at that time there rested great and naturally completely mistaken revolutionary hopes)—here were the three groups that suffered. The fourth group is youth, their friend, helper, inspirer, and teacher. Corresponding to these, roles were assigned in the following way. Chernyshevskii, as the expert on the peasant question, which he really knew in its entirety, was to write a proclamation to the peasants; Shelgunov and Nikolai Obruchev took upon themselves the address to the soldiers; the schismatics they charged to Shchapov and then, I do not recall by what circumstances, gave [it] also to Nikolai Gavrilovich [Chernyshevskii]; Shelgunov and Mikhailov took the young generation. In the beginning of 1861, Chernyshevskii himself told me about such a plan and its execution. Also N. M. Obruchev knew about it, then, fearing to be discovered, removed himself from participation in the general undertaking.[52]

As Steklov and others have noted, there are several points at which the accuracy of this report is open to serious doubt. Sleptsov's reference to a conversation with Chernyshevskii in the beginning of 1861 contradicted another part of his memoirs which stated that he first met Chernyshevskii in July 1861, at which time Chernyshevskii denied trying to write any proclamations.[53] Also Sleptsov's mention of A. P. Shchapov's original part in the plan seems to have no foundation in fact. Shchapov only met Chernyshevskii in December 1861, and prior to Sleptsov's report, the sole mention of his participation had been one of the most doubtful parts of V. D. Kostomarov's attestation to the police.[54] After so many years, Sleptsov had to seek confirmation of his memory in other sources, which raises the question of how much of what he wrote came from memories of direct experience.[55] Moreover, Sleptsov's inclusion of "To the Young Generation" in the original plan, which he claimed to hear from Chernyshevskii, specifically contradicts Shelgunov, who wrote earlier and was in a far better position to know.

Admittedly, Sleptsov was much concerned with his own historical reputation, and in addition to lapses in memory, he wrote with the obvious desire to play up his own role in the revolutionary movement of the 1860's. Yet it is difficult to think that he would have relied on an official version of Chernyshevskii's involvement were it not in part reinforced by his own recollection. Even though inaccurate in details, it is not possible to dismiss his evidence on the larger question of whether Chernyshevskii took direct part in this series of proclamations. One can only regret that Sleptsov, in mentioning the plan, gave so little attention to the plan's execution.

In order to establish the authorship of the extant text of "To the Landlords' Peasants," which is not in Chernyshevskii's hand, attempts have been made to analyze the internal evidence in the document. Unfortunately the results are inconclusive: nothing in the text would definitely bar Chernyshevskii's authorship or, conversely, definitely establish it.[56] The proclamation's general depreciation of the peasant reform and its suggestion that only united mass revolutionary action would bring authentic freedom did express openly the position Chernyshevskii hinted at in the pages of *The Contemporary*. But anyone under his influence and familiar with his thought could have expressed the same thing, including Mikhailov, in whose hand the extant text is written. From an opposite point of view, in an attempt to question Chernyshevskii's authorship,

N. A. Alekseev, the compiler of the best book of documents on his trial, argued that it was unlikely that Chernyshevskii would have considered France under Napoleon III an example of a "free" society, as did the author of the proclamation.[57] However, in a document of this sort, whose purpose was clearly to agitate and to hold up certain goals of freedom in terms that would be understood, strict fidelity to fact may not have been the primary concern. Chernyshevskii may simply have wanted to use names that would most likely strike a familiar chord in the countryside. Nor were there so many other examples of "free" societies in the 1860's for the author of the proclamation to use. It is also possible to argue that the author of the extant text was unfamiliar with some of the terminology and conditions of the reform settlement. One would hardly expect this to have been true of Chernyshevskii, which may indicate that he did not write all of the proclamation as we know it. But it may equally well indicate, as M. V. Nechkina maintained, that he wrote the proclamation before the appearance of the reform manifesto.[58]

Barring what was most probably false witness and evidence at his trial, one can be reasonably sure only that Chernyshevskii planned and to some extent cooperated with Shelgunov and Mikhailov in an attempt to rouse the Russian nation with a series of revolutionary appeals. On this general point, Shelgunov's memoirs, especially when supported by Sleptsov, are conclusive. Some doubt remains as to whether the appeal to the peasants survives in the exact form that Chernyshevskii wrote it, but in view of the fact that "To the Landlords' Peasants" corresponds to other indications of his views at the time, this point has secondary importance.

The execution of the plan itself does very little credit to the reputation of Chernyshevskii, Shelgunov, and Mikhailov as conspirators, and belies the existence of a large, well-organized revolutionary group. The contents of "To the Young Generation," which appeared without Chernyshevskii's participation and perhaps even without his knowledge, shows that the group did not work closely together. Furthermore, the casual, indeed reckless, dealings with Kostomarov almost defy belief. It may well be, as Chernyshevskii maintained at his trial, that his own contacts with Kostomarov were limited to his efforts to help the impoverished young man publish his writings, or at least find some other employment.[59] If this was true, Chernyshevskii lost control of the undertaking by turning the important task of printing the proclamations over to Shelgunov and Mikhailov, with whom his communications were inadequate, as evidenced by their willingness to act on their own without consulting him. These men in turn, with or without Chernyshevskii's agreement, placed tremendous confidence in Kostomarov, even though they had little reason to trust him. Early in 1861, when they included Kostomarov in their plans, they had to recommend him only a general letter from the poet A. N. Pleshcheev and their own recently gained impressions. Kostomarov apparently expressed his radical views freely, but he also complained of his dire financial needs and told both Shelgunov and Mikhailov that his brother had threatened to report his secret printing press to the police. Neither Shelgunov nor Mikhailov took this threat seriously, and in Shelgunov's account, at least, it appears that Kostomarov told of the danger from his brother before he was given the revolutionary appeals to print.[60] A more haphazard approach to the serious matter of revolution could scarcely be imagined. Since the only evidence to the contrary is the dubious testimony of Kostomarov and Iakovlev at Chernyshevskii's trial, it is most likely that Chernyshevskii did not negotiate directly with Kostomarov about the printing of the proclamations, and also that the responsibility for such a poor choice of fellow-conspirator rested primarily with Mikhailov. This interpretation would help account for an alleged cooling in Chernyshevskii's relationship with Mikhailov, noticed by contemporaries, but it would not explain why, once having taken the risk of illegal action, Chernyshevskii carelessly let control of the situation slip from his hands.[61]

A final criticism of the appeal "To the Landlords' Peasants" is its obvious lack of realism. In order to incite the Russian peasants to a large-scale revolution, the proclamation had to attack the myth of the tsar's loving concern for his people and place squarely on him the blame for the peasants' condition. Although it is difficult to gauge how a politically unsophisticated audience might have responded to the language of the appeal, its author tried imaginatively to achieve this end, besides offering sound and needed advice on the importance of coordinating revolutionary activity. But "To the Landlords' Peasants" also included the claim that a well-organized revolutionary party existed, which had members everywhere, and that, when the proper moment came, it would be able to provide overall leadership. Though considerable opposition and even radical sentiment existed, it found expression only in scattered groups, so that it was either terribly naive or misleading to the point of dishonesty to claim that an overall organization existed in early 1861.[62]

Although the planning and abortive efforts of Chernyshevskii, Mikhailov, and Shelgunov occurred some months before, it was only in the early summer of 1861 that a group within Russia, calling itself the Committee of "The Great Russian," succeeded in printing and giving significant circulation to an illegal proclamation that openly condemned the government and expressed the need for drastic change. Thus began what Shelgunov labeled the "era of proclamations" and, with it, yet another aspect of the still unsettled argument about Chernyshevskii's direct revolutionary activity.

Three brief issues of "The Great Russian" appeared in July, September, and October of 1861. Within Russia, according to one recent estimate, they were distributed in numbers of six hundred copies each.[63] Soon after each issue appeared, Herzen reprinted it in *The Bell* and thus greatly increased its circulation; he also gave space in his journal to a discussion of "The Great Russian's" program and tactics.[64] The first issue of "The Great Russian," the shortest of all, established its fundamental position and directed an appeal to the "educated classes." It stated that the peasants were dissatisfied with the burdensome changes produced by the government in the name of freedom. This dissatisfaction had already led to outbreaks and, if Russia continued on its present path, would cause great turmoil in the future. The "foolish and uninformed" government had brought Russia to the verge of a new Pugachev revolt. In these circumstances, the educated classes must act, both to save the people from torment and themselves from terrorism, because otherwise the government, incapable of conducting affairs rationally, would be forced to use compulsion to maintain the system. In effect, the proclamation stated that this was the last chance of the educated classes:

If the educated classes believe themselves without strength, and do not sense in themselves the decisiveness to bridle the government and lead it, then the patriots will be obliged to call the people to the task which the educated classes refused. First let us try; perhaps the enlightened part of the nation does not consider itself without strength. In fact, it is much stronger than the stupid and cowardly government. Thus enlightened people need only say loudly to the government: We wish to change such and such things, we wish to replace them by such and such. The demand will be fulfilled. We are not Poles and we are not peasants. It is impossible to shoot at us.[65]

Although the society itself would have to determine a program of action, the proclamation suggested two of the most important questions to decide: "Shall the essence of the new order of things, which the people and the educated classes alike desire, consist in the setting aside of arbitrary rule, and its replacement by legality?—and Is the present dynasty capable of giving up arbitrary power honestly and firmly?"[66]

The two succeeding issues of "The Great Russian" offered answers to these two questions. The second issue considered the link between the peasant and the Polish questions, on the one hand, and the desire for constitutional reform on the other. A legal order could not be built in Russia alongside the armed repression of the peasants and the Poles. Although the greater part of the peasantry expected that all the land, including land held directly by the landlord, would pass into peasant hands, it might be possible to avoid an uprising with a more moderate minimum program. The peasants might be pacified if they at least received all of the land and facilities that they used under serfdom, entirely without redemption payments, which would be borne by the whole nation. For the Poles, nothing less than unconditional liberation was acceptable. Such liberation would be to Russia's advantage, not only because it was essential to Russia's own freedom, but because the Poles were bound to liberate themselves in any case.[67]

The third issue of "The Great Russian" returned to the question of the existing dynasty, its willingness and ability to carry through the needed reforms.[68] The Committee noted a deep division of opinion in the public. Those called "constitutionalists" believed that the tsar was inclined toward a constitutional order and capable of conforming to that kind of rule. Opposed to the constitutionalists were the "republicans," who could admit good in the tsar as a person but did not think it possible for him to adhere to a constitution. They considered him hostile to freedom, pointing to such evidence as the "bureaucratic" handling of peasant affairs, the arbitrary control of literature, hostility toward the universities, the bloodshed in Kazan and other provinces, and the treatment of Poland. As presented by the Committee, the position of the republicans seemed much more persuasive than that of the constitutionalists. Yet the Committee concluded that the good of the nation would best be served by allowing the tsar one last chance. It argued that if the present ruler, in good conscience, turned away from arbitrary rule, the loss to the republican party would not be great, because a true constitutional monarchy was little different from a republic. Thus, the Committee proposed further educational and organizational work among the public, and to the tsar it made a relatively moderate proposal, which included a land settlement that relieved the peasants of any payments or obligations but gave them no additional land and allowed compensation to the landlords at state expense. It also called for an assembly of representatives of the nation to compose a constitution for Russia. This call for political change was more basic and far-reaching than the other reform suggestions. Although the tone of the address remained moderate and respectful throughout, behind it loomed the threat of revolution:

With this number and with this proposed address our paper discontinues for the time being. We will see what results from our invitation to the educated classes. We turned to them as we promised. But, if we see that they do not decide to act, we will have no choice: we will then have to work upon the common people and with them it will be necessary to speak in a different language about other things. It is impossible to delay the decision for long: if the educated classes do not form a peaceful opposition that will oblige the government, before the spring of 1863, to remove the reasons for rebellion—then the people will inevitably revolt in the summer of 1863. The patriots will not have the strength to ward off the uprising and will have to concern themselves only with trying to direct it in a way beneficial to the nation.[69]

To this day, the certain identity of the group behind the publication of these issues of "The Great Russian" has not been established. Early in October 1861, the police arrested V. A. Obruchev, then a contributor to *The Contemporary*, Dr. P. I. Bokov, a family friend of Chernyshevskii's, and the students V. V. Lobanov, F. R. Dannenberg, and M. I. Svari-chevskii, for distributing the second issue of the proclamation. Little came of the investigation, and of those arrested, only V. A. Obruchev received serious punishment for denying knowledge of the group that printed "The Great Russian" and refusing to reveal the name of the person who had given him copies for distribution.[70] While these men awaited trial, the third issue appeared, indicating that the police were still far from unraveling the mystery. Later historians have mentioned other names in relation to this illegal publication: V. F. Luginin, the brothers N. A. and A. A. Serno-Solov'evich, N. N. Obruchev, A. V. Za-kharin and N. P. Trubetskoi.[71] Yet even this brief list cannot be definitely established. Both N. N. Obruchev and N. P. Trubets-koi were out of the country in 1861, and N. A. Serno-Solov'evich is generally credited with writing the "Reply to 'The Great Russian,'" which appeared anonymously in *The Bell* in September 1861 and took a significantly different stand on tactics. Only against this background of inadequate knowledge and specu-lation can the question of Chernyshevskii's participation in the Committee of "The Great Russian" be raised. Many of the arguments for and against his involvement seem equally to lack conviction and, on balance, tend only toward a tentative conclusion.

An unsigned letter to Chernyshevskii, found in his possession at the time of his arrest, displayed a suspicion among some contemporaries that he had written "The Great Russian," but at the time of his trial, the government offered no further evidence to support this suspicion. Nor have subsequent memoirs added significantly to the argument favoring Chernyshevskii's participation. The two memoirists most often mentioned in support, L. F. Panteleev and S. G. Stakhevich, had no direct contact with "The Great Russian," and their comments seem only to be informed guesses. Panteleev thought it possible that Chernyshevskii had taken part merely because of his close acquaintance with A. V. Zakharin and because his style of writing could be likened to that of the proclamations.[72] Stakhevich also suspected that Chernyshevskii had written some illegal works, and when the two men discussed illegal publications in prison, in the late 1860's Stakhevich noted that Chernyshevskii showed sympathy toward "The Great Russian" and in conversation used similar ideas and expressions. On these meager grounds, Stakhevich concluded that Chernyshevskii must have been either its author or one of its authors.[73]

The opposing view, denying Chernyshevskii's direct participation, finds only slightly better support in two other memoirs, those of P. D. Ballod, who like Stakhevich knew Chernyshevskii in prison, and V. A. Obruchev, who alone among these memoirists may have been in a position to speak with authority on the matter. Ballod held that Chernyshevskii took no part in any revolutionary activity, and he even claimed that those who published "The Great Russian" did not look on Chernyshevskii with sympathy.[74] This latter assertion seems doubtful, especially in view of the personal ties between Chernyshevskii and many of the persons named as possible participants. But apart from this consideration, Ballod's denial of Chernyshevskii's direct action, a guess based on his impression of a man who consistently chose to be secretive about his past, is no more creditable than the guess of Stakhevich, who came to the opposite conclusion. Much more compelling are the statements of V. A. Obruchev, published in 1907, long after Chernyshevskii's death and after his own retirement from a successful military career. Obruchev continued to shield the identity of the person who had given him a packet of the second issue of "The Great Russian" for distribution, but he claimed not to have known the person well and subsequently to have heard nothing more about him. Furthermore, he specifically denied any relation between Chernyshevskii and himself in regard to "The Great Russian." In fact, he belittled the proclamation as "schoolboyish" and considered it unworthy to be linked with the name of so profound a thinker as Chernyshevskii.[75] If one could be sure that Obruchev had played a central role in the undertaking, his testimony would be persuasive, especially in the absence of any strong motive on his part for distorting the historical record. But Obruchev continued to minimize his own role in the affair, and as Steklov has suggested, he might simply have been unaware of Chernyshevskii's contribution.[76]

With so little firm evidence available, arguments based on internal evidence and analysis of content have assumed greater importance, even though in their own right these arguments are inconclusive.[77] At first glance, content would seem to indicate that Chernyshevskii was not directly involved in "The Great Russian," since the proclamation appealed to reform pressure by the "educated classes" as an alternative to peasant revolt, accepted a less extreme agrarian program, and proposed a constitutional order that might be considered more "liberal" than "revolutionary." Considerations such as these make it difficult to accept the possibility that the same man who was significantly involved in the composition of "To the Landlords' Peasants" could have worked on "The Great Russian" at almost the same time. Steklov stated this point of view forcefully when he contrasted the "liberal aspirations" of "The Great Russian" with Chernyshevskii's "revolutionary-socialist" position.[78] More recent Soviet writers, such as S. A. Pokrovskii or E. S. Vilenskaia, use the current term "revolutionary democrat" to describe Chernyshevskii but, on this general question of authorship, take a position similar to that of Steklov.[79]

In the past decade, however, there has been an attempt to revive the view of some early Soviet historians that Chernyshevskii was not only involved in writing "The Great Russian," but that these proclamations were in fact part of a larger, well-conceived plan of revolution.[80] Essential to this view is an interpretation of the content of "The Great Russian" that relieves it of any suspicion of liberal inclinations. N. N. Novikova, for example, treats the relatively moderate proposals of the proclamations simply as a tactical maneuver, designed to show those who might be wavering before a fully revolutionary position that their hopes for any other solution were in vain.[81] In a different variation, I. S. Miller suggests the possibility that Chernyshevskii, without any intention of seeking a coalition with liberals, nonetheless realized that they were a factor worthy of attention in the political struggle against autocracy.[82]

In a situation where specific evidence is lacking, there is surely value in speculation about how "The Great Russian" might have been designed to fit into a revolutionary plan of action, despite the moderation of its tone and most of its immediate recommendations. But these speculations tend to assume Chernyshevskii's participation rather than to establish it on any basis of certainty. Behind the claims of Chernyshevskii's leading role in "The Great Russian," one often finds argument that is specious and evidence strained beyond the point of credibility.[83] Perhaps the most important contribution of these speculations, therefore, is a negative one. They show that the surface dissimilarity between "To the Landlords' Peasants" and "The Great Russian" is not in itself sufficient reason to dismiss the possibility that Chernyshevskii composed them both. "The Great Russian" need not necessarily be interpreted as the product of a liberal rather than a revolutionary position.

Since neither the memoir material relating to "The Great Russian" nor analysis of the proclamation's content gives sufficient grounds for a definite statement, one can only reach a tentative conclusion. Although nothing in the documents would automatically rule out Chernyshevskii's authorship, it would appear that the best case can be made against his direct involvement. Denial of Chernyshevskii's authorship has the advantage of coinciding with the best of the memoir references, that of V. A. Obruchev, and it receives additional support from the direct statement of N. V. Shelgunov that the proclamations, including specifically "The Great Russian," "To the Young Generation," and "Young Russia," had no common center or directing leadership. Shelgunov claimed that the proclamations were the partisan actions of obscure, separate groups, which had no links among themselves. Insofar as Chernyshevskii cooperated with Shelgunov and M. I. Mikhailov to plan a series of proclamations, his participation in "The Great Russian" would thereby appear to be ruled out.[84]

The most significant consideration, however, remains a comparison of the content of "The Great Russian" with what is known of Chernyshevskii's views at the time. This comparison shows that "The Great Russian," taken at face value, expressed a point of view considerably less radical than the message Chernyshevskii expounded not only in "To the Landlords' Peasants" but also on the pages of *The Contemporary*. Since well before the February nineteenth reform, he had given up serious hope of cooperation with more moderate reformers, because of their indecision and timid refusal to make the needed appeal to popular revolution. His most bitter denunciations of moderate illusions were made in the course of 1861, when he reached the conclusion that only a popular movement, aided by a sympathetic radical elite, could achieve the needed destruction of autocracy. It is difficult to believe that at the very same time, during the summer and early fall of 1861, Chernyshevskii would have ventured the dangerous undertaking of an illegal, underground proclamation only to show that the views he had just managed to express openly, with great daring and cleverness, were too extreme, and that there was in fact hope that the more moderate approach of the "constitutionalists" might yet serve a purpose or even win the day.

Though it is possible that "The Great Russian" represented a tactical maneuver by a group that actually desired or expected a more radical solution, the evidence thus far assembled does not give this possibility a high degree of probability, and the fact that "The Great Russian" did not go unanswered indicates that there was a distinct sentiment to its left. Although the evidence is not undisputed, there is good reason to believe that the objection came from a source close to Chernyshevskii. The criticism from the left found expression in a brief article entitled "Reply to 'The Great Russian,'" printed by Herzen in *The Bell* on September 15, 1861, under the signature "One of many." Appearing at that date, the "Reply" could only comment on the first issue of "The Great Russian," yet its major criticism would have applied to the other issues with only slightly less force. The "Reply" praised the bold appearance of "The Great Russian" as a sign of resistance to slavery in Russian life and an indication of the government's weakness, but it took a different position on the immediate action needed. Since elements hostile to the government were growing every day, they must be united and inspired to mount an uninterrupted, unsparing campaign against established authority. The "Reply" admitted that "The Great Russian" recognized the inevitability of struggle, but it had mistakenly tried to agitate "society," whereas to face the task seriously, it was necessary to turn not to society, but to the people; and it was necessary not to ask questions, but to work out from the principle that the present order was intolerable and that none better would be achieved until power was taken from the tsar's hands.[85]

The "Reply" indicated that within society, or the so-called educated classes, only a minority had real concern for the people, but this minority could reach its goal if it created a secret society of dedicated men to unite with the people, who had ample discontent but too little initiative and organization. A relatively few men could achieve a great deal if they focused on such activities as writing so as to be understood by the masses, printing secret literature and distributing it to the people and the troops, and establishing ties among discontented groups. In conclusion, the "Reply" belittled the significance of a constitution. It proposed neither to help nor hinder the constitutional effort. Though a constitution that guaranteed the right of assembly and free speech would be easier to work under, it was not the final goal. That goal was rather the full liberation of the peasants, the right of the peasants to the land (presumably all the land), the people's right to rule themselves, and a free federative system of government.[86]

A significant tactical difference thus existed between "The Great Russian" and the "Reply," and the position Chernyshevskii expounded in his published writings, admittedly in disguised form, appears closer in sentiment to the "Reply" than to the original proclamation. The authorship of the "Reply" suggests an additional link to Chernyshevskii.[87] Despite dissenting opinion, the general consensus is that N. A. Serno-Solov'evich wrote the "Reply." N. A. Serno-Solov'evich, one of the founders of the first "Land and Liberty" organization, had in the course of 1861 moved decidedly to the left in his political position and drawn close to the radical circle of *The Contemporary*. From the time of the initial appearance of "The Great Russian" to the time of their joint arrest in 1862, he was in close contact with Chernyshevskii and had ample opportunity to know his views. There is every reason to believe he shared those views.

One final consideration fits less easily into the tentative conclusion that Chernyshevskii did not take part in the composition of "The Great Russian," but can nevertheless be reasonably well explained. In February 1862, Chernyshevskii wrote the "Letters Without Address," which, though rejected by the censor and therefore not known to the public at the time, like "The Great Russian" allowed the possibility of significant opposition to the government from quarters other than the peasantry, namely from the Tver nobility, and similarly urged the government to act to avoid a mass revolution. The question arises whether the "Letters" do not invalidate the argument that the general tendency of "The Great Russian" is counter to what is known of Chernyshevskii's contemporary views. If the "Letters" had been written a half-year before, they would do just that, so the question of timing is decisive. Whereas Chernyshevskii clearly favored a revolutionary alternation of Russian society and government, he was not a dogmatic revolutionist in tactics, who would automatically deny the value of temporary cooperation with other groups working for progressive change. But these groups had to show serious determination in their efforts, and it was the failure to see such determination that brought Chernyshevskii, in 1859 to 1861, to make his strongest statements about totally polarized alternatives: stagnation or mass revolution. If Chernyshevskii is to be relieved of the suspicion of self-contradiction, and if the argument about the incompatibility of "The Great Russian" and his other known views is to be used, it is necessary to assume that the protest movement among the Tver nobility early in 1862 made a significant impression upon him. Without altering his fundamental view of the need for revolution, these short-lived signs of determined resistance, the most impressive show of opposition from the nobility since the Decembrists, most likely caused him to reconsider the value of giving tactical support to alternate forms of opposition. At the time of the appearance of "The Great Russian," however, several months earlier, there is no indication that he felt such optimism.

During the latter part of 1861 and the early months of 1862, there were signs in many areas of Russian life that gave determined opponents of autocracy realistic grounds for hope. Although the announcement of the February nineteenth reform manifesto had failed to trigger wide-scale peasant rebellion, and Chernyshevskii himself, in his "Letters Without Address," made ironic reference to the fact that both he and the tsar had reason to be disappointed in the people's apathy, neither had the peasants indicated that they would necessarily accept their fate passively (X, 91). The revolt at Bezdna in April 1861, and numerous signs of resistance elsewhere, showed that the gap between what the peasants expected and what the government and landlords were prepared to concede remained wide indeed. Thus, there were reasonable grounds to expect that the revolutionary forces of the countryside might yet be mobilized. As the writers of "The Great Russian" reported, rumors had already spread among the peasants that when the two-year period of temporary obligation ended in 1863, the long-awaited freedom would come. Surely the peasants would resist once they discovered that their slavery was to continue in a different form.

There were indications of unrest in other areas of Russian

life as well. Disorders at the universities, even when confined
largely to issues of corporate rights, showed a young generation
ever more willing to challenge traditional values and patterns
of behavior, as well as to relate their parochial concerns to
broader social and political questions. As they began to reject
their own society, these youth might become a source of leadership to give organization and direction to peasant discontent.
Nor did it seem that those who struggled against autocracy
would have to stand without allies. Events in Poland appeared
to be moving toward a direct challenge of the government's
apparatus of repression through a movement of national liberation. Even in the most favored segment of Russian society,
the nobility, the government's bureaucratic handling of the
reform settlement had brought wide-spread dissatisfaction. Although much of this dissatisfaction represented no more than
the selfish protection of class privilege, a small group of the
nobility opposed the government under the banner of genuinely
liberal principles. In either case, their opposition weakened the
government's position. Finally, the very appearance of illegal
proclamations offered grounds for hope. Not only did they
indicate the existence of protest and perhaps revolutionary
groups, but as N. A. Serno-Solov'evich noted in the "Reply to
'The Great Russian,'" they revealed the weakness of the authorities, which had been unable to suppress them.[88]

Against these indications that there might yet be hope for
change, stood an imposing set of problems and obstacles. Primary among them was the enormous cultural gulf that separated members of the radical educated elite from the people,
whose needs they felt and whose interests they wanted to serve.
Even the most radical groups had hardly begun the difficult
task of crossing over into what was essentially a distinct culture, in order to establish significant contacts with the dark
world of the peasant village. Moreover, within the radical
movement, the ranks could not easily be closed. Separate groups
and leading individuals took different positions on a series of
important questions, and this disunity could paralyze con-
certed action. The question of whether Europe should be regarded as a model or a warning remained unresolved. Nor could

agreement be found on the capacity of the peasants to show initiative, the degree of constructive direction they required from without, or even the possibility of influencing the course of a mass social upheaval. There were many problems concerning the relationship of radicals to moderate reformers, such as the degree of tactical cooperation to be employed in the short run. Questions about immediate programs proved equally troublesome. At this time it was still possible to be radical without being socialist. But even if one favored socialism, the choice must be made as to whether socialism should be demanded immediately or left to a later time, in the manner of "To the Landlords' Peasants." Further disagreement developed over the question of a land settlement, with regard to the amount of land distributed and the compensation received.

The fact that diverse answers to these questions found expression in late 1861 and early 1862 indicated the desperate need of greater organization among opposition groups. If possible, common agreement had to be reached on a program, and lines of communication and discipline had to be established, both among existing groups and new groups to be created in different parts of Russia. The need for such an organization was recognized by N. A. Serno-Solov'evich in his article in *The Bell* on September 15, 1861, and in the following issue, for October 1, N. P. Ogarev expressed his agreement. But Ogarev, in his article "Reply to the Reply to 'The Great Russian,'" clearly disagreed with Serno-Solov'evich on certain tactics. He divided the Russian population into three categories: the great majority of the oppressed people, the landlords and bureaucrats who oppressed them, and the educated minority from amidst the landlords, bureaucrats, and men of varied rank (raznochintsy) who sympathized with the people. Recognizing divergences among those who felt that the existing order had to be changed, Ogarev, unlike Serno-Solov'evich, thought it was important for these groups to work together. The constitutionalists, because they recognized the bankruptcy of autocracy, could serve as useful allies, without altering the future course. On the question of organization, Ogarev warned of dangers and introduced thoughtful qualifications. As he was wary of an organization that imposed common goals and assumptions from above, he stressed the need for groups to form within the varied regions of Russia, in close contact with local conditions and problems. These must then unite and cooperate, so it might not happen that a movement in St. Petersburg would succeed before the regional forces were prepared. If the regions had to be organized from above on the day after victory, the danger loomed of a new kind of tsarist power or dictatorship. Yet for all his qualifications and differences, Ogarev greeted the call to organize with genuine enthusiasm. For a long time he had quietly waited for a voice from Russia to say that the time for fear had passed, and that the time to act had arrived. He had long believed the appearance of such a voice to be inevitable.[89]

These two statements by Serno-Solov'evich and Ogarev symbolize the early attempt to create a nationwide revolutionary organization. Realistically, initiative had to come from within Russia, as it did from a small group of men in St. Petersburg who stood close to Chernyshevskii and *The Contemporary*. But this initiative was given encouragement and support from Ogarev and later Herzen in London. The appearance of these two articles in the fall of 1861 did not necessarily preclude the possibility that there had been prior discussions between individuals from London and St. Petersburg, but it indicated that plans were still far from translation into action and that nothing like agreement had been reached.

The full story of the first organization to be called "Land and Liberty" may never be known. Not only do the relatively few direct sources leave many questions unanswered, but to some extent they appear contradictory. A. A. Sleptsov, for example, was goaded into composing his memoirs by the appearance of memoirs by L. F. Panteleev, which Sleptsov felt gave a false view of the movement, as well as an uncomplimentary impression of his own role. Yet these two memoirs, along with the program documents of the organization that appeared within Russia and abroad, are among the most important sources. Nevertheless, the main outlines of Land and Liberty, as well as of Chernyshevskii's involvement, can be described with reasonable confidence.[90]

In 1868, N. I. Utin gave an account of the founding of Land and Liberty, in the earliest published review of its activities by a participant. He described the fear aroused in government circles by the student unrest, the proclamations, and the St. Petersburg fires in the spring of 1862. These fears led to repressive measures, and just when government and social reaction was most intense, the revolutionary cause entered a new phase with the formation of a secret society, known to the public as Land and Liberty.[91] That the spring of 1862 was a time of organization and recruitment is confirmed by Panteleev, who along with Utin made his way into the organization at this time.[92] But by then, as Utin noted, local revolutionary groups already existed, so that the task of the new effort was to bring all of these groups into a unified whole, capable of coordinated action on the basis of a common program.

The genesis of the effort to form a nationwide revolutionary organization goes well back into 1861 and has been the subject of considerable speculation and disagreement. The date of origin depends on one's definition of "organization," as well as on estimates of how closely key individuals worked together. These estimates, however, given the paucity of evidence, are rarely more than informed, and sometimes uninformed, guesses. It is known, for example, that N. N. Obruchev, who later was an active organizer of Land and Liberty in St. Petersburg, collaborated with Ogarev in writing "What Do the People Need?" which was printed in *The Bell* in July 1861. In time, this article became a program statement of the organization and, indeed, supplied its title and slogan, for in answer to their question of what the people needed, Ogarev and Obruchev replied that it was very simple: the people needed "land and liberty." [93] Yet the collaboration behind "What Do the People Need?" cannot be taken as evidence that an organization already existed; it seems rather to show a growing realization that one was needed. The same can be said for evidence from A. A. Sleptsov about his first conversation with Chernyshevskii in the late spring or early summer of 1861. Although the question of organizing a secret society appeared in the record of the conversation (recalled some forty years after the event), this is scarcely reason to argue, as one historian does, that plans and organizational efforts were underway at this early date, because otherwise Chernyshevskii, an "experienced conspirator," would surely have been more cautious.[94]

One other piece of evidence which shows that the need of an organization was under discussion in the summer of 1861 also reveals the differences that prevented a comfortable cooperation among elements opposed to autocracy at the time. This evidence is a cryptic remark contained in a letter sent by Ogarev to Shelgunov in late July or early August 1861, which was later found in Chernyshevskii's possession at the time of his arrest.[95] Ogarev complained that Chernyshevskii had sent someone to tell him not to entice youth into a "literary alliance," because nothing would come of such an attempt. Here "literary alliance" referred to a secret political organization, as admitted by Chernyshevskii at his trial, when he tried to use the document as an indication that he was not in league with the London emigrés (XIV, 725–726).[96] One can speculate on why Chernyshevskii might have discouraged Ogarev's initiative at this time. Certainly he distrusted the position taken by *The Bell* on several important issues, and he continued to harbor personal feelings against its editors. Or he may honestly have believed that nothing would come of the attempt. But the point is that Ogarev in this letter obviously took Chernyshevskii's warning as a sign of the latter's skepticism and refusal to act.[97] This fact, along with Chernyshevskii's having issued the warning at all, seems ample proof that, by the summer of 1861, many suspicions had yet to be overcome if a truly united effort were to be mounted.

It is most likely that the first significant attempt to meet the recognized need for organizational unity came after the appearance of "Reply to 'The Great Russian'" and "Reply to the Reply to 'The Great Russian,'" in the early fall of 1861. By October, N. A. Serno-Solov'evich and N. N. Obruchev were back in St. Petersburg, and according to A. A. Sleptsov, by the spring of 1862 these two had joined with A. A. Serno-Solov'evich, V. S. Korochkin, and himself to form the basic nucleus that grew into Land and Liberty.[98] Regardless of the question of Chernyshevskii's direct participation in this organizational effort, it is beyond question that these men stood close to him in their fundamental ideas, and had many personal ties as well.[99]

The tasks faced by the initial nucleus in the following months were many. They had to recruit and organize new members and to broaden their base of support, through legal and illegal publications and through participation in public groups like the Chess Club and the Literary Fund.[100] Finally, and perhaps most difficult of all, they faced the imposing task of establishing contact with new or existing groups in other parts of Russia and abroad. Although important progress was made in the spring of 1862, especially in recruitment among the youth of St. Petersburg, the basic organization of a large-scale secret society and the definition of a united program was far from complete when the government, without actually knowing of the existence of the secret nucleus, struck at its heart.[101] In July, N. A. Serno-Solov'evich and another early member, S. S. Rymarenko, were arrested, along with Chernyshevskii, and A. A. Serno-Solov'evich was forced to flee abroad. Thus, the organization had to continue deprived of some of its best leadership.

It is difficult to determine precisely the relationship of the nucleus in St. Petersburg with the London emigrés during the first half of 1862. Ogarev, whose articles in *The Bell* showed an increasingly radical tendency, probably preceded Herzen in the hope he placed in the enterprise, but even he, realizing that the essential work had to be done in Russia, could only offer advice from the outside. In the middle of June 1862, he sent a letter to N. A. Serno-Solov'evich, which urged that the demand for a representative assembly (zemskii sobor) be made a central part of the secret society's program, and which stressed the need of organizational effort in the provinces, in line with the warning he had given in "Reply to the Reply to 'The Great Russian.'"[102] The fact that the efforts of the two centers, London and St. Petersburg, were not yet closely coordinated was revealed in a curious document, a penitent "Confession" by V. I. Kel'siev, who, as a close collaborator of Herzen and Ogarev, made a clandestine trip to Russia in the spring of 1862 to arrange for the transport of publications from London, at which time he met with N. A. Serno-Solov'evich in St. Petersburg.[103] As Linkov points out, there are parts of Kel'siev's account that do not seem creditable, such as his suggestion that Herzen was to assume a "dictatorial" leadership once the network of organizations had been perfected. But Kel'siev's record of N. A. Serno-Solov'evich's disappointment with Herzen's refusal to be drawn immediately into "practical activity" does carry conviction.[104] Except for support given in the pages of *The Bell* for points of a program that might be shared, the men involved in organizational work within Russia were essentially on their own.

Despite the arrests in St. Petersburg in July, the organization grew and extended its influence, as young men like N. I. Utin came to play a more important role. There is a record of attempts to reach out to other parts of Russia, a task that proved more difficult than anyone had anticipated.[105] Not only were the technical problems of communication and coordination over such great distances imposing, but it soon became obvious that the extent of organizational influence depended on finding a common program that would unite the broadest possible spectrum of opposition sentiment. From the radical point of view, compromises were made to gain the cooperation of diverse groups. Some years later N. I. Utin identified this policy as a tactical error, because it weakened the capacity of the organization as an instrument of revolution.[106]

Although there is disagreement on this point, the name Land and Liberty was apparently used first in August 1862.[107] And only by the fall of that year had something like a cooperating network of organizations been established. It was then that the leading group in St. Petersburg reconstituted itself as the Russian Central National Committee, with the implication that it directed the activities of the whole. Probably this assertion went beyond the reality of the Central Committee's authority. From the latter part of 1862 into 1863, however, a secret press within Russia and presses in safer locations abroad produced publications that can with partial justification be called program statements of an organization.[108] With this greater degree of unity, thought could be given to strengthening ties between St. Petersburg and London which, for all the early interest of Ogarev, had weakened after the arrest of N. A. Serno-Solov'evich. In January 1863, A. A. Sleptsov arrived in London for conversations with Herzen, on whom he did not make a favorable impression. Herzen was put off by Sleptsov's arrogance and pride, as well as by Sleptsov's suggestion that Herzen should become an "agent" of Land and Liberty. Nor did Herzen have confidence in Sleptsov's claim that the organization already had several hundred men in St. Petersburg and three thousand in the provinces.[109] Skeptical of the strength of an organization that a few months later he was to call a myth that lived on only because its members believed in it, Herzen nonetheless gave publicity and support to Land and Liberty, especially in relation to the sad events that were unfolding in Poland.[110] On the basis of this tenuous liaison, the organization reached the peak of its influence and unity.

The year 1863 saw the temporary collapse of all the hopes on which Land and Liberty had been founded. Its political program calling for a classless popular assembly to replace autocracy, which in itself represented a considerable concession by members who favored more radical programs of social revolution, had no chance of realization without the serious threat of a popular revolution. Yet contrary to the expectation of many who joined the organization, the countryside remained relatively quiet. Clearly the peasant movement had subsided after 1861, and in its short life, Land and Liberty had neither the time nor the organization necessary to stimulate a revolutionary consciousness from outside.[111] The second major source of disappointment was the inability to coordinate any revolutionary effort in Russia with the revolution that broke out in the Polish provinces under Russian domination. Efforts had been made to link the two movements in the latter part of 1862, but it was just as impossible for the Russian revolutionary leaders to hasten a popular upheaval in Russia as it was for the Polish leaders to delay an outbreak in Poland.[112] As it turned out, the Poles had to face a brutal defeat and repression, with little more than symbolic gestures of help from their only supporters within Russia, while the Russians in Land and Liberty, who tried to give at least verbal support to the Polish cause, lost stature in their own society where that cause aroused only antagonism and nationalist passion.

During most of the time that Land and Liberty was making

its bid to achieve unity among the groups opposed to autocracy, Chernyshevskii was fighting a losing legal battle to regain his freedom. The government, along with the rest of society, only knew about the organization from its publications, which appeared months after Chernyshevskii's arrest, so that it had no grounds for suspicion of his complicity. However, in later years the publication of memoirs raised the issue of Chernyshevskii's participation and showed beyond a reasonable doubt that Chernyshevskii kept abreast of the attempts to form a secret society and generally favored and supported the effort. There is also no doubt about his close relation to many of the early organizers, especially N. A. Serno-Solov'evich. But there is still a wide difference of opinion on the question of Chernyshevskii's initiative in the enterprise and also on the degree to which he engaged directly in organizational work.

Writing in 1928, Iu. M. Steklov made a reasonable evaluation of Chernyshevskii's relationship to Land and Liberty. Steklov at first found it difficult to think that Chernyshevskii could have stood to the side in this attempt to rally revolutionary forces on a broad scale, because on the basis of his ideas Chernyshevskii should have been the rightful leader, if not the initiator of the organization. But Steklov admitted that the only evidence which spoke specifically to this question, by a direct participant, was the recollections of A. A. Sleptsov, who maintained that Chernyshevskii had declined to become a member of Land and Liberty because of the priority of his important commitment to *The Contemporary.* According to this account, however, Chernyshevskii continued to show interest in the organization and to advise its leaders concerning their plans. Relying on Sleptsov's recollections, even though he admitted they were not always accurate, Steklov had no choice but to conclude that Chernyshevskii's role was limited to the guidance of his ideas on the men who were at the center of the secret society. Steklov supported this view with the reminder that neither N. I. Utin nor L. F. Panteleev, both of whom knew Chernyshevskii and also worked in the organization, gave further evidence of his direct participation.[113]

Steklov used the version of Sleptsov's recollections prepared by M. K. Lemke from conversations with Sleptsov and from extracts of a notebook written by Sleptsov shortly before his death, which has never been recovered. In Lemke's version, there is little room for diverse interpretation. Sleptsov did not mention Chernyshevskii among the early founders, whose preparatory work began at the end of October 1861. However, he did note the special effort made by the early leaders to reach out to Russian journalists for their cooperation. Some of the writers approached joined the secret society; others, like P. L. Lavrov and G. Z. Eliseev who were somewhat older, became consulting members. Then Sleptsov told of the approach made to Chernyshevskii:

> It was different with Chernyshevskii. Nikolai Gavrilovich talked with A. and N. Serno-Solov'evich, listened to them very attentively, with grieved eyes and unflagging interest, and, when they had finished their communication, said: "For me the matter must be decided by the illness of Nikolai Aleksandrovich [Dobroliubov] and the inability of Nekrasov to conduct the present-day journal by himself. To work at the same time on *The Contemporary* and with you, excuse me with you all, I do not see as physically possible. Let us wait and see what happens with our sick one. When I see that he is in a condition to work as before, then after a month, as a friend, I will be with you, but all the same with *The Contemporary*. It is valuable to me as a tribune which must not be forfeited either for me or for you, insofar as you share its general tone." [114]

This conversation, if it has been accurately reported, occurred sometime in early November 1861, because Dobroliubov died on the seventeenth of that month, and preparatory work had begun only in late October. It is true that Chernyshevskii would still have had eight months of freedom to change his mind and, despite this initial refusal, both join the secret society and work on *The Contemporary*. But Sleptsov's subsequent comments, which claimed that "nevertheless" Chernyshevskii took interest in the society and offered advice, indicate the contrary. Nor did Sleptsov mention Chernyshevskii among the organizing group at work in the spring of 1862. Though the distinction between joining and advising at that stage may not have been great, it is reasonable to conclude from Lemke's version of Sleptsov's recollections that Chernyshevskii was not the initiator of the efforts to form a secret society, and that, despite his sympathies, he preferred to remain on the sidelines.

In 1933, five years after Steklov's work, this reasonable conclusion was challenged by the publication of another set of recollections by Sleptsov's wife, M. N. Sleptsova. Sleptsova described her husband's first meeting with Chernyshevskii in May of 1861 (not in June as Lemke indicated) and his reacquaintance with N. A. Serno-Solov'evich, whom he had known earlier in school. Then Sleptsova told of the earliest steps toward organization:

After a month or two, that is, in the beginning of July or August, Chernyshevskii proposed with his young adepts the organization of a fundamental circle of five (piatërka) as the basis of an "underground," a society as it was called in those days. Besides it was not only an underground, inasmuch as they also worked out entirely legal courses of action on all social strata.

I do not know why Lemke, in his extracts from the lost notebook of Sleptsov, was not aware that Chernyshevskii not only participated in the initial circle of five, but was the initiator of them and a member of the first one. Its composition was as follows: Chernyshevskii, Nikolai Serno-Solov'evich, Aleksander Sleptsov, Nikolai Obruchev and Dmitrii Putiata. Nikolai Obruchev, a member of the Moscow circle of "The Great Russian," thus appeared as a link which united the Moscow organization with Chernyshevskii's circle of five.[115]

In a footnote to this paragraph, Sleptsova added:

It is true, Chernyshevskii said that as yet he could not participate in the practical work of the society that was coming into being, but this it seems [meant] practical work in Land and Liberty which was organized somewhat later. And really, could Chernyshevskii have thrown aside his literary work in order to travel to Kiev, for example, to organize regional committees and circles? But he was a member of the Central Committee.[116]

Sleptsova described the "legal" activities of this initial group, including attempts to reach the masses through the publication of popular books, inexpensive reading rooms, and a network of Sunday Schools, as well as the "illegal" efforts to propagate revolutionary ideas. The actual formation of Land and Liberty in 1862, Sleptsova described as an extension of Chernyshevskii's initial circle of five, with each member forming other circles, and so on. Furthermore, this organization carried out its affairs with such conspiratorial skill that members of the St. Petersburg regional committee did not even know the members of the Central Committee. As a consequence, the question arose whether Chernyshevskii actually took part in the revolutionary society. In restating her view about the centrality of Chernyshevskii's role, Sleptsova admitted that Dobroliubov's death prevented him from working actively in the new organization, so that he became primarily its consultant and theoretician. But she insisted on his practical activity in forming the first circle of five and in joining that circle to the Central Committee of Land and Liberty, of which he was himself a member.[117] Since it would appear that Chernyshevskii's general sympathy with Land and Liberty and his willingness to give advice are nowhere in question, the issues raised by Sleptsova's version are limited to Chernyshevskii's initiative in the genesis of that organization and to his direct involvement in its Central Committee. Recent writers, who stress Chernyshevskii's role as a revolutionary organizer as well as a theoretician, necessarily rely on Sleptsova's account as a major source of evidence.[118] Even Venturi, who at one point recognizes Chernyshevskii's opposition to early attempts to organize a secret society, refers to Sleptsova to support his claim that Chernyshevskii entered the central group of five in Land and Liberty.[119]

Despite this growing tendency to rely on Sleptsova's recollections, there is little about them to merit confidence. She was born in 1861, and began to hear about the events she described only twenty years later when she became Sleptsov's third wife, long after he had left the revolutionary movement.[120] By the time she wrote about Land and Liberty, a half-century later, she admitted that her only sources were her own remembrance of secondhand accounts, heard at least twenty years after the event, some unidentified papers of her husband, which apparently did not include the notebook used by Lemke, and vaguely defined information from supporting literature. This did not stop her from including verbatim conversations, however, although she admitted at one point that her husband may not have used exactly those words. Nor is the existing version of her work complete. In a cautious introduction, her editors explained that they used only those parts of an extensive manuscript which, with "more or less grounds," might be considered as echoes of stories by those who had participated directly in the events described. The editors also noted that Sleptsova's recollections could not be considered an "authentic historical document," because of her uncritical, subjective attitude toward her husband, and because so much of what she wrote relied on memory and an "unskillful" use of her written materials.[121] The editors might have gone even further to note Sleptsova's obvious errors, which seriously undercut the value of her contribution. Since Sleptsova was wrong about including N. N. Obruchev (who was out of the country at the time) in the first group of five, organized in July or August 1861, she might also have been wrong about Chernyshevskii's leadership. Or if the career of A. D. Putiata, whom she also included in this early group, was so well known to her, she should have known that his arrest took place in 1866, not 1862.[122] Furthermore, if she had a reasonable grasp of the events of the early 1860's, she would have hesitated to write that Chernyshevskii showed Sleptsov his letter from "A Russian Man" before sending it to Herzen, because she had identified the date of Chernyshevskii and Sleptsov's first meeting as May 1861, and the letter was published in *The Bell* more than a year before.[123]

With so many sound reasons to doubt the accuracy of Sleptsova's account, it is difficult to see how the increased use of her recollections can be justified. There are problems enough with Lemke's version of her husband's testimony, yet wherever the two versions conflict, it certainly merits greater belief. Following this line of reasoning, one must conclude that the organizational initiative of Chernyshevskii in beginning a small conspiratorial group that in time developed into Land and Liberty, and his participation in the Central Committee of that organization, cannot yet be accepted as fact.

At the current stage of knowledge of the events of the early 1860's, the question of Chernyshevskii's direct involvement in the revolutionary movement cannot be fully answered. The lack of sound evidence, and the conflicting nature of the available evidence, leaves the way open to subjective speculation and guesswork that has little scientific value. The facts permit a reasonably strong negative conclusion rather than a positive one. Enough is known about what happened among the divergent groups that sought radical change to reject the suggestion that, in 1861 and the first half of 1862, a well-organized revolutionary center existed in St. Petersburg. The several attempts made to translate thought into action were hesitant, contradictory, and conspicuously devoid of careful plan and organization. As for Chernyshevskii's relation to these efforts, it seems obvious that his intellectual contribution was paramount. He, more than anyone else, provided the general framework of radical thought and the goads to action that led other men to leave the comfortable realm of passive speculation. But at best, direct action by him probably went little further than his participation in a poorly planned and even more poorly executed effort to circulate revolutionary proclamations, and his willingness to give encouragement and advice to those who tried desperately if unsuccessfully to form a strong, nationwide revolutionary organization, Land and Liberty. It would be difficult to overestimate the general importance of Chernyshevskii's contribution to this early phase of the revolutionary movement in Russia, but the significant nature of his contribution was not his work as an organizer, but rather in the fact that other men, who read his words and knew him personally, found in his message the inspiration to act.

# X. Prison and Exile
## (1862–1889)

By means of the arrest, rigged trial, and punishment of Chernyshevskii, the Russian government sought a way out of a difficult situation that was largely of its own making. For several years prior to his arrest, the annoying but unimaginative and ineffective censorship had permitted him to express and popularize a point of view more radical than could safely be allowed by a government ruled by traditional autocracy. Then in 1862, when reasons of state required that his influential voice be silenced, the government acted with ruthlessness, inflicting a cruel, prolonged punishment on this offender whose published works had all passed through the censorship. Once they had committed themselves to undisguised repression, one would at least have expected the Russian authorities to have made a thorough job of it. Instead, revealing a decided inability to learn from past mistakes, for some time they continued to treat Chernyshevskii with a bizarre combination of inhumane, sometimes senseless severity and careless, inefficient laxness. He was held for eight months without knowing the main charge that was to be brought against him; he had only the meagerest opportunity to defend himself, without aid of legal council; and until he began a determined hunger strike, he was not allowed the comfort of a visit from his wife (XIV, 470, 473). Yet at the very same time, even though writing

312

had been his main threat to the established order, he was allowed to continue work and, unbelievable as it seems, through a bureaucratic confusion of censorship responsibility he was given one final opportunity to influence Russian public opinion. *What Is To Be Done?*, without question Chernyshevskii's most influential single work, was written and legally published while the author was in prison and completely under the government's power.[1]

Chernyshevskii began *What Is To Be Done?* in December 1862, and according to his habit worked at a furious pace. A few months later, the novel was printed in three installments in the March, April, and May issues of *The Contemporary*, which by 1863 had been allowed to resume publication.[2] Unexpected good fortune had accompanied the attempt to have the work printed, for not only was it a most unlikely work ever to slip through prepublication censorship, but Avdot'ia Panaeva, whose husband was for long the legally responsible editor of *The Contemporary*, later reported that Nekrasov had at one point actually lost the packet containing Chernyshevskii's manuscript on the street. A few days later, in response to the announcement of a reward, the packet was returned to Nekrasov and publication plans resumed.[3]

More than a decade earlier, Chernyshevskii had experienced nothing but disappointment and frustration when trying his hand at belles-lettres, and that experience had left him with serious doubts regarding his artistic talent. Yet other motives now impelled him to write *What Is To Be Done?* Practically, if he wanted to maintain the influence he had built up over the years, he needed to find a way through the censorship. Furthermore, Chernyshevskii had only his pen to ensure the support of his family, a problem that now weighed heavily on him. Both these considerations coincided with his belief that enlightenment had to be spread in society by works at several levels of sophistication, ranging from vast compendia of scientific knowledge to thoroughly popularized literature, or sugared pill versions of the enlightened point of view (XIV, 456).

To the modern reader, the novel *What Is To Be Done?* is an awkward and flimsy construction, whose obvious purpose

313

was to provide a platform for the author's instructions to the reader on a variety of social and personal problems. Crude melodrama and hopelessly contrived literary devices were employed, which might suggest that Chernyshevskii sought to parody the frivolous, sentimental novels that ran counter to his own work.[4] Yet the line between intended parody and Chernyshevskii's own unintended artistic failings is difficult to draw. In a sense, the book produces the same confusion as one of his personal interviews sometimes produced in his contemporaries, who were never quite sure whether Chernyshevskii was being serious or was making fun of them, or indeed of himself.

The novel opens with the apparent suicide of an unidentified traveler, the report of which causes terrible feelings of guilt in a man and woman who are the two other corners of an ill-fated love triangle. After assuring his readers that all will end joyously "in drinking and song," Chernyshevskii proceeds for two-thirds of the novel to explain the background of this tragic turn of events, and then constructs a bizarre, but eminently rational happy ending.

Vera Pavlovna, the young heroine of the story and the apex of the triangle, has remained marvelously uncorrupted by the hypocritical and oppressive family environment in which she was raised. Trapped by traditional family domination, she nevertheless yearns for freedom and fights her strong-willed mother to a standstill by threatening suicide rather than submitting to an arranged marriage. But her actual salvation comes only with the fortuitous appearance of Lopukhov, a struggling medical student of great promise and a personification of the new morality of rational egoism.

Lopukhov, motivated by barely admitted feelings of affection along with a desire to do the rational thing, marries Vera Pavlovna so as to remove her from her family's control. Their life together is unlike anything seen up to that time in Russian literature—a relationship consistent with the morality of a new breed of men and women who have been liberated from the tyranny and hypocrisy of the past. For several years they know happiness, while Vera Pavlovna develops a deeper understanding of the need for rationality in social as well as personal relationships. With remarkable ease she organizes a successful cooperative of seamstresses and thereby demonstrates the mutual advantage of rational, nonexploitive economic theory.

Trouble appears only when Vera Pavlovna matures in self-understanding and realizes that something is lacking in her relation to her husband, whose work keeps him in a constant state of preoccupation. When she dares to recognize the truth, she finds herself drawn to her husband's good friend Kirsanov, who feels a like attraction and has struggled heroically to keep his feelings hidden. Kirsanov is also a "new man," no more nor less worthy than Lopukhov, but simply more suited to Vera Pavlovna. The old morality never gave a satisfactory solution to this age-old dilemma, and now the "new people" offer one.

Their answer returns the reader to the suicide at the beginning of the novel, and it soon becomes evident that the tragedy is not a tragedy at all. The suicide is a hoax carried off by Lopukhov to remove himself from the scene and thus grant freedom to his wife and friend. He must have Vera Pavlovna experience and display real grief for a time, so that the hoax will be convincing, and her legal right to remarry will appear to be above suspicion. But at the proper time, the truth is revealed to Vera Pavlovna by an extraordinary character named Rakhmetov, bearing a message from her husband who has fled abroad. Chernyshevskii describes Rakhmetov as a giant among other "new people," who are themselves heroes when compared to ordinary men. Rakhmetov is the "rigorist," who has developed the new ideas to their logical conclusion and has dedicated himself totally to achieve their realization. From this lofty vantage point he soon convinces Vera Pavlovna and Kirsanov that their guilt is irrational and thus frees them for a happy, creative life together.

Vera Pavlovna's second marriage offers further opportunity for Chernyshevskii to develop his theme of rational love among the new people. Lopukhov, the reader is relieved to learn, is not to be left simply as the victim of self-sacrifice. After a sojourn in America, he returns to Russia as a foreign business representative with the assumed name of Beaumont. In Russia he soon marries another young woman of emancipated views, Katerina, and as luck would have it, Lopukhov-Beaumont's new love had earlier been saved from the well-meaning but nonetheless destructive domination of her father by the timely intervention of Kirsanov. In this way, the stage is set for the two couples finally to come together, and as the novel ends, Vera Pavlovna and Kirsanov are living in delightful and innocent harmony with Lopukhov-Beaumont and Katerina. What the old morality would condemn as bigamy, the new morality reveals as an authentic and truly uncompromised love.

The novel might well have ended here, but Chernyshevskii saw fit to add some closing pages in which his happy new people meet a mysterious "lady in mourning" while on a frolicking winter picnic. The symbolism is too obscure and the suggestions too veiled to be certain what the author was trying to express in this incoherent section. In a final remark he suggests that in two years, in 1865, there will be a time of rejoicing, a time to "change decorations." By this, Chernyshevskii might have meant anything from a simple statement of hope in the future to a declaration of imminent political revolution (XI, 336).

Chernyshevskii's general treatment of characters and his awkward employment of hackneyed literary devices compound the difficulties of establishing the line between intended parody and his incapacity as a writer. Ironically, this man who once argued that art reached its highest pinnacle in the imitation of nature, populated his own novel with a host of characters representing abstract virtues and vices, who rarely appear to the reader as believable human beings. One is reminded of those sections of Chernyshevskii's diary where he revealed that he could never relate to a person apart from the particular world view held by that person. Of course, Chernyshevskii may have intended to poke fun at the second- or third-rate literature of his day by imitating it from a completely different point of view. But the fact remains that the characters of *What Is To Be Done?* are wooden, predictable, and unconvincing.

Chernyshevskii's use of tired literary devices is best exemplified by his development of the character of Vera Pavlovna, whose growth from an oppressed but defiant victim to a shining example of the liberated woman provides the strongest thread of continuity in the novel. The stages of Vera's growth are marked by four dream sequences, which in Chernyshevskii's own time were a target for mockery by his opponents and a source of embarrassment to some of his friends. The mysterious and edifying figures that populate the world of Vera's dreams remind one of the ghosts of Christmas Past, Present, and Future used by Dickens to reform Ebenezer Scrooge. With each dream, the heroine rises another rung on the ladder of self-understanding, enlightenment, and emancipation. Thus, in two encounters with the female figure "Love of Mankind," Vera learns of the pleasure to be gained from helping to liberate the oppressed, and discovers how wickedness is tied to a misunderstanding of one's own best interest. Later she is helped by another apparition (this time in the form of an Italian opera singer) to realize that her relation to Lopukhov is falsely based on gratitude rather than love. And finally in Vera's fourth dream, two figures, both gloriously beyond description, complete her education: one shows her the long uphill struggle of women to achieve true equality; the other grants her the ultimate beatitude, a vision of the rational society of the future (XI, 77–78, 119–125, 166–172, 269–284).

However one judges the relative balance of intended parody and literary failure in *What Is To Be Done?*, the question of the value of the novel as a piece of literature perhaps misses the point, for Chernyshevskii wrote with the primary intention of instructing his readers in a world view, and his own intention provides the most useful standard by which to measure the novel's success.[5] Only if the merit of the novel as novel is made secondary to the impact it had on a particular audience can one give Chernyshevskii's effort its due. In this regard it cannot be denied that for a significant portion of the Russian youth of the 1860's and 1870's the novel was an important formative experience that helped shape their attitudes and values, and occasionally even guided their social action. The important question, therefore, is why the work had this impact, despite its serious limitations as a piece of literature.

There were doubtless aspects of fad and notoriety in the novel's success. The story is so naive and gentle by modern standards that it is difficult to understand the sense of shock it aroused in hostile contemporary critics, who saw the work as a daring statement of the moral laxity of youth. Yet according to many standards of their day, they were right. For example, in Chernyshevskii's tale the sacrament of marriage was subordinated to a rational criterion of legitimacy in love, and illegal bigamy was praised over proper marriage if that bigamy represented a more authentic relationship. One might also point to a faint suggestion in Vera's fourth dream that in the rational utopia of the future, men and women would enjoy even freer, more casual love relationships.

But such considerations ought not to be overemphasized. Primarily the novel's success rested on positive acceptance of its message by part of a generation that had already suffered a crisis of confidence in the traditional functioning and values of society. Chernyshevskii's message may have been simplistic, but in context this very weakness became part of the novel's appeal. The reader had only to recognize the universal validity of the one great truth—that rational egoism had the power to correct the evils inherent in existing personal relationships and society—and problems could ultimately be solved. At the same time, by describing this advanced morality as the special insight of a new generation, Chernyshevskii pampered his young readers' self-esteem and offered them an easily won position of moral superiority to their elders.

A further explanation of the positive reception of Chernyshevskii's message must be found in the optimism and hopeful expectancy that pervaded the novel. The reality of the problems he identified was undeniable, as sensitive persons were aware. In his day traditional morality often served as a mask for hypocrisy and unfair advantage. Parents often manipulated the lives of the children they professed to love. Society allowed the exploitation of many for the benefit of a few, and the position of woman was far from exhibiting reasonable equality.

In view of these problems, it was probably not the workability of a given scheme that comprised Chernyshevskii's strongest appeal, but rather his underlying idea that men need not be captives of their heritage. They could organize their relationships in work and daily life in a manner that would correct the gross inequalities. Injustice did not have to be, simply because it always had been. Men could use their reason with not only the promise but the certainty of success. Thus, a good part of the appeal of *What Is To Be Done?* was in the challenge it presented to its readers. The future would not bring improvement of its own accord; men of the present would have to work and fight for change. But a better world was within human grasp if, instead of accepting life blindly, men used reason to evaluate the present and think through alternatives.

In addition to its arguments for a new morality and for the power of reason over tradition, *What Is To Be Done?* appealed to young readers by offering them a model of commitment. All of the so-called new people of the novel could be taken as possible models of conduct, but Chernyshevskii reserved his greatest praise for the towering figure of Rakhmetov, who can best be described as a revolutionary ascetic. This overdrawn hero realized the extraordinary demands that would be made in the struggle for a better world and, through giant feats of self-denial and mental and physical training, prepared himself for complete dedication to the cause. For later generations, he became the model for a professional revolutionary (XI, 195–210).

Besides these inherent appeals, the government contributed to the success of the novel by its treatment of Chernyshevskii himself. To the extent that his conviction and punishment became a cause célèbre, appearing as yet another example of tsarist injustice, the appreciation of *What Is To Be Done?* increased. The generosity and human concern that found expression in its pages, despite any awkwardness of style, stood in so great a contrast to the vindictive punishment inflicted on its author as not to go unnoticed.

During the two years of his imprisonment in the fortress of St. Peter and St. Paul while awaiting trial, Chernyshevskii maintained a consistent pose of injured innocence. He sent a number of defiant notes to the prison commandant, A. F. Sorokin, and refused to comply with the demand that he modify and soften his tone (XIV, 465–466, 468–481). Respectfully, but nonetheless firmly, he wrote at least one note directly to Alexander II, complaining of the long interval between his arrest and first interrogation, which he took as proof that the authorities could make no firm accusation (XIV, 460–461). Early in 1863, probably before he realized the seriousness of his situation, he reached a pinnacle of defiance when he wrote a letter (never delivered) to the governor-general of St. Petersburg, Prince A. A. Suvorov. Chernyshevskii claimed to be turning to Suvorov because the prince combined two qualities that were rare among Russian public officials: common sense and a knowledge of the government's real interests. Chernyshevskii then asserted that his own fate was important to the government's reputation, and scornfully suggested that a way out of this difficult situation might be for the government to exonerate itself by placing the blame for the whole mistake on underlings (XIV, 470–471).

Separated from his family while awaiting the outcome of his trial, Chernyshevskii began a long series of personal letters which continued from Siberia until the time of his return in the 1880's. Through these letters one again becomes aware of his personal concerns and aspirations, which during the active years of his career were reflected only in his journalistic writing or in the reports of the few who knew him well. Unfortunately, even these family letters are not always a satisfactory source. He knew that his letters passed through the hands of the police, both in St. Petersburg and later in Siberia, and he knew they were read and sometimes delayed (XIV, 465). Thus he would hardly have been entirely frank in expressing his views in any case where they might have undercut his stance of total innocence. Moreover, to this externally imposed limitation Chernyshevskii added a limitation of his own. Because of the need to comfort his family, especially Olga, with encouraging reports of his situation, he generally tried to convey to them the most optimistic picture possible. In reading this correspondence, therefore, one is never entirely sure when

Chernyshevskii believed his own words and when he wrote simply for a calculated effect on his reader.

One example is the earliest extant letter to Olga written after his arrest, wherein he expressed something akin to exultation as he anticipated the future. He claimed that her name along with his own belonged to history, and predicted that in one hundred years they would be remembered with gratitude when others around them were forgotten. To explain this anticipation of renown, he told Olga of his writing plans, now that he would have time for the work he had long dreamed about and was no longer required to write simply to live. His ambition seemed boundless: he would write a multivolumed "History of the Material and Intellectual Life of Man," a work of broader scope and better execution than the efforts of Guizot, Buckle, and Vico; a "Critical Dictionary of Ideas and Facts" based on this history, which would be for scholars; and a smaller "Encyclopedia of Knowledge and Life" intended for the public. Altogether his works, written in French, the language of the learned world, would compare in value to those of Aristotle (XIV, 456). It is known that Chernyshevskii had for long thought of making a significant scholarly contribution of an encyclopedic nature and continued to think along these lines until shortly before his death. But in this letter, as in a number of others, exactly where honest self-revelation left off and fantasy, or a desire to make a brave show of his lack of despondency, began is impossible to say.

By early February 1864, the Senate had examined Chernyshevskii's case, at least to its own satisfaction, and had reached a conclusion. The sentence read that Chernyshevskii, for his evil intention to overthrow the existing order, for his undertaking of agitation, and for his composition and attempt to circulate a seditious appeal to the landlords' peasants, was to be deprived of all rights of rank and sent to the mines for fourteen years of penal labor, to be followed by lifelong exile in Siberia. Apparently some consideration was given to the possibility of imprisoning him nearby in the Schlüsselburg fortress, but the Senate's original recommendation was carried out, with the one change that the length of his initial prison term was cut in half, from fourteen to seven years.[6] However, this standard, ritualistic act of imperial mercy had been assumed in determining the original length of the sentence.

Of Chernyshevskii's life in St. Petersburg, the city that had once wakened him to the world beyond his provincial Saratov and which had provided the setting for his extraordinary career, nothing now remained except to play out a last scene of public humiliation. On May 19, 1864, Chernyshevskii was subjected to the ceremony called "civil execution." After the announcement of his sentence, he was pilloried and publicly identified as a state criminal. The assembled crowd, which in memoir reports and police records was variously estimated at between two or three hundred and several thousand, witnessed a gruesome demonstration of the helplessness of the individual before the massed power of an autocracy that had not yet been seriously challenged.[7] And for the man, this demonstration of oppressive power tragically foreshadowed what he was to experience throughout the next quarter-century.

After its absurd blunder of allowing publication of *What Is To Be Done?*, the government had in fact achieved its objective, even though at considerable cost to its own reputation, of making Chernyshevskii suffer for his affront and threat to the established order and traditions of Russian society. Moreover, the direct line of his influence was cut, never to be re-established. What remained was the legacy of his earlier published writing and a myth of the man based on his martyrdom for the radical cause. Neither his work nor the myth could be completely stamped out, but successive governments made strenuous efforts to see that nothing new was added, and generally they succeeded. No new writing appeared in Russia over his name until well after his death. In the 1880's, when a few new translations and articles were printed, they bore a pseudonym instead of Chernyshevskii's own name.[8] Nor could there be any serious possibility of direct ties between his distant places of imprisonment and exile and the ongoing radical movement either in Russia or abroad. His movements and contacts were too easily controlled, and effective restrictions were too easily placed on his correspondence. Although in the earlier years of his imprisonment he had contact with other political prisoners, these men were not free to write of their experiences when released, and generally their memoirs appeared only after 1905.[9]

The main outlines of the long and dreary closing decades of Chernyshevskii's life are spare. He spent the years from 1864 to 1871, the official period of penal labor, in the trans-Baikal region near Chita.[10] Because of his tendency to send only encouraging reports back to his family, it is difficult to get an accurate picture of his condition during these years. His health, which was never robust, suffered under the general rigors and privations of prison life, and perhaps most damaging of all, he did not have the materials or situation to continue the sustained and purposeful work that once had so completely dominated his way of life, and which his personality required. Yet in other ways these early years were easier to bear than what followed. Chernyshevskii had the community of other political prisoners, and more important, he could sustain himself with the hope and expectation that after his prison term of seven years he would be allowed to return to some part of European Russia, live with his family, and continue at least scholarly if not journalistic work. From the late 1860's up through 1871, Chernyshevskii's letters to Olga spoke of his impending return and his plans to become active again (XIV, 497–511). Nor did these hopes seem unrealistic. He felt that, at best, the government had only a flimsy case against him, and for seven years he had conducted himself in a way to avoid reproach. Furthermore, other offenders, with as much or more proven guilt on their heads, had been allowed to return after expiration of the prison term of their sentence.[11]

But to the degree that Chernyshevskii seriously expected to be allowed to return to Russia, he must have been unaware of or simply unable to evaluate the government's fear of his influence on the radicals who continued the revolutionary struggle. The sustained radical agitation for Chernyshevskii's release merely reinforced the suspicion of the authorities that, despite the passage of years, he still represented a dangerous revolutionary threat. The several daring, but blundering and ineffective, attempts to liberate him worked in the same direction.

There was brutal irony in the fact that the handful of young men who wanted to repay their ideological leader by securing his release succeeded only in displaying their own thoughtless bravado and inability to keep a secret, and thus in hurting the very man they wanted passionately to help. Strong views against Chernyshevskii's release had been expressed in government circles even before discovery of the liberation attempt by G. A. Lopatin in 1870 and 1871; but it was not long after that attempt, later in 1871, that orders were issued to send Chernyshevskii to a more secure outpost, the desolate town of Viliuisk, on one of the tributaries of the Lena River, at a latitude only slightly below that of Archangel.[12]

It is generally agreed that the eleven dreary years spent in Viliuisk, from 1872 to 1883, hurt Chernyshevskii's health and spirit to such a degree that he never completely recovered. Added to the hardship of a more severe climate was the terrible isolation, the poverty, and the total lack of intellectual stimuli. Although he continued to minimize his own discomforts, one can read between the lines of his descriptions of the wretched life of the local inhabitants what it must have meant to live among them (XIV, 518–519). And following the collapse of his hopes for an improvement in his situation after the first seven years of his sentence, Chernyshevskii had to live with the prospect of spending the rest of his life separated from the family he loved and the serious work he craved. Under these circumstances, it is not surprising that he experienced a threat to his equilibrium; the surprise is that he held up so well. Occasionally, the anguish he experienced broke through the surface of his quiet resignation and expressed itself in unexpected ways.[13] He burned many of his literary efforts from this period, the reason for which, one suspects, was only partly his fear that they would be considered politically dangerous. But though he frequently withdrew, and found it difficult to focus his intellectual concern or to maintain his old intellectual vigor, Chernyshevskii managed to weather the crisis of boredom and despair. His psyche and world view remained intact.

Chernyshevskii's personal situation in Viliuisk continued to vary according to factors over which he had no control. Changes in local personnel, as well as changes in government policy, affected the degree of surveillance and the number of restrictions placed on him. Once again his situation worsened because of an ill-conceived liberation attempt, carried out by I. N. Myshkin in 1875, which resulted in tighter control of his movements and contacts. This must have been an especially painful blow, because during the previous two years he had tried to inform the authorities through his letters, which he knew they read, that he wanted no part of any plan to escape (XIV, 553). It was only during the final years in Viliuisk, from 1879 to 1883, that the surveillance and restrictions were relaxed so that his situation resembled exile more than imprisonment.

There may have been one occasion, in the summer of 1874, when Chernyshevskii had an opportunity to alter his fate. V. Ia. Kokosov, who for many years served as a prison doctor in eastern Siberia, described the episode in memoirs published about thirty years later. Kokosov had never met Chernyshevskii, but he had heard a secondhand account of a note, allegedly sent by the governor-general of Siberia to the hapless prisoner, which invited him to petition for mercy, thereby offering him freedom in return for admission of his guilt. Chernyshevskii, as the story was told, refused outright, insisting again that he had done nothing for which to ask mercy. This proud and highly principled reply has been widely accepted as true.[14] Yet in the absence of support from any other sources, and considering the fact that such an offer would seem to contradict all else that is known of the government's fear and treatment of Chernyshevskii at the time, there are good grounds to doubt that the offer was ever made. Although, Chernyshevskii was surely capable of such a reply, Kokosov's secondhand story requires further corroborative evidence before it can be accepted as fact.[15]

It is impossible to evaluate the weight of the several factors that finally influenced the decision to recall Chernyshevskii from his Siberian exile. Appeals and petitions came from Chernyshevskii's family, but these long remained without effect. In the early 1880's, the pressure of public opinion to have his case reconsidered increased both in Russia and abroad. There is also record of secret negotiations conducted indirectly between government officials and terrorists of the revolutionary group "People's Will," who offered to refrain from violence at the coronation of Alexander III in exchange for Chernyshevskii's return from Siberia.[16] Whereas it is difficult to think of the government's yielding to this kind of pressure, especially since Chernyshevskii was moved only after the real threat of the People's Will had been broken, the terrorist demands may have added a note of urgency to more moderate appeals. Clearly the government had no intention of allowing him to return to one of the centers of Russian intellectual and political life. Excessive fear of his influence even ruled out the possibility of returning to his home town of Saratov. At the end of the summer in 1883, Chernyshevskii, excited by the hope that his dreadful isolation might at last be at an end, was sent back to European Russia under strict guard. After a brief stop in Saratov, he was taken to Astrakhan, a new place of exile.

The life Chernyshevskii led for six years in Astrakhan could scarcely have fulfilled his hopes for authentic freedom and intellectually rewarding work. However, his immediate conditions of life improved. He lived in a private dwelling, with permission to have his family with him, although his sons pursued their own careers outside of Astrakhan, and even Olga made a number of extended trips.[17] But the problem of financial support bore heavily on him. He wanted to earn his way and to provide his wife with a living style previously denied her during his unproductive exile in Siberia. Yet he could not publish under his own name, and the only path open to him meant spending long and tedious hours in the frustrating task of translating other writers for whom he rarely had respect. Nor was he in any sense a free man. So strong was the fear that he might yet become a rallying point for opposition sentiment, that for several years he was kept under close surveillance, a fact that he knew and resented. Only gradually did this surveillance lessen, as the authorities realized that this once powerful voice of Russian radicalism was no longer a serious threat.[18]

It is impossible to gauge how significantly this watchfulness of the government affected his continued isolation from stimulating personal contacts. In the political context of Russia in the 1880's, one may assume that some men would have held back from advertising their sympathy with Chernyshevskii. In fact, the number of visitors from outside Astrakhan was relatively small, and he did not find a community of intellectuals there with whom to share ideas.[19] But it is also true that Chernyshevskii himself did little to encourage such contact. To a large degree he withdrew to a self-imposed isolation, which at one point led Olga to complain that they lived like hermits.[20] It was not that he was denied human contact, but rather that he found no one on his own level with whom to talk. Nor did the situation improve with time. In a letter of August 1888 to A. N. Pypin, he explained his indifference to Russian literature and current affairs by a comparison of his own condition with that of Robinson Crusoe on an island. Chernyshevskii knew some agreeable friends, but they were all "Fridays," with whom he could only discuss such matters as the size of the fish catch or the price it might bring at market (XV, 730). Despite its light tone, this note showed the scars of a depressing intellectual loneliness.

By the time that the government finally relented and allowed Chernyshevskii to return to Saratov, he had little time left to live. He arrived in Saratov in June 1889, and four months later he was dead. His secretary noted that despite delirium, he characteristically tried to continue work up to a few days before his death.[21]

No straightforward account of the treatment received by Chernyshevskii at the hands of the government can convey the full measure of the torment he endured. Every man confronts his experiences with a unique combination of strengths and weaknesses. Chernyshevskii's tendency toward self-effacement and self-denial helped him to live through a prolonged period of physical discomfort and personal privation, which might have broken other men. Yet this same tendency made him vulnerable to a terrible feeling of guilt in relation to Olga, whose way of life, so different from his own, depended on his freedom and his financial support. He suffered from a painful sense of unfulfilled responsibility, and the torture of this feeling was never far from the surface of his letters. Although reality occasionally broke into Chernyshevskii's correspondence with Olga, his general tendency was to treat her like a pampered child, whose every wish and need had to be met, and who had to be shielded from all unpleasantness.

From the time of Chernyshevskii's banishment to Siberia in 1864 to his return to Astrakhan in 1883, he saw Olga only once, during a brief visit in 1866, and because of his intense concern for her comfort and well-being, the meeting brought him as much grief as joy. The round trip from St. Petersburg for Olga and her eight-year-old son Mikhail lasted over five months; the actual visit lasted only four days. Chernyshevskii found it difficult to bear the sight of his wife and child, accompanied by a gendarme, in a setting which he could endure himself more readily than he could impose on those he loved. He soon requested that they return and not attempt the trip again. In a version of the visit given much later by his son Mikhail, Chernyshevskii was grieved by the length, expense, and unpleasantness of the journey undertaken by others for his benefit. It would have been easier for him if that effort and expenditure had been spared, or used to make Olga's life more comfortable.[22]

If a reference in one of Chernyshevskii's letters several years later may be taken at face value, it was during Olga's brief visit that he first urged her to seek another marriage (XIV, 589). Over the next several years he clung to this possibility, and indeed, in 1868 and 1869 he tried to force the issue by breaking off all correspondence with his family (XIV, 600). The fact that he made such an attempt so close to the time of his impending release indicates the doubt that was mixed with his desperate hope. The pain it must have caused him was probably no worse than the pain of his guilt over being responsible for Olga's misfortune. One extant letter of Chernyshevskii's from April 1868 (just before he tried to break contact with his family) gives a pathetic illustration of what was troubling him. He pleaded for Olga's forgiveness because he had not left her in a "secure situation," for which he blamed his impracticality. Admitting that he had long anticipated what might happen to himself, he lamented that he had not considered how such a change in his circumstances might affect her. Earlier, he had not thought that he would lose the opportunity to work for her benefit over so long a period of time. He had thought that after a year, or a year and a half, the journals would again be filled with the "nonsense" (vzdor) of his works, and that she would then have as much income as before, or even more (XIV, 496). The pathetic aspect of this letter was not only Chernyshevskii's inclination to assume an excessive burden of guilt, but also his apparent willingness to equate his importance to Olga with his capacity to supply her with money.

With the passage of time, the problem of his family's support became more troublesome. In his desperate concern for Olga's happiness, Chernyshevskii at times showed a distinct loss of contact with reality. He responded to Olga's complaints about her health with a repeated plea that she take up residence in Italy, as if such a decision were simply a matter of free choice. He even put pressure on his sons to change their own life plans and accompany her so that his wife's needs might best be served. This motive was revealed in a series of letters he sent to his sons in 1876 and 1877 recklessly belittling Russian education and culture, which most likely Chernyshevskii calculated would convince his sons of the advantage of going abroad with their mother.[23]

The main responsibility for the support of Olga and the children while Chernyshevskii was in Siberia fell to his cousin, A. N. Pypin, who readily put aside ideological differences to prove the depth and staying power of his affection in this way. Yet even this display of generous loyalty on Pypin's part did not pass without friction and crisis during the 1870's, for Olga and Pypin's family did not get along. When Olga complained of them to Chernyshevskii in 1874, he was profoundly hurt and troubled.[24] But there was little he could do, although he tended in immediate response to take his wife's side. In September 1874, he told his son Aleksandr not to allow other family members to reproach Olga because she had not joined him in Siberia. In fact, Chernyshevskii advised, it was his son's obligation to break with anyone who offended Olga (XIV, 568). Cruelly trapped in his own situation, Chernyshevskii could only suggest blindly to his wife and children that they cut themselves off from their major source of aid and means of support.

The strained feelings between Olga and the Pypin family affected Chernyshevskii's own relationship with his cousins. Without knowing the exact content of the letters between Chernyshevskii and his wife and children, A. N. Pypin guessed that Olga had complained to her husband about her treatment, which threatened the ties between Chernyshevskii and his other relatives. Near the end of 1874, he wrote Chernyshevskii a long letter telling his side of the story.[25] Clearly Pypin was troubled by the thought that he might lose Chernyshevskii's trust even though his family had done so much to help. He again asserted his love and concern for Chernyshevskii, claiming that neither he nor his family wanted to engage in arguments with Olga, which often had no point or clearly understood cause. In effect, Pypin blamed Olga's nervous irritability for bringing arguments on herself.

The letter Chernyshevskii wrote in response to Pypin's explanation, as well as one he wrote in 1878 in response to what must have been a similar situation, showed the seriousness of the unhappy man's dilemma (XIV, 600–604; XV, 136–150). On one level, he simply could not afford to offend Pypin if he wanted to be realistic about the affairs of his immediate family. Such a consideration may well have influenced his efforts to smooth matters over, minimize the seriousness of Olga's complaints, and generally play the peacemaker. But it would appear that Chernyshevskii's dilemma went considerably deeper. One suspects that, for a change, he was being honest with himself and with Pypin when in both letters he expressed sympathy with the Pypins and admitted that Olga was not an easy person. In fact, in the letter of 1878 he went further than ever before in revealing the difficulties Olga had brought into their marriage (XV, 146). He claimed that nothing could interfere with his own feelings for the woman he valued far above even his children, but driven by a conflict among those he loved, which he could neither reconcile nor deny, he had finally to admit that he could not expect others to share those feelings. Perhaps at this point he realized that the idealized image of Olga lodged at the center of his affection was only a product of his own imagination.

Though there is no adequate way to compare the personal experience of essentially different kinds of suffering, any sympathetic attempt to understand what Chernyshevskii lived through during the last decades of his life must include this consideration of family strife and the guilt he felt when thinking of the effect of his actions on Olga. One can at least question whether the loss of his freedom and his personal loneliness were the worst he had to bear.

Beyond the loss of his freedom and of his ability to serve those he loved, the final element in the tragedy of Chernyshevskii's life in prison and exile was his separation from the world of journalism. For about a decade, the challenge of current questions, the excitement of polemics, and even the monthly demands for copy had enlivened his efforts. Although he often had reason to complain of the lack of time for reflection, his position on *The Contemporary* encouraged a prodigious amount of writing. The momentum of this activity carried over into the two-year period of his trial, after which, at a stroke, his situation was changed by the bleak prospects of prison and separation from an audience and purposeful work.[26]

Initially, Chernyshevskii probably had serious hopes that he might be able to engage in scholarship and perhaps even fulfill his lifelong intention to write encyclopedic works. But in Siberia, cut off from intellectual stimulation and adequate resources, he found himself blocked. In the early years, when he retained the greatest intellectual vigor, he was in the least convenient situation and had the least free time. Later, when the dreary isolation of Viliuisk bore heavily upon him, he went through periods when it seemed extremely difficult to focus his attention. Before his return to Astrakhan, for example, in a letter to his sons he tried to give them an outline of how he intended to organize a major work on world history. Several pathetic attempts to define his position were filled with testy name-calling and pointless repetition (e.g. XV, 118–135). Clearly, during some of these years he was simply unequal to the task.

Resources proved another problem. At no time in Siberia could he accumulate an adequate library. Books were allowed him, but they were not easily acquired, and even for this purpose he was reluctant to put further financial demands upon his family. The spotty library he managed to assemble seemed more suitable for filling up time during the endless months than for sustained and concentrated study in one field.[27]

Furthermore, Chernyshevskii soon realized that he had no immediate prospect of publishing any work on a subject that might include the views for which he was being punished. Yet in his desperate desire to help support his family, he clung to the hope that he might be allowed to publish belle-lettres. At various times he expressed faith in his literary talent and told of his plans to earn badly needed money through literature. At other times, more realistically, he expressed justifiable doubts (XIV, 505; XV, 20). Neither on their own intrinsic merit nor in their ability to help his financial plight were these efforts successful. For whatever reason, he destroyed much of his own writings, and Venturi did not exaggerate in calling others that survived "incredibly muddled."[28] One can find passages in them that express Chernyshevskii's values, but his message was often obscure. In some instances, he employed allegory, which could be given almost any kind of interpretation; elsewhere there were paradoxical statements, flashes of skepticism, and a tendency to laugh at his own writing. Even in the best of these works, the novel *Prologue*, alongside cutting political commentary and an imaginative reconstruction of his beliefs and actions in the late 1850's, the reader finds passages where it is not exactly clear what Chernyshevskii meant to ridicule, or indeed when he meant to be serious. For all of these limitations, anything published under Chernyshevskii's name in the 1860's and 1870's would certainly have found an ample market, but after the experience of *What Is To Be Done?*, it was unthinkable that the government would grant permission, least of all for a novel like *Prologue*, which dealt with social themes in recent times. As it happened, during Chernyshevskii's lifetime only the first part of the novel was published, in London in 1877 by the emigré group "Forward." Appearing in this way, it could scarcely contribute, as he had hoped, to his family's support.[29]

During the 1870's, the crushing disappointment of being re-settled in Viliuisk instead of returning to European Russia, and the oppressive loss of hope for any future improvement in his situation, placed a terrible tax on his spirit and energy. Cut off from adequate resources and stimulation, he could not keep abreast of events, and there was a temporary and partial eclipse of his intellectual powers, which doubtless left some traces throughout his remaining years. In 1876, he complained bitterly of having to rely on the Brockhaus *Encyclopedia* as his sole reference work. At other times, he refused to become involved in books that were sent to him. On two separate occasions, for instance, in 1877 and 1878, he rejected books on aspects of the peasant and land question, though he realized his family had chosen these books especially because of his earlier interest. In one case he belittled the value of the specialist's study of details; in the other, besides dismissing one author summarily as a "jackass," he admitted that the subject itself nauseated him (XV, 70, 282–283).

His letters of the 1870's and 1880's, as well as other attempts at serious writing, varied greatly in quality. Amidst some pages that retained his earlier vigorous expression, there were many in which he wandered and lost track of the point. Although N. S. Rusanov has argued persuasively that during the Siberian period Chernyshevskii's thought underwent a shift in emphasis from a position that stressed activism to one emphasizing the primary power of ideas in historical and social change, there can be no question but that he held to his former views.[30] Indeed, in a desperate rear-guard action he tended to reassert his long-held opinions against any questioning or innovation. In letters to his sons, Chernyshevskii frequently assumed the pose of a generalist, who commanded the "correct" point of view and was therefore free to pass quick, usually damning judgments on narrow specialists whose detailed work was distorted by "incorrect" theory.[31] In such fields as mathematics and natural science, he ventured opinions without legitimate base. In 1878, for example, he noted that for over twenty years he had read almost nothing in natural science (XV, 128). In another extreme example, although his own background in mathematics admittedly went little past arithmetic, he saw fit to advise his son Aleksandr to disregard the work of most of his university professors (XIV, 689–690).

Generally the touchstone of Chernyshevskii's evaluations was adherence to certain social values or to his fundamental world view of materialism, but not all of his condemnations were so determined. He showed an unfortunate, if understandable, inclination to be suspicious of almost all innovation. Even when new views were compatible with his own philosophical assumptions, he did not accept them readily. Thus, he scorned the work of the Russian mathematician N. I. Lobachevskii for daring to question the obvious truths of Euclidean geometry. What was "geometry without the axiom of parallel lines," he asked. It was like hopping on one foot—praiseworthy as the prank of a child, but utterly foolish for a grown man (XV, 192–193).

The same impression of fighting a rear-guard action against present-day opinions is gained from Chernyshevskii's brief original writings in the 1880's, after his return from Viliuisk to Astrakhan. His article "The Character of Human Knowledge," published under a pseudonym in 1885, angrily condemned the recent attempts of natural scientists, like Emil Du Bois-Reymond and Rudolph Virchow, to reconsider the question of the human mind's ability to know reality (X, 720–736). Another example of his defense of an older view was Chernyshevskii's attack on the application of Darwinian theory to relations among men. His article in 1888, "Origin of the Theory of the Beneficence of the Struggle for Life," was signed "an old transformist," and although clearly intended as an ethical protest against social Darwinism rather than as a work of natural science, it put Chernyshevskii in the position of defending older Lamarckian theories of evolution against the socially dangerous new slogans of "natural selection" and "survival of the fittest" (X, 737–772).[32]

These articles, and the few other extant works of Chernyshevskii from his period in Astrakhan, show only occasional flashes of the ability that had earlier given him a prominent position in Russian journalism. The years had taken their toll, and he lacked the support of contact with a reading public. Dreams of what he might yet do were kept alive by Chernyshevskii until a few months before his death.[33] Realistically, however, he could earn his livelihood only in the dreary and humiliating work of translating. Over several years, he translated more than eleven volumes of the massive world history of Georg Weber, a writer for whom he had scant respect. For his own part, Chernyshevskii contributed only a short condensation of Weber's text, which sometimes aroused the ire of his publisher, and a few brief commentaries. Indicative of the pathos of his situation, he at one time conceived of using a second edition of Weber as a mask to cover an original work of his own, but nothing came of this bizarre plan (XV, 844).

Just as Chernyshevskii clung desperately to his earlier views, so too he cherished the memories of former years on *The Contemporary*. In Astrakhan, under A. N. Pypin's constant urging, he wrote some literary memoirs, and in the last year of his life he returned to the task of publishing "Material for the Biography of N. A. Dobroliubov," which he had begun a few months before his arrest. Perhaps it was fitting that he should give this attention to the past, for in many ways the present had passed him by.

The unrelieved sadness that pervaded the final quarter-century of Chernyshevskii's life in itself claims a sympathetic evaluation of his career. For the role he chose to play in the radical movement of his day, he paid a high price. He sacrificed personal freedom, the family relations that alone brought him personal satisfaction, and the opportunity for intellectual fulfillment, essentially because he chose to express his views of right and wrong. A lesser man would have devised a safer course.

Yet sympathetic appreciation ought not to suggest uncritical glorification, which has too often been Chernyshevskii's fate at the hands of his fellow-countrymen, in his own time and today. Chernyshevskii himself usually judged other men by their ideology, so that when his well-intentioned, latter-day admirers have done the same to him, they have with poetic justice produced a wooden hero and an unbelievable caricature. His humanity is affirmed only by recognizing his weaknesses and limitations as well as his strengths. The staying power of his character balanced his continual hesitation and self-doubt. Some of his most generous acts toward like-minded associates were matched by a dogmatic intolerance toward opponents and a petty delight in intellectual ascendancy. The same man who spoke as the conscience of society could at times be unaware of the sensitivities of the person standing next to him. And finally, although he literally gave his life to a cause, he was often goaded into his most intense activity by a desire to gratify the frivolous pleasures of a self-seeking woman who in no serious way shared his goals. The complexities and contradictions of the man do not in any significant way discredit his achievement; they merely indicate that he was fallible and therefore human.

Through the years of his exile, Chernyshevskii must have experienced keen frustration and disappointment. His exalted visions of his destiny as a young man (when he was not tormented by crippling doubts) indicated an appreciation of his own intellect and an expectation of making a scholarly contribution to his nation. Yet circumstances had thrust him into the exhausting arena of Russian journalism, with its never-ending pressure of monthly deadlines, its demand for hastily written polemics, and its requirement that he spread his efforts over a large number of fields. He was often forced into the position of popularizing other men's ideas or simply of reworking other men's scholarship to conform to the "correct view." Even in such presentations he was rarely allowed the luxury of careful and orderly exposition. He wrote as the situation demanded and with an eye to penetrating the screen of censorship. To add to his disappointment, the goal of a just society, for which he had sacrificed himself, was never achieved in his lifetime.

But Chernyshevskii had a coherent rationalization for the role that he played, which may have given him comfort. He recognized the importance of the journalist in the popularization of ideas, a process that had to take place if those ideas were to operate as factors for progressive change. Viewing the situation in mid-century Russia, he judged that the time was ripe for just such activity. He saw the state and society as ruled by concepts that had long since lost legitimacy, and he saw many of his fellow Russian intellectuals as clinging to ideas that belonged properly to an earlier generation. At the same time, the world's leading thinkers had made significant breakthroughs in human understanding. If these truths became widely known, and if men incorporated them into their own world view and used them as guides to action, men could be freed. To popularize the new truths, to show their relevance in areas that were not immediately obvious—in short, to be a Russian version of the Encyclopedists—was in Chernyshevskii's mind an honorable and much needed calling. It is in relation to this undertaking, rather than to his brief involvement with revolutionary conspiracy, that the final judgment of his career should be made.

In making a judgment, one need not consider one criterion that Chernyshevskii himself would probably have applied. He often made reference to the unity of his ideas, as if they were all related parts of an internally consistent whole. There is no doubt that Chernyshevskii's materialistic monism helped him, as it did writers of the French Enlightenment, to mount an attack on the past. With its use, many traditional ideals and values that could not be derived scientifically from nature were automatically declared invalid, and the slate rubbed clean to start afresh. Similarly, the morality of utilitarianism, which naturally follows in a world thus defined, proved to be a powerful weapon in the examination of economic and political systems. Nevertheless, when Chernyshevskii made his criticisms, and especially when he looked to the future, despite the scientific cast of his statements, he implied values that did not stem directly or necessarily from his basic materialistic philosophy. And when his thought led him to choose between consistency of argument and personally cherished values and aspirations, he clearly preferred the latter.

Fortunately consistency is not the determining factor in assessing the significance of ideas in history, and that is the question here. Taken together, Chernyshevskii's writings formed a massive onslaught against the institutions of the Russian state and society, and against the ideas that gave those institutions a claim to legitimacy. He urged his readers to a different way of looking at the world and a different kind of reasoning. He pointed out specific injustices in Russian life and proposed radical alternatives, which had as their common basis the assumption that every man had equal claim to a life of freedom and abundance. He argued that a new morality, based on a rational view of one's own best interest, could achieve what centuries of high-sounding moralizing had failed to bring about, namely, decent human relationships among men and women. Moreover, he proclaimed his message with passionate urgency, demanding that no area of life remain untouched. In a sense, everything, including art, had to be either politicized or judged according to its contribution to the struggle. Chernyshevskii's writings shattered belief in the old moral system and offered as inspiration a new dream of utopia.

However, although Chernyshevskii achieved brief control over Russia's most popular journal, his audience was necessarily limited. Popularization was relative, aiming only at a select minority who were far removed from the common people he longed to reach. In his day his influence was felt among an alienated segment of an already small intellectual elite, including many students who, when conditions or their own situation changed, passed out of his sphere as easily as they had entered it.

But a core of followers remained, both at that time and in the decades that followed. Several who devoted their lives to the revolutionary movement, not the least of whom was Lenin, gave evidence of his ongoing influence. For them, the ideas he represented, though modified, had an impressive staying power, and the model of his life continued to inspire personal sacrifice.

The Russian revolutionaries who were part of this tradition could not themselves initiate a revolution. At first, because of the hopelessness of their isolation, the most they probably achieved was an invitation to repression and counterrevolution. But later, toward the end of the century, more effective groups were formed, and contact was established with the Russian masses to inform them of the relation between their local distress and the overall state of society. When revolution finally came, leadership was provided by men who had been reared in the long tradition of protest inspired in part by Chernyshevskii.

*Bibliography*
*Notes*
*Index*

# Bibliography

Abramovich, A. F., et al., eds. *N. G. Chernyshevskii: Sbornik statei k 50-letiiu so dnia smerti velikogo revoliutsionera-demokrata.* Saratov: Saratovskoe oblastnoe gosudarstvennoe izd-vo, 1939.

Alekseev, N. A., ed. *Protsess N. G. Chernyshevskogo: Arkhivnye dokumenty.* Saratov: Saratovskoe oblastnoe gosudarstvennoe izd-vo, 1939.

Annenkov, P. V. *Literaturnye vospominaniia.* S. N. Golubov et al., eds. Moscow: Goslitizdat, 1960.

Annenskii, N. F. "N. G. Chernyshevskii i krest'ianskaia reforma." In *Velikaia reforma,* A. K. Dzhivelegov et al., eds., IV, 220–279. Moscow: Tovarishchestvo I. D. Sytina, 1911.

Antonov, M. *N. G. Chernyshevskii: Sotsial'no-filosofskii etiud.* Moscow: Tovarishchestvo tipografii A. I. Mamontova, 1910.

Antonovich, M. A., and G. Z. Eliseev. *Shestidesiatye gody.* Moscow– Leningrad: Academia, 1933.

Balabanov, M. *Ocherk istorii revoliutsionnogo dvizheniia v Rossii.* Leningrad: Priboi, 1929.

Barghoorn, Frederick C. "D. I. Pisarev and the Russian Intellectual Movement." Ph.D. dissertation, Harvard University, 1941.

_____. "The Philosophic Outlook of Chernyshevsky: Materialism and Utilitarianism," *The American Slavic and East European Review,* VI (1947), 42–55.

_____. "The Russian Radicals of the 1860's and the Problem of the Industrial Proletariat," *The Slavonic and East European Review* (American Series II), XXI, part I (1943), 57–69.

Baskakov, V. G. *Mirovozzrenie Chernyshevskogo.* Moscow: Izd-vo AN SSSR, 1956.

343

Belinskii, V. G. *Sobranie sochinenii v trekh tomakh.* F. M. Govoven-
chenko, ed. 3 vols. Moscow: Ogiz, 1948.
Berdyaev, Nicolas. *The Origin of Russian Communism.* London:
Geoffrey Bles, 1948.
———. *The Russian Idea.* New York: Macmillan, 1948.
Berlin, Isaiah. "A Marvellous Decade, 1838–1848: The Birth of the
Russian Intelligentsia," *Encounter,* no. 21 (1955), 27–39.
———. "A Marvellous Decade, 1838–1848: German Romanticism in
Petersburg and Moscow," *Encounter,* no. 26 (1955), 21–29.
———. "A Marvellous Decade: Belinsky—Moralist and Prophet," *En-
counter,* no. 27 (1955), 22–43.
———. "A Marvellous Decade: Herzen and the Grand Inquisitors,"
*Encounter,* no. 32 (1956), 20–34.
———. "Russia and 1848," *The Slavonic and East European Review,*
XXVI (1948), 341–360.
Berliner, G. *N. G. Chernyshevskii i ego literaturnye vragi.* L. B.
Kamenev, ed. Moscow-Leningrad: Gosudarstvennoe izd-vo, 1930.
Billington, James H. *The Icon and the Axe: An Interpretive History
of Russian Culture.* New York: Alfred A. Knopf, 1966.
Boborykin, P. D. *Za polveka (moi vospominaniia).* Moscow-Leningrad:
Zemlia i fabrika, 1929.
Bogdanovich, T. A. *Liubov' liudei shestidesiatykh godov.* Leningrad:
Academia, 1929.
Bogoslovskii, N. *Nikolai Gavrilovich Chernyshevskii, 1828–1889.*
2nd ed. Moscow: Molodaia gvardiia, 1957.
Bograd, V. E. "O memuarakh A. A. Sleptsova," *Literaturnoe nasled-
stvo,* no. 67 (1959), 669–684.
———. *Zhurnal "Sovremennik" 1847–1866: Ukazatel' soderzhaniia.*
Moscow-Leningrad: Goslitizdat, 1959.
Bowman, Herbert E., "Art and Reality in Russian 'Realist' Criticism,"
*The Journal of Aesthetics and Art Criticism* (March 1954), 386–
391.
———. "Revolutionary Élitism in Černyševskij," *The American Slavic
and East European Review,* XIII (1954), 185–199.
———. *Vissarion Belinski, 1811–1848: A Study in the Origins of
Social Criticism in Russia.* Cambridge: Harvard University Press,
1954.
Bukhshtab, B. "Iz vospominanii A. I. Artem'eva o N. G. Chernyshev-
skom," *Literaturnoe nasledstvo,* no. 25/26 (1936), 230–234.
Bursov, B. I. "Literaturno-esteticheskie vzgliady N. G. Chernyshevskogo." In N. G. Chernyshevskii, *Estetika i literaturnaia kritika,*
pp. III–XXVIII. Moscow-Leningrad: Goslitizdat, 1951.
———. *Masterstvo Chernyshevskogo-kritika.* Leningrad: Sovetskii
pisatel', 1959.
Chamberlain, William B. *Heaven Wasn't His Destination: The Phi-*

*losophy of L. Feuerbach*. London: George Allen & Unwin, 1941.

Cherno, Melvin. "Ludwig Feuerbach and the Intellectual Basis of Nineteenth Century Radicalism." Ph.D. dissertation, Stanford University, 1955.

Chernyshev, V. R. *N. G. Chernyshevskii i G. V. Plekhanov: Ocherk ikh ekonomicheskikh vozzrenii*. Moscow-Leningrad: Moskovskii rabochii, 1926.

Chernyshevskaia-Bystrova, N. M. *Letopis' zhizni i deiatel'nosti N. G. Chernyshevskogo*. Moscow-Leningrad: Academia, 1933.

_____. *Letopis' zhizni i deiatel'nosti N. G. Chernyshevskogo*. Moscow: Goslitizdat, 1953.

_____. *N. G. Chernyshevskii v Saratove: Detskie i iunosheskie gody*. Saratov: Ogiz, 1948.

_____. *N. G. Chernyshevskii v Saratove*. Saratov: Saratovskoe oblastnoe gosudarstvennoe izd-vo, 1949.

Chernyshevskii, N. G. *Dnevnik*. N. A. Alekseev, ed. Parts I and II. Moscow: Izd-vo Politkatorzhan, 1931–1932.

_____. *Estetika i literaturnaia kritika*. B. I. Bursov, ed. Moscow-Leningrad: Goslitizdat, 1951.

_____. *Izbrannye ekonomicheskie proizvedeniia*. I. D. Udal'tsov, ed. 3 vols. (vol. III in two parts.) Moscow: Ogiz, 1948–1949.

_____. *Izbrannye filosofskie sochineniia*. M. M. Grigor'ian, ed. 3 vols. Moscow: Gospolitizdat, 1950–1951.

_____. *Izbrannye pedagogicheskie proizvedeniia*. V. Z. Smirnov, ed. Moscow: Izd-vo Akademii pedagogicheskikh nauk RSFSR, 1953.

_____. *Literaturnoe nasledie*. N. A. Alekseev et al., eds. 3 vols. Moscow: Gosudarstvennoe izd-vo, 1928–1930.

_____. *Polnoe sobranie sochinenii*. V. Ia. Kirpotin et al., eds. 16 vols. Moscow: Goslitizdat, 1939–1953.

_____. *Polnoe sobranie sochinenii N. G. Chernyshevskogo*. M. N. Chernyshevskii, ed. 10 vols. (vol. X in two parts.) St. Petersburg: Izdanie M. N. Chernyshevskogo, 1906.

[Cheshikhin]-Vetrinskii, [V. E.] "'Kolokol' i krest'ianskaia reforma." In *Velikaia reforma*, A. K. Dzhivelegov et al., eds., IV, 194–219. Moscow: Tovarishchestvo I. D. Sytina, 1911.

_____. "Literaturnoe i kriticheskoe dvizhenie shestidesiatykh godov." In *Istoriia russkoi literatury XIX v.*, D. N. Ovsianiko-Kulikovskii, ed., III, 70–130. Moscow: Mir, 1910.

_____. *N. G. Chernyshevskii, 1828–1889*. Petrograd: Kolos, 1923.

Chizhevskii, D. I. *Gegel' v Rossii*. Paris: Dom Knigi, 1939.

Coquart, Armand. *Dmitri Pisarev (1840–1868) et l'idéologie du nihilisme russe*. Paris: Institut d'études slaves de l'Université de Paris, 1946.

Corbet, Charles. "Černyševskij estheticien et critique," *Revue des études slaves*, XXIV (1948), 107–128.

Corbet, Charles. "Dobroljubov et Herzen," *Revue des études slaves,* no. 27 (1951), 70–77.

————. *Nekrasov l'homme et le poète.* Paris: Institut d'études slaves de l'Université de Paris, 1948.

Croce, Benedetto. *Aesthetic.* Rev. ed. New York: The Noonday Press, 1956.

Denisiuk, N. *Kriticheskaia literatura o proizvedeniiakh N. G. Chernyshevskago.* Moscow: Izdanie A. S. Panafidinoi, 1908.

Dobroliubov, N. A. *Sobranie sochinenii.* B. I. Bursov et al., eds. 9 vols. Moscow: Goslitizdat, 1961–1964.

————. *Sochineniia.* 5th ed. 4 vols. St. Petersburg, 1896.

Dodonov, I. K. "N. G. Černyševskij als Historiker," *Jahrbuch für Geschichte der Deutsch-Slawischen Beziehungen und Geschichte Ost- und Mitteleuropas,* I (1956), 171–213.

Dostoievsky, F. M. *Diary of a Writer.* Boris Brazol, trans. New York: George Braziller, 1954.

Druzhinin, A. V. *Sobranie sochinenii.* N. V. Gervel, ed. 8 vols. St. Petersburg, 1865–1867.

Druzhinina, E. I. "Kritika samoderzhaviia i krepostnogo prava v legal'nykh proizvedeniiakh N. G. Chernyshevskogo nakanune revoliutsionnoi situatsii (1853–1857gg.)." In *Revoliutsionnaia situatsiia v Rossii v 1859–1861 gg.,* M. V. Nechkina et al., eds., pp. 361–388. Moscow: Izd-vo AN SSSR, 1962.

Dukhovnikov, F. V. "Nikolai Gavrilovich Chernyshevskii, ego zhizn' v Saratove," *Russkaia starina,* no. 67 (1890), 531–568.

————. "Nikolai Gavrilovich Chernyshevskii," *Russkaia starina,* no. 11 (1910), 501–517; no. 1 (1911), 68–96.

Dzhivelegov, A. K., et al., eds. *Velikaia reforma.* 6 vols. Moscow: Tovarishchestvo I. D. Sytina, 1911.

Evgen'ev-Maksimov, V. E., A. A. Voznesenskii, and Sh. I. Ganelin, eds. *N. G. Chernyshevskii (1889–1939): Trudy nauchnoi sessii k piatidesiatiletiiu so dnia smerti.* Leningrad: Izdanie Leningradskogo gosudarstvennogo universiteta, 1941.

————. *'Sovremennik' pri Chernyshevskom i Dobroliubove.* Leningrad: Goslitizdat, 1936.

Evgrafov, V. E. "Filosofskie vzgliady N. G. Chernyshevskogo." In *Iz istorii russkoi filosofii: Sbornik statei,* I. Ia. Shchipanov, ed., pp. 304–401. Moscow: Gospolitizdat, 1952.

Fedorov, K. M. *N. G. Chernyshevskii.* Askhabad: Electropechatiia K. M. Fedorova, 1904.

Fomin, A. "N. G. Chernyshevskii i ego znachenie v istorii russkoi obshchestvennoi zhizn'," *Istoricheskii vestnik* (1907), no. 5, pp. 503–521; no. 6, pp. 851–872.

Gerschenkron, Alexander. "The Problem of Economic Development in Russian Intellectual History of the Nineteenth Century."

In *Continuity and Change in Russian and Soviet Thought*, Ernest J. Simmons, ed., pp. 11–39. Cambridge: Harvard University Press, 1955.

Gertsen, A. I. *Polnoe sobranie sochinenii i pisem.* M. K. Lemke, ed. 22 vols. Petrograd: Gosizdat, 1919–1925.

———. *Sochineniia v deviati tomakh.* V. P. Volgin et al., eds. 9 vols. Moscow: Goslitizdat, 1958.

Gifford, Henry. *The Hero of His Time: A Theme in Russian Literature.* London: Edward Arnold & Co., 1950.

Gorodetskii, B. P., A. Lavretskii, and B. S. Meilakh, eds. *Istoriia russkoi kritiki v dvukh tomakh.* 2 vols. Moscow-Leningrad: Izd-vo AN SSSR, 1958.

Granjard, Henri. *Ivan Tourguénev et les courants politiques et sociaux de son temps.* Paris: Institut d'études slaves de l'Université de Paris, 1954.

Grigoryan, M. N. *G. Chernyshevsky's World Outlook.* Moscow: Foreign Languages Publishing House, 1954.

Hare, Richard. *Pioneers of Russian Social Thought.* London-New York-Toronto: Oxford University Press, 1951.

Harper, Kenneth E. "Criticism of the Natural School in the 1840's," *The American Slavic and East European Review,* XV (1956), 400–414.

Hecht, David. *Russian Radicals Look to America, 1825–1894.* Cambridge: Harvard University Press, 1947.

Hecker, Julius F. *Russian Sociology.* New York: John Wiley and Sons, 1934.

Hegarty, Thomas J. "Student Movements in Russian Universities, 1855–1861." Ph.D. dissertation, Harvard University, 1965.

Herbert, Eugenia W. *The Artist and Social Reform.* New Haven: Yale University Press, 1961.

Hook, Sidney. *From Hegel to Marx: Studies in the Intellectual Development of Karl Marx.* New York: The Humanities Press, 1950.

Iurkevich, P. D. "Iz nauki o chelovecheskom dukhe," *Trudy Kievskoi dukhovnoi akademii,* I (1860), 367–511.

Ivanov, Ivan. *Istoriia russkoi kritiki.* Parts 3 and 4. St. Petersburg: Tipografiia I. N. Skorokhodova, 1900.

Ivanov-Razumnik, R. V. *Istoriia russkoi obshchestvennoi mysli.* 3rd ed. 2 vols. St. Petersburg: Tipografiia M. M. Stasiulevicha, 1911.

———. "Obshchestvennyia i umstvennyia techeniia 60-kh godov i ikh otrazhenie v literature." In *Istoriia russkoi literatury XIX v.,* D. N. Ovsianiko-Kulikovskii, ed., pp. 45–69. Moscow: Mir, 1910.

Kagan, M. S. *Esteticheskoe uchenie Chernyshevskogo.* Leningrad-Moscow: Iskusstvo, 1958.

Kamenev, Iu. *Gertsen i Chernyshevskii.* Petrograd, 1916.

347

Karpovich, Michael M. "N. G. Chernyshevski Between Socialism and Liberalism," *Cahiers du monde russe et soviétique*, I (1960), 569–583.

Katkov, M. N. "Starye bogi i novye bogi," *Russkii vestnik*, XXXI (February 1861), 891–904.

Kavelin, K. D. *Pis'ma K. D. Kavelina i I. S. Turgeneva k A. I. Gertsenu.* Geneva, 1892.

Khomentovskaia, A. I. "N. G. Chernyshevskii i podpol'naia literatura 60-kh gg.," *Istoricheskii arkhiv*, no. 1 (1919), 324–413.

Kizevetter, Aleksandr Aleksandrovic. "Herzen und der 'Kolokol'," *Zeitschrift für Osteuropäische Geschichte*, VII (1933), 389–400.

Klevenskii, M. "Novye materialy po istorii 'Sovremennika'," *Literaturnoe nasledstvo*, no. 25/26 (1936), 359–360.

Klochkov, M. V. "Protsess N. G. Chernyshevskogo," *Istoricheskii vestnik* (1913), no. 9, pp. 889–919; no. 10, pp. 157–190.

Klochkov, V. M. "Skhodstvo i razlichie v eticheskikh vzgliadakh L. Feierbakha i N. G. Chernyshevskogo," *Voprosy filosofii*, no. 6 (1957), 47–58.

Kolbasin, E. Ia. "Teni starago 'Sovremennika'," *Sovremennik*, no. 8 (1911), 221–240.

*Kolokol.* See Nechkina, M. V.

Kornilov, A. A. "Chernyshevskii i krest'ianskaia reforma," *Russkaia mysl'*, no. 1 (1910), 1–26.

———. "Istoricheskii ocherk epokhi 60-kh godov." In *Istoriia russkoi literatury XIX v.*, D. N. Ovsianiko-Kulikovskii, ed., pp. 9–44. Moscow: Mir, 1910.

———. *Obshchestvennoe dvizhenie pri Aleksandre II, 1855–1881.* Moscow: Tovarishchestvo tipografii A. I. Mamontova, 1909.

Korolenko, V. G. *Vospominaniia o Chernyshevskom.* Berlin: Hugo Stein Verlag, 1904.

Koshovenko, A. E. "K voprosu o londonskoi vstreche N. G. Chernyshevskogo s A. I. Gertsenom v 1859 g. i formule 'Kavelin v kvadrate'." In *Revoliutsionnaia situatsiia v Rossii v 1859–1861gg.*, M. V. Nechkina et al., eds., pp. 271–282. Moscow: Izd-vo AN SSSR, 1960.

Kostomarova, A. L. *Avtobiografiia N. I. Kostomarova.* V. Kotel'nikov, ed. Moscow: Zadruga, 1922.

Kotliarevskii, Nestor. *Kanun osvobozhdeniia.* Petrograd: Tipografiia M. M. Stasiulevicha, 1916.

Koyré, Alexandre. *Études sur l'histoire de la pensée philosophique en Russie.* Paris: Librairie philosophique J. Vrin, 1950.

Koz'min, B. P. "Byl li N. G. Chernyshevskii avtorom pis'ma 'Russkogo cheloveka' k Gertsenu," *Literaturnoe nasledstvo*, no. 25/26 (1936), 576–585.

_____. *Iz istorii revoliutsionnoi mysli v Rossii: Izbrannye trudy.* V. P. Volgin et al., eds. Moscow: Izd-vo AN SSSR, 1961.

_____. "N. G. Chernyshevskii i M. I. Mikhailov (K istorii ikh vzaimootnoshenii)," *Voprosy istorii,* no. 7 (1946), 19–25.

_____, ed. "N. G. Chernyshevskii i III otdelenie," *Krasnyi arkhiv,* no. 4 (1928), 175–190.

_____. "N. G. Chernyshevskii v redaktsii 'Voennogo sbornika' iz vospominanii D. A. Miliutina," *Literaturnoe nasledstvo,* no. 25/26 (1936), 234–235.

_____. *Russkaia sektsiia pervogo internatsionala.* Moscow: Izd-vo AN SSSR, 1957.

_____. "Vystuplenie Gertsena protiv 'Sovremennika' v 1859 gody," *Izvestiia AN SSSR, Otdelenie literatury i iazyka,* XI, no. 4 (1952), 366–384.

Krasnoperov, I. M. *Zapiski raznochintsa.* Moscow-Leningrad: Molodaia gvardiia, 1929.

Kucherov, Alexander. "N. G. Chernyshevskii on Capitalism and Russia's Shortcut to Socialism." Ph.D. dissertation, Columbia University, 1953.

Kulczycki, Ludwig. *Geschichte der russischen Revolution.* 2 vols. Gotha: Friedrich Andreas Perthes A.-G., 1910–1911.

Labry, Raoul. *Alexandre Ivanovic Herzen, 1812–1870: Essai sur la formation et le developpement de ces idées.* Paris: Editions Bossard, 1928.

Lampert, Eugene. *Sons Against Fathers.* Oxford: Oxford University Press, 1965.

_____. *Studies in Rebellion.* New York: Frederick A. Praeger, 1957.

Lange, Frederick Albert. *The History of Materialism and Criticism of Its Present Importance.* Ernest Chester Thomas, trans. 3rd ed. New York: The Humanities Press, 1950.

Laserson, Max M. *The American Impact on Russia—Diplomatic and Ideological—1784–1917.* New York: Macmillan, 1950.

Lavretskii, A. "Chernyshevskii." In *Istoriia russkoi kritiki v dvukh tomakh,* B. P. Gorodetskii, A. Lavretskii, and B. S. Meilakh, eds., II, 42–89. Moscow-Leningrad: Izd-vo AN SSSR, 1958.

Lazerson, B. I. "Publitsistika Chernyshevskogo v gody revoliutsionnoi situatsii." In *N. G. Chernyshevskii: Stat'i, issledovaniia i materialy,* E. I. Pokusaev and N. M. Chernyshevskaia, eds., no. 3, pp. 62–91. Saratov: Izd-vo Saratovskogo universiteta, 1962.

Lebedev-Polianskii, P. I. "Chernyshevskii." In *Istoriia russkoi literatury,* M. P. Alekseev et al., eds. Vol. VIII, Part I, *Literatura shestidesiatykh godov,* pp. 113–174. Moscow-Leningrad: Izd-vo AN SSSR, 1956.

Lemke, M. K. *Ocherki osvoboditel'nago dvizheniia "shestidesia-*

*tykh godov."* St. Petersburg: Izdatel'stvo O. H. Popovoi, 1908.

Lemke, M. K., ed. *Politicheskie protsessy M. I. Mikhailova, D. I. Pisareva, i N. G. Chernyshevskogo.* St. Petersburg, 1907.

————, ed. *Politicheskie protsessy v Rossii 1860-kh gg.* Moscow-Petrograd: Gosudarstvennoe izdatel'stvo, 1923.

Levin, Sh. M. "K voprosu ob istoricheskikh osobennostiakh russkogo utopicheskogo sotsializma," *Istoricheskie zapiski,* XXVI (1948), 217–257.

————. *Obshchestvennoe dvizhenie v Rossii v 60-70-e gody XIX veka.* Moscow: Izd-vo sotsial'no-ekonomicheskoi literatury, 1958.

Lew, Emanuel. "Uber den Einfluss der schönen Literatur auf die Russische soziale Bewegung," *Jahrbücher für Kultur und Geschichte der Slaven,* n.s., VIII (1932), 231–292.

Liatskii, E. A. "Chernyshevskii-Uchitel," *Sovremennik,* no. 6 (1912), 343–368.

————, ed. *Chernyshevskii v Sibiri: Perepiska s rodnymi.* 3 vols. St. Petersburg: Izdanie tovarishchestva Ogin, 1912–1913.

————. "Liubov' i zaprosy lichnogo schast'ia v zhizni N. G. Chernyshevskogo," *Sovremennik* (1912), no. 9, pp. 174–199; no. 10, pp. 28–38; no. 11, pp. 1–15; no. 12, pp. 86–106.

————. "Na pereput'e k novoi zhizni," *Sovremennik,* no. 5 (1912), 139–159.

————. "N. G. Chernyshevskii i ego dissertatsiia ob iskusstve," *Golos minuvshago,* no. 1 (1916), 5–34.

————. "N. G. Chernyshevskii i I. I. Vvedenskii," *Sovremennyi mir,* no. 6 (1910), 148–164.

————. "N. G. Chernyshevskii i Sh. Fur'e," *Sovremennyi mir,* no. 11 (1909), 161–187.

————. "N. G. Chernyshevskii i uchitelia ego mysli," *Sovremennyi mir* (1910), no. 10, pp. 138–162; no. 11, pp. 135–154.

————. "N. G. Chernyshevskii na poroge semeinoi zhizni," *Sovremennik* (1913), no. 1, pp. 200–228; no. 4, pp. 108–154.

————. "N. G. Chernyshevskii, v gody ucheniia i na puti v universitet," *Sovremennyi mir* (1908), no. 5, pp. 45–74; no. 6, pp. 37–67; no. 12, pp. 28–58; (1909), no. 3, pp. 51–70.

————. "N. G. Chernyshevskii v redaktsii 'Sovremennika'," *Sovremennyi mir* (1911), no. 9, pp. 141–192; no. 10, pp. 154–188; no. 11, pp. 161–201.

————. "N. G. Chernyshevskii v 1848–50 gg.," *Sovremennyi mir* (1912), no. 2, pp. 177–197; no. 3, pp. 156–178.

Lind, V. N. "Moskovskoe studenchestvo v 1861 g. i ego otnoshenie k osvobozhdeniiu krest'ian (iz vospominanii)." In *Velikaia reforma,* A. K. Dzhivelegov et al., eds., V, 269–278. Moscow: Tovarishchestvo I. D. Sytina, 1911.

Linkov, Ia. I. "Ideinye i takticheskie raznoglasiia v riadakh revo-

liutsionnoi demokratii v epokhu padeniia krepostnogo prava,"
*Voprosy istorii*, no. 6 (1959), 47–68.

———. "O politicheskoi programme N. G. Chernyshevskogo v period
revoliutsionnoi situatsii 1859–1861 godov," *Voprosy istorii*, no. 5
(1955), 110–116.

———. "Osnovnye etapy istorii revoliutsionnogo obshchestva 'Zemlia
i volia' 1860-kh godov," *Voprosy istorii*, no. 9 (1958), 33–57.

———. "Problema revoliutsionnoi partii v Rossii v epokhu padeniia
krepostnogo prava," *Voprosy istorii*, no. 9 (1957), 57–70.

———. *Revoliutsionnaia bor'ba A. I. Gertsena i N. P. Ogareva i tainoe
obshchestvo "Zemlia i volia" 1860-kh godov.* Moscow: Izd-vo
Nauka, 1964.

Lotman, L. M. "Chernyshevskii-romanist." In *Istoriia russkoi literatury*, M. P. Alekseev et al., eds. Vol. VIII, Part I, *Literatura shestidesiatykh godov*, pp. 484–535. Moscow-Leningrad: Izd-vo
AN SSSR, 1956.

Lukacs, Georg. *Der russische Realismus in der Weltliteratur.* Berlin:
Aufbau Verlag, 1949.

Lunacharskii, A. V. *Stat'i o Chernyshevskom.* E. M. Mel'nikova, ed.
Moscow: Goslitizdat, 1958.

Lyashchenko, Peter I. *History of the National Economy of Russia
to the 1917 Revolution.* L. M. Herman, trans. New York: Macmillan, 1949.

Makeev, N. *N. G. Chernyshevskii-redaktor 'Voennogo sbornika'.*
Moscow: Voennoe izd-vo Voennogo Ministerstva Soiuza S.S.R.,
1950.

———. "N. G. Chernyshevskii-redaktor 'Voennogo sbornika'," *Voprosy
istorii*, no. 4 (1949), 65–82.

Malia, Martin E. *Alexander Herzen and the Birth of Russian Socialism, 1812–1855.* Cambridge: Harvard University Press, 1961.

———. "Herzen and the Peasant Commune." In *Continuity and
Change in Russian and Soviet Thought*, Ernest J. Simmons, ed.,
pp. 197–217. Cambridge: Harvard University Press, 1955.

Masaryk, T. G. *The Spirit of Russia: Studies in History, Literature,
and Philosophy.* Eden and Cedar Paul, trans. 2nd ed. 2 vols.
London-New York: George Allen & Unwin Ltd., Macmillan, 1955.

Mathewson, Rufus W. "The Hero and Society: The Literary Definitions
(1855–1865, 1934–1939)." In *Continuity and Change in Russian
and Soviet Thought*, Ernest J. Simmons, ed., pp. 255–276. Cambridge: Harvard University Press, 1955.

———. *The Positive Hero in Russian Literature.* New York: Columbia University Press, 1958.

Mavor, James. *An Economic History of Russia.* 2nd ed. 2 vols. London-
Toronto: J. M. Dent & Sons, 1925.

Medvedev, A. P. "N. G. Chernyshevskii v kruzhke I. I. Vvedenskogo."

In *N. G. Chernyshevskii: Stat'i, issledovaniia i materialy,* E. I. Pokusaev et al., eds., pp. 42–104. Saratov: Saratovskoe knizhnoe izd-vo, 1958.

Mikhailov, M. L. *Sochineniia v trekh tomakh.* B. P. Koz'min, ed. 3 vols. Moscow: Goslitizdat, 1958.

Miller, I. S. "Vokrug 'Velikorussa'." In *Revoliutsionnaia situatsiia v Rossii 1859–1861 gg.,* M. V. Nechkina et al., eds., pp. 84–123. Moscow: Izd-vo AN SSSR, 1965.

Moser, Charles A. *Antinihilism in the Russian Novel of the 1860's.* The Hague: Mouton, 1964.

Nabokov, Vladimir. *The Gift.* New York: G. P. Putnam's Sons, 1963.

Nahirny, Vladimir C. "The Russian Intelligentsia: From Men of Ideas to Men of Convictions," *Comparative Studies in Society and History,* IV (1962), 403–435.

Nechkina, M. V., et al., eds. *Kolokol: Gazeta A. I. Gertsena i N. P. Ogareva.* Facsimile ed. 11 vols. Moscow: Izd-vo AN SSSR, 1962.

———. "N. G. Chernyshevskii v bor'be za splochenie sil russkogo demokraticheskogo dvizheniia v gody revoliutsionnoi situatsii (1859–1861)," *Voprosy istorii,* no. 7 (1953), 56–73.

———. "N. G. Chernyshevskii v gody revoliutsionnoi situatsii," *Istoricheskie zapiski,* no. 10 (1941), 3–39.

———, et al., eds. *Revoliutsionnaia situatsiia v Rossii v 1859–1861 gg.* Moscow: Izd-vo Akademii nauk S.S.S.R., 1960.

———. *Revoliutsionnaia situatsiia v Rossii v 1859–1861 gg.* Moscow: Izd-vo Akademii nauk S.S.S.R., 1962.

———. *Revoliutsionnaia situatsiia v Rossii v 1859–1861 gg.* Moscow: Izd-vo Akademii nauk S.S.S.R., 1963.

———. *Revoliutsionnaia situatsiia v Rossii v 1859–1861 gg.* Moscow: Izd-vo Nauka, 1965.

———. "Vozniknovenie pervoi 'Zemli i voli'." In *Revoliutsionnaia situatsiia v Rossii v 1859–1861 gg.,* M. V. Nechkina et al., eds., pp. 283–298. Moscow: Izd-vo AN SSSR, 1960.

Nekrasov, N. A. *Sochineniia.* Kornei Chukovskii, ed. 3 vols. Moscow: Izd-vo Pravda, 1954.

Neupokoev, V. I. "'Zemlia i volia' 60-kh godov po materialam Dinaburgskogo protessa." In *Revoliutsionnaia situatsiia v Rossii v 1859–1861 gg.,* M. V. Nechkina et al., eds., pp. 305–334. Moscow: Izd-vo AN SSSR, 1962.

*N. G. Chernyshevskii (1828–1928): Sbornik statei, dokumentov i vospominanii.* Moscow: Izd-vo Politkatorzhan, 1928.

Nikitenko, A. V. *Dnevnik v trekh tomakh.* I. Ia. Aizenshtok, ed. 3 vols. Moscow: Goslitizdat, 1955–1956.

Nikoladze, N. Ia. "Vospominaniia o shestidesiatykh godakh," *Katorga i ssylka* (1927), no. 4, pp. 29–52; no. 5, pp. 28–46.

Nikolaev, M. P. *N. G. Chernyshevskii: Seminarii.* 2nd ed. Leningrad: Uchpedgiz, 1959.

Normano, J. F. *The Spirit of Russian Economics.* New York: John Day, 1945.

Novich, I. S. *Zhizn' Chernyshevskogo.* Moscow: Izd-vo khudozhestvennaia literatura, 1939.

Novikova, N. N. "Komitet 'Velikorussa' i bor'ba za sozdanie revoliutsionnoi organizatsii v epokhu padeniia krepostnogo prava," *Voprosy istorii,* no. 5 (1957), 132–142.

_____. "N. G. Chernyshevskii i komitet 'Velikorussa'." In *Revoliutsionnaia situatsiia v Rossii v 1859–1861 gg.,* M. V. Nechkina et al., eds., pp. 299–326. Moscow: Izd-vo AN SSSR, 1960.

Obruchev, V. A. "Iz perezhitogo," *Vestnik Evropy* (1907), no. 5, pp. 122–155; no. 6, pp. 565–595.

Ogarev, N. P. *Izbrannye sotsial'no-politicheskie i filosofskie proizvedeniia.* M. T. Iovchuk and N. G. Tarakanov, eds. 2 vols. Moscow: Gospolitizdat, 1952–1956.

Oksman, Iu. G., ed. *N. G. Chernyshevskii v vospominaniiakh sovremennikov.* 2 vols. Saratov: Saratovskoe knizhnoe izd-vo, 1958–1959.

Ovsianiko-Kulikovskii, D. N. *Istoriia russkoi intelligentsii.* 2nd ed. Moscow: Izdanie V. M. Sablina, 1907.

_____, ed. *Istoriia russkoi literatury XIX v.* 5 vols. Moscow: Mir, 1910.

_____. "Nikolai Aleksandrovich Dobroliubov." In *Istoriia russkoi literatury XIX v.,* D. N. Ovsianiko-Kulikovskii, ed., III, 204–217. Moscow: Mir, 1910.

Panaeva, Avdot'ia (E. Ia. Golovacheva). *Vospominaniia, 1824–1870.* Kornei Chukovskii, ed. 3rd ed. Leningrad: Academia, 1929.

Panteleev, L. F. *Vospominaniia.* S. N. Golubov et al., eds. Moscow: Goslitizdat, 1958.

Pashkov, A. I., ed. *Istoriia russkoi ekonomicheskoi mysli.* Vol I: *Epokha feodalizma,* part 2. Moscow: Gospolitizdat, 1958.

Pelles, Geraldine. *Art, Artists and Society: Origins of a Modern Dilemma.* Englewood Cliffs, N.J.: Prentice-Hall, 1963.

Pipes, Richard. "Narodnichestvo: A Semantic Inquiry," *Slavic Review,* XXIII (September 1964), 441–458.

Plekhanov, G. V. *Sochineniia.* D. Riazanov, ed. 2nd ed., vols. V, VI. Moscow: Gosudarstvennoe izd-vo, 1923–1927.

_____. "N. G. Chernyshevskii." In *Istoriia russkoi literatury XIX v.,* D. N. Ovsianiko-Kulikovskii, ed., III, 160–203. Moscow: Mir, 1910.

Pokrovskii, S. A. "O roli Chernyshevskogo i Gertsena v sozdanii revoliutsionnoi organizatsii," *Voprosy istorii,* no. 9 (1954), 81–88.

_____. *Fal'sifikatsiia istorii russkoi politicheskoi mysli v sovremennoi reaktsionnoi burzhuaznoi literature.* Moscow: Izdatel'stvo Akademii nauk S.S.S.R., 1957.

Pokusaev, E. I., et al., eds. *N. G. Chernyshevskii: Stat'i, issledovaniia i materialy*. No. 1. Saratov: Saratovskoe knizhnoe izdatel'stvo, 1958.

Pokusaev, E. I., ed. *N. G. Chernyshevskii: Stat'i, issledovaniia i materialy*. No. 2. Saratov: Izd-vo Saratovskogo universiteta, 1961.

———— and N. M. Chernyshevskaia, eds. *N. G. Chernyshevskii: Stat'i, issledovaniia i materialy*. No. 3. Saratov: Izd-vo Saratovskogo universiteta, 1962.

————, ed. *N. G. Chernyshevskii: Stat'i, issledovaniia i materialy*. No. 4. Saratov: Izd-vo Saratovskogo universiteta, 1965.

Prutskov, N. I. "'Esteticheskaia' kritika (Botkin, Druzhinin, Annenkov)." In *Istoriia russkoi kritiki v dvukh tomakh*, B. P. Gorodetskii, A. Lavretskii, and B. S. Meilakh, eds., I, 444–469. Moscow-Leningrad: Izd-vo AN SSSR, 1958.

Pypin, A. N. *Moi zametki*. E. A. Liatskii, ed. Moscow: Izdanie L. E. Bukhgeim, 1910.

————. *N. A. Nekrasov*. St. Petersburg: Tipografiia M. M. Stasiutevicha, 1905.

Pypina, V. A. *Liubov' v zhizni Chernyshevskogo*. Petograd, Izd-vo put' k znaniiu, 1923.

Randall, Francis B. *N. G. Chernyshevskii*. New York: Twayne Publishers, 1967.

Randall, John Herman, Jr. *The Career of Philosophy*. 2 vols. New York and London: Columbia University Press, 1962, 1965.

Razumovskii, N. N. *Pedagogicheskie idei N. G. Chernyshevskogo*. Moscow: Uchpedgiz, 1948.

Reingardt, N. V. "N. G. Chernyshevskii (po vospominaniiam i rasskazam raznykh lits)," *Russkaia starina*, no. 2 (1905), 447–476.

Reiser, S. A. "Byl li N. A. Dobroliubov avtorom pis'ma 'russkogo cheloveka'?" *Voprosy istorii*, no. 7 (1955), 128–131.

————. "Vospominaniia A. A. Sleptsova." In *N. G. Chernyshevskii: Stat'i, issledovaniia i materialy*, E. I. Pokusaev and N. M. Chernyshevskaia, eds., no. 3, pp. 249–282. Saratov: Izd-vo Saratovskogo universiteta, 1962.

Riasanovsky, Nicholas V. *Nicholas I and Official Nationality in Russia, 1825–1855*. Berkeley and Los Angeles: University of California Press, 1959.

————. *Russia and the West in the Teaching of the Slavophiles: A Study of Romantic Ideology*. Cambridge: Harvard University Press, 1952.

Robinson, Geroid Tanquary. *Rural Russia under the Old Regime*. New York: Macmillan, 1949.

Romanov, I. M. *N. G. Chernyshevskii v viliuiskom zatochenii*. Iakutsk: Iakutskoe knizhnoe izd-vo, 1957.

Rozenshtein, D. M. "N. G. Chernyshevskii i klassicheskaia nemetskaia filosofiia." In *N. G. Chernyshevskii (1889–1939): Trudy nauchnoi sessii k piatidesiatiletiiu so dnia smerti,* V. E. Evgen'ev-Maksimov, A. A. Voznesenskii, and Sh. I. Ganelin, eds., pp. 68–88. Leningrad: Izdanie Leningradskogo gosudarstvennogo universiteta, 1941.

Rozental', M. *Filosofskie vzgliady N. G. Chernyshevskogo.* Moscow: Gospolitizdat, 1948.

Rubinshtein, N. L. *Russkaia istoriografiia,* pp. 367–374. Moscow: Gospolitizdat, 1941.

Ruirikov, B. *N. G. Chernyshevskii: Kritiko-biograficheskii ocherk.* Moscow: Goslitizdat, 1961.

Rusanov, N. S. "Chernyshevskii i Rossiia 60-kh godov," *Russkoe bogatstvo,* no. 3 (1905), 166–207.

———. "Chernyshevskii v Sibiri," *Russkoe bogatstvo* (1910), no. 3, pp. 173–205; no. 4, pp. 92–125; no. 5, pp. 162–195; no. 6, pp. 60–82; no. 7, pp. 63–82.

Scheibert, Peter. "Der junge Černyševskij und sein Tagebuch," *Jahrbücher für Geschichte Osteuropas,* V (1957), 190–197.

Schermann, I. *N. G. Tschernischewsky als Socialpolitiker.* Heidelberg: Carl Pfeffer, 1909.

Schwarz, Solomon M. "Populism and Early Russian Marxism on Ways of Economic Development of Russia (the 1880's and 1890's)." In *Continuity and Change in Russian and Soviet Thought,* Ernest J. Simmons, ed., pp. 40–62. Cambridge: Harvard University Press, 1955.

Seton-Watson, Hugh. "The Intellectuals: Russia," *Encounter,* no. 24 (1955), 43–53.

Shapiro, A. L. "Voprosy russkoi istorii v proizvedeniiakh Chernyshevskogo." In *N. G. Chernyshevskii: Sbornik statei k 50-letiiu so dnia smerti velikogo revoliutsionera-demokrata,* A. F. Abramovich et al., eds., pp. 130–181. Saratov: Saratovskoe oblastnoe gosudarstvennoe izd-vo, 1939.

Shebunin, A. "K voprosu o roli N. G. Chernyshevskogo v revoliutsionnom dvizhenii 60-kh godov," *Katorga i ssylka,* no. 11 (1929), 7–34.

Shelgunov, N. V. *Vospominaniia.* A. A. Shilov, ed. Moscow-Petrograd: Gosudarstvennoe izd-vo, 1923.

Shilov, A., ed. "N. G. Chernyshevskii v doneseniiakh agentov III otdeleniia (1861–1862 gg.)," *Krasnyi arkhiv,* no. 14 (1926), 84–127.

Shpet, Gustav. *Ocherk razvitiia russkoi filosofii.* Part I. Petrograd: Kolos, 1922.

Shtein, V. M. *Ocherki razvitiia russkoi obshchestvenno-ekonomicheskoi mysli XIX–XX vekov.* Leningrad, 1948.

Shul'gin, V. N. *Ocherki zhizni i tvorchestva N. G. Chernyshevskogo.* Moscow: Goslitizdat, 1956.

Sikorskii, N. M. *Zhurnal "Sovremennik" i krest'ianskaia reforma 1861 g.* Moscow: Izd-vo AN SSSR, 1957.

Silberstein, Leopold. "Belinskij und Černyševskij: Versuch einer geistesgeschichtlichen Orientierungsskizze," *Jahrbücher für Kultur und Geschichte der Slaven*, n.s., VII (1931), 163–189.

Simmons, Ernest J. *Continuity and Change in Russian and Soviet Thought*. Cambridge: Harvard University Press, 1955.

Skerpan, Alfred A. "The Russian National Economy and Emancipation," In *Essays in Russian History*, Alan D. Ferguson and Alfred Levin, eds., pp. 161–229. Hamden, Connecticut: Archon Books, 1964.

Skorikov, N. F., "N. G. Chernyshevskii v Astrakhani," *Istoricheskii vestnik*, no. 5 (1905), 477–495.

Sladkevich, G. N. "Problema reformy i revoliutsii v russkoi publitsistike nachala 60-kh godov." In *Revoliutsionnaia situatsiia v Rossi v 1859–1861 gg*, M. V. Nechkina et al., eds., pp. 509–521. Moscow: Izdatel'stvo Akademii nauk S.S.S.R., 1960.

Sladkevich, N. G. *Ocherki istorii obshchestvennoi mysli Rossii v kontse 50-kh—60-kh godov XIX veka*. Leningrad: Izd-vo Leningradskogo universiteta, 1962.

Sleptsova, M. [N.] "Shturmany griadushchei buri (Iz vospominanii)," *Zven'ia*, II (1933), 386–464.

Solov'ev, E. A. (Andreevich, pseud.) *Ocherki iz istorii russkoi literatury XIX veka*. St. Petersburg: Tipografiia A. E. Kolpinskago, 1903.

———. *Opyt' filosofii russkoi literatury*. St. Petersburg: Znanie, 1905.

Solov'ev, V. S. *Pis'ma Vladimira Sergeevicha Solov'eva*. E. L. Radlov, ed. 3 vols. St. Petersburg: Tipografiia Obshchestvenniia pol'za, 1908–1911.

Steklov, Iu. M. *N. G. Chernyshevskii: Ego zhizn' i deiatel'nost', 1828–1889*. 2nd ed. 2 vols. Moscow-Leningrad: Gosudarstvennoe izd-vo, 1928.

Stilman, Leon. "Freedom and Repression in Prerevolutionary Russian Literature." In *Continuity and Change in Russian and Soviet Thought*, Ernest J. Simmons, ed., pp. 417–432. Cambridge: Harvard University Press, 1955.

Taubin, R. A. "K voprosu o roli N. G. Chernyshevskogo v sozdanii 'revoliutsionnoi partii' v kontse 50-kh nachale 60-kh godov XIX v.," *Istoricheskie zapiski*, no. 39 (1952), 59–97.

Tsagolov, N. A., and N. V. Khessin. "Ekonomicheskaia teoriia N. G. Chernyshevskogo—vershina ekonomicheskoi nauki domarksovskogo perioda." In *Istoriia russkoi ekonomicheskoi mysli*: Vol. I. *Epokha feodalizma*, Part 2, A. I. Pashkov, ed., pp. 592–786. Moscow: Gospolitizdat, 1958.

Tschernyschewskij, N. G. *Was Tun?* Berlin: Aufbau-Verlag, 1954.

Tuchkova-Ogareva, N. A. *Vospominaniia*. S. N. Golubov et al., eds. Moscow: Goslitizdat, 1959.

Tun, A. *Istoriia revoliutsionnykh dvizhenii v Rossii*. Vera Zasulich,

D. Kol'tsov, et al., trans. N.p.: Izdanie "Biblioteki dlia vsekh," n.d.

Turgenev, Ivan. *Literary Reminiscences and Autobiographical Fragments*. David Magarshack, trans. New York: Farrar, Straus and Cudahy, 1958.

_____. *Sobranie sochinenii*. G. A. Bialyi et al., eds. 12 vols. Moscow: Goslitizdat, 1958.

Turin, S. P. "Nicholas Chernyshevsky and John Stuart Mill," *The Slavonic and East European Review*, IX (1930), 29–33.

Usakina, T. I. "Stat'ia Gertsena 'Very Dangerous!!!' i polemika vokrug 'oblichitel'noi literatury' v zhurnalistike 1857–1859 gg." In *Revoliutsionnaia situatsiia v Rossii v 1859–1861 gg.*, M. V. Nechkina et al., eds., pp. 246–270. Moscow: Izd-vo AN SSSR, 1960.

Utin, N. I. "Propaganda i organizatsiia," *Narodnoe delo*, no. 2/3 (Geneva, 1868), 25–51.

Venturi, Franco. *Roots of Revolution: A History of the Populist and Socialist Movements in Nineteenth Century Russia*. Francis Haskell, trans. London: Weidenfeld and Nicolson, 1960.

Vilenskaia, E. S. "N. G. Chernyshevskii i A. I. Gertsen o roli narodnykh mass v osvoboditel'noi bor'be," *Voprosy filosofii*, no. 8 (1960), 108–119.

_____. *Revoliutsionnoe podpol'e v Rossii (60-e gody XIX v.)*. Moscow: Izd-vo nauka, 1965.

Volodarskii, I. B. " 'Otvet Velikorussu' i ego avtor." In *Revoliutsionnaia situatsiia v Rossii 1859–1861 gg.*, M. V. Nechkina et al., eds., pp. 52–83. Moscow: Izd-vo AN SSSR, 1965.

Volynskii, A. *Russkie kritiki*. St. Petersburg, 1896.

Wellek, René. *A History of Modern Criticism, 1750–1950*. 4 vols. New Haven: Yale University Press, 1955–1965.

_____. "Social and Aesthetic Values in Russian Nineteenth-Century Literary Criticism (Belinskii, Chernyshevskii, Dobroliubov, Pisarev)." In *Continuity and Change in Russian and Soviet Thought*, Ernest J. Simmons, ed., pp. 381–397. Cambridge, 1955.

Wiedeman, Marie. "Herzen und der Kolokol." Charlottenburg, 1935.

Yarmolinsky, Avrahm. *Road to Revolution: A Century of Russian Radicalism*. London: Cassell, 1957.

Zamiatnin, V. N. *Ekonomicheskie vzgliady N. G. Chernyshevskogo*. Moscow: Gospolitizdat, 1951.

Zamotin, I. I. "Ocherk istorii zhurnalistiki za pervuiu polovinu XIX veka." In *Istoriia russkoi literatury XIX v.*, D. N. Ovsianiko-Kulikovskii, ed., II, 374–397. Moscow: Mir, 1910.

Zapadov, A. V., ed. *Istoriia russkoi zhurnalistiki XVIII–XIX vekov*. Moscow: Gosudarstvennoe izd-vo Vysshaia shkola, 1963.

Žekulin, G. "Forerunner of Socialist Realism: The Novel 'What To Do?' by N. G. Chernyshevsky," *The Slavonic and East European Review*, XLI (1963), 467–483.

Zenkovsky, V. V. *A History of Russian Philosophy*. George L. Kline, trans. 2 vols. London: Routledge & Kegan Paul, 1953.

Zevin, V. Ia. *Politicheskie zvgliady i politicheskaia programma N. G. Chernyshevskogo*. Moscow: Gospolitizdat, 1953.

Zlatovratskii, N. N. *Vospominaniia*. Moscow: Goslitizdat, 1956.

# Notes

## I. Boyhood in Saratov (1828–1846)

1. Chernyshevskii knew about the traditions of the Golubev family from stories told by his maternal grandmother (I, 567–580).

2. For accounts of Chernyshevskii's family background and early years, see V. E. Cheshikhin-Vetrinskii, *N. G. Chernyshevskii 1828–1889* (Petrograd, 1923), pp. 7–31; F. V. Dukhovnikov, "Nikolai Gavrilovich Chernyshevskii, ego zhizn' v Saratove," *Russkaia starina*, no. 67 (1890), 531–568; E. A. Liatskii, "N. G. Chernyshevskii v gody ucheniia i na puti v universitet," *Sovremennyi mir* (1908), no. 5, pp. 45–75, no. 6, pp. 37–67; N. M. Chernyshevskaia-[Bystrova], *N. G. Chernyshevskii v Saratove: Detskie i iunosheskie gody* (Saratov, 1948).

3. A. N. Pypin, *Moi zametki* (Moscow, 1910), p. 5.

4. Three years earlier a daughter had been born to the Chernyshevskiis, but she lived only three weeks.

5. A younger cousin of Chernyshevskii's left a description of the family home. E. N. Pypina, "Besedy o proshlom," in Iu. G. Oksman, ed., *N. G. Chernyshevskii v vospominaniiakh sovremennikov* (Saratov, 1958–1959), I, 88–92.

6. Pypin, *Moi zametki*, p. 7. Chernyshevskii remarked on his father's heavy burden of preparing official reports and noted that the fathers of both households worked from morning to night (I, 702; XV, 152).

7. Oksman, ed., *N. G. Chernyshevskii*, I, 19, 32–33. See also Cheshikhin-Vetrinskii, *N. G. Chernyshevskii*, pp. 12–14; Liatskii, "N. G. Chernyshevskii v gody," *Sovremennyi mir*, no. 5 (1908), 51–53.

8. Some of Gavriil's writings on his church work were later published. Oksman, ed., *N. G. Chernyshevskii*, I, 52n23.

9. Oksman, ed., *N. G. Chernyshevskii*, I, 97; Iu. M. Steklov, *N. G.*

*Chernyshevskii: Ego zhizn' i deiatel'nost', 1828–1889* (2nd ed.; Moscow-Leningrad, 1928), I, 4.

10. I. Novich, *Zhizn' Chernyshevskogo* (Moscow, 1939), p. 18. In general, recent Soviet biographers tend to stress the impact of the social environment on young Chernyshevskii more than Plekhanov, who wrote correctly that Nikolai could view the outer world without himself becoming soiled. G. V. Plekhanov, *Sochineniia,* ed. D. Riazanov (2nd ed.; Moscow, 1923–1927), V, 142.

11. Chernyshevskii's autobiographical fragments (I, 566–713) are extremely difficult to use as a source, for they appear as a haphazard, confused body of recollections with consistency neither of theme nor of attitude.

12. Liatskii, "N. G. Chernyshevskii v gody," Sovremennyi mir, no. 5 (1908), 61–65.

13. Oksman, ed., *N. G. Chernyshevskii,* I, 35, 97.

14. Pypin, *Moi zametki,* pp. 17–18.

15. Oksman, ed., *N. G. Chernyshevskii,* I, 36; Pypin, *Moi zametki,* p. 13. In a diary entry in 1848, Chernyshevskii wrote that "earlier" he had been "educated" or "brought up" on *Notes of the Fatherland,* but the exact period he referred to is not clear (I, 84).

16. In his autobiographical fragments Chernyshevskii referred to his childhood reading as not yet reflecting "satisfactory convictions." Along with V. G. Belinskii, Charles Dickens, and George Sand, he mentioned reading medieval religious writings, "Russian theologians," "French historians," and "scholars of all tendencies" (I, 597, 632–634).

17. See also I. Iu. Krachkovskii, "Chernyshevskii i orientalist G. S. Sablukov," in V. E. Evgen'ev-Maksimov et al., eds., *N. G. Chernyshevskii (1889–1939)* (Leningrad, 1941), pp. 34–45.

18. Novich, *Zhizn' Chernyshevskogo,* p. 19.

19. Some writers try unsuccessfully to establish a strong current of materialism in Chernyshevskii's thinking before his attendance at the university. For example, see V. G. Baskakov, *Mirovozzrenie Chernyshevskogo* (Moscow, 1956), pp. 330–337.

20. Oksman, ed., *N. G. Chernyshevskii,* I, 20, 43, 47. I find no evidence for Venturi's claim that young Chernyshevskii "had constant clashes with his superiors." Franco Venturi, *Roots of Revolution,* trans. Francis Haskell (London, 1960), p. 132.

21. These theme notebooks were analyzed by Liatskii, "N. G. Chernyshevskii v gody," *Sovremennyi mir,* no. 6 (1908), 37–42.

22. Oksman, ed., *N. G. Chernyshevskii,* I, 76, 29–32. Pypin spoke fondly of Nikolai as a kindly older brother. Pypin, *Moi zametki,* p. 5.

23. Oksman, ed., *N. G. Chernyshevskii,* I, 36–37. Looking back over this period, Chernyshevskii later described himself as a "bibliophile" (I, 632).

24. N. G. Chernyshevskii, *Literaturnoe nasledie,* ed. N. A. Alekseev et al. (3 vols.; Moscow, 1928–1930), I, 171.

25. Oksman, ed., *N. G. Chernyshevskii*, I, 20.
26. Liatskii, "N. G. Chernyshevskii v gody," *Sovremennyi mir*, no. 5 (1908), 73–74.
27. Oksman, ed., *N. G. Chernyshevskii*, I, 41.
28. Oksman, ed., *N. G. Chernyshevskii*, I, 20, 45.
29. Pypin, *Moi zametki*, p. 22.
30. On Levitskii, see Oksman, ed., *N. G. Chernyshevskii*, I, 41–42, 52n27.
31. The only other significant mention Chernyshevskii made of Levitskii was in 1847, after receiving news that his friend had lost his scholarship, probably for drunkenness. Chernyshevskii's first reaction was to lament that poor handling by teachers had hurt Levitskii, who might otherwise have brought honor to Russia. Later, after learning the details, Chernyshevskii admitted that Levitskii probably had only himself to blame (XIV, 101–102, 111).
32. Oksman, ed., *N. G. Chernyshevskii*, I, 78,
33. Oksman, ed., *N. G. Chernyshevskii*, I, 48, 77.
34. Pypin, *Moi zametki*, pp. 22–23.
35. Thus, I see little justification for Lampert's claim that at this time, "to the dismay of his mentors," Chernyshevskii was given to "dangerous thoughts." Eugene Lampert, *Sons Against Fathers* (Oxford, 1965), p. 95.

## *II. University Years: The Making of a Radical (1846–1851)*

1. E. A. Liatskii, "N. G. Chernyshevskii v gody ucheniia i na puti v universitet," *Sovremennyi mir*, no. 6 (1908), 58–59. In Moscow, Chernyshevskii and his mother stayed at the home of G. S. Klientov, a priest from a Saratov family. The Klientovs noted Evgeniia Egorovna's fussy concern for her son and her tendency to treat him like a small child. V. E. Cheshikhin-Vetrinskii, *N. G. Chernyshevskii, 1828–1889* (Petrograd, 1923), pp. 30–31.
2. Liatskii, "N. G. Chernyshevskii v gody," no. 6 (1908), 58.
3. A. N. Pypin, *Moi zametki* (Moscow, 1910), p. 25.
4. In a diary entry for September 7, 1848, in which Chernyshevskii considered a possible theme for Nikitenko, he first mentioned the problem of the relation of poetry to reality (I, 108). His undergraduate dissertation, a study of Fonvizin's *Brigadier*, also written for Nikitenko, dealt with the naturalness rather than the artistry of the work (II, 792–805).
5. S. A. Reiser, "Chernyshevskii v Peterburge," in E. I. Pokusaev et al., eds., *N. G. Chernyshevskii: Stat'i, issledovaniia, i materialy* (Saratov, 1958), pp. 391–411. This article outlines Chernyshevskii's living conditions in the capital.
6. Vladimir C. Nahirny, "The Russian Intelligentsia: From Men of

Ideas to Men of Convictions," *Comparative Studies in Society and History,* IV (1962), 426.

7. M. L. Mikhailov, *Sochineniia v trekh tomakh* (Moscow, 1958), I, 6.

8. N. V. Shelgunov, *Vospominaniia* (Moscow-Petrograd, 1923), pp. 94–95.

9. Iu. G. Oksman, ed., *N. G. Chernyshevskii v vospominaniiakh sovremennikov* (Saratov, 1958–1959), I, 70.

10. A. P. Medvedev, "N. G. Chernyshevskii i V. P. Lobodovskii," in E. I. Pokusaev, ed., *N. G. Chernyshevskii: Stat'i, issledovaniia i materialy* (Saratov, 1961), no. 2, pp. 3–34.

11. See, e.g., Iu. M. Steklov, *N. G. Chernyshevskii: Ego zhizn' i deiatel'nost', 1828–1889* (2nd ed.; Moscow-Leningrad, 1928), I, 24–28.

12. Steklov praises Khanykov's knowledge of Western socialists and places him, as a person, above Lobodovskii. Steklov, *Chernyshevskii,* I, 28.

13. For Chernyshevskii's involvement with the Vvedenskii circle, see E. A. Liatskii, "N. G. Chernyshevskii i I. I. Vvedenskii," *Sovremennyi mir,* no. 6 (1910), 148–164; A. P. Medvedev, "N. G. Chernyshevskii v kruzhke I. I. Vvedenskogo," in Pokusaev et al., eds., *N. G. Chernyshevskii* (1958), pp. 42–104.

14. Lampert, for example, claims that Chernyshevskii joined the Vvedenskii circle as early as his second year at the university. Eugene Lampert, *Sons Against Fathers* (Oxford, 1965), p. 96.

15. By the end of 1850, Chernyshevskii could write to M. I. Mikhailov that Vvedenskii was treating the young man's friends as his own (XIV, 212).

16. Oksman, ed., *N. G. Chernyshevskii,* I, 106–107.

17. Liatskii, "N. G. Chernyshevskii i I. I. Vvedenskii," *Sovremennyi mir,* no. 6 (1910), 159.

18. Oksman, ed., *N. G. Chernyshevskii,* I, 107n4.

19. Oksman, ed., *N. G. Chernyshevskii,* I, 109–110.

20. The question is not whether Belinskii and Herzen influenced Chernyshevskii, but rather when this influence was first felt. The general tendency of Soviet writers to insist on early dates for this influence seems to reflect a piqued national pride because foreign writers played so great a part in Chernyshevskii's transformation into a radical.

21. Medvedev, "N. G. Chernyshevskii v kruzhke," in Pokusaev et al., eds., *N. G. Chernyshevskii* (1958), pp. 50–99 *passim.*

22. For a discussion of earlier editions of the diary and the problems of deciphering, see I, 24–28.

23. See, for example, V. G. Baskakov, *Mirovozzrenie Chernyshevskogo* (Moscow, 1956), pp. 330–337.

24. Although neither Venturi nor Lampert suggests that Chernyshevskii experienced a Hegelian period in his development, they both claim greater Hegelian influence than is justified. See, e.g., Lampert, *Sons*

Notes to Pages 51–63

*Against Fathers*, p. 140; Franco Venturi, *Roots of Revolution*, trans. Francis Haskell (London, 1960), p. 134.

25. P. V. Annenkov, *Literaturnye vospominaniia* (Moscow, 1960), p. 274.

26. A. L. Kostomarova, *Avtobiografiia N. I. Kostomarova*, ed. V. Kotel'nikov (Moscow, 1922), p. 331; Chernyshevskii, *Sochineniia* (1939–1953), I, 424.

27. E. A. Liatskii, "N. G. Chernyshevskii i uchitelia ego mysli," *Sovremennyi mir*, no. 11 (1910), 152.

28. For the view that Feuerbach considered a new philosophy to be the prerequisite for political and social change, see Melvin Cherno, "Ludwig Feuerbach and the Intellectual Basis of Nineteenth Century Radicalism" (Ph.D. diss., Stanford University, 1955), p. 22.

29. Sidney Hook notes, however, that Feuerbach's almost classic refutation of "absolute" materialism in 1838 did not prevent his own later acceptance of a "degenerate" sensationalism. Sidney Hook, *From Hegel to Marx* (New York, 1950), pp. 237, 267.

30. As Chernyshevskii usually recorded his reactions to books, it is significant that his student diary contains few comments on the original works of socialist writers. In 1850, he traced his disposition toward socialism to opinions acquired from newspapers (I, 373).

31. On the general question of Fourier's influence on Chernyshevskii, see E. A. Liatskii, "N. G. Chernyshevskii i Sh. Fur'e," *Sovremennyi mir*, no. 11 (1909), 167–187.

32. Eight months later, Chernyshevskii spoke to a cabman about serfdom and the need to support demands for liberation with force (I, 362).

33. In the same diary entry, Chernyshevskii seemed to find hope in the oppression of one class by another, because oppression would increase the desire of those who suffered to change the existing order.

34. Steklov, *Chernyshevskii*, I, 92.

35. E. A. Liatskii, "N. G. Chernyshevskii v 1848–50 gg.," *Sovremennyi mir*, no. 2 (1912), 182–184.

36. For the fragment itself and useful notes, see XI, 696–699, 740–742.

37. For the story itself, see XI, 640–695.

*III. The Teacher (1851–1853)*

1. Few writers defend the school. An exception is V. E. Cheshikhin-Vetrinskii, *N. G. Chernyshevskii, 1828–1889* (Petrograd, 1923), pp. 66–67.

2. Iu. G. Oksman, ed., *N. G. Chernyshevskii v vospominaniiakh sovremennikov* (Saratov, 1958–1959), I, 171.

3. Sh. I. Ganelin, "Pedagogicheskie idei N. G. Chernyshevskogo i

ego deiatel'nost' v Saratovskoi gimnazii," in V. E. Evgen'ev-Maksimov et al., eds., *N. G. Chernyshevskii (1889–1939)* (Leningrad, 1941), p. 131.

4. F. V. Dukhovnikov, "Nikolai Gavrilovich Chernyshevskii," *Russkaia starina*, no. 1 (1911), 69.

5. For Chernyshevskii's writings on education, see N. G. Chernyshevskii, *Izbrannye pedagogicheskie proizvedeniia*, ed. V. Z. Smirnov (Moscow, 1953). See also Ganelin, "Pedagogicheskie idei," in Evgen'ev-Maksimov et al., eds., *N. G. Chernyshevskii;* N. N. Razumovskii, *Pedagogicheskie idei N. G. Chernyshevskogo* (Moscow, 1948).

6. E. G. Bushkanets, "N. G. Chernyshevskii-uchitel' Saratovskoi gimnazii," in E. I. Pokusaev, ed., *N. G. Chernyshevskii: Stat'i, issledovaniia i materialy*, no. 4 (Saratov, 1965), p. 196.

7. Dukhovnikov, "N. G. Chernyshevskii," *Russkaia starina*, no. 1 (1911), 70–72.

8. Cheshikhin-Vetrinskii, *N. G. Chernyshevskii*, p. 73.

9. Iu. M. Steklov, *N. G. Chernyshevskii: Ego zhizn' i deiatel'nost', 1828–1889* (2nd ed.; Moscow-Leningrad, 1928), I, 99.

10. A. N. Pypin, *Moi zametki* (Moscow, 1910), pp. 88–90.

11. See, e.g., Ganelin, "Pedagogicheskie idei," in Evgen'ev-Maksimov et al., eds., *N. G. Chernyshevskii*, pp. 137–141.

12. Dukhovnikov, "N. G. Chernyshevskii," *Russkaia starina*, no. 1 (1911), 82–83.

13. E. A. Liatskii, "Chernyshevskii-Uchitel," *Sovremennik*, no. 6 (1912), 361–362.

14. Steklov, *Chernyshevskii*, I, 100.

15. Oksman, ed., *N. G. Chernyshevskii*, I, 164–168.

16. A. L. Kostomarova, *Avtobiografiia N. I. Kostomarova*, ed. V. Kotel'nikov (Moscow, 1922), p. 330.

17. Dukhovnikov, "N. G. Chernyshevskii," *Russkaia starina*, no. 1 (1911), 80.

18. Oksman, ed., *N. G. Chernyshevskii*, I, 150.

19. Dukhovnikov, "N. G. Chernyshevskii," *Russkaia starina*, no. 1 (1911), 80–83.

20. Steklov, *Chernyshevskii*, I, 101–102.

21. E. A. Belov, Chernyshevskii's friend and fellow-teacher, noted that his mother doted on him at this time. Oksman, ed., *N. G. Chernyshevskii*, I, 170–171.

22. After a year he described the other teachers as "kind, but dull," and made fun of their petty arguments. Oksman, ed., *N. G. Chernyshevskii*, I, 164.

23. Dukhovnikov, "N. G. Chernyshevskii," *Russkaia starina*, no. 1 (1911), 84.

24. Oksman, ed., *N. G. Chernyshevskii*, I, 164.

25. Dukhovnikov, "N. G. Chernyshevskii," *Russkaia starina*, no. 1

(1911), 89. For a recent study of Chernyshevskii's relationship with Kostomarov, see L. V. Domanovskii, "K saratovskim vzaimootnosheniiam N. G. Chernyshevskogo i N. I. Kostomarova," in E. I. Pokusaev and N. M. Chernyshevskii, eds., *N. G. Chernyshevskii: Stat'i, issledovaniia i materialy*, no. 3 (Saratov, 1962), pp. 213–232.

26. Oksman, ed., *N. G. Chernyshevskii*, I, 166.

27. A. L. Kostomarova, *Avtobiografiia*, p. 330.

28. Dukhovnikov, "N. G. Chernyshevskii," *Russkaia starina*, no. 1 (1911), 85–86.

29. E. Lampert, *Sons Against Fathers* (Oxford, 1965), p. 102.

30. An early reference to Sand in 1846 was less complimentary than one to Eugene Sue, but in the next few years Chernyshevskii's appreciation of Sand grew (XIV, 45; I, 297).

31. For the best treatment of this episode, see E. A. Liatskii, "Na pereput'e k novoi zhizni," *Sovremennik*, no. 5 (1912), 139–159.

32. In his later novel *Prologue*, Chernyshevskii placed the character Levitskii (Dobroliubov) in so many situations where marriage to an unfortunate young woman was the only way to help her that the result was almost a farce.

33. E. A. Liatskii, "Liubov' i zaprosy lichnogo schast'ia v zhizni N. G. Chernyshevskogo," *Sovremennik*, no. 9 (1912), 192–198.

34. On Chernyshevskii's courtship and marriage, see E. A. Liatskii, "Liubov' i zaprosy lichnogo schast'ia v zhizni N. G. Chernyshevskogo," *Sovremennik* (1912), no. 10, pp. 28–58; no. 11, pp. 4–15; no. 12, pp. 86–107; E. A. Liatskii, "N. G. Chernyshevskii na poroge semeinoi zhizni," *Sovremennik* (1913), no. 1, pp. 200–228; no. 4, pp. 108–154; V. A. Pypina, *Liubov' v zhizni Chernyshevskogo* (Petrograd, 1923); T. A. Bogdanovich, *Liubov' liudei shestidesiatykh godov* (Leningrad, 1929), pp. 67–263.

35. Liatskii, "Liubov'," *Sovremennik*, no. 10 (1912), 46.

36. Liatskii, "N. G. Chernyshevskii na poroge," *Sovremennik*, no. 1 (1913), 203–204.

37. Oksman, ed., *N. G. Chernyshevskii*, I, 171.

38. Bogdanovich, *Liubov' liudei shestidesiatykh godov*, pp. 104–105.

39. Nahirny uses Chernyshevskii's reaction to the news that Olga was a democrat and not very religious as evidence of the "extent to which he depersonalized other human beings and standardized his attitude to them." Vladimir C. Nahirny, "The Russian Intelligentsia: From Men of Ideas to Men of Convictions," *Comparative Studies in Society and History*, IV (1962), 427.

40. Liatskii, "Liubov'," *Sovremennik*, no. 12 (1912), 91, 98–99, 106.

41. Bogdanovich, *Liubov' liudei shestidesiatykh godov*, p. 132.

42. Steklov, *Chernyshevskii*, I, 116.

43. The list appeared in two earlier editions of Chernyshevskii's diary, but has been conspicuously omitted from the most recent edition.

See, N. G. Chernyshevskii, *Literaturnoe nasledie,* ed. N. A. Alekseev et al. (Moscow, 1928–1930), I, 680.

## IV. The Journalist and Editor (1853–1862)

1. In some respects it is strange that the transfer was approved at all. In an official report, Meier blamed Chernyshevskii's failure to complete the term and his many absences from class in the months before his departure for the lower performance of literature students. E. G. Bushkanets, "N. G. Chernyshevskii-uchitel' Saratovskoi gimnazii," in E. I. Pokusaev, ed., *N. G. Chernyshevskii: Stat'i, issledovaniia i materialy,* no. 4 (Saratov, 1965), p. 197.

2. For two versions of this episode, see Iu. G. Oksman, ed., *N. G. Chernyshevskii v vospominaniiakh sovremennikov* (Saratov, 1958–1959), I, 81, 85n30.

3. N. V. Shelgunov, *Vospominaniia,* ed. A. A. Shilov (Moscow-Petrograd, 1923), pp. 163–166. For a detailed and somewhat exaggerated account, see N. K. Piksanov, "Universitetskii disput Chernyshevskogo kak obshchestvennoe sobytie," in V. E. Evgen'ev-Maksimov et al., eds., *N. G. Chernyshevskii (1889–1939): Trudy nauchnoi sessii k piatidesiatiletiiu so dnia smerti* (Leningrad, 1941), pp. 20–33.

4. Iu. M. Steklov, *N. G. Chernyshevskii: Ego zhizn' i deiatel'nost', 1828–1889* (2nd ed.; Moscow-Leningrad, 1928), I, 142–143. In January 1859, Chernyshevskii wrote to his father that he might consider taking a university chair, providing he would not have to go on for a doctor's degree, but one suspects he was merely trying to humor his father's preference (XIV, 370).

5. Chernyshevskii's earliest years in journalism, see G. Berliner, *N. G. Chernyshevskii i ego literaturnye vragi,* ed. L. B. Kamenev (Moscow-Leningrad, 1930), pp. 8–43.

6. A. V. Zapadov, ed., *Istoriia russkoi zhurnalistiki XVIII-XIX vekov* (Moscow, 1963), pp. 245–246. In a later memoir on Nekrasov, Chernyshevskii noted that from the beginning of his association with *The Contemporary* he had understood that Nekrasov was clearly the more important of the two when it came to making decisions (I, 715).

7. V. E. Evgen'ev-Maksimov, *'Sovremennik' pri Chernyshevskom i Dobroliubove* (Leningrad, 1936), pp. 15–16. See also Charles Corbet, *Nekrasov l'homme et le poète* (Paris, 1948), pp. 139–147.

8. Kolbasin, who worked on *The Contemporary* at the time, described Druzhinin as a kind, well-educated Anglomaniac, but one who in principle defended serfdom and had no thought of liberating his own serfs. E. Kolbasin, "Teni starago 'Sovremennika'," *Sovremennik,* no. 8 (1911), 238.

9. Evgen'ev-Maksimov, *'Sovremennik' pri Chernyshevskom i Do-broliubove*, p. 19.

10. Corbet, *Nekrasov*, p. 201.

11. For these early attempts to remove Chernyshevskii, see Corbet, *Nekrasov*, pp. 203–207.

12. Evgen'ev-Maksimov, *'Sovremennik' pri Chernyshevskom i Do-broliubove*, p. 75.

13. Henri Granjard, *Ivan Tourguénev et les courants politiques et sociaux de son temps* (Paris, 1954), p. 271.

14. Venturi overstates the speed with which Chernyshevskii made his influence felt when he writes that "within a few months he had imposed his own personality and ideas on the review." Franco Venturi, *Roots of Revolution,* trans. Francis Haskell (London, 1960), p. 141.

15. M. Klevenskii, "Novye materialy po istorii 'Sovremennika'," *Literaturnoe nasledstvo,* no. 25/26 (1936), 359–360.

16. N. A. Nekrasov, *Sochineniia,* ed. Kornei Chukovskii (Moscow, 1954), III, 424.

17. I. S. Turgenev, *Sobranie sochinenii,* ed. G. A. Bialyi et al. (Moscow, 1958), XII, 247.

18. Corbet, *Nekrasov,* pp. 218–221.

19. A. N. Pypin, *N. A. Nekrasov* (St. Petersburg, 1905), p. 180.

20. Steklov stresses the importance of working with Chernyshevskii and Dobroliubov to Nekrasov's own development. Steklov, *Cherny-shevskii,* I, 167–168. In contrast, Chernyshevskii, with his typical self-effacement, later denied that he was an influence on Nekrasov (I, 746). For the complexity of Nekrasov's character and the troubled course of his career, see Corbet, *Nekrasov,* esp. pp. 441–455.

21. Evgen'ev-Maksimov, *'Sovremennik' pri Chernyshevskom i Dobroliubove,* p. 467.

22. I. Novich, *Zhizn' Chernyshevskogo* (Moscow, 1939), p. 64.

23. For an analysis of how much the different sections of the journal reflected the thinking of Chernyshevskii during the period 1858–1860, see Evgen'ev-Maksimov, *'Sovremennik' pri Chernyshevskom i Do-broliubove,* pp. 215–474. Once the victory of the new men was complete, Nekrasov was willing to join them in ridicule of his former comrades-in-arms. Corbet, *Nekrasov,* p. 268.

24. Chernyshevskii later claimed that he had warned Dobroliubov against offending the school administration by working on the journal before graduation (I, 756).

25. There is evidence in the memoir literature that Dobroliubov came to have a wider cirlce of readers than Chernyshevskii himself. See, e.g., L. F. Panteleev, *Vospominaniia* (Moscow, 1958), p. 531; N. N. Zlatovratskii, *Vospominaniia* (Moscow, 1956), p. 189.

26. N. A. Dobroliubov, *Sobranie sochinenii,* ed. B. I. Bursov et al.

(Moscow, 1961–1964), IX, 248. For Chernyshevskii's role in the formation of Dobroliubov's ideas, see Charles Corbet, "Dobroljubov et Herzen," *Revue des études slaves,* no. 27 (1951), 70–77.

27. M. A. Antonovich and G. Z. Eliseev, *Shestidesiatye gody* (Moscow-Leningrad, 1933), p. 40.

28. For a perceptive statement on Dobroliubov's personal difficulties, see Eugene Lampert, *Sons Against Fathers* (Oxford, 1965),
pp. 226–242.

29. Later, on February 25, 1878, Chernyshevskii wrote to his cousin
Pypin that he knew little of Dobroliubov except his writing (XV, 138).

30. For example, Dobroliubov made no effort to hide his dislike of
Turgenev. Once he told Turgenev to his face that he was bored by his
talk and he desired to stop talking altogether. Lampert, *Sons Against
Fathers,* pp. 238–239.

31. Avdot'ia Panaeva (E. Ia. Golovacheva), *Vospominaniia, 1824–
1870,* ed. K. Chukovskii (3rd ed.; Leningrad, 1929), pp. 372–373.

32. Corbet, *Nekrasov,* p. 257. See also Berliner, *N. G. Chernyshevskii,* pp. 83–104.

33. Corbet, *Nekrasov,* p. 205.

34. A former coworker on *The Contemporary* quoted Nekrasov as
saying, "it is better to be last among the youth, than first among the
aged." E. Kolbasin, "Teni starago 'Sovremennika'," *Sovremennik,*
no. 8 (1911), 240.

35. D. A. Miliutin in his memoirs indicated clearly that Chernyshevskii was forced to resign the editorship of the *Military Compendium.* B. P. Koz'min, "N. G. Chernyshevskii v redaktsii 'Voennogo
sbornika' iz vospominanii D. A. Miliutina," *Literaturnoe nasledstvo,*
no. 25/26 (1936), 234–235. For a version of this episode that stresses
Chernyshevskii's desire to spread revolutionary ideas in the army,
see N. Makeev, *N. G. Chernyshevskii-redaktor 'Voennogo sbornika'*
(Moscow, 1950).

36. N. Ia. Nikoladze, "Vospominaniia o shestidesiatykh godakh,"
*Katorga i ssylka,* no. 5 (1927), 30.

37. V. A. Pypina, *Liubov' v zhizni Chernyshevskogo* (Petrograd,
1923). There is considerable support for this criticism of Olga in T. A.
Bogdanovich, *Liubov' liudei shestidesiatykh godov* (Leningrad, 1929),
pp. 67–263 passim.

38. See, e.g., V. N. Shul'gin, *Ocherki zhizni i tvorchestva N. G. Chernyshevskogo* (Moscow, 1956).

39. Chernyshevskii is said to have remarked that Olga preferred his
following a career in journalism to teaching because he could earn
more money. Bogdanovich, *Liubov' liudei shestidesiatykh godov,*
pp. 139–140.

40. According to Pypina, Olga later reported that Chernyshevskii

would stop at the door of her room, not daring to enter without permission. Pypina, *Liubov' v zhizni Chernyshevskogo*, p. 121.

41. Lampert, *Sons Against Fathers*, p. 123. See also Steklov, *Chernyshevskii*, I, 125.

42. Many years later, according to Pypina, Olga claimed to have had a lover of whom Chernyshevskii was aware. Pypina, *Liubov' v zhizni Chernyshevskogo*, p. 105.

43. Steklov, *Chernyshevskii*, I, 123–127.

44. Antonovich and Eliseev, *Shestidesiatye gody*, pp. 34–35.

45. For example, Antonovich described Chernyshevskii's sympathy and concern when he thought that Antonovich did not have sufficient money to buy a warm coat. As it happened, Antonovich was merely dressing according to what he considered the fashion. Antonovich and Eliseev, *Shestidesiatye gody*, p. 42.

46. The evidence is strong that these characteristics were a part of Chernyshevskii's personality. See, e.g., Shelgunov, *Vospominaniia*, pp. 27–28; B. Bukhshtab, "Iz vospominanii A. I. Artem'eva o N. G. Chernyshevskom," *Literaturnoe nasledstvo*, no. 25/26 (1936), 230–234; Nikoladze, "Vospominaniia," *Katorga i ssylka*, no. 5 (1927), 41–42; V. E. Cheshikhin-Vetrinskii, *N. G. Chernyshevskii, 1828–1889* (Petrograd, 1923), pp. 161–162.

47. Antonovich and Eliseev, *Shestidesiatye gody*, p. 36.

48. As an example of the bitter hostility Chernyshevskii encountered, see an anonymous letter he received in the early 1860's, which was found in his possession at the time of his arrest. N. A. Alekseev, ed., *Protsess N. G. Chernyshevskogo* (Saratov, 1939), pp. 54–56.

49. A. V. Nikitenko, *Dnevnik v trekh tomakh*, ed. I. Ia. Aizenshtok (Moscow, 1955–1956), II, 110, 211.

50. K. D. Kavelin, *Pis'ma K. D. Kavelina i I. S. Turgeneva k. A. I. Gertsenu* (Geneva, 1892), p. 82. Vladimir Solov'ev noted that his father, the historian, was less pleased with Chernyshevskii during their second meeting in 1862, feeling that Chernyshevskii had changed for the worse, because of the idolatry he received from his admirers. V. S. Solov'ev, *Pis'ma Vladimira Sergeevicha Solov'eva*, ed. F. L. Radlov (St. Petersburg, 1908), I, 275.

51. A. I. Gertsen, *Sochineniia v deviati tomakh*, ed. V. P. Volgin et al. (Moscow, 1958), VII, 347.

52. Lampert recognizes that some of Chernyshevskii's utterances appeared opinionated, but in his presentation of Chernyshevskii as "saint and revolutionary," he underplays the provocative intolerance of Chernyshevskii's writing style. Lampert maintains, "there are no signs that he took his achievements very seriously," but I doubt if Chernyshevskii's readers would have agreed. Lampert, *Sons Against Fathers*, p. 116.

53. For a yearly listing of the number of pages cut out by the censor from copy submitted by *The Contemporary*, see V. G. Baskakov, *Mirovozzrenie Chernyshevskogo* (Moscow, 1956), p. 351.

54. See, e.g., Chernyshevskii's reviews of books by Gustav Molinari and Wilhelm Roscher (VII, 466–475, 969–983).

55. Charles E. Moser, *Antinihilism in the Russian Novel of the 1860's* (The Hague, 1964), p. 17; Oksman, ed., *N. G. Chernyshevskii*, I, 413–414n2.

56. Nikoladze, "Vospominaniia," *Katorga i ssylka*, no. 5 (1927), 33–34.

57. Panteleev, *Vospominaniia*, pp. 223, 522.

58. Shelgunov, *Vospominaniia*, pp. 29, 36.

59. See, e.g., Panteleev, *Vospominaniia*, p. 525; N. N. Zlatovratskii, *Vospominaniia* (Moscow, 1956), pp. 189–190; Oksman, ed., *N. G. Chernyshevskii*, I, 388.

60. For a general account of this polemic, see Berliner, *N. G. Chernyshevskii*, pp. 105–162. Opposition to *The Contemporary* did not necessarily mean that other writers wanted the journal closed, however. Evgen'ev-Maksimov refers to a letter of June 1862, in which A. A. Kraevskii and B. D. Skariatin warned the Minister of Education, A. V. Golovnin, of the harmful effects on public opinion and a free press if the journal were closed. Evgen'ev-Maksimov, *'Sovremennik' pri Chernyshevskom i Dobroliubove*, pp. 515–517.

61. N. M. Chernyshevskaia, *Letopis' zhizni i deiatel'nosti N. G. Chernyshevskogo* (Moscow, 1953), p. 236.

62. Nikitenko, *Dnevnik v trekh tomakh*, II, 211.

63. For Dostoevskii's record of the meeting, see F. M. Dostoievsky, *The Diary of a Writer* (New York, 1954), pp. 23–30.

64. Antonovich and Eliseev, *Shestidesiatye gody*, pp. 169–170.

65. Evgen'ev-Maksimov, *'Sovremennik' pri Chernyshevskom i Dobroliubove*, pp. 503–504. Early the following month Panaev and Nekrasov received a strong warning based on this criticism (pp. 504–505).

66. These reports, which have been printed, show a high degree of police suspicion, but they give no direct evidence of underground or illegal activity by Chernyshevskii. A. Shilov, ed., "N. G. Chernyshevskii v doneseniiakh agentov III otdeleniia (1861–1862 gg.)," *Krasnyi arkhiv*, no. 14 (1926), 84–127.

67. M. K. Lemke, *Politicheskie protsessy v Rossii 1860-kh gg.* (Moscow-Petrograd, 1923), p. 199.

68. Oksman, ed., *N. G. Chernyshevskii*, II, 95–96; Bogdanovich, *Liubov' liudei shestidesiatykh godov*, p. 176n1.

69. Venturi suggests that Chernyshevskii's decision to continue his work may have been related to a desire to give himself one more

proof of his resolution, a problem that troubled his conscience since boyhood. Venturi, *Roots of Revolution,* p. 177.

70. Alekseev, ed., *Protsess N. G. Chernyshevskogo,* pp. 24, 36.

71. Oksman, ed., *N. G. Chernyshevskii,* II, 271. N. V. Reingardt claimed to have heard this directly from Chernyshevskii.

72. The irony of this accusation was bitter, since for several years Herzen's position had been less radical than Chernyshevskii's.

## V. Philosophy

1. Censorship alone cannot be blamed for this delay, for in 1858 Dobroliubov was allowed to print a scathing attack on dualism in philosophy, which by implication criticized Christianity. N. A. Dobroliubov, *Sochineniia* (5th ed.; St. Petersburg, 1896), I, 525–533.

2. Among non-Soviet writers, see, e.g., M. Antonov, *N. G. Chernyshevskii: Sotsial'no-filosofskii etiud* (Moscow, 1910), pp. 12, 43–54. More recently, Rozental' has given one kind of dialectical thinking an important place in Chernyshevskii's philosophy. M. Rozental', *Filosofskie vzgliady N. G. Chernyshevskogo* (Moscow, 1948), pp. 105–141.

3. E. A. Liatskii, "N. G. Chernyshevskii i uchitelia ego mysli," *Sovremennyi mir,* no. 10 (1910), 154. Chernyshevskii added that, while there was progress in essence, the final state resembled the beginning in form.

4. See, e.g., Iu. M. Steklov, *N. G. Chernyshevskii: Ego zhizn' i deiatel'nost', 1828–1889* (2nd ed.; Moscow-Leningrad, 1928), I, 261–265. Steklov here made an unconvincing comparison between Chernyshevskii and Bakunin, to the effect that they both appreciated the destructive, revolutionary aspect of the dialectic.

5. Chernyshevskii here also referred to the contradiction between the spirit and the content of Hegel's work. The short-lived *Moscow Observer,* under Belinskii's editorship in 1838–1839, was an organ of Russian Hegelianism.

6. Frederick Engles, *Ludwig Feuerbach and the Outcome of Classical German Philosophy* (London, 1947), pp. 18–19.

7. Without direct evidence of Chernyshevskii's denial of a necessary three-stage pattern of development, the issue must be left open. But I cannot believe that he would have accepted on faith a pattern of change, when he scorned the system that gave rise to belief in that pattern, and when he had no alternative system to explain it.

8. Chernyshevskii, *Sochineniia* (1939–1953), VII, 222–295. Whenever Chernyshevskii used the term "transcendental philosophy," he was referring directly to German idealism, but he at the same time implied religion.

9. A summary of this argument is given in Rozental', *Filosofskie vzgliady N. G. Chernyshevskogo,* pp. 70–104; G. Berliner, *N. G. Chernyshevskii i ego literaturnye vragi,* ed. L. B. Kamenev (Moscow-Leningrad, 1930), pp. 105–126.

10. Dobroliubov, *Sochineniia,* I, 526.

11. I cannot agree with Lampert, who argues from the same evidence that Chernyshevskii's underlying idea was not "an allegedly all-material of all-spiritual universe" but rather of man "who is both spirit and matter." See Eugene Lampert, *Sons Against Fathers* (Oxford, 1965), p. 155.

12. From a different point of view, Chernyshevskii's critics have been quick to assert that neither can one prove monism merely by showing that dualism cannot be proved scientifically. Ivanov called such an assertion "metaphysical." Ivan Ivanov, *Istoriia russkoi kritiki,* Parts 3 and 4 (St. Petersburg, 1900), pp. 515–516.

13. Lampert admits that this section does not take the reader far in understanding how knowledge is possible, but he explains Chernyshevskii's "naive realism" as a weapon for eliminating complexities, which he tended to regard as narrow and obstructive pedantry. Chernyshevskii's account of human knowledge was an attempt to look reality in the face, instead of trying to explain it away with a myth, a word, an impression, or a preconceived idea. Lampert, *Sons Against Fathers,* p. 149.

14. Steklov made a strong case for Chernyshevskii's debt to the eighteenth century enlighteners in the field of ethics. Steklov, *Chernyshevskii,* I, 279–287. Kotliarevskii called Chernyshevskii's ethics a simple repetition of Bentham and Mill. Nestor Kotliarevskii, *Kanun osvobozhdeniia* (Petrograd, 1916), p. 307.

15. Some of the calculations of Chernyshevskii's heroic characters appear so forced that perhaps he had come to look upon his own theory with amusement. Steklov, *Chernyshveskii,* I, 297.

16. By "fantastic errors of former times," Chernyshevskii meant idealistic philosophy and religion. In the version quoted here, these words were followed by a comparison of "fantastic errors" with Greek myths. N. G. Chernyshevskii, *Izbrannye filosofskie sochineniia,* ed. M. M. Grigor'ian (Moscow, 1950–1951), III, 202–203. In the full edition of Chernyshevskii's works the paragraph is not included (VII, 253–254).

17. This statement speaks against the claims of both Kotliarevskii, who felt that Chernyshevskii was little interested in philosophical questions and knowingly spread false doctrines for their utility, and Baskakov, who credits Chernyshevskii with an understanding of *partiinost'* (party-mindedness) in philosophy. Kotliarevskii, *Kanun osvobozhdeniia,* p. 290; V. G. Baskakov, *Mirovozzrenie Chernyshevskogo* (Moscow, 1956), pp. 413–456.

18. The theme of Chernyshevskii as an "enlightener" runs throughout Plekhanov's works. See, e.g., G. V. Plekhanov, *Sochineniia*, ed. D. Riazanov (2nd ed.; Moscow, 1923–1927), VI, 251. For Chernyshevskii's plans to write compendiums of knowledge and works of popularization, see his letter to Olga written shortly after his arrest (XIV, 455–457).

19. L. F. Panteleev, *Vospominaniia* (Moscow, 1958), p. 525.

20. P. D. Iurkevich, "Iz nauki o chelovecheskom dukhe," *Trudy Kievskoi dukhovnoi akademii,* I (1860), 367–511.

21. Iurkevich, "Iz nauki," *Trudy Kievskoi dukhovnoi akademii,* I (1860), 370–371, 383–388, 437–442, 462, 493.

22. Iurkevich, "Iz nauki," *Trudy Kievskoi dukhovnoi akademii,* I (1860), 508–511. Chizhevskii referred to Iurkevich's criticism of materialism as "quiet and skillful." D. I. Chizhevskii, *Gegel' v Rossii* (Paris, 1939), p. 253. Lampert's curt dismissal of Iurkevich's objections falls far short of a fair restatement of his position. Lampert, *Sons Against Fathers,* pp. 162–163.

23. Antonovich wrote a negative review of S. S. Gogotskii's *Philosophical Lexicon.* Rozental', *Filosofskie vzgliady N. G. Chernyshevskogo,* p. 74.

24. M. N. Katkov, "Starye bogi i novye bogi," *Russkii vestnik,* XXXI (February 1861), 894, 897, 902–904.

25. *Russkii vestnik,* XXXII (April 1861), 79–105; XXXIII (May 1861), 26–59.

26. Berliner, *N. G. Chernyshevskii,* pp. 114–116.

27. Lavrov, for example, said he was disappointed at Chernyshevskii's performance in this polemic. M. Antonov, *N. G. Chernyshevskii: Sotsial'no-filosofskii etiud* (Moscow, 1910), p. 41.

28. Rozental', *Filosofskie vzgliady N. G. Chernyshevskogo,* p. 98.

29. See, e.g., Steklov, *Chernyshevskii,* II, 171; Berliner, *N. G. Chernyshevskii,* p. 112. Lampert comes closer to the truth when he speaks of Chernyshevskii as losing his head in his concern to rebut a socially compromised and therefore untenable position. Lampert, *Sons Against Fathers,* p. 164. The burden of proof should be on those who blame the censorship conditions exclusively for Chernyshevskii's unimpressive performance.

30. John Herman Randall, Jr., *The Career of Philosophy* (New York and London, 1962–1965), II, 366.

31. Randall notes that in the early 1840's Feuerbach wrote a "classic" criticism of metaphysical materialism, some parts of which speak directly against what Chernyshevskii tried to do in "The Anthropological Principle in Philosophy." Randall, *The Career,* II, 369.

32. Chizhevskii, *Gegel' v Rossii,* p. 249.

VI. *Aesthetics and Literary Criticism*

1. René Wellek, *A History of Modern Criticism, 1750–1950* (New Haven, 1955–1965), II, 321. This volume, subtitled *The Romantic Age*, provides an excellent treatment of the school of aesthetics and criticism Chernyshevskii sought to dislodge.

2. Geraldine Pelles, *Art, Artists and Society: Origins of a Modern Dilemma* (Englewood Cliffs, N.J., 1963), p. 19; Eugenia W. Herbert, *The Artist and Social Reform* (New Haven, 1961), pp. 11–14.

3. Steklov discusses in some detail which sections of Feuerbach's works might have been of use to Chernyshevskii in his aesthetic theory. He also suggests the influence of French enlighteners, especially Diderot. Iu. M. Steklov, *N. G. Chernyshevskii: Ego zhizn' i deiatel'nost'* (2nd ed.; Moscow-Leningrad, 1928), I, 307–312. See also V. M. Klochkov, "Skhodstvo i razlichie v eticheskikh vzgliadakh L. Feierbakha i N. G. Chernyshevskogo," *Voprosy filosofii,* no. 6 (1957), 47–58.

4. Croce calls Vischer's concept of aesthetic activity "Hegel's concept debased." Benedetto Croce, *Aesthetic* (rev. ed.; New York, 1956), p. 337. Wellek refers to Vischer as the "tombstone of German aesthetics." Wellek, *A History of Modern Criticism,* II, 335.

5. N. G. Chernyshevskii, *Izbrannye filosofskie sochineniia,* ed. M. M. Grigor'ian (Moscow, 1950–1951), I, 802. Wellek describes Chernyshevskii's thesis as an argument against "isolated Hegelian formulas." Wellek, *A History of Modern Criticism,* IV, 239.

6. This discussion was in many ways misleading, because Chernyshevskii implied that his opponents valued art above reality in a moral sense. The question had been posed in this way before, however. See M. S. Kagan, *Esteticheskoe uchenie Chernyshevskogo* (Leningrad-Moscow, 1958), p. 60.

7. Plekhanov lamented that Chernyshevskii did not go on from here to speak of changes in aesthetic theory in relation to changes in the ruling class of society. G. V. Plekhanov, *Sochineniia,* ed. D. Riazanov (2nd ed.; Moscow, 1923–1927), V, 319.

8. This reference is a good example of Chernyshevskii's arguments of expediency. He found support for his immediate point at the cost of contradicting his usual view that dreaming of luxury represented a form of upper class escapism.

9. Kagan suggests that Chernyshevskii believed Vischer's concept of the comic was too restricted. Kagan, *Esteticheskoe uchenie Chernyshevskogo,* p. 78.

10. There is a question as to whether "contradiction" is too strong a word here. But I cannot agree with the statement of Kagan, quoted approvingly by Lampert, that Chernyshevskii disavowed the "notion of art as 'imitation of nature' which dominated all previous mate-

rialistic aesthetics." Eugene Lampert, *Sons Against Fathers* (Oxford, 1965), p. 215.

11. Kagan, *Esteticheskoe uchenie Chernyshevskogo*, p. 87.

12. Chernyshevskii wrote, "By real life, naturally, is meant not only the relation of man to the objects and beings of the objective world, but also the inner life of man. Sometimes man lives with dreams,— then dreams have for him (to a certain degree and for a certain time) the significance of something objective. Even more often a man lives in the world of his own feelings. These states, if they achieve interest, also are reproduced by art" (II, 85).

13. In this same section Chernyshevskii blamed the introduction of a false concept of idealization on Plotinus, "one of those nebulous thinkers called Neo-Platonists."

14. Wellek underplays the extent to which Chernyshevskii believed in a social mission for art. Wellek, *A History of Modern Criticism*, IV, 239, 243.

15. Chernyshevskii's use of the word scientific (nauchnyi) was not limited to the sphere of natural science, but implied all learning.

16. In defense of Chernyshevskii, it must be added that I am here applying a systematic analysis to hastily written journalistic articles. He scarcely had time for adequate systematization.

17. Chernyshevskii, in a review of Pisemskii's *Sketches of Peasant Life,* defended Belinskii and, by implication, himself from charges that they favored didacticism in art (IV, 562–563).

18. These lines were part of a paragraph disallowed by the censor.

19. Significantly, this show of concern for form was part of a discussion of Pushkin, in whom Chernyshevskii felt artistic form triumphed over content.

20. Wellek, who is generally critical of Chernyshevskii's aesthetics, describes these "Essays" as showing that Chernyshevskii had the makings of an intellectual historian. Wellek, *A History of Modern Criticism,* IV, 241.

21. Chernyshevskii used a quotation from an 1847 article by Belinskii to show the temporary value of European influence (III, 249).

22. In addition to these articles, which appeared in nos. 2, 3, 7, and 8 of *The Contemporary* for 1855, Chernyshevskii wrote a short analysis of Pushkin's life and work intended for young readers and published the following year (III, 310–339).

23. The paragraph is taken from Belinskii's "Survey of Russian Literature for 1847."

24. See, e.g., Plekhanov, *Sochineniia,* V, 360–362; Evg. Solov'ev (Andreevich, pseud.), *Ocherki iz istorii russkoi literatury XIX veka* (St. Petersburg, 1903), p. 222.

25. It is difficult to tell in these letters when Chernyshevskii was being honest. As he clearly wanted to get on the right side of Turgenev,

he may have merely been playing on the ill feeling between Turgenev and Tolstoi.

26. Georg Lukacs, *Der russische Realismus in der Weltliteratur* (Berlin, 1949), p. 34.

27. Charles Corbet, "Černyševskij estheticien et critique," *Revue des études slaves*, XXIV (1948), 126.

28. It was because of Chernyshevskii's utilitarian tendency to view art as a "textbook of life," a means to serve the intellectual development of society, that he earned Plekhanov's reproachful label "enlightener." Plekhanov, *Sochineniia*, VI, 251.

29. E. A. Liatskii, "N. G. Chernyshevskii v redaktsii 'Sovremennika'," *Sovremennyi mir*, no. 9 (1911), 170.

30. G. Berliner, *N. G. Chernyshevskii i ego literaturnye vragi* (Moscow-Leningrad, 1930), p. 45.

31. See, e.g., Steklov, *Chernyshevskii*, II, 16–17.

32. Chernyshevskii published his own review of his dissertation in the June 1855 issue of *The Contemporary*, under the initials "N. P." (II, 93–118).

33. Berliner, *N. G. Chernyshevskii*, pp. 22–23.

34. Berliner, *N. G. Chernyshevskii*, p. 24. See also Turgenev's negative comments in a letter to V. P. Botkin and N. A. Nekrasov. I. S. Turgenev, *Sobranie sochinenii v dvenadtsati tomakh*, ed. G. A. Bialyi et al. (Moscow, 1958), XII, 186.

35. Iu. G. Oksman, ed., *N. G. Chernyshevskii v vospominaniiakh sovremennikov* (Saratov, 1958–1959), II, 383.

36. Ivan Turgenev, *Literary Reminiscences and Autobiographical Fragments*, trans. David Magarshack (New York, 1958), p. 196.

37. Charles A. Moser, *Antinihilism in the Russian Novel of the 1860's* (The Hague, 1964), pp. 86–88.

38. B. P. Gorodetskii, A. Lavretskii, and B. S. Meilakh, eds., *Istoriia russkoi kritiki v dvukh tomakh* (Moscow-Leningrad, 1958), I, 444–469.

39. A. V. Druzhinin, *Sobranie sochinenii*, ed. N. V. Gervel (St. Petersburg, 1865–1867), VII, 189–192.

40. Druzhinin, *Sobranie sochinenii*, VII, 214–222.

41. Druzhinin, *Sobranie sochinenii*, VII, 57; Gorodetskii et al., eds., *Istoriia russkoi kritiki*, I, 462.

42. A. N. Pypin, *N. A. Nekrasov* (St. Petersburg, 1905), p. 29. In Pypin's interpretation both of these tendencies had their origin in Belinskii's writing.

43. Quoted in Rufus W. Mathewson, Jr., *The Positive Hero in Russian Literature* (New York, 1958), p. 123.

44. Wellek, *A History of Modern Criticism*, III, 244.

45. V. G. Belinskii, *Sobranie sochinenii v trekh tomakh*, ed. F. M. Golovenchenko (Moscow, 1948), III, 789.

46. In his "Essays on the Gogol Period," Chernyshevskii noted the wider implications of differences in aesthetic theories (III, 25).

47. Kagan equates the views of Chernyshevskii and Dobroliubov so closely that he suggests the younger man's articles were essentially what Chernyshevskii would have written, if he had continued to write much in the field of criticism. Kagan, *Esteticheskoe uchenie Chernyshevskogo*, p. 46.

48. Wellek summarizes Dobroliubov's views on the relation of art to society as follows: "Thus Dobrolyubov runs the gamut from complete pessimism to messianic hopes; from the view that literature is a passive mirror to the view that it incites to direct action, transforms society." Wellek, *A History of Modern Criticism*, IV, 247.

49. N. A. Dobroliubov, *Sobranie sochinenii v deviati tomakh*, ed. B. I. Bursov et al. (Moscow-Leningrad, 1961–1964), VI, 96–99. Wellek notes the value of Dobroliubov's distinction between the overt and latent meaning of a work. Wellek, *A History of Modern Criticism*, IV, 250.

50. Mathewson, *The Positive Hero in Russian Literature*, pp. 57–79. For a discussion of Dobroliubov with a different emphasis, see Lampert, *Sons Against Fathers*, pp. 242–271.

51. Wellek, *A History of Modern Criticism*, IV, 256. For other useful works on Pisarev, see Armand Coquart, *Dmitri Pisarev (1840–1868) et l'ideologie du nihilisme russe* (Paris, 1946), pp. 251–272; Frederick C. Barghoorn, "D. I. Pisarev and the Russian Intellectual Movement" (Ph.D. diss., Harvard University, 1941), pp. 151–174; Lampert, *Sons Against Fathers*, pp. 329–338.

52. D. I. Pisarev, "Razrushenie estetiki," in N. Denisiuk, ed., *Kriticheskaia literatura o proizvedeniiakh N. G. Chernyshevskogo* (Moscow, 1908), pp. 26–53.


*VII. Economics and Social Theory*

1. For an outline of European theories that had influence in Russia, see J. F. Normano, *The Spirit of Russian Economics* (New York, 1945), pp. 1–77.

2. In 1848, John Stuart Mill published the first edition of his *Principles of Political Economy*, in which he argued that distribution of the economic product was a matter of human arrangement rather than the reflection of a necessary law.

3. Gerschenkron notes that a strong current of humanitarian concern kept many nineteenth-century Russian writers from a profound understanding of the economic life of their times. Alexander Gerschenkron, "The Problem of Economic Development in Russian Intellectual History of the Nineteenth Century," in Ernest J. Simmons,

ed., *Continuity and Change in Russian and Soviet Thought* (Cambridge, 1955), p. 34.

4. Herzen once justified this expectation by reference to the injustice of history, which granted latecomers the advantage of the experience of others. A. I. Gertsen, *Polnoe sobranie sochinenii i pisem*, ed. M. K. Lemke (Petrograd, 1919–1925), VIII, 151. Chernyshevskii, in turn, spoke of the love of history for its youngest grandchildren (V, 387).

5. See, e.g., A. A. Kornilov, "Chernyshevskii i krest'ianskaia reforma," *Russkaia mysl'*, no. 1 (1910), 1–26; V. E. Evgen'ev-Maksimov, *'Sovremennik' pri Chernyshevskom i Dobroliubove* (Leningrad, 1936), p. 292; Alexander Kucherov, "N. G. Chernyshevskii on Capitalism and Russia's Shortcut to Socialism" (Ph.D. diss., Columbia University, 1953), pp. 237–259.

6. V. N. Zamiatnin, *Ekonomicheskie vzgliady N. G. Chernyshevskogo* (Moscow, 1951), p. 131. See also N. M. Sikorskii, *Zhurnal "Sovremennik" i krest'ianskaia reforma 1861 g.* (Moscow, 1957), pp. 6–7.

7. Despite his claim of Chernyshevskii's consistent revolutionary intent, Sikorskii provides a valuable catalogue of the positive, practical suggestions made in *The Contemporary* for an equitable liberation settlement short of revolution. Sikorskii, *Zhurnal "Sovremennik,"* pp. 8–123 passim. For other views of Chernyshevskii's writings on the reform settlement, see N. F. Annenskii, "N. G. Chernyshevskii i krest'ianskaia reforma," in A. K. Dzhivelegov et al., eds., *Velikaia reforma* (Moscow, 1911), IV, 220–279; Zamiatnin, *Ekonomicheskie vzgliady N. G. Chernyshevskogo*, pp. 126–212; N. A. Tsagolov, "Agrarnaia programma N. G. Chernyshevskogo: Otnoshenie ego k reforme 1861 g.," in A. I. Pashkov, ed., *Istoriia russkoi ekonomicheskoi mysli:* vol. I. *Epokha feodalizma* (Moscow, 1955–1958), part 2, pp. 747–769.

8. In 1857, for example, Ivan Aksakov's journal *Molva* was closed for mentioning the question of liberation of the serfs. A. A. Kornilov, *Obshchestvennoe dvizhenie pri Aleksandre II (1855–1881)* (Moscow, 1909), pp. 40, 74.

9. The rescripts and accompanying instructions are reprinted as they appeared in *The Contemporary* in N. G. Chernyshevskii, *Izbrannye ekonomicheskie proizvedeniia* (Moscow, 1948–1949), I, 504–523. Liberation with land, other than the peasants' house plots, was thus part of the intention of the original rescript and not, as Venturi maintains, a later concession made in response to a united campaign of the liberals and socialists. Franco Venturi, *Roots of Revolution*, trans. Francis Haskell (London, 1960), p. 152.

10. Despite this consideration by the government, the Moscow nobles replied cynically that they did not see what advantages would accrue to them from the proposed measure. James Mavor, *An Economic History of Russia* (2nd ed.; London and Toronto, 1925), I, 386.

11. Zamiatnin minimizes the importance of this praise of Alexander with the reminder that Chernyshevskii considered Peter's reforms to have been "progressive" but also burdensome to the people. Zamiatnin, *Ekonomicheskie vzgliady N. G. Chernyshevskogo*, 135. For another attempt to belittle these statements, see Sikorskii, *Zhurnal "Sovremennik,"* pp. 14–17.

12. Chernyshevskii, *Izbrannye ekonomicheskie proizvedeniia*, I, 538–564. According to the latest scholarship, this article and a few others included in earlier collections of Chernyshevskii's work were not written by him. V. E. Bograd, *Zhurnal "Sovremennik" 1847–1866: Ukazatel' soderzhaniia* (Moscow-Leningrad, 1959), p. 341. The important point, however, is that he included them in the journal.

13. See, e.g., his comments on an article by Iurii Samarin about the peasants in Prussia. Chernyshevskii, *Izbrannye ekonomicheskie proizvedeniia*, I, 566–567.

14. A. A. Kornilov, "Chernyshevskii i krest'ianskaia reforma," *Russkaia mysl'*, no. 1 (1910), 13–14.

15. For a brief review of the validity of this widely-held liberal assumption, see Alfred A. Skerpan, "The Russian National Economy and Emancipation," in Alan D. Ferguson and Alfred Levin, eds., *Essays in Russian History* (Hamden, Conn., 1964), pp. 202–211.

16. In July 1857, Chernyshevskii had given a hint of his true feelings on the rights of landlords to compensation, in a review of an article by V. P. Bezobrazov. In effect, he compared the Russian landlords to robber barons in the realm of Rudolph of Hapsburg, who deserved no compensation simply because, under pressure, they had ceased to rob (IV, 798–800).

17. One might question the logic of Chernyshevskii's calculations, for one of the totals used included the amount of money needed to support the peasants, which he compared to another total from which the support of the peasants had been deducted.

18. The actual settlement of 1861 priced the land in the non-black soil provinces (that is, where land had marginal productivity, and where obrok payments usually substituted for the performance of barshchina) at almost twice its market value, in order to compensate the landlords for their loss of obrok payments. Geroid Tanquary Robinson, *Rural Russia under the Old Regime* (New York, 1949), p. 88.

19. In fact, the peasant debt to the government for the land received in 1861 was divided into payments over a forty-nine-year period, including 6.5% for interest and amortization. Peter I. Lyashchenko, *History of the National Economy of Russia to the 1917 Revolution*, trans. L. M. Herman (New York, 1949), p. 386.

20. In the 1861 settlement, the peasants of the black soil provinces generally received less land than in their prereform allotments, and in the non-black soil provinces peasant landholdings generally in-

creased. Lyashchenko, *History of the National Economy of Russia,* pp. 382–383.

21. In describing the American South, Chernyshevskii also implied a comparison with Russia. For his views on the American slave states, see David Hecht, *Russian Radicals Look to America, 1825–1894* (Cambridge, 1947), pp. 97–120.

22. Many years after the event, Chernyshevskii wrote about a discussion he had with Nekrasov early in 1861. When Nekrasov expressed disappointment with the terms of the reform settlement, Chernyshevskii replied, "But what did you expect? For a long time it has been clear that it would be just this way" (I, 747).

23. It is not always clear when Chernyshevskii used such issues as Austrian legislation or American slavery as Aesopian language for Russian affairs and when he considered them in their own right. Sikorskii, *Zhurnal 'Sovremennik',* pp. 145–146.

24. For example, in 1857 Chernyshevskii engaged in a polemic with *The Economic Indicator,* which under the editorship of I. V. Vernadskii supported the position of economic liberalism.

25. Kucherov argues persuasively that Chernyshevskii never really made up his mind whether to attribute the capitalist system to historical necessity or to human weakness and folly. Kucherov, "N. G. Chernyshevskii on Capitalism," pp. 92–94.

26. This section is a good example of Chernyshevskii's tendency to establish his position with deductive reasoning rather than statistical evidence.

27. Chernyshevskii criticized the effect on production of different forms of private property in response to claims by I. V. Vernadskii that communal ownership hindered production (IV, 395–402, 427–428).

28. These suggestions for state action are counterparts of Chernyshevskii's campaign to keep the redemption payments low during the preparation of the serf reform. Karpovich makes the point that though the censor could prevent Chernyshevskii from expressing his radical views, no censor could force him to make positive statements of a reformist nature. Michael M. Karpovich, "N. G. Chernyshevskii Between Socialism and Liberalism," *Cahiers du monde russe et soviétique,* I (1960), 582.

29. For a summary statement on the Slavophile view of the commune, see Nicholas V. Riasanovsky, *Russia and the West in the Teaching of the Slavophiles* (Cambridge, 1952), pp. 133–135.

30. In order to disassociate Chernyshevskii from the populist position, Plekhanov argued, with little success, that he wrote this article after he had already "washed his hands of the Russian commune." G. V. Plekhanov, *Sochineniia,* ed. D. Riazanov (2nd ed.; Moscow, 1923–1927), VI, 34.

31. In an attempt to minimize the difference between this suggestion and the basic views of Marxism, Steklov tried to link Chernyshevskii's interest in the commune with his hope for a socialist revolution in the West, which would in turn aid Russia's transition. Iu. M. Steklov, *N. G. Chernyshevskii: Ego zhizn' i deiatel'nost'* (2nd ed.; Moscow-Leningrad, 1928), I, 581. For a similar view, see V. M. Shtein, *Ocherki razvitiia russkoi obshchestvenno-ekonomicheskoi mysli XIX–XX vekov* (Leningrad, 1948), p. 203.

32. This shift of position is noted in Kucherov, "N. G. Chernyshevsky on Capitalism," pp. 218–219.

33. The parallel between Chernyshevskii's views on the commune and those of Marx, as expressed in his March 8, 1881, letter to Vera Zasulich, is noted in V. R. Chernyshev. *N. G. Chernyshevskii i G. V. Plekhanov: Ocherk ikh ekonomicheskikh vozzrenii* (Moscow-Leningrad, 1926), pp. 89–90.

34. Karl Marx, *Capital: A Critique of Political Economy*, ed. Frederick Engels, revised according to the fourth German edition by Ernest Untermann (New York, 1906), p. 19.

35. Chernyshevskii was not so naive as to expect the tsarist government to take such action, but neither did he think of these plans in terms of a program for a revolutionary party dictatorship, as Steklov maintained. Steklov, *Chernyshevskii*, I, 589. Chernyshevskii merely wanted to popularize the principle of association.

36. The impact of these words on young people was apparently great. N. I. Utin, then a young man very much under Chernyshevskii's influence, wrote in 1864 on the reception of the novel: "He [Chernyshevskii] wanted to show the youth a visible and attractive picture of that utility and those advantages that were contained in the realization of socialist aspirations . . . And if only you had seen with what enthusiasm youth seized upon his novel and how he forced them to think and to reach conclusions!" E. S. Vilenskaia, *Revoliutsionnoe podpol'e v Rossii (60-e gody XIX v.)* (Moscow, 1965), p. 177.

37. The censor cut out this section. Similar statements appear in Chernyshevskii's notes on Mill's *Principles of Political Economy*, which were not intended for publication (IX, 832).

38. According to the report of M. I. Pisarev, who visited Chernyshevskii in Astrakhan in 1884, he considered *What Is To Be Done?* his poorest work, and his notes on Mill's *Principles of Political Economy* his best. Steklov, *Chernyshevskii*, II, 600.

39. Chernyshevskii's translation, summary, and comments on Mill comprise the whole of Volume IX of the 1939–1953 edition of his works. In addition to the general studies of Chernyshevskii's economic views, see S. P. Turin, "Nicholas Chernyshevskii and John Stuart Mill," *The Slavonic and East European Review*, IX (1930), 29–33.

40. Steklov insisted that Chernyshevskii abandoned the historical point of view here because he apparently assumed that his economic "laws" served to judge any economic system. Steklov, *Chernyshevskii*, I, 510–513.

41. Plekhanov argued that in fact Chernyshevskii was trying not to understand the bourgeois economy, but rather to preach socialism. This may be true as a value judgment on the quality of Chernyshevskii's effort, but it is not a fair statement of his intent. Plekhanov, *Sochineniia* (1923–1927), VI, 70, 90.

42. In this respect, Chernyshevskii resembled Marx.

43. See, e.g., Plekhanov, *Sochineniia* (1923–1927), VI, 76–78; Steklov, *Chernyshevskii*, I, 523.

44. Chernyshevskii made little use of reliable statistical information, and in some cases his calculations were in error. Plekhanov, *Sochineniia* (1923–1927), VI, 381–382; Kucherov, "N. G. Chernyshevskii on Capitalism," p. 304. Kucherov remarked (pp. 55–56) on the "naive, almost childish manner" in which Chernyshevskii made use of the hypothetical method, as a warning against Chernyshevskii's tendency to oversimplify complex questions.

45. Nor was Chernyshevskii always consistent in his analysis of these self-destructive tendencies. For a devastating critique of his confusion on the subject of profits in the competitive system, see Kucherov, "N. G. Chernyshevskii on Capitalism," pp. 127–135.

46. This view is most evident in Plekhanov's studies of Chernyshevskii. See, e.g., G. V. Plekhanov, "N. G. Chernyshevskii," in D. N. Ovsianiko-Kulikovskii, ed., *Istoriia russkoi literatury XIX v.* (Moscow, 1910), III, 198.

47. Kucherov, "N. G. Chernyshevskii on Capitalism," pp. 301–302.

48. V. I. Lenin, *Sochineniia* (3rd ed.; Moscow-Leningrad, 1928–1937), XV, 144.

49. Venturi, *Roots of Revolution*, p. 470. Schwarz also employs this expanded definition. Solomon M. Schwarz, "Populism and Early Russian Marxism on Ways of Economic Development of Russia (the 1880's and 1890's)," in Ernest J. Simmons, ed., *Continuity and Change in Russian and Soviet Thought* (Cambridge, 1955), p. 43. For the origins of this definition, see Richard Pipes, "Narodnichestvo: A Semantic Inquiry," *Slavic Review*, XXIII (1964), 441–458.

50. In an argument on Chernyshevskii's views of history that does not correspond to my own, Lampert comes close to this kind of assertion. Eugene Lampert, *Sons Against Fathers* (Oxford, 1965), p. 172.

51. Chernyshevskii frequently complained about the backwardness of Russian learning and science (see, e.g., XIV, 529).

52. N. S. Rusanov, "N. G. Chernyshevskii i Rossiia 60-kh godov," *Russkoe bogatstvo*, no. 3 (1905), 185–186.

## VIII. *Politics and the Theory of Revolution*

1. Chernyshevskii's major essays dealt with France, under the titles "Cavaignac" (1858), "The Party Struggle in France under Louis XVIII and Charles X" (1858), "Turgot: His Scientific and Administrative Activity" (1858), "France under Louis Napoleon" (1859), and "The July Monarchy" (1860). The section "Politics" appeared in every issue from January 1859 to April 1862. "France under Louis Napoleon" was based on an article originally appearing in the *Westminster Review*. For the articles "Turgot," "The July Monarchy," and "The Party Struggle in France," Chernyshevskii relied extensively on the works of Louis Blanc. In the opening page of "The July Monarchy," he admitted that the work was close to being a translation (VII, 64).

2. Because Michael Karpovich sought to establish the tactical flexibility in Chernyshevskii's approach to political questions, he has been accused in recent Soviet scholarship of repeating a now "demolished" view that Chernyshevskii hoped for revolution from above. Cf. Michael M. Karpovich, "N. G. Chernyshevskii Between Socialism and Liberalism," *Cahiers du monde russe et soviétique*, I (1960), 569–583; E. I. Druzhinina, "Kritika samoderzhaviia i krepostnogo prava v legal'nykh proizvedeniiakh N. G. Chernyshevskogo nakanune revoliutsionnoi situatsii (1853–1857 gg.)," in M. V. Nechkina et al., eds., *Revoliutsionnaia situatsiia v Rossii v 1859–1861 gg.* (Moscow, 1962), pp. 361–362.

3. For a useful article that provides both insight and occasional overstatement, see B. I. Lazerson, "Publitsistika Chernyshevskogo v gody revoliutsionnoi situatsii," in E. I. Pokusaev and N. M. Chernyshevskaia, eds., *N. G. Chernyshevskii: Stat'i, issledovaniia i materialy*, no. 3 (Saratov, 1962), pp. 62–91.

4. See, e.g., V. Ia. Zevin, *Politicheskie vzgliady i politicheskaia programma N. G. Chernyshevskogo* (Moscow, 1953), pp. 108–144 passim; V. G. Baskakov, *Mirovozzrenie Chernyshevskogo* (Moscow, 1956), pp. 11–81 passim.

5. See, e.g., Nestor Kotliarevskii, *Kanun Osvobozhdeniia* (Petrograd, 1916), p. 340; M. Antonov, *N. G. Chernyshevskii; Sotsial'no-filosofskii etiud* (Moscow, 1910), pp. 226–227.

6. Iu. G. Oksman, ed., *N. G. Chernyshevskii v vospominaniiakh sovremennikov* (Saratov, 1958–1959), II, 72–73.

7. Thus, Chernyshevskii could speak of monarchists in the United States, or partisans of European civilization in China, as radicals (V, 216).

8. Steklov suggested that in Siberia Chernyshevskii became deeply pessimistic, because he felt the masses were indifferent to the need for political change and thought only of improvement in their material

condition, which he realized was not enough. Iu. M. Steklov, *N. G. Chernyshevskii: Ego zhizn' i deiatel'nost', 1828–1889* (2nd ed.; Moscow-Leningrad, 1928), II, 450.

9. Plekhanov distinguished between Chernyshevskii's theoretical position as a "utopian socialist" and his practical activity as a publicist. From the former position, hope for reform from above was possible. Plekhanov thus explained some of Chernyshevskii's statements which, more recently, Soviet scholars tend either to ignore or to reinterpret freely to show hidden revolutionary meaning. G. V. Plekhanov, *Sochineniia*, ed. D. Riazanov (2nd ed.; Moscow, 1923–1927), VI, 64.

10. If Chernyshevskii's early articles (before 1858) really had the serious revolutionary intent suggested by Druzhinina, one can only wonder at the length of time needed to discover it. Druzhinina, "Kritika," in Nechkina et al., eds., *Revoliutsionnaia situatsiia v Rossii* (1962), pp. 361–388.

11. Druzhinina, "Kritika," in Nechkina et al., eds., *Revoliutsionnaia situatsiia v Rossii* (1962), p. 372.

12. Lazerson introduces a list of such hints from Chernyshevskii's study of Lessing with a sentence taken from one of Chernyshevskii's letters to Nekrasov, in which he compares Germany in the eighteenth century with Russia in his own day. In its original context, however, the sentence referred to the literary scene. Lazerson, "Publitsistika," in Pokusaev and Chernyshevskaia, eds., *N. G. Chernyshevskii*, no. 3 (1962), p. 71.

13. Zevin at least recognizes this tactic, but only to belittle it. Zevin, *Politicheskie vzgliady i politicheskaia programma N. G. Chernyshevskogo*, pp. 232–233.

14. Yet Druzhinina comes to an opposite conclusion with reference to the same comments by Chernyshevskii on Bentham. Druzhinina, "Kritika," in Nechkina et al., eds., *Revoliutsionnaia situatsiia v Rossii* (1962), pp. 387–388.

15. L. F. Panteleev, *Vospominaniia* (Moscow, 1958), p. 524.

16. In a paragraph cut out by the censor, Chernyshevskii claimed that those who lived in want represented ninety out of every hundred persons (VI, 337).

17. Venturi notes that Chernyshevskii reached this conclusion with Russia in mind. Franco Venturi, *Roots of Revolution*, trans. Francis Haskell (London, 1960), p. 162.

18. Yet Chernyshevskii did not simply lump his enemies together. If liberals and moderates were considered fools, reactionaries were knaves or worse. For example, in the later novel *Prologue*, he mocked the ineffective tactics of the liberals, but reserved his most bitter comments for the supporters of serfdom and autocracy, one of whom he described as a "butcher" (XIII, 167).

19. For further discussion of Chernyshevskii's comments on Speranskii, see G. N. Sladkevich, "Problema reformy i revoliutsii v russkoi publitsistike nachala 60-kh godov," in M. V. Nechkina et al., eds., *Revoliutsionnaia situatsiia v Rossii v 1859–1861 gg.* (Moscow, 1960), pp. 509–521.

20. Karpovich notes that Chernyshevskii's criticism of Western bourgeois liberalism, intended as an object lesson to his own compatriots, might have seemed premature in the Russian setting, yet he saw it as the task of Russian radicals to prevent the formation of a powerful, class-conscious bourgeoisie and an organized liberal party. This is true so far as it goes, but it is also true that Chernyshevskii used the example of Western liberals and moderates as a vehicle to discredit a pattern of political behavior at issue in his own time, even if Western class categories did not readily apply. Karpovich, "N. G. Chernyshevskii," *Cahiers du monde russe et soviétique,* I (1960), 581.

21. An interesting technique of his, which cut both ways, was to give a mock defense of the actions of monarchy, on the grounds that it acted as one would expect it to act (VIII, 120–122, 184).

22. A useful guide to this article, but one that goes too far in interpreting it as a direct call to revolutionary action, is Ia. I. Linkov, "O politicheskoi programme N. G. Chernyshevskogo v period revoliutsionnoi situatsii 1859–1861 godov," *Voprosy istorii,* no. 5 (1955), 110–116.

23. As late as October 1861, in a discussion of affairs in Western Europe, Chernyshevskii noted that the lack of a clear political tendency accompanied illiteracy (VIII, 561).

24. Chernyshevskii concluded with the statement that it was not difficult for educated persons to be understood by the common people and gain their sympathy, if the educated really loved the people in more than just words. With the aid of passages disallowed by the censor, Vilenskaia makes a good case for the theory that Chernyshevskii wanted the intelligentsia to help the people to develop a revolutionary consciousness, even though when the time came, the people would raise up their own leaders. E. S. Vilenskaia, "N. G. Chernyshevskii i A. I. Gertsen o roli narodnykh mass v osvoboditel'noi bor'be," *Voprosy filosofii,* no. 8 (1960), 108–115.

25. Until news came of the repression in Poland, Herzen was prepared to toast Alexander II as the "liberator of the peasants." A. I. Gertsen, *Sochineniia v deviati tomakh,* ed. V. P. Volgin et al. (Moscow, 1958), VII, 362.

26. There has been a dramatic reversal of opinion on Herzen in recent Soviet scholarship, especially in relation to his role in the organization of the underground revolutionary movement. See, e.g., Ia. I. Linkov, *Revoliutsionnaia bor'ba A. I. Gertsena i N. P. Ogareva i tainoe obshchestvo "Zemlia i volia" 1860-kh godov* (Moscow, 1964), pp. 6–17. Although there may still be differences of emphasis and

evaluation, there is no support for the angry claim of Steklov that Herzen was the "initiator of the liberal attack" against Chernyshevskii. Steklov, *Chernyshevskii*, II, 43.

27. Gertsen, *Sochineniia v deviati tomakh*, VII, 98, 172.

28. For Herzen's disagreement with *The Contemporary* in 1859, see B. P. Koz'min, *Iz istorii revoliutsionnoi mysli v Rossii: Izbrannye trudy*, ed. V. P. Volgin et al. (Moscow, 1961), pp. 606–637.

29. Charles Corbet, "Dobroljubov et Herzen," *Revue des études slaves*, no. 27 (1951), 73–74; V. E. Evgen'ev-Maksimov, *"Sovremennik" pri Chernyshevskom i Dobroliubove* (Leningrad, 1936), pp. 337–343.

30. Gertsen, *Sochineniia v deviati tomakh*, VII, 254–259. For an attempt to broaden the target of Herzen's attack, see T. I. Usakina, "Stat'ia Gertsena 'Very Dangerous!!!' i polemika vokrug 'oblichitel'noi literatury' v zhurnalistike 1857–1859 gg.," in Nechkina et al., eds., *Revoliutsionnaia situatsiia v Rossii* (1960), pp. 246–270.

31. N. A. Dobroliubov, *Sobranie sochinenii v deviati tomakh*, ed. B. I. Bursov et al. (Moscow-Leningrad, 1961–1964), VIII, 568–570.

32. M. A. Antonovich and G. Z. Eliseev, *Shestidesiatye gody*, ed. V. Evgen'ev-Maksimov (Moscow-Leningrad, 1923), pp. 79, 83.

33. According to one report, Herzen said that Chernyshevskii was too quick to bury men of the older generation, who were still very much alive, while Chernyshevskii referred to Herzen as clever and backward. A. A. Kizevetter, "Herzen und der 'Kolokol'," *Zeitschrift für Osteuropäische Geschichte*, VII (1933), 400.

34. For a valiant but unsuccessful effort to minimize this statement of difference, see A. E. Koshovenko, "K voprosu o londonskoi vstreche N. G. Chernyshevskogo s A. I. Gertsenom v 1859 g. i formule 'Kavelin v kvadrate'," in Nechkina et al., eds., *Revoliutsionnaia situatsiia v Rossii* (1960), pp. 271–282.

35. Antonovich and Eliseev, *Shestidesiatye gody*, pp. 90–92. Antonovich also included an account of Chernyshevskii's difficulty in making the journey (pp. 93–96).

36. Oksman, *N. G. Chernyshevskii*, II, 90–91.

37. Gertsen, *Sochineniia v deviati tomakh*, VII, 260.

38. For a review of the debate among Soviet scholars, see Linkov, *Revoliutsionnaia bor'ba A. I. Gertsena i N. P. Ogareva*, p. 121n61.

39. Gertsen, *Sochineniia v deviati tomakh*, VII, 329.

40. Gertsen, *Sochineniia*, VII, 324.

41. Gertsen, *Sochineniia*, VII, 342–353.

42. Gertsen, *Sochineniia*, VII, 389.

43. For further discussion of this difference of opinion, see E. S. Vilenskaia, "N. G. Chernyshevskii i A. I. Gertsen o roli narodnykh mass v osvoboditel'noi bor'be," *Voprosy filosofii*, no. 8 (1960), 108–119.

44. Gertsen, *Sochineniia*, VII, 410.
45. For Marxist criticisms of the "idealism" in Chernyshevskii's views of history, see Plekhanov, *Sochineniia*, VI, 27; I. K. Dodonov, "N. G. Černyševskij als Historiker," *Jahrbuch für Geschichte Ost- und Mitteleuropas*, I (1956), 193; V. E. Evgrafov, "Filosofskie vzgliady N. G. Chernyshevskogo," in I. Ia. Shchipanov, ed., *Iz istorii russkoi filosofii: Sbornik statei* (Moscow, 1952), p. 378. Lampert discusses both the utopian and scientific, or deterministic, elements in Chernyshevskii's views on history, in an interpretation that varies considerably from my own. Eugene Lampert, *Sons Against Fathers* (London, 1965), pp. 171–181.
46. Despite improved knowledge, Chernyshevskii recognized the institutional obstacles to progress (IX, 415, 627–628).
47. Herbert E. Bowman, "Revolutionary Élitism in Černyševskij," *The American Slavic and East European Review*, XIII (1954), 185–199.
48. A. A. Kornilov, *Obshchestvennoe dvizhenie pri Aleksandre II (1855–1881)* (Moscow, 1909), pp. 113–116.

## IX. *Chernyshevskii and the Revolutionary Movement (1860–1862)*

1. I. S. Miller argues for Chernyshevskii's part in the authorship of "The Great Russian." I. B. Volodarskii, on the other hand, argues that N. A. Serno-Solov'evich, in his "Reply to 'The Great Russian'," expressed Chernyshevskii's ideas. Both claims cannot be true. See M. V. Nechkina et al., eds., *Revoliutsionnaia situatsiia v Rossii v 1859–1861 gg.* (Moscow, 1965), pp. 52–123.
2. Nikoladze reported hearing Olga say that Chernyshevskii was opposed to the way Mikhailov spoke openly of his part in illegal activities at the time of his arrest. Chernyshevskii apparently felt that silence was of greater value than speech-making. N. Ia. Nikoladze, "Vospominaniia o shestidesiatykh godakh," *Katorga i ssylka*, no. 5 (1927), 29–30.
3. For a review of the different versions of this document, see S. A. Reiser, "Vospominaniia A. A. Sleptsova," in E. I. Pokusaev and N. M. Chernyshevskaia, eds., *N. G. Chernyshevskii: Stat'i, issledovaniia i materialy*, no. 3 (Saratov, 1962), pp. 249–282.
4. A. V. Nikitenko, *Dnevnik v trekh tomakh*, ed. I. Ia. Aizenshtok (Moscow, 1955–1956), II, 441–442.
5. N. I. Utin, "Propaganda i organizatsiia," *Narodnoe delo*, no. 2/3 (Geneva, 1868), 25–51.
6. Iu. M. Steklov, *N. G. Chernyshevskii: Ego zhizn' i deiatel'nost', 1828–1889* (2nd ed.; Moscow-Leningrad, 1928), II, 223–232.
7. See, e.g., the unconvincing claims in R. A. Taubin, "K voprosu o

roli N. G. Chernyshevskogo v sozdanii 'Revoliutsionnoi partii' v kontse 50-kh nachale 60-kh godov XIX v.," *Istoricheskie zapiski,* no. 39 (1952), 86–93.

8. See Thomas J. Hegarty, "Student Movements in Russian Universities, 1855–1861" (Ph.D. diss., Harvard University, 1965).

9. Several contemporaries called the student movement a "barometer" of public opinion or of the times. Franko Venturi, *Roots of Revolution,* trans. Francis Haskell (London, 1960), p. 220.

10. V. N. Lind, "Moskovskoe studenchestvo v 1861 g. i ego otnoshenie k osvobozhdeniiu krest'ian (iz vospominanii)," in A. K. Dzhivelegov et al., eds., *Velikaia reforma* (Moscow, 1911), V, 269–270.

11. Lind claimed that in Moscow the most influential journal among students was *The Bell.* Lind, "Moskovskoe," in A. K. Dzhivelegov et al., eds., *Velikaia reforma,* V, 273. In St. Petersburg, *The Contemporary* held first place.

12. Lind, "Moskovskoe," in A. K. Dzhivelegov et al., eds., *Velikaia reforma,* V, 274.

13. L. F. Panteleev, *Vospominaniia* (Moscow, 1958), p. 527.

14. Levin suggests that official suspicion of Chernyshevskii's involvement in student unrest was one reason that he was not released from prison and exile in 1870. Sh. M. Levin, *Obshchestvennoe dvizhenie v Rossii v 60–70-e gody XIX veka* (Moscow, 1958), p. 179.

15. Lately, these police suspicions have been buttressed by writers who would exaggerate the least hint of Chernyshevskii's revolutionary agitation. V. G. Baskakov, for example, in perhaps the least reliable full-scale study devoted specifically to Chernyshevskii, claims that working through the St. Petersburg student committee, he "organized" the protests of students against the repression of the tsarist government. V. G. Baskakov, *Mirovozzrenie Chernyshevskogo* (Moscow, 1956), p. 226. So blatant a claim will probably never be supported by direct evidence, even if it cannot be dismissed out of hand. At best the evidence is suggestive, but inconclusive, and to some extent contradictory.

16. P. D. Boborykin, *Za polveka (moi vospominaniia)* (Moscow-Leningrad, 1929), p. 170.

17. Panteleev, *Vospominaniia,* p. 272.

18. Panteleev quotes N. I. Utin on Chernyshevskii's reaction to this suicide, which was that if Piotrovskii did not value his own life, he should at least have sacrificed it to a rational purpose. Panteleev, *Vospominaniia,* p. 296.

19. Panteleev, *Vospominaniia,* pp. 533–534.

20. Panteleev, *Vospominaniia,* p. 534.

21. Venturi, *Roots of Revolution,* p. 230.

22. Nikoladze, "Vospominaniia," *Katorga i ssylka,* no. 4 (1927), 49.

23. N. V. Reingardt, "N. G. Chernyshevskii (Po vospominaniiam

i razskazam raznykh lits)," *Russkaia starina,* no. 2 (1905), 454.

24. Panteleev, *Vospominaniia,* pp. 272–273.

25. Chernyshevskii's proposal for these lectures appears in V. E. Cheshikhin-Vetrinskii, *N. G. Chernyshevskii, 1828–1889* (Petrograd, 1923), pp. 148–155.

26. Panteleev, *Vospominaniia,* pp. 261–262.

27. In a later autobiographical sketch, Chernyshevskii contrasted his own version of this encounter to the version given by Kostomarov (I, 759–763).

28. Antonovich later claimed that the editors of *The Contemporary* believed that Eval'd's article had originated in the Ministry of Education. M. A. Antonovich and G. Z. Eliseev, *Shestidesiatye gody* (Moscow-Leningrad, 1933), p. 103.

29. Panteleev, *Vospominaniia,* pp. 261–266.

30. One can only agree with Nikoladze's surprise that Chernyshevskii's sharply worded article ever passed censorship. Nikoladze, "Vospominaniia," *Katorga i ssylka,* no. 5 (1927), 36.

31. A. I. Gertsen, *Polnoe sobranie sochinenii i pisem,* ed. M. K. Lemke (Petrograd, 1915–1925), XVI, 76.

32. See, e.g., M. V. Nechkina, "N. G. Chernyshevskii v bor'be za splochenie sil russkogo demokraticheskogo divizheniia v gody revoliutsionnoi situatsii (1859–1861)," *Voprosy istorii,* no. 7 (1953), 56–73.

33. N. A. Alekseev, ed., *Protsess N. G. Chernyshevskogo* (Saratov, 1939), p. 101.

34. The proclamation's generally favorable treatment of France under Napoleon III has led some scholars to doubt whether Chernyshevskii could have written it. In this case, I agree with Nechkina that the author of "To the Landlords' Peasants" probably intended simply to show that people were better off under other systems. M. V. Nechkina, "N. G. Chernyshevskii v gody revoliutsionnoi situatsii," *Istoricheskie zapiski,* no. 10 (1941), 11–12.

35. The trial documents collected in Alekseev, ed., *Protsess N. G. Chernyshevskogo,* are more complete and better edited than the earlier volume, N. K. Lemke, *Politicheskie protsessy v Rossii 1860-kh gg.* (2nd ed.; Moscow-Petrograd, 1923), pp. 163–502. The record of the interrogations of Chernyshevskii are reprinted in (XIV, 722–772).

36. Antonovich gives an eyewitness account of the arrest in Antonovich and Eliseev, *Shestidesiatye gody,* pp. 125–133.

37. Nikitenko, *Dnevnik v trekh tomakh,* II, 441.

38. M. V. Klochkov, "Protsess N. G. Chernyshevskogo," *Istoricheskii vestnik* (1913), no. 9, pp. 889–919; no. 10, pp. 157–190.

39. During the trial, Chernyshevskii maintained that his diary was in fact simply preparatory material for a novel he intended to write (XIV, 760).

40. Alekseev, ed., *Protsess N. G. Chernyshevskogo*, pp. 170–181, 190–191.

41. For photocopies of these letters, see Klochkov, "Protsess," *Istoricheskii vestnik*, no. 9 (1913), 893, 897–899.

42. Alekseev, ed., *Protsess N. G. Chernyshevskogo*, pp. 104, 117.

43. For evidence that Iakovlev's testimony was highly suspect, see Alekseev, ed., *Protsess N. G. Chernyshevskogo*, pp. 189–190, 202–203.

44. Klochkov, "Protsess," *Istoricheskii vestnik*, no. 10 (1913), 180–181.

45. Steklov, *Chernyshevskii*, II, 452–455, 446–447.

46. N. V. Shelgunov, *Vospominaniia*, ed. A. A. Shilov (Moscow-Petrograd, 1923), p. 32.

47. Shelgunov, *Vospominaniia*, p. 33.

48. Shelgunov, *Vospominaniia*, p. 141.

49. Panteleev indicated that Chernyshevskii knew of Mikhailov and Shelgunov's activities abroad, but as Steklov noted, there is no indication he had knowledge of their intention beforehand. Panteleev, *Vospominaniia*, pp. 342–343; Steklov, *Chernyshevskii*, II, 286. Steklov also indicated that Dobroliubov had no prior knowledge.

50. For the text of "To the Young Generation," see Shelgunov, *Vospominaniia*, pp. 287–302. See also E. S. Vilenskaia, *Revoliutsionnoe podpol'e v Rossii (60-e gody XIX v.)* (Moscow, 1965), pp. 90–92.

51. M. K. Lemke, who cooperated with Sleptsov in editing these memoirs, admitted that Sleptsov was confused on many points and had forgotten much. Iu. G. Oksman, ed., *N. G. Chernyshevskii v vospominaniiakh sovremennikov* (Saratov, 1958–1959), I, 282. At one point, Koz'min doubted the very existence of the notebook Lemke claimed to have used. B. P. Koz'min, "Byl li N. G. Chernyshevskii avtorum pis'ma 'Russkogo cheloveka' k Gertsenu," *Literaturnoe nasledstvo*, no. 25/26 (1936), 578. It would seem, however, that the issue has been settled by Reiser, "Vospominaniia," in Pokusaev and Chernyshevskaia, eds., *Chernyshevskii*, no. 3 (1962), 249–282.

52. Lemke, *Politicheskie protsessy*, p. 318.

53. For Lemke's version of this part of Sleptsov's memoirs, see Gertsen, *Polnoe sobranie sochinenii i pisem*, X, 425–427. The date of July 1861 is given for the encounter because of reference to "The Great Russian," which had just appeared. Another version of the encounter, allegedly copied from Sleptsov's notebook by M. N. Chernyshevskii, varies somewhat in its wording and does not include Chernyshevskii's statement that he had not written a proclamation. Similar words are instead attributed to Sleptsov. V. E. Bograd, "O memuarakh A. A. Sleptsova," *Literaturnoe nasledstvo*, no. 67 (1959), 681–682.

54. T. A. Bogdanovich, *Liubov' liudei shestidesiatykh godov* (Leningrad, 1929), pp. 167–168.

55. Bograd, "O memuarakh," *Literaturnoe nasledstvo*, no. 67 (1959), 674.

56. See, e.g., the inconclusive quibbling of Nechkina, "N. G. Chernyshevskii," *Istoricheskie zapiski*, no. 10 (1941), 12–13.

57. Alekseev, ed., *Protsess N. G. Chernyshevskogo*, pp. 283–284.

58. Nechkina, "N. G. Chernyshevskii," *Istoricheskie zapiski*, no. 10 (1941), 19–28.

59. Alekseev, ed., *Protsess N. G. Chernyshevskogo*, pp. 235–239. Two of Chernyshevskii's letters show his interest in Kostomarov and his attempt to offer help (XIV, 424, 436).

60. Shelgunov, *Vospominaniia*, p. 33.

61. The cooling of relations between Chernyshevskii and Mikhailov, reported by Panteleev, is denied by B. P. Koz'min, "N. G. Chernyshevskii i M. I. Mikhailov (K istorii ikh vzaimootnoshenii)," *Voprosy istorii*, no. 7 (1946), 19–25.

62. Nechkina insists that there must have been an organization behind "To the Landlords' Peasants," because otherwise Chernyshevskii would have acted like an adventurist, a possibility alien to him. Nechkina, "N. G. Chernyshevskii," *Istoricheskie zapiski*, no. 10 (1941), 18–19. However, Shelgunov specifically stated that at the time there was no overall organization. Shelgunov, *Vospominaniia*, p. 135.

63. N. N. Novikova, "Komitet 'Velikorussa' i bor'ba za sozdanie revoliutsionnoi organizatsii v epokhu padeniia krepostnogo prava," *Voprosy istorii*, no. 5 (1957), 138.

64. The three issues of "The Great Russian" appeared in *The Bell* on September 15, October 15, and December 8, 1861. The two leading commentaries, "Reply to 'The Great Russian'" and "Reply to the Reply to 'The Great Russian'," appeared on September 15 and October 1, 1861.

65. *Kolokol* (September 15, 1861), no. 107, p. 900. This and subsequent citations for *Kolokol* refer to M. V. Nechkina et al., eds., *Kolokol: Gazeta A. I. Gertsena i N. P. Ogareva* (Moscow, 1962).

66. *Kolokol* (September 15, 1861), no. 107, p. 900.

67. *Kolokol* (October 15, 1861), no. 109, pp. 913–914.

68. *Kolokol* (December 8, 1861), no. 115, pp. 961–963.

69. *Kolokol* (December 8, 1861), no. 115, p. 963.

70. On the trial of those arrested, see M. K. Lemke, *Ocherki osvoboditel'nago dvizheniia "shestidesiatykh godov"* (St. Petersburg, 1908), pp. 357–398.

71. Venturi, *Roots of Revolution*, p. 239; Levin, *Obshchestvennoe dvizhenie*, p. 192.

72. Panteleev, *Vospominaniia*, p. 340.

73. Oksman, ed., *N. G. Chernyshevskii,* II, 99.

74. For this section of Ballod's memoirs, see Cheshikhin-Vetrinskii, *N. G. Chernyshevskii,* pp. 157–158.

75. V. A. Obruchev, "Iz perezhitogo," *Vestnik Evropy,* no. 5 (1907), 123–124. Novikova minimizes the importance of this evidence. N. N. Novikova, "N. G. Chernyshevskii i komitet 'Velikorussa,'" in M. V. Nechkina et al., eds., *Revoliutsionnaia situatsiia v Rossi v 1859–1861 gg.* (Moscow, 1960), pp. 311–314.

76. Steklov, *Chernyshevskii,* II, 261.

77. One of the most valuable parts of Vilenskaia's recent study of the revolutionary underground in the early 1860's is a systematic study of the positions taken in leading legal and illegal writings on the central questions of organization, objectives, and tactics. Vilenskaia, *Revoliutsionnoe podpol'e,* pp. 97–131.

78. Steklov, *Chernyshevskii,* II, 253.

79. S. A. Pokrovskii, "O roli Chernyshevskogo i Gertsena v sozdanii revoliutsionnoi organizatsii," *Voprosy istorii,* no. 9 (1954), 86; Vilenskaia, *Revoliutsionnoe podpol'e,* pp. 106, 115–116.

80. For example, Khomentovskaia saw a similarity between "The Great Russian" and "To the Landlords' Peasants." Shebunin argued that "The Great Russian" was not a liberal document. A. Khomentovskaia, "N. G. Chernyshevskii i podpol'naia literatura nachala 60-kh g.g.," *Istoricheskii arkhiv,* no. 1 (1919), 388–413; A. N. Shebunin, "K voprosu o roli N. G. Chernyshevskogo v revoliutsionnom dvizhenii 60-kh godov," *Katorga i ssylka,* no. 11 (1929), 23.

81. Novikova, "Komitet," *Voprosy istorii,* no. 5 (1957), 137.

82. I. S. Miller, "Vokrug 'Velikorussa,'" in Nechkina et al., eds., *Revoliutsionaia situatsiia,* (1965), p. 92.

83. For example, Novikova attempted to trace names on a mailing list for "The Great Russian" to Chernyshevskii. Novikova, "N. G. Chernyshevskii," in Nechkina et al., eds., *Revoliutsionnaia situatsiia* (1960), pp. 318–319.

84. Shelgunov, *Vospominaniia,* p. 135. The different attitude toward secrecy in the two documents is also of import: "To the Landlords' Peasants" cautioned the peasants to be quiet about their preparations in order to achieve surprise; "The Great Russian" warned openly of a peasant rising in 1863.

85. *Kolokol* (September 15, 1861), no. 107, pp. 895–897.

86. *Kolokol* (September 15, 1861), no. 107, p. 897.

87. For a review of this argument, see I. B. Volodarskii, "'Otvet Velikorussu' i ego avtor," in Nechkina et al., eds., *Revoliutsionnaia situatsiia* (1965), pp. 52–83.

88. *Kolokol* (September 15, 1861), no. 107, p. 895.

89. *Kolokol* (October 1, 1861), no. 108, pp. 901–903.

90. For recent work on the organization by Soviet historians, see

Vilenskaia, *Revoliutsionnoe podpol'e;* Ia. I. Linkov, *Revoliutsionnaia bor'ba A. I. Gertsena i N. P. Ogareva i tainoe obshchestvo "Zemlia i volia" 1860-kh godov* (Moscow, 1964).

91. Utin, "Propaganda," *Narodnoe delo,* no. 2/3 (Geneva, 1868), 33.

92. Panteleev, *Vospominaniia,* pp. 290–291.

93. *Kolokol* (July 1, 1861), no. 102, supplement.

94. M. V. Nechkina, "Vozniknovenie pervoi 'Zemli i voli'," in Nechkina et al., eds., *Revoliutsionnaia situatsiia* (1960), pp. 292–293.

95. N. P. Ogarev, *Izbrannye sotsial'no-politicheskie i filosofskie proizvedeniia,* ed. M. T. Iovchuk and N. G. Tarakanov (Moscow, 1952–1956), II, 451.

96. Chernyshevskii also referred to Ogarev's letter in a petition for release addressed to the tsar on November 20, 1862 (XIV, 460–461).

97. Ogarev wrote with a clear sense of outrage, describing Chernyshevskii's skepticism as shameful. Ogarev, *Izbrannye sotsial'no-politicheskie i filosofskie proizvedeniia,* II, 451.

98. Gertsen, *Polnoe sobranie sochinenii i pisem,* XVI, 72, 76.

99. Linkov also notes the ties of these men with Herzen and Ogarev. Linkov, *Revoliutsionnaia bor'ba A. I. Gertsena i N. P. Ogareva,* p. 272.

100. For a summary of these activities, see Vilenskaia, *Revoliutsionnoe podpol'e,* pp. 141–155.

101. Panteleev, who came into contact with the organizers of Land and Liberty only around Easter 1862, recorded the comment of Sleptsov that the organization was then in its initial, preparatory stage of development. Panteleev, *Vospominaniia,* pp. 291–293.

102. Ogarev, *Izbrannye sotsial'no-politicheskie i filosofskie proizvedeniia,* II, 462–463.

103. For Kel'siev's "Confession," see *Literaturnoe nasledtsvo,* no. 41/42 (Moscow, 1941), 253–470.

104. Linkov, *Revoliutsionnaia bor'ba A. I. Gertsena i N. P. Ogareva,* pp. 266–268.

105. See, e.g., the trip described in Panteleev, *Vospominaniia,* pp. 299–308. Levin notes how difficult it is to evaluate the claims of organizational success made by Sleptsov. Levin, *Obshchestvennoe dvizhenie v Rossii,* pp. 209–210.

106. Utin, "Propaganda," *Narodnoe delo,* no. 2/3 (1868), 50.

107. Gertsen, *Polnoe sobranie sochinenii i pisem,* XVI, 83.

108. On the operation of one such press in the town of Mariengauzen, province of Vitebsk, see V. I. Neupokoev, "'Zemlia i volia' 60-kh godov po materialam Dinaburgskogo protsessa," in M. V. Nechkina et al., eds., *Revoliutsionnaia situatsiia v Rossii v 1859–1861 gg.* (Moscow, 1962), pp. 305–334.

109. Levin, *Obshchestvennoe dvizhenie v Rossii,* pp. 211–212.

110. *Kolokol* (March 1, 1863), no. 157, p. 1302.

111. Panteleev could speak only of the group in St. Petersburg with certainty, but he claimed that no direct propaganda was undertaken among the people. Panteleev, *Vospominaniia*, pp. 316–317.

112. On the ties of Land and Liberty with Polish revolutionaries, see Utin, "Propaganda," *Narodnoe delo*, no. 2/3 (1868), 34–39.

113. Steklov, *Chernyshevskii*, II, 271. Comparable reasonableness is not shown by Steklov in a subsequent section (II, 274–281), where he tries to show the closeness between Chernyshevskii's position and that expressed in the proclamation "Young Russia."

114. Gertsen, *Polnoe sobranie sochinenii i pisem*, XVI, 75.

115. M. N. Sleptsova, "Shturmany griadushchei buri (Iz vospominanii)," *Zven'ia*, no. 2 (1933), 403–404. Later in her article (p. 433), Sleptsova explained the term *piatërka* as an organizational procedure to minimize the danger of discovery by the police.

116. Sleptsova, "Shturmany," *Zven'ia*, no. 2 (1933), 404.

117. Sleptsova, "Shturmany," *Zven'ia*, no. 2 (1933), 433, 443, 448.

118. See, e.g., Vilenskaia, *Revoliutsionnoe podpol'e*, p. 148; Nechkina, "Vozniknovenie," in Nechkina et al., eds., *Revoliutsionnaia situatsiia* (1960), pp. 294–296.

119. Venturi, *Roots of Revolution*, pp. 171, 269n41.

120. Reiser, "Vospominaniia," in Pokusaev and Chernyshevskaia, eds., *N. G. Chernyshevskii*, no. 3 (1962), 252.

121. Sleptsova, "Shturmany," *Zven'ia*, no. 2 (1933), 386, 402–403.

122. Vilenskaia, *Revoliutsionnaia podpol'e*, p. 149.

123. Sleptsova, "Shturmany," *Zven'ia*, no. 2 (1933), 449.

## X. *Prison and Exile (1862–1889)*

1. The novel is published in two slightly different versions (XI, 5–336, 337–639).

2. Although in the following decades the novel was published abroad, it did not appear legally in Russia again until 1900. In April 1863, Chernyshevskii wrote to A. N. Pypin and N. A. Nekrasov that he planned to write a second part to the novel, which he hoped to finish by that fall or winter. It was never done (XIV, 479–480).

3. Avdot'ia Panaeva (E. Ia. Golovacheva), *Vospominaniia, 1824–1870*, ed. K. Chukovskii (3rd ed.; Leningrad, 1929), pp. 446–451.

4. See, e.g., the introductory essay by Georg Lukács in N. G. Tschernyschewskij, *Was Tun?* (Berlin, 1954), p. 27. For a recent evaluation of the novel, see Francis B. Randall, *Chernyshevskii* (New York, 1967), pp. 104–130.

5. Plekhanov argued that it is of little use to compare *What Is To Be Done?* with a novel like *Anna Karenina*. A fairer comparison would

be with the philosophical novels of Voltaire. G. V. Plekhanov, *Sochineniia*, ed. D. Riazanov (2nd ed.; Moscow, 1923–1927), V, 179.

6. N. A. Alekseev, ed., *Protsess N. G. Chernyshevskogo* (Saratov, 1939), pp. 330, 333.

7. For reports on Chernyshevskii's civil execution, see Iu. G. Oksman, ed., *N. G. Chernyshevskii v vospominaniiakh sovremennikov* (Saratov, 1958–1959), II, 19–51.

8. For a valuable year-by-year list of Chernyshevskii's published works, see XVI, 758–828.

9. For a summary list of the memoir literature that appeared after 1905, see Oksman, ed., *N. G. Chernyshevskii*, II, 9–12.

10. For several versions of this later phase of Chernyshevskii's life, see Iu. M. Steklov, *N. G. Chernyshevskii: Ego zhizn' i deiatel'nost', 1828–1889* (2nd ed.; Moscow-Leningrad, 1928), II, 481–666; E. A. Liatskii, ed., *Chernyshevskii v Sibiri: Perepiska s rodnymi*, notes by M. N. Chernyshevskii (St. Petersburg, 1912–1913), I, pp. iii–lxiii; II, pp. v–xlvii; III, pp. iii–xlix; N. S. Rusanov, "Chernyshevskii v Sibiri," *Russkoe bogatstvo* (1910), no. 3, pp. 173–205, no. 4, pp. 92–125, no. 5, pp. 162–195, no. 6, pp. 60–82, no. 7, pp. 63–82; I. M. Romanov, *N. G. Chernyshevskii v viliuiskom zatochenii* (Iakutsk, 1957); Konstantin Erymovskii, *Chernyshevskii v Astrakhani* (Astrakhan, 1964).

11. Steklov, *Chernyshevskii*, II, 525.

12. More incredible than Lopatin's attempt itself was the fact that he finally admitted all to the authorities. The same had been true of members of the Karakazov group, who admitted considering ways of liberating Chernyshevskii. N. M. Chernyshevskaia, *Letopis' zhizni i deiatel'nosti N. G. Chernyshevskogo* (Moscow, 1953), pp. 357, 408.

13. Oksman, ed., *N. G. Chernyshevskii*, II, 218.

14. This story has been accepted at face value not only in Soviet hagiography but by both Lampert and Venturi. Eugene Lampert, *Sons Against Fathers* (Oxford, 1965), p. 133; Franco Venturi, *Roots of Revolution*, trans. Francis Haskell (London, 1960), p. 183.

15. Kokosov's story is reprinted in Oksman, ed., *N. G. Chernyshevskii*, II, 195–196. An introductory note (p. 187) comments on the lack of supporting evidence.

16. Steklov, *Chernyshevskii*, II, 571–576.

17. The dates on Chernyshevskii's letters to Olga indicate that she was generally away during the summers. See also Chernyshevskii's letter to his son Aleksandr, asking him to come to Astrakhan to live (XV, 425–426).

18. Some secret surveillance continued up to February 1887. Chernyshevskaia, *Letopis' zhizni i deiatel'nosti N. G. Chernyshevskogo*, p. 560.

19. For a brief list of outside visitors, see Oksman, ed., *N. G. Chernyshevskii*, II, 279.

20. Chernyshevskaia, *Letopis' zhizni i deiatel'nosti N. G. Chernyshevskogo*, p. 536.

21. K. M. Fedorov, *N. G. Chernyshevskii* (Askhabad, 1904), p. 67.

22. Liatskii, ed., *Chernyshevskii v Sibiri*, I, 175–177.

23. N. S. Rusanov, "Chernyshevskii v Sibiri," *Russkoe bogatstvo*, no. 4 (1910), 101–103. Chernyshevskii did, in fact, have a low opinion of formal education.

24. Olga's letters are not extant, but her complaints are obvious from Chernyshevskii's responses.

25. Liatskii, ed., *Chernyshevskii v Sibiri*, I, 110–118.

26. Venturi notes that "the end of his daily political journalism and controversies in St. Petersburg meant the end of his true life as a writer." Venturi, *Roots of Revolution*, p. 183.

27. For books in Chernyshevskii's possession at different periods of his exile, see Chernyshevskaia, *Letopis' zhizni i deiatel'nosti N. G. Chernyshevskogo*, pp. 396, 508–509, 525–526. In view of the difficulties in Chernyshevskii's situation, Masaryk's criticism of his lack of scientific output in Siberia is needlessly harsh. T. G. Masaryk, *The Spirit of Russia*, trans. Eden and Cedar Paul (London-New York, 1955), II, 42.

28. Venturi, *Roots of Revolution*, p. 184.

29. On this entire episode, see Liatskii, ed., *Chernyshevskii v Sibiri*, II, pp. xxxii–xlviii.

30. N. S. Rusanov, "Chernyshevskii v Sibiri," *Russkoe bogatstvo* (1910), no. 5, pp. 191–195; no. 6, pp. 61–64.

31. Chernyshevskii's scorn could reach impressive heights. He called Malthus "a charlatan, worth only to spit upon" (XV, 35).

32. A decade earlier, he had described himself to his son Mikhail as an old man whose views on botany and zoology had been formed by eighteenth century books, especially Lamarck (XIV, 643).

33. Oksman, ed., *N. G. Chernyshevskii*, II, 342.

# Index